Modern China and International Economic Law

This book series offers an essential forum for Chinese economic law scholars, as well as international scholars interested in China's practice in the context of international economic law. It is thus the aim of this book series to publish essential monographs/compilations in the field of international economic law that focus on China, or on uniquely Chinese characteristics. This book series above all focuses on research that closely relates current practices with past history, and future policies with current circumstances, pursuing a philosophy of understanding legal practices by combining the past and present. Accordingly, top scholars in China and beyond its borders will be invited to contribute to this project from their respective areas of focus, which can cover broad topics related to international law in the current context of China's peaceful rise, such as China's economic policy with various countries, its participation in the WTO legal system and bilateral investment treaty practices, etc.; as well as more specific topics such as China's domestic legislation regarding foreign business, its unique "one country, two systems" policy and its implications on external economic interactions between different "systems" within China.

Leo Zeng

A Study on the Creation, Impact and Legal Issues of Crypto Special Drawing Rights

中国国际经济法学会
Chinese Society of International Economic Law, CSIEL

Springer

Leo Zeng
Delta, BC, Canada

ISSN 2364-8317 ISSN 2364-8325 (electronic)
Modern China and International Economic Law
ISBN 978-981-99-9974-3 ISBN 978-981-99-9975-0 (eBook)
https://doi.org/10.1007/978-981-99-9975-0

This Springer imprint is published by the registered company Springer Nature Singapore Pte Ltd.
The registered company address is: 152 Beach Road, #21-01/04 Gateway East, Singapore 189721, Singapore

Paper in this product is recyclable.

Acknowledgements

I extend my heartfelt gratitude to Professor Li Guo'an for his invaluable guidance and to Professor Chen An for his kind recommendation, which has allowed this book to be presented in its best light to the world. I am deeply indebted to the esteemed faculty members of the International Law Department at Xiamen University Law School for their unwavering support and mentorship throughout this endeavor. I would also like to express my sincere appreciation to Bao Ningzhen, a doctoral student in the class of 2021 within the International Law program at Xiamen University Law School, for diligently translating the first and second chapters, comprising a total of 51,391 words, Wu Yikai, a doctoral student in the class of 2020 within the International Law program at Xiamen University Law School, for diligently translating the third chapters, comprising a total of 50,561 words, and to Ma Yuxi, a doctoral student in the class of 2018 within the International Law program at Xiamen University Law School, for her dedicated efforts in translating the fourth and fifth chapters, totaling 52,879 words.

Contents

Chapter 1
The Reform of the IMF and the Origin of CryptoSDRs

The current international monetary system has serious flaws, including the "Triffin Dilemma" and other factors that have led to frequent global financial crises. These flaws have forced countries and international organizations to consider how to reform the international monetary system. Therefore, this chapter proposes the creation of crypto Special Drawing Rights (hereafter referred to as "cryptoSDRs") as a possible solution to reform the current international monetary system and address its inherent flaws.

1.1 Defects in the IMF and SDRs

Currently, the international monetary system, the International Monetary Fund (hereafter referred to as the "IMF"), and Special Drawing Rights (hereafter referred to as the "SDRs") all have significant flaws, which have resulted in long-term instability in the international monetary system. The IMF and SDRs have not fully fulfilled their role in maintaining a stable international monetary order.

1.1.1 The Evolution of International Monetary System and the Creation of SDRs

To fully explore the deficiencies of the international monetary system, the IMF and the SDRs, it is first necessary to understand the concept of the SDRs and the development history of the international monetary system.

L. Zeng, *A Study on the Creation, Impact and Legal Issues of Crypto Special Drawing Rights*, Modern China and International Economic Law,
https://doi.org/10.1007/978-981-99-9975-0_1

(1) The concept of SDRs

In 1969, the IMF issued SDRs, also known as "paper gold." It is a book-entry asset that can be used to repay IMF debts and offset member countries' balance of payments deficits. Under the Bretton Woods system established after World War II, the international monetary and financial market quickly became trapped due to the setting of the US dollar as the major international currency and the dual-peg system. On the one hand, the US dollar was linked to gold, giving it international recognition and serving as the primary international reserve asset. On the other hand, the US dollar was also the domestic currency of the United States (hereafter referred to as the "US") and subject to the country's monetary policy. However, for the US, its domestic and international goals were often inconsistent or even at odds. First, it needed to ensure a stable exchange relationship between the US dollar and gold to maintain the US dollar's position as the international reserve asset and major international currency, thereby making more countries crave more US dollars and requiring the US to maintain a long-term trade surplus. Second, the world's demand for US dollars required the US to continuously export dollars through trade deficits. To solve this contradiction and ease the pressure on the US dollar as an international reserve currency, SDRs were created as a special international asset. Initially, SDRs were introduced to address the problem of insufficient reserve currency and liquidity in the international monetary system.[1] Because it only supplemented the IMF's existing general drawing rights, it was named Special Drawing Rights.

The IMF Executive Board reviews the SDR basket every five years to ensure that the SDRs can relatively accurately reflect the current economic, trade, and financial landscape of the world. During the SDRs' five-year fixed-value period, the amount of various currencies in the currency basket remains unchanged, but the actual weight of these currencies will fluctuate due to changes in the exchange rates between currencies in the basket. The value of the SDRs is determined daily based on market exchange rates. At the beginning of the issuance of SDRs, each unit was equal to 0.888 g of gold, equivalent to one US dollar at the time. After the collapse of the Bretton Woods system in 1974, the SDRs were redefined as a basket of currencies, including sixteen sovereign currencies. By 1981, the number of currencies in the basket had been reduced to five sovereign currencies, namely, the currencies of the five major industrial countries. By 1999, due to the birth of the euro, the basket of currencies was reduced to four sovereign currencies, namely, the US dollar, euro, Japanese yen, and British pound. In the review that ended in November 2015, Chinese yuan was officially included in the basket of currencies. On October 1, 2016, the value of the SDRs was determined by the current exchange rates of the currency basket, which consists of the following five currencies: US dollar, euro, Chinese yuan, Japanese yen, and British pound, with weights of 41.73%, 30.93%, 10.92%, 8.33%, and 8.09%, respectively.[2]

[1] Li Xiang. The Establishment of Asian Monetary Unit from the Development of Artificial Currency SDR and European Currency Unit. (Shanghai: Fudan University, 2008), p. 23.

[2] Nie Lin. IMF reform plan officially takes effect, China becomes the third largest shareholder [EB/OL]. http://www.jiemian.com/article/527073.html. Accessed 4 July 2020.

In essence, SDRs are a potential claim to an international reserve currency that the IMF distributes among its member countries. Upon receiving SDRs, member countries classify them as their own reserve assets and can use them at any time in the event of a balance of payments deficit. Additionally, SDRs can be used directly to pay for IMF loans, interest, and other expenses.[3]

The distribution of the SDRs is categorized into two types: general allocation and special allocation. According to the agreement of the IMF, the IMF can allocate the SDRs to member countries in proportion to their quotas under certain conditions, which is called a general allocation. Special allocations occurred in 2009 when a special allocation was made to countries that joined the IMF after 1981, based on their previously allocated quotas, with the aim of ensuring that all member countries could participate fairly in the SDR system. As of now, there have been several allocations of SDRs, including a general allocation of 9.3 billion SDRs from 1970 to 1972, a general allocation of 12.1 billion SDRs from 1979 to 1981, a general allocation of 161.2 billion SDRs in August 2009, and a special allocation of 21.5 billion SDRs in September 2009. In 2016, the IMF increased the total size of the fund from the original 204.1 billion SDRs to 477 billion SDRs (equivalent to approximately 682.9 billion US dollars) through the "Board of Executive Directors Reform Amendment."[4] In August 2021, the IMF approved the largest ever allocation of SDRs, totaling approximately 456 billion SDRs (equivalent to approximately 650 billion US dollars).[5] Previously, the size of the SDRs was only equivalent to 0.3% of global Gross Domestic Product (hereafter referred to as the "GDP"), less than 1% of global trade volume, and only 4% of total international reserves.[6] Therefore, some scholars believe that the current total amount of the SDRs is not sufficient to support its role as a circulating currency, and its holders are not sufficiently diversified, almost all of which are "official" holders. This limits its usefulness as a trading medium in international trade and finance. However, the author believes that with the development of technology and changes in the political landscape, the disadvantages of SDRs will be greatly improved and eventually thoroughly resolved.

(2) The Development History of the International Monetary System

The modern international monetary system originated from the monetary system of developed Western countries. Prior to the Nineteenth century, the international monetary system operated under the gold and silver standard. In the Nineteenth century, Britain gained world dominance and implemented the gold standard as the international settlement currency. As the economy and international trade of developed

[3] Research Team of the Research Bureau of the People's Bank of China. Literature Review on International Monetary System Reform. Financial Development Review, 2010(3), pp. 143–158.

[4] According to the IMF website data of March 12th, 2021, 1SDR = 1.431610 US Dollars, https://www.imf.org/external/np/fin/data/rms_mth.aspx?SelectDate=2021-03-31&reportType=CVSDR.

[5] IMF, 2021 General SDR Allocation. https://www.imf.org/en/Topics/special-drawing-right/2021-SDR-Allocation. Accessed 6 May 2022.

[6] Li Guoan. The Fragility of the International Monetary System and the Dilemma and Way Out of the Prevention and Control of International Financial Crises [J]. Strait Law, 2010(1), pp. 6–12.

countries in the West grew explosively, demand for gold as an international currency increased sharply. However, gold production was limited and unevenly distributed. At the same time, Western developed countries continued to plunder gold for war preparations, wars, and colonization, further reducing the amount of gold available for circulation and undermining the foundation of the gold standard. The great crises of the 1930s further destabilized the gold standard, eventually leading to the collapse of the gold-based international monetary system. On July 1, 1944, the US organized and invited 44 countries to the International Monetary and Financial Conference in Bretton Woods, New Hampshire, where they passed the "International Bank for Reconstruction and Development Agreement" and the "International Monetary Fund Agreement" (hereafter referred to as the "IMF Agreement"), establishing the "Bretton Woods international monetary system." The system's basic principles were established on the "dual pegs" mechanism, where the US dollar was linked to gold, and each country's sovereign currency was linked to the US dollar, establishing the dominance of the US dollar in the international monetary system.[7]

The establishment of the Bretton Woods International Monetary System stabilized the chaotic international monetary order after the 1930s and played a positive role in the recovery and development of the postwar world economy. However, due to the US' need to compensate for its international trade deficit, it printed a large amount of dollars, which resulted in the devaluation of the dollar in reality. Although the Bretton Woods system established the principle of "Linking the dollar to gold," which meant that the issuance and circulation of the dollar were restricted by the amount of its gold reserves, in fact, the US was able to achieve its goal of effectively plundering other countries by unrestricted printing and use of the dollar, increasing its investment in other countries, importing goods and resources from other countries, and buying gold from other countries. At the beginning of the establishment of the Bretton Woods system, the US held a monopoly on the world's gold reserves, accounting for 59% of the world's total gold reserves. However, by 1960, the US's short-term foreign debt had skyrocketed to $21 billion, far exceeding its $17.8 billion in gold reserves, causing the US's international credit to hit rock bottom. Therefore, in the late 1950s, there was widespread oversupply and devaluation of the dollar, and there was a large-scale sale of dollars in the international currency market. In October 1960, the market behavior of selling dollars and buying gold and other currencies continued, triggering the first "dollar crisis" since World War II. By the end of 1972, the US's short-term foreign debt had reached 8 times its total gold reserves, and the creditworthiness of the US's debt repayment capacity had reached its lowest point in history, triggering another large-scale sale of the dollar in the international financial market. In December 1971, the US announced a 7.89% devaluation of the dollar against gold. In February 1973, the US announced a further devaluation of the dollar against gold by 10%, but the "dollar crisis" could not be resolved. This was followed by a wave of large-scale sales of dollars and purchases of gold and other currencies, causing the price of gold on the London gold market to more than double from $42.22/ounce (1 ounce = 28.35 g)

[7] Liao Fan. New Developments in International Financial Law [M]. Beijing: China Social Sciences Press, 2013, pp. 62–65.

to $96 and causing the foreign exchange markets in Japan and Western Europe to close for 17 days. Finally, the currencies of some traditional industrialized countries in the West were converted from fixed exchange rates tied to the dollar to separate floating exchange rates or joint floating exchange rates. At the same time, the US unilaterally announced the cessation of the exchange of gold for dollars by countries around the world, leading to the complete collapse of the Bretton Woods system.[8] In 1972, the IMF established a "Special Committee on the Reform of the International Monetary System and Related Issues," also known as the "G20," which included 11 developed countries such as the US, the United Kingdom (hereafter referred to as the "UK"), Japan, and nine developing countries such as Brazil and India. In January 1976, the G20 held a summit in Kingston, the capital of Jamaica, to discuss and revise certain provisions of the IMF Agreement. In the end, the leaders of the G20 countries reached and signed the Jamaica Agreement. The Jamaica system established based on the Jamaica Agreement, which took effect in 1978, was the successor to the Bretton Woods system. First, under the Jamaica system, there has been an increase in the number of international reserve currencies alongside the US dollar, with SDRs serving as the primary reserve asset. However, the US dollar still retains its status as the major international currency, and its position remains unassailable. Second, the IMF, established under the Bretton Woods system, continues to play a significant role on the international economic and political stage.[9] Since the collapse of the Bretton Woods system in 1971 and the withdrawal of precious metals from international circulation, international trade has begun to use multiple sovereign currencies as settlement currencies, no longer relying solely on the US dollar. The diversification of the global landscape has also become apparent within the monetary system. The currencies of each country now have not only nominal value but also real value, which reflects a country's creditworthiness and is protected by national laws and supported by national banks. The specific value of a currency depends on a country's comprehensive strength. Through credit-based currency, trading goods has become more convenient, meeting the daily economic needs of individuals.

With the advancement of science and technology, the economies of various countries are experiencing rapid development, and the trend of globalization is continuous. Industrialization cannot be achieved without resources, and currency has continuously developed alongside the progress of the times. Currency can estimate people's potential for the future and can be transformed into resources that can be obtained in the present. When someone needs funds, they can obtain a certain amount of loans through credit, and their credit activity can be evaluated through market behavior. Essentially, currency can achieve the goal of transforming various forms of credit into social resources, which is crucial for the development of market economies and

[8] Chen Fengying, Tao Jian. Changes in the International Financial System and Reflections. Modern International Relations, 1998(12), pp. 33–35.

[9] Zhang Liqing. Research on Global Financial Governance Should Start from Eight Major Issues [EB/OL]. https://a.d4t.cn/NYGzwc or https://mp.weixin.qq.com/s?__biz=MjM5NDg1Nzk3NA==&mid=2652560491&idx=1&sn=b537902e887f28d38714c25b19ec3388&chksm=bd6f2af28a18a3e4ca406f802e43bffd3923a60d93f96843bbc4a133ba105de37499a6eca7f5&scene=27. Accessed 6 May 2022.

credit economies. However, it is important to note that the use of currency also carries risks, as it can lead to overborrowing and unsustainable debt if not managed properly.

However, the issuance and policy formulation of currencies in various countries are dominated by central banks, and the lack of universal regulations for the circulation of currencies due to different policies in different countries has made it difficult to manage. To cope with the impact of the international financial crisis, many countries have implemented loose monetary policies, especially the US Federal Reserve, which has launched loose monetary policies four times in a row, leading to global liquidity flooding. Hayek believed that during the period when precious metals such as gold and silver were used for coinage, the issuance of currency did not pose significant problems. However, with the appearance of paper currency, the defects of national monopoly on currency issuance gradually emerged. With the expansion of the circulation scale, paper currency gradually detached from its relationship with coinage, and its issuance was no longer restricted by precious metal reserves but purely based on the government's demand. All kinds of data show that regardless of which government issues paper currency, it will ultimately lead to depreciation. As long as the government can issue currency and there is no external constraint to restrict its issuance, it will issue an amount that satisfies its own needs, rather than the amount the country can withstand. Therefore, the government lacks the self-control ability of paper currency issuance, which means that it is difficult to issue an "appropriate" amount of currency for circulation without any restrictions. In other words, if a country does not establish a currency issuance supervision system, it is easy to lead to an economic crisis.[10] In this case, an external supervisory mechanism is needed to restrain the country's currency issuance. The currency supervision systems of various countries are all imperfect, which makes the currency constraints of each country a mere empty talk. Due to the lack of self-restraint ability and no external force to control it, the government often issues excessive amounts of currency from the perspective of its own interests rather than those of the country, and this uncontrolled currency printing only leads to nationwide inflation and various serious economic problems.

After analyzing past economic crises, Hayek pointed out that deflation has a smaller impact on the economy than inflation, with deflationary effects being more localized and temporary, while inflationary effects are more widespread and prolonged. Governments control the issuance of currency in circulation, and when faced with deficits, they may implement policies to increase the amount of currency in circulation to cover daily operational expenses. This leads directly to economic crises, resulting in market slump, economic standstill, soaring prices, and rising unemployment.[11] Therefore, some scholars suggest that the inherent flaw in the current international monetary system is the objective economic foundation for the

[10] Sergio Rossi, Global imbalances and international monetary disorder: supranational, Berlin: Paper for the 13th international conference of the Research Network on Macroeconomics and Macroeconomic Policies "The World Economy in Crisis: The Return of Keynesianism?" 2009, pp. 4–13.

[11] FRIEDRICHA. Von HAYEK, *Denationalization of Money*, London: Institute of Economic Affairs, 1976, pp. 40–55.

emergence of Bitcoin. However, the legitimacy of Bitcoin is questioned in many countries and regions, and it is difficult to achieve global recognition of Bitcoin as a currency in the short term. Thus, finding a supersovereign currency combined with blockchain technology as a fundamental tool to solve the problems of the current international monetary system is relatively more feasible.

1.1.2 Defects in the International Monetary System

The current international monetary system relies on sovereign currencies as the major international currency and reserve assets. However, the existence of paper currency has caused governments to unconsciously overissue money, leading to periodic inflation and financial crises. Therefore, the current international monetary system has many flaws, and SDRs cannot fully play their role in the current monetary system.

In 1976, the IMF held a member country conference and reached the famous "Jamaica Agreement," which laid the foundation for the current international monetary system. The agreement includes several main points: first, the sovereign currencies of several economically strong developed countries are designated international reserve currencies, and the US dollar is determined to be the major international currency; second, gold is determined to be nonmonetary, and international currencies are mainly backed by the issuing country's government credit. Gold is no longer directly linked to international currencies. Third, different national currencies are allowed to have floating exchange rates, which can fluctuate freely according to supply and demand in the foreign exchange market. The specific floating mechanism can be set by each country according to its own situation.[12] From the above content, many flaws in the "Jamaica system" can be seen, including a lack of constraints on the issuance of international currencies, a lack of regulatory mechanisms, an unstable exchange rate system, unbalanced rights and responsibilities, and major deficiencies in the decision-making mechanism.

(1) The Triffin Dilemma under the Jamaica System

Although the Jamaica system was much more flexible than the previous Bretton Woods system and made up for the issue of international liquidity, it still faced many challenges, one of which was the unsolved "Triffin Dilemma." The concept of the "Triffin Dilemma" was first introduced by American scholar Robert Triffin in his article "Gold and the Dollar Crisis." Specifically, after the US dollar became the major international currency, other countries wanted to earn more dollars in international trade. This required the US to maintain a long-term trade deficit, which conflicted with the stability and strength of the international currency. To maintain the value and attractiveness of the US dollar as the major international currency, the US needed to

[12] Li Chong. Study on the Construction of Supersovereign International Monetary System [J]. Academic Research, 2014(2), pp. 62–70 + 159.

maintain a long-term trade surplus in international trade. The contradiction between these two requirements is known as the "Triffin Dilemma."[13]

Under the Jamaica Agreement, the "Triffin Dilemma" still existed, but in a different form from its manifestation under the Bretton Woods system. Under the Jamaica system, the US dollar continued to play a central role in international trade, serving as a medium for connecting countries around the world, while other countries obtained dollars through trade, labor, or asset exchanges. In this way, the US was able to benefit from international relationships, for example, through seigniorage, while other countries had to bear the risk of inflation due to fluctuations in the value of the dollar. When there was an excess of dollars in the international trade market, the US usually responded by devaluing the dollar to avoid financial risks. However, this approach could cause significant losses to other countries' dollar reserves and damage their interests. The "Triffin Dilemma" is an issue that arises whenever a sovereign currency serves as an international currency.[14] Therefore, any reform of the international monetary system under the Jamaica Agreement should focus on the problem of a sovereign currency serving as the major international currency.

(2) Imbalance of rights and responsibilities of international currency issuing country

In the principles of international law, every country is supposed to be equal and have the same rights, including equal participation and decision-making power on the same issues. However, the establishment of the Bretton Woods system was clearly influenced by the will of Western developed countries, especially the US. The IMF Agreement was designed almost entirely according to the will of the US, thanks to its strong political, military, and economic power, and therefore solidified the position of the US dollar as the major international currency. Even the former "Empire on which the sun never sets," Britain, had to submit to this arrangement, while most developing countries with weaker capabilities had no choice but to be manipulated by the US. Therefore, the Bretton Woods system, which allowed the US dollar to firmly occupy the position of the major international currency, and even the later Jamaica system, were not a reflection of the common will and interests of all countries in the world. The core logic of serving the strong is also the inevitable result of their collapse.[15]

After the signing of the "Jamaica Agreement," the US dollar became the major international currency. As the biggest beneficiary, the US had an obligation to maintain the existing international monetary system while also shouldering certain responsibilities and obligations. However, when US interests conflicted with the interests of other countries, the US naturally prioritized its own interests. This led to a significant imbalance between the responsibilities it assumed and the rights it obtained and ultimately resulted in the international monetary system's inability to fulfill its fair

[13] TRIFFEN, ROBERT, *Gold and Dollar Crisis*, New Haven: Yale University Press, 1960, pp. 50–67.

[14] Xu Shan, Luo Yangyang, Zhao Zheng. Analysis of Domestic and Foreign Research Status of Currency Internationalization [J]. Economic Research Reference, 2019(11), pp. 49–58.

[15] Li Pengcheng. Micro-Exploration of the International Financial System Crisis. Journal of Guangdong Agricultural and Commercial Administrative Cadre Institute, 2000(3), pp. 50–54.

role.[16] For example, the US increased the issueness of dollars globally through trade deficits with other countries to achieve the goal of transferring domestic debt and increasing its own economic benefits.[17] Other countries, on the other hand, could only passively accept the effects of the dollar's devaluation, which led to resources being somewhat depleted and being subject to US domination in international trade.

In addition, as the provider of the world's main reserve asset, the US can use its currency advantage in financial markets to obtain higher macroeconomic policy control through lower-cost foreign borrowing, thereby enjoying great policy-making privileges. Since the US' assets are primarily domestic and foreign assets, tax revenue, and foreign currency, and its liabilities are foreign exchange and debt denominated in US dollars, it can acquire capital gains through the depreciation of the US dollar. In the years leading up to the 2008 financial crisis, the US used the gradual depreciation of the US dollar to seize capital gains of more than $1 trillion.[18] In addition, the US has gained the privilege of asymmetric adjustment, meaning that when a financial crisis occurs, the US, as the issuing country of the international currency, needs to bear less policy adjustment pressure than noninternational currency issuing countries.[19]

(3) Unstable World Pattern and Volatile Foreign Exchange Market

Despite significant economic imbalances between countries, the globalized economic system has facilitated their collaborative development. However, no country can sustain rapid economic growth indefinitely. Thus, it follows that the currency of any sovereign nation cannot serve as a long-term international currency.

The Bretton Woods system was established during a time when the US held an absolute dominant position in the global economy. However, just 20 years later, the US's relative position in the international economy began to decline, and it experienced multiple currency crises. To protect itself, the US terminated its commitment to exchange gold for dollars, hastening the collapse of the Bretton Woods system.

Subsequently, the Jamaica system was established, which abandoned the use of precious metals as currency and maintained the stability of the international monetary system for a considerable period. However, this system also faced significant problems. Particularly as the US's international influence waned, the value of the US dollar in international trade diminished, leading to volatile exchange rates and a long-term depreciation trend. This situation inflicted severe economic harm upon countries around the world.[20]

The weaknesses of the fixed exchange rate system in the Bretton Woods system were alleviated in the Jamaica system through a floating exchange rate system, which allowed exchange rate tools to play a regulatory role in international economic

---

[16] See footnote 12.

[17] See footnote 14.

[18] Richard Clarida. With Privilege Comes …? At http://www.pimco.com/LeftNav/Global+Markets/Global. Accessed 6 May 2022.

[19] Wang Shuji. The Historical Evolution and Design Ideas of Super-Sovereign Reserve Currency [J]. Wuhan Finance, 2015(4), pp. 8–11.

[20] See footnote 12.

activity to a certain extent. During the period when the US dominated the international economic order, fluctuations in the value of the dollar were adjusted based on the needs of its own economic development. For the US, both upward and downward exchange rates of the dollar could be beneficial, while other countries faced economic risks and losses due to fluctuations in the dollar. However, due to the large fluctuations in the exchange rates of major international currencies, emerging economies and developing countries bear too much risk, which can lead to currency and debt crises.[21] In recent years, particularly after the outbreak of the COVID-19 pandemic, traditional developed countries and regions such as the US, Europe, and Japan have successively adopted multiple rounds of loose monetary policies, monetizing their debt and transferring their internal economic crises through "currency wars" and other means. Because there are only one or two sovereign currencies with the function of major international currency in the current international monetary system, there is an imbalance in the exchange rate risk faced by the issuing countries of international currencies and noninternational currency issuing countries. Emerging economies and developing countries have always relied on international currencies for settlement, pricing, loans, and investments in long-term foreign trade. It is precisely this dependence on economic and financial development that makes emerging economies passive in their choice to peg their currencies to a few currencies such as the US dollar. Their exchange rate system lacks flexibility and is extremely fragile. Developed countries often adjust their exchange rates based on their own circumstances and interests, which leads to great risks in the exchange rates of developing countries and emerging economies that adopt fixed exchange rate systems and makes it difficult to reflect their true economic situation. As a result, the regulatory role of exchange rate tools in these countries is greatly weakened, and asset risks and exchange rate risks caused by currency mismatches cannot be avoided. At the same time, frequent large fluctuations in the exchange rates of major international currency issuing countries not only seriously interfere with the normal conduct of international trade and investment but also cause the exchange rates of other noninternational currency issuing countries to change dramatically, which can lead to currency and debt crises in these countries. In response, Mundell believes that the violent fluctuations in the exchange rates of emerging economies and developing countries are caused by frequent fluctuations in the exchange rates of major international currencies, which provide opportunities for international speculative capital to engage in foreign exchange speculation and ultimately become a direct cause of their currency crises. It is precisely because of the dual impact of foreign exchange speculation and exchange rate shocks that emerging economies in Asia and Latin America experienced debt and currency crises in the 1980s and 1990s, leading to social unrest and economic development difficulties.[22] In addition, frequent fluctuations in the international exchange rate system also affect the normal conduct of international

[21] See footnote 14.

[22] He Shulan. The Rise of Emerging Economies and the Reform of the International Monetary System [J]. International Economic Cooperation, 2012(10), pp. 80–86.

economic activity. In particular, individuals, institutions, or organizations specializing in international economic activity face changes in international exchange rates, either paying additional costs to mitigate risks through hedging strategies or not taking protective measures and suffering losses due to exchange rate fluctuations. At the same time, frequent fluctuations in international exchange rates will also lead to foreign exchange speculation, which has also been one of the root causes of frequent financial crises worldwide since the 1990s.[23]

(4) Unfair to Developing Countries

In the Bretton Woods and Jamaica systems, global economic crises were frequent occurrences, leaving emerging economies with no other option but to protect themselves by amassing large foreign exchange reserves. Moreover, due to the increasingly stringent loan conditions imposed by international financial institutions such as the IMF and the World Bank, developing countries have become increasingly reluctant to accept their loans. As a result, they have accumulated massive foreign exchange reserves over the past few decades.

Between 2003 and 2007, countries worldwide accumulated an average of $177 billion in foreign exchange reserves per year, which amounts to approximately 1.6% of global GDP. By 2007, foreign exchange reserves had grown to account for 11.7% of global GDP. As of 2008, developing countries and emerging economies had amassed between $4 trillion and $4.5 trillion in foreign exchange reserves for insurance purposes, which represented two-thirds of their total foreign exchange reserves and exceeded the growth rate of the previous decade.[24]

As of May 2021, China had accumulated a total of $3221.803 billion in foreign exchange reserves, accounting for 25.6% of the world's total foreign exchange reserves.[25] The US, Russia, Brazil, and Mexico held foreign exchange reserves of $433.26 billion, $435.984 billion, $336.905 billion, and $185.161 billion, respectively. The total foreign exchange reserves of developing countries and emerging economies account for more than half of the world's foreign exchange reserves.[26]

Emerging economies and developing countries hold vast foreign exchange reserves, which means that they transfer a significant amount of their resources to the international currency issuing countries. This phenomenon not only distorts global capital flows, but it also reduces the benefits of capital account liberalization. When the reduction in foreign exchange reserves is caused not only by a decrease in foreign private capital inflows but also by current account surpluses, it can lead to a decline in global aggregate demand.[27]

---

[23] See footnote 12.

[24] M. Odstfeld & J. C. Shambaugh & A. M. Taylor, Financial Stability, the Trilemma, and International Reserves, NBER Working Paper, No. 14217 2008.

[25] China's State Administration of Foreign Exchange, Official Reserve Assets [EB/OL]. http://www.safe.gov.cn/safe/whcb/index.html. Accessed 6 May 2022.

[26] CEIC DATA. US foreign exchange reserves. https://www.ceicdata.com/zh-hans/indicator/united-states/foreign-exchange-reserves. Accessed 6 May 2022.

[27] See footnote 19.

According to the "original sin of small country currencies" theory proposed by American economist McKinnon in 1963, if a small country has a long-term trade surplus in its current account, its foreign exchange reserves will inevitably continue to increase, leading to appreciation of its local currency. However, this can result in rapid increases in domestic asset prices and liquidity, ultimately leading to an even larger economic bubble. For example, Japan experienced this situation after signing the Plaza Accord. On the other hand, if a small country consistently has a trade deficit in its current account, it needs to borrow from abroad to cover its budget deficits, resulting in a sustained depreciation of its local currency. As foreign debt accumulates, this can lead to a debt crisis or currency crisis. The 1995 peso crisis in Mexico is a typical example of this situation. Therefore, a small country's noninternational currency must be consistent with the international currency. When there is international financial turmoil, small countries often experience massive capital outflows, leading to currency and debt crises. In addition, fluctuations in the exchange rate of the international currency can create opportunities for arbitrage in the small country's currency market, leading to international speculators targeting the small country's currency.[28]

Therefore, the only way for a small noninternational currency issuing country to avoid losses or being targeted is to maintain a balance in its current account and strictly align with international currencies. Even in the case of continuous overissuance of the US dollar, the small country's currency must follow the speed of the US dollar's issuance to avoid the risk of currency speculation caused by the small country's currency appreciation or depreciation being too small or too large, which could result in an economic impact on the country and lead to economic recession. Thailand was a good example of this during the Southeast Asian financial crisis in the twentieth century. If a small country's currency takes unilateral action to resist the US dollar, the inevitable result is self-destruction. This is the inequality and tragedy of the fate of small country currencies under the current international monetary system dominated by large countries with international currency powers.[29]

Meanwhile, the GDP of emerging economies has approached 50% of the global total GDP, while their financial assets account for only 19% of the global total financial assets, which is significantly lower than their proportion of GDP. This means that emerging economies need to bear more financial risks than larger countries. Moreover, since the currencies of most emerging economies are pegged to the US dollar, their monetary policy independence has been greatly weakened. Furthermore, after the financial crisis, a large amount of hot money flowed into emerging economies, not only further increasing their foreign exchange reserves but also exacerbating their input-oriented inflation risks, making them increasingly vulnerable to US debt risks.[30]

[28] Liu Junmin, Li Lingyun. The "Dual Standard" International Monetary System and the Global Financial Crisis. Asia–Pacific Economy, 2009(5), pp. 22–26.

[29] Li Lingyun. Formation and Influence of the "Dual Standard" International Monetary System [D]. Tianjin: Nankai University, 2010, pp. 186–189.

[30] See footnote 22.

(5) "Currency Overissuance Trap"

When discussing the "currency trap," one must first understand "Gresham's law," which is one of the few recognized and widely discussed laws in the field of economics related to the circulation of money. It refers to the tendency of people to hoard higher-value coins and use lower-value coins for transactions when both types of coins are in circulation, leading to the disappearance of higher-value coins from the market. When paper currency is introduced, this creates a "currency trap." In today's multicurrency system, the overissuance of any international currency will force other more stable currencies to follow. Otherwise, countries with more stable currencies will not only suffer significant losses in asset gains from overseas but also face the risk of economic recession due to currency appreciation and declining exports.[31]

Therefore, in the current international monetary system, once a sovereign currency is issued, there is no automatic mechanism for it to exit circulation, and central banks around the world often use "liquidity hedging" to reduce excess cash in circulation. However, since currency cannot be automatically removed from circulation once it is issued, its ultimate fate can only be devaluation.

After the birth of the Euro, the world entered the era of international currency diversification. If the US dollar is overissued, causing its exchange rate to continuously decline, but the euro is not overissued, the euro will continue to appreciate, leading to a decline in European exports and a continuous increase in inflation. Therefore, in a diversified international monetary system, the overissue of any international currency will force other international currencies to overissue as well and thus cause the entire international monetary system to fall into a serious "currency trap."

Meanwhile, countries that obtain current account surpluses in their trade with the US often use foreign exchange reserves to purchase US Treasury bonds, government agency bonds, and other relatively safe financial products denominated in US dollars. This creates a world flow of US dollars, as the cash flows back to the US. For these countries with current account surpluses, there are not only large amounts of US dollar reserves but also equivalent amounts of US dollar bonds and their own currencies. This also indicates that offshore US dollars have created at least twice their broad liquidity.

Additionally, when offshore dollars flow back to the US through various dollar-denominated bonds, a portion of these dollars will flow out of the US again through transfer payments and government spending on overseas products and services. Another portion of the dollars can flow back to the US in the form of nonofficial financial products, such as purchasing stocks and corporate bonds of American companies or being deposited in American banks or financial institutions. Some dollars remain in the US in the form of resident loans, stocks, funds, and others flow overseas by purchasing foreign products, which eventually flow back to the US through investments, loans, and other means, further increasing global liquidity.

From the above description of the circulation of the US dollar both inside and outside the US, it can be seen that offshore dollars can cause the basic currency

[31] See footnote 28.

of other countries to increase by at least twice. In addition, taking into account the different currency multipliers of each country, the inflation of money is bound to become increasingly serious. As international liquidity continues to be invested or speculated on in commodity futures markets, capital markets, and currency markets, the liquidity of international currencies abroad will be magnified three to five times and will be further multiplied through financial leverage tools. This cycle of the circulation of US dollars both inside and outside the country will continue to exist and intensify, ultimately leading to increasingly severe global inflation. After the euro was introduced, it began playing the same cyclic game as the US dollar, but at a faster pace, further exacerbating the inflation of liquidity in the entire world.[32]

When gold is no longer used as currency, the issuance of the US dollar is no longer restricted. As the US dollar flows continuously to the world through the US trade deficit, its fate is no longer solely in the hands of the US government but is increasingly tied to overseas speculative activities. The US Federal Reserve's control over the direction and fate of the US dollar's development becomes increasingly inadequate. The confidence of global private equity funds, sovereign wealth funds, mutual funds, hedge funds, and other international investment institutions in US government bonds and agency bonds has become a force that determines the direction and fate of the US dollar.[33]

(6) Frequent Financial Crises

Since the 1980s, a series of financial crises have exposed inherent flaws and systemic risks in the current international monetary system. The Latin American debt crisis, the Asian financial crisis of 1997, the global financial crisis of 2008, and the ongoing Eurozone crisis have all had a significant impact. According to data from the World Bank, there were a total of 108 financial crises of varying scales from the 1980s to the late 1990s. Of these, there were 45 financial crises in the 1980s and 63 financial crises in the 1990s, a 40% increase from the previous decade. The vast majority of countries severely impacted by these crises were economically underdeveloped.[34]

The "dollar crisis" was a frequent occurrence in the later period of the Bretton Woods system, with 9 instances happening in just 13 years in the 1960s and 1970s. Despite triggering these crises, the US did not suffer the anticipated losses but instead emerged as the ultimate beneficiary. The US government and monopolistic financial groups continuously appropriated seigniorage and currency exchange profits, leading to persistent trade deficits and inflation, ultimately resulting in the "dollar crisis." Although the US experienced serious fiscal deficits and debts during this time, two large-scale public devaluations of the dollar were carried out, the position of the dollar as the core international currency remained unshaken. This suggests that these

[32] Liu Junmin, Zhang Yun. Liquidity Expansion Dilemma and Its Response from the Perspective of Virtual Economy. Reform, 2008(1), pp. 18–25.

[33] Liu Junmin, Li Lingyun. Global Economic Imbalances and Financial Crisis in the Virtualization of World Economy. Social Sciences, 2009(1), pp. 3–11.

[34] Jamus Jerome Lim & Geoffrey Minne, Learning from Financial Crises, Word Bank Policy Research Working Papers, April 2014, pp. 5–11.

dollar devaluations and "dollar crises" were foreseeable by the US government and its monopolistic financial groups.[35] While some "dollar crises" could ease the US domestic economy and asset bubbles, creditor countries of the dollar suffered greatly, which was grossly unfair to emerging economies and developing countries that were major dollar creditors.

(7) Defects of the IMF

A reasonable and efficient international monetary system is crucial for maintaining a stable global financial order. However, the existing international monetary and financial systems, including the IMF, have inherent flaws that hinder their effectiveness.

First, the establishment of a sound and reasonable international monetary system is the basis for ensuring the stable operation of the international financial order. However, the international monetary and financial systems established thus far, as well as the IMF itself, have inherent flaws.

When the IMF was established, its primary responsibility was to promote cooperation in the international monetary field, provide ways and means for countries to address international monetary issues, and address short-term foreign exchange shortages and imbalances in international payments for developing countries and regions. It also aimed to improve the international trade system and ensure the smooth flow of economic and trade activities among countries. However, after the collapse of the Bretton Woods system, the IMF failed to adopt appropriate mechanisms to fulfill its core function of maintaining exchange rate stability. Consequently, the legitimacy of its mechanisms has been questioned by many developing countries.

Although the IMF has made modifications to its articles of agreement to enhance its adaptability and self-regulatory capacity, it is still unable to cope with changes in the international economic landscape. Over the past few decades, the economic structure of countries around the world has undergone fundamental changes, and the trend of economic globalization has become a consensus. If we continue to adhere to the international governance mechanism of the IMF created based on the international situation and environment at the end of World War II, it is evident that we will be unable to overcome the inherent flaws of the international monetary system.

Second, the IMF also suffers from serious lagging in its early warning and emergency response mechanisms. For example, in 1997, the IMF did not detect the upcoming financial crisis in Southeast Asia in its "World Economic Survey." In August of that year, the IMF even gave high praise to Thailand's economic policies, calling them safe and sound.[36] However, shortly thereafter, Thailand's economy collapsed, triggering a widespread economic crisis throughout Southeast Asia. It is clear that the IMF's early warning mechanism is severely lagging and is no longer able to cope with the current financial environment. Furthermore, it may even make

---

[35] He Bingmeng, Li Qian. Correct Understanding of the Essence of the Contemporary International Monetary and Financial System. Red Flag Manuscripts, 2007(11), pp. 35–38.

[36] Chen An, Li Guoan. International Monetary and Financial Law [M]. Beijing: Peking University Press, 1999, p. 17, 71, 73.

erroneous judgments about the economic situation of the international community or individual countries, providing misleading reports on international economic development. At the same time, the IMF's regulatory lag and inaccurate information gathering limit its predictive ability, resulting in its inability to fully fulfill its role.

The IMF typically implements rigid "austerity + openness" plans without distinguishing between countries when faced with economic crises. When the IMF provided assistance to different countries affected by the Latin American debt crisis and the Southeast Asian financial crisis, it used the same rescue plan, which was not ideal because the two crises had significant differences in their times and nature. Latin America and Africa's overall economies are relatively backward, with government loans and budget deficits remaining at high levels. Therefore, they need to choose the method of using austerity policies to reduce local financial burdens. In contrast, Southeast Asian countries' economic development is relatively good, with each country basically able to maintain a balance between income and expenditure, with relatively low government debt levels and high savings levels. The reason for their high debt levels is mainly due to blind borrowing by private companies and reckless lending by foreign capital. Another important reason for the Southeast Asian financial crisis was the lack of confidence in the market and the deliberate suppression of capital, which triggered factors that led to the crisis. Without conducting a specific analysis of each country's situation, the IMF adopted the same rescue plan for all countries receiving assistance, and the consequences had to be borne by the recipient countries. This approach may even bring adverse effects to the recipient countries. In this situation, many developing countries have expressed dissatisfaction with the current international monetary system and have called for reform.

Meanwhile, except for Japan and the UK, most noninternational currency issuing countries are developing countries and emerging economies. When a financial crisis hits, these countries often suffer the most severe impact. However, developed countries frequently turn around and blame them for their slow response and improper actions, as was the case in the 1997 financial crisis. In a sense, these emerging economies and developing countries are innocent victims, bearing punishment and paying a huge price for the improper behavior of some developed economies and the government's inadequate regulation. Therefore, these countries hope that the design and reform of the international monetary system can take into account the weak position of small noninternational currency issuing countries and establish corresponding protection mechanisms for them, rather than waiting until they are on the brink of bankruptcy before they receive limited help from the IMF. In addition, the high conditions set by the IMF for receiving financial assistance have also led many developing countries to believe that this is not truly saving them.[37]

According to international practice, if a country violates international law, it is required to bear the legal consequences. Although the international financial sector is also part of the adjustment of international law, the binding force of the international monetary system is far lower than that of ordinary international law. Even if there is a breach of contract, it usually does not lead to serious legal consequences, and

---

[37] See footnote 29.

the corresponding country does not need to bear significant legal responsibilities. This also results in the rules of the international monetary system lacking mandatory force internationally. Although the IMF stipulates the obligations of member countries, requiring them to avoid restrictions on current payments, avoid discriminatory currency arrangements and multiple exchange rate practices, etc., such provisions do not have corresponding international legal binding force. Therefore, even if member countries do not fulfill their obligations as stipulated, the IMF can only implement "remedies" rather than mandatory "sanction" measures. However, precisely because of this, it can maintain a long-term harmonious relationship between the IMF and its member countries. The IMF usually has two ways to deal with member countries that do not fulfill their obligations: one is to publicly judge and adjudicate their behavior, which is a nonmandatory measure; the other is to stop financial support for them and force them to withdraw from the IMF, which is a mandatory measure.

In actual operations, when a member state fails to fulfill its obligations under the agreement, the IMF does not immediately implement mandatory measures but instead adopts remedial measures. Even if serious problems arise, the IMF seeks more appropriate solutions through peaceful negotiations.[38] As a result, the IMF typically does not impose any sanctions when faced with a member state's failure to fulfill its obligations, which has led to more developed countries blatantly violating the relevant provisions of the agreement. The consequences of member states failing to fulfill their obligations often result in currency devaluation, foreign exchange sales, and the transfer of financial crises, but member states do not have to bear any legal responsibility for the serious consequences they have caused. In sharp contrast, the IMF takes a tough stance on developing countries, even intervening in their domestic policies in the name of aiding disaster-stricken countries. The IMF's loan conditions are a good example of this. For instance, when a country accepts a loan from the IMF, it must also accept harsh conditions that may seriously damage its interests and even provoke opposition from its people. In 1998, the IMF demanded that South Korea reduce its economic growth rate from 6 to 3%, control its inflation rate within 5%, restructure its domestic financial institutions, implement tight monetary policies nationwide, change the insurance system between parent and subsidiary companies, allow foreign financial institutions to enter South Korea, and increase the limit on foreign entities' ownership of Korean enterprises from 26 to 50%, as well as requiring South Korea to open its capital markets.[39]

The IMF often uses special procedures with member countries to strengthen its "soft law" system and achieve its goal of restraining member countries. However, the effectiveness of this approach only applies to developing countries. The IMF is powerless in regard to developed countries, especially economic powers, which enjoy an absolute advantage in the international financial market. This has resulted in developing countries being to some extent restricted by institutional arrangements.

[38] See footnote 36.

[39] Shao Jie, Qian Yong. IMF Economic Assistance Plan and the Reform of International Financial Institutions [J]. New Finance, 1998(4), p. 871.

It can be seen that the IMF's institutional flaws have caused enormous contradictions between different countries and have led to constantly intensifying conflicts of interest, even to the extent of impacting the existing international financial system and exacerbating financial crises.

Therefore, from the perspective of internal mechanisms, the international monetary system has deviated greatly from its original conception. Financial superpowers and strong economies have increasingly gained power in international financial markets and are able to influence the order of the global financial market through their monetary policies while transferring their financial crises to other countries. Meanwhile, most developing countries are left to bear the consequences. This inequality caused by the existing international monetary system shows that reform is necessary.

Last, there are obvious flaws in the IMF's weighted voting system. Although the system was established to promote equality among nations and the IMF distributed 250 basic votes to its member countries to represent their equal rights, the votes with decision-making power are mainly weighted votes, which are allocated based on each member country's contribution to the fund. This system clearly favors economically developed countries. In particular, the US, as the world's only superpower, holds absolute veto power in the IMF. Although the US has reduced its voting share in the IMF under pressure from other countries, it still holds 16.51% of the voting power[40] and thus maintains its veto power. Many economic researchers from various countries propose that the current system should be changed to ensure that the amount of funds a country contributes is directly related to its voting power. Additionally, the IMF's selection mechanism for its management team is not transparent enough, and there is a low representation of developing countries. Although the IMF implemented the "Executive Board Reform Amendment" in 2016, which ended the tradition of designating an executive director and shifted to an elected executive board,[41] the power imbalance among the management team still exists, and developing countries still occupy an unfairly small position. All these factors have resulted in a "democratic deficit" in the decision-making and operational processes of the IMF, weakening its legitimacy, effectiveness, and fairness. Therefore, to change this widely criticized situation, the international monetary system must re-examine its legal foundation and undergo reform.[42]

---

[40] IMF. IMF Members' Quotas and Voting Power, and IMF Board of Governors at https://www.imf.org/external/np/sec/memdir/members.aspx. Accessed 6 May 2022.

[41] The Executive Board is a permanent body responsible for managing the daily business of the IMF, composed of 24 Executive Directors. Prior to this, eight Executive Directors were appointed by the five member countries with the largest shares in the fund—the United States, the United Kingdom, Germany, France, and Japan each appointed one, and China, Russia, and Saudi Arabia each appointed one. The remaining 16 Executive Directors were elected by 16 constituencies of other member countries. For reference, see the "Fifteenth General Review of Quotas—Report of the Executive Board to the Board of Governors" at https://www.imf.org/en/Publications/Policy-Papers/Issues/2016/12/31/Fifteenth-General-Review-of-Quotas-Report-of-the-Executive-Board-to-the-Board-of-Governors-PP5016. Accessed 6 May 2022.

[42] See footnote 15.

(8) The Launch of the Euro Has a Huge Impact on the Current International Financial System

On January 1, 1999, the euro was officially introduced, marking the beginning of the coexistence of the euro and the US dollar in the international monetary system. This event posed a strong challenge to the unipolar dominance of the US dollar and ushered in a new "bipolar" era of international currency. Although the US dollar still maintains its dominance among major international currencies and remains the preferred currency for settling international transactions in areas such as oil trading and bulk commodities, it is important to note that the euro is gradually gaining recognition and acceptance in international trade, reserves, and investment. As a result, the international status of the euro is gradually rising, and its use is becoming increasingly common.

In 1999, statistical data indicated that the combined GDP of the 11 countries in the Eurozone already represented 20% of the world's total economic output, with a stock and bond market size exceeding 21 trillion US dollars. While still falling short of the US's 23 trillion US dollars, this figure had already surpassed that of Japan, which was then the world's third-largest economy, with a GDP of 16 trillion US dollars. Following the unification of the Eurozone's financial markets, the relative cost of financial transactions decreased, and financial assets traded in euros became popular among people in the world. As a result, the euro has become the second most favored international currency for investors, after the US dollar.

The usage and influence of the euro in the international financial market continue to grow, which is leading to significant impacts on the reform of the international monetary system. It is foreseeable that the future international exchange rate system will depend heavily on market fluctuations of both the US dollar and the euro. Any changes in the exchange rate between these two currencies can have enormous effects on the value of assets priced in either of them. The euro's rapid ascension and important role in the market will inevitably challenge the current flawed international monetary system. As a result, some experts even predict that the euro may eventually replace the US dollar as the primary international currency. They believe that the euro's stability and resilience will increasingly play a significant role in the international financial market, while the US dollar may continue to lose its strength.[43]

For a considerable period of time, the US has benefited from its dominant position in the international financial market by continuously printing US dollars, causing their value to decrease and generating international trade benefits for the country. However, this approach has resulted in significant economic losses for other countries under the existing international monetary system. Despite this, other countries had no choice but to accept the situation. The rise of the euro has played a critical role in curbing the US dollar's dominance and balancing the responsibilities of international currencies. This means that any changes in the leading international currencies will have a direct impact on the prospects for reform of the international monetary system. Unfortunately, despite initial hopes that the euro would help balance the international

[43] Li Shuren. European Monetary Integration and the International Monetary System. World Economy, 1998(1), p. 421.

monetary system, events such as Brexit and the Greek debt crisis have shown that the euro has not lived up to expectations. In fact, it has further destabilized the already volatile and "multipolar" international monetary landscape.

The rise of the euro has had a significant impact on the US dollar, leading to increased instability in the global financial system and volatility in the international monetary system. This instability can be seen as a systemic root cause of potential global economic crises. Nonetheless, it is important to acknowledge that the emergence of the euro has also acted as a catalyst for the reform of the current international monetary system, signaling the need for change.[44]

1.1.3 Problems with SDRs

As previously mentioned, the SDR was issued by the IMF in the late 1960s to alleviate the pressure of the US dollar as an international reserve asset. Its function is similar to that of gold and foreign exchange, becoming a major reserve asset for various countries. As a form of international reserve asset that differs from other international reserve assets, SDRs have become assets with stable value, low cost, high international visibility, and high international recognition. However, it still has many defects and shortcomings, and it is precisely because of these shortcomings that it cannot yet become a supersovereign currency in the international monetary system.[45]

(1) Narrow Usage Scope

According to the IMF Agreement, SDRs are primarily used for member countries to repay IMF loans and settle trade between themselves. SDRs cannot be directly used as a currency for financial transactions or personal payments in economic transactions. Furthermore, their role in global trade is minimal, resulting in low demand and acceptance in the international market.[46] Some scholars have criticized SDRs for their narrow usage and limited scope, which prevents them from playing a larger role in balancing the international monetary and financial system.

Despite its limitations, SDRs are different from traditional currencies because they have no physical form and can only be reflected in financial settlements. This similarity can be drawn with cryptocurrencies that do not have a material medium. SDRs could have been developed and applied in private markets with the support of relevant policies, but this has not yet been achieved. They have also not developed into a widely accepted and recognized currency such as the US dollar or the euro.

---

[44] See footnote 15.

[45] He Qufu, Xu Xijing, Peng Rong. Prospects for the Development of Bitcoin in the Background of the Reform of the International Monetary System with a Supersovereign Currency Orientation [J]. Economist, 2017(4), pp. 15–17 + 19.

[46] Ge Zhaoqiang. Research on International Monetary System Reform and RMB Internationalization. Journal of Capital University of Economics and Business, 2009(5), pp. 29–38.

Although the trade flow of SDRs has increased since the 1980s due to the IMF's reciprocal agreements, only a few economically developed countries recognize SDRs. These countries represent only approximately one-tenth of the IMF member countries, with the rest being economically underdeveloped countries that require financial support.[47] This means that the current usage of SDRs is still very limited, and there is a need to further increase their usability and liquidity to enable them to play a more significant role in the international monetary system.

(2) Insufficient Currency Basket and Few Currency Types

Currently, the currency basket of SDRs is still incomplete. This is primarily because fixed-value currencies rely solely on the five major reserve currencies, with the US dollar continuing to occupy a dominant position. Furthermore, there is a significant disparity in distribution between developed and developing countries. Although the Chinese yuan became a fixed-value currency in the SDR currency basket eight years ago, it is not enough to meet the demands of a rapidly developing global economy that is becoming increasingly diverse. Relying solely on the five major reserve currencies does not provide sufficient balance and stability to effectively cope with economic crises. This approach also limits its recognition and acceptance in developing countries and regions. Therefore, it is crucial to develop a more diverse and stable currency basket to ensure stability and resilience in the international financial system.

(3) Lack of a Material Basis for Maintaining Currency Stability

SDRs are used solely as a unit of account, as they lack a corresponding tangible asset to provide value. Unlike gold, SDRs do not have a stable value attribute, nor do they possess the national credit and tax base backing of the US dollar, which is considered a hard currency due to the US's strong gross domestic product and tax collection capabilities. In contrast, the IMF does not have gross domestic product or tax collection capabilities and thus lacks the fundamental conditions for creating monetary credit.

Moreover, SDRs are not currently a market-oriented asset. The IMF entirely controls their pricing, yield, holding, and use. As a result, their value and income are not determined by the market, and they do not reflect changes in the value and income of the basket currencies that comprise their value base due to supply and demand changes. Therefore, SDRs do not integrate well with the market and lack a basis for maintaining their currency stability or the ability to interact and adjust with the market.

In summary, while SDRs are a valuable tool for international reserve diversification and supplementing global liquidity, they face significant limitations due to their lack of a tangible asset, market-oriented characteristics, and interaction with the global financial system.

[47] See footnote 1.

(4) The United States Has Effective Veto Power

According to the operational rules of the IMF, the higher the share of a member country is, the greater its influence. Therefore, for a long time, the US held the majority of shares and power in the IMF, firmly controlling the organization. After the IMF's capital increase in 2010, the US subscribed to 17.67% of the total funds. As of May 2023, the US holds 829.942 billion SDRs, accounting for 17.43% of the total shares and 16.5% of the total voting rights.[48] According to IMF rules, decisions on major issues must receive more than 85% of the voting rights in favor of being passed, which means that the US has de facto veto power within the IMF. Especially in regard to events related to major interests and economic decisions, the support of the US must be obtained.

Although the US has gradually declined in its position in the global economy since the 1990s, its share and voting weight in the IMF have also been decreasing, and the other developed countries that have an interest in the US still have a significant influence. Even though the US's influence on the IMF has shifted more behind the scenes since the 1990s, it does not change the fact that the US controls the operation and decision-making of the IMF.[49]

(5) Insufficient Currency Attributes

SDRs are a type of artificial currency unit that has not yet developed into a fully fledged currency and can at best be referred to as a "crippled currency." SDRs mainly serve as a unit of account currency in international transactions. If SDRs are to further develop into a true international currency, the IMF would have to lower its usage restrictions and increase its total issuance, as it is difficult to imagine a currency unit that accounts for less than 1% of international reserves becoming a major international currency.[50] Scholars such as Bergsten argue that SDRs do not possess the characteristics of a currency because they are just derivatives of five currencies (the US dollar, Japanese yen, euro, British pound, and Chinese yuan), and derivatives are not currencies. Additionally, the IMF explicitly states that SDRs cannot be used as a currency or represent the debt owed by member countries to the IMF. Rather, SDRs have significance in international trade as a potential claim to freely circulating currencies. Politicians from the US and the EU may agree to expand the circulation scope and central position of SDRs, but they have been reluctant to cede currency issuing rights to the IMF. Developing countries, on the other hand, have smaller SDR allocations and are less willing to cede currency issuing rights. Therefore, the current SDRs do not possess the attributes of a currency and are not yet a true currency.

---

[48] See footnote 40.

[49] Liu Cheng. How China is dismantling US financial hegemony [EB/OL]. http://www.banbijiang.com/book/story.php?id=46946. Accessed 6 May 2022.

[50] See footnote 1.

(6) Lack of Liquidity

In the real world, the liquidity of the US dollar and the euro asset markets is already very strong, and the cost of increasing the liquidity of SDRs is very high.[51] SDRs are a nonlegal and intangible currency, and upgrading them to a tangible currency would be extremely expensive. At the same time, the transportation and circulation costs of distributing tangible currency to countries around the world are very high, and they may face blockades from certain sovereign nations, increasing their circulation costs and even rendering them noncirculating. Therefore, if SDRs are to follow the path of global circulation like the US dollar and euro, it is not only costly to issue and circulate but also face heavy resistance, making it difficult to truly materialize and implement.

(7) Small Scale

Currently, the total amount of SDRs is only equivalent to 0.33% of global GDP, less than 1% of global trade volume and 4% of global currency reserves. Its size is completely inadequate to meet the basic demand for currency volume in international economic transactions. In addition, the unfair distribution ratio, where developed countries receive a larger proportion than developing countries,[52] makes it difficult for SDRs to become an international currency. Furthermore, the small size of SDRs also severely limits their application and promotion.

1.2 Reform Plans of the IMF and SDRs

The current international monetary system is plagued by several problems, including the "Triffin Dilemma," unequal treatment of different countries, and the self-interest of the US as the sole major international currency issuer. These issues have contributed significantly to the instability of the global international monetary and financial order. Experts such as Zhang Tao and Tao Kunyu argue that the failure to address the "Triffin Dilemma" in the current system will perpetuate conflicts of interest among member countries of the IMF and jeopardize the stability of the global financial environment. Moreover, inadequate regulation and a lack of effective regulatory mechanisms further exacerbate the problems with the system. Therefore, it is crucial to address these shortcomings and implement reforms aimed at improving the functionality of SDRs, constructing a robust global financial security network, and establishing and strengthening regulatory mechanisms applicable at an international level.[53]

---

[51] Barry Eichengreen, The Dollar Dilemma: The World's Top Currency Faces Competition, 88 Foreign Affairs 2009(5), pp. 47–49. anbijiang.com/book/story.php?id=46946. Accessed 6 May 2022.

[52] See footnote 51.

[53] Zhang Tao. "SDR Boosts International Monetary System Reform." [N]. First Financial Daily, September 5, 2016, p. A11.

Currently, the need for reforming the international monetary system has become increasingly urgent, and scholars have proposed various reform proposals to address the issues within the system. The theoretical viewpoints can be broadly classified into two camps: the "radical camp" proposes the establishment of a single, supersovereign currency to solve the "Triffin Dilemma" faced by the US dollar, while the "reformist camp" believes that the existing international monetary system can be improved by increasing the diversity of international currencies and implementing measures to ensure mutual constraints among all factors within the system.[54]

There are three different views among the "radical" camp. The first view is to establish a supersovereign currency within the current international monetary system framework but still based on the current sovereign currency. This could be achieved by restoring the monopoly position of the US dollar and gold or directly designating the euro as a supersovereign currency. However, this proposal cannot convince other countries, as it is essentially a regression in the system, and this proposition is almost impossible to implement. The second view is to expand the role of SDRs and elevate their status to a supersovereign currency. Some scholars, including the former governor of the Central Bank of China Zhou Xiaochuan, have suggested using SDRs as an international currency to address the deficiencies and "Triffin Dilemma" of the current international monetary system.[55] The third view is to create a completely new supersovereign currency. Advocates of this proposal include scholars such as He Qufu. They have conducted a comprehensive analysis of the characteristics, development status, advantages, and disadvantages of Bitcoin and believe that Bitcoin can be defined as a supersovereign currency because it has neutrality and fairness that other sovereign currencies cannot match and can meet the requirements of decentralization and other attributes of a supersovereign currency in the international financial market.[56] However, some scholars have raised doubts about the concept of a supersovereign currency, questioning whether it can become an ideal currency and whether it can truly be achieved. For example, scholar Zheng Jianhua holds a pessimistic attitude toward the realization of a supersovereign currency, believing that in the current international financial market structure, if major economies and economic powers cannot benefit from the system, they are likely to form alliances to resist the emergence of a supersovereign currency, causing the birth of a supersovereign currency to lose its proper environment.[57]

On the other hand, the "reformist" camp suggests implementing measures such as the diversification of international currencies within the existing framework of the international monetary system. This would ensure that various factors within the system constrain each other, preventing any one country from having too much

[54] See footnote 14.

[55] Zhou Xiaochuan. Thoughts on Reforming the International Monetary System. Theoretical Reference, 2009(10), pp. 4–5.

[56] See footnote 45.

[57] Zheng Jianhua. Discussion on International Monetary System Reform: On the Internationalization of RMB. Macroeconomic Research, 2014(7), pp. 112–121 + 135.

power in the issuance of international currency and thereby maintaining stability in the overall international financial environment.

Currently, the international trend is toward establishing a diversified international monetary system, increasing the internationalization of sovereign currencies such as the Chinese yuan, and establishing a basket of currencies mechanism. Scholars such as Li Daokui believe that due to the influence of currency and economic cycles, the hegemonic position of the US dollar will remain dominant for a long time and that in the future, the international financial market will evolve toward a tri-polar system consisting of the US dollar, the euro, and the Chinese yuan. To continue promoting the reform of the international monetary system, China should maintain a long-term balance of payments surplus, improve the domestic financial market environment, follow the trend of international monetary system reform, and assume the responsibilities and obligations of an international currency issuing country.[58]

1.2.1 Reform Plans of the International Monetary System

Since the twentieth century, due to the extreme instability of the international monetary system and frequent financial crises, governments and experts around the world have proposed various reform plans. Among them, some of the typical reform proposals are as follows.

(1) Return to the Gold Standard

Restoring the gold standard requires all countries to join a gold-based international union, in which they would confirm or simultaneously change their stable relationship between their currencies and gold and determine the gold content of each country's currency. This would prevent currency overissuance and maintain the stability of each country's currency value. The gold standard would also take advantage of the fixed and natural value of gold production to combat inflation, adjust currency balances, and eliminate fiscal deficits in each country. Furthermore, it would operate automatically through the "price-coin flow mechanism" to regulate the balance of payments in the international economy and ensure sustainable development of the world economy.

However, the gold standard system also had many inherent flaws that could not be overcome. First, each country only cared about maintaining its own economic balance and did not pay attention to maintaining the international economic balance. Second, it was difficult for countries to reject the use of the gold exchange standard, which was a substitute for gold that reduced transaction costs offered by the world's superpowers. This inevitably led to the accumulation of gold by these powers, which undermined the "price-coin flow mechanism" and ultimately led to the collapse of the gold standard. Third, as the world's superpowers eventually accumulated large amounts of gold and built up sufficient gold reserves to stabilize their economies,

[58] Li Daokui, Yin Xingzhong. New Structure of the International Monetary System: Research on the PostFinancial Crisis Era [J]. Financial Research, 2010(2), pp. 31–43.

other countries would bear the brunt of exchange rate fluctuations and the adjustment of international balances. Finally, since the global growth of gold production was far lower than the growth of the world's total output, it could not meet the demands of global economic growth and maintain price stability. As a result, it would ultimately lead to global deflation.[59]

Meanwhile, gold has always been an international reserve currency and the foundation of the international monetary system, performing the function of some supersovereign currencies and occupying an important position in the international monetary system. Member countries can exchange their sovereign currency for gold based on the value of their currency, maintaining relative stability between gold and currency. At the same time, because gold has a regulating function, it can adjust a country's inflation and exchange rate fluctuations. However, with the continued and stable growth of the global economy, the existing gold reserves are insufficient to meet the total demand for currency, making gold as the sole supersovereign currency unrealistic and only suitable as a supplement to international currency reserves. The emergence of sovereign currencies has further weakened gold's function as a super-sovereign reserve currency. Although some scholars have called for a return to the gold standard after the 2008 financial crisis, it is clearly impractical and, in fact, a step back in terms of the existing system.[60]

(2) Keynes' "Bancor" Proposal

The plan proposed by Triffin to address the "Triffin Dilemma" is similar to Keynes' International Clearing Union plan. Triffin suggested that the liquidity of international reserves be increased to alleviate the dilemma. This involved transferring the foreign exchange balances of member countries' currency reserves to the IMF, obtaining a creditor balance in the IMF account, and finally settling debts denominated in US dollars and British pounds with the US and the UK through a unified institution, the IMF. Unfortunately, Triffin's idea was not adopted and never came to fruition.

In Triffin's proposal, member countries first had to pay a deposit to the IMF to obtain a balance in the IMF account, which replaced the original quota system. Second, the IMF would absorb surplus foreign exchange reserves. Third, through these two steps, the IMF would reabsorb nearly $15 billion worth of US dollars and British pounds in reserve, which were kept in various banks in the US and the UK in the form of deposits, bonds, and bills of exchange. Finally, the IMF's lending authority would be restricted, such as by setting limits on its net borrowing amount within 12 months to avoid inflation, and further refinement of the multilateral clearing mechanism proposed by Keynes' International Clearing Union plan would be made.[61]

(3) SDR Alternative Accounts

A substitution account for SDRs refers to a special account established by member countries in the IMF. Member countries can exchange their international reserve

---

[59] See footnote 45.

[60] See footnote 19.

[61] See footnote 19.

currencies, such as the US dollar, for SDRs and deposit them into the substitution account. They then receive SDR certificates issued by the IMF. The IMF uses the US dollars in the substitution account to purchase US government bonds and distributes the earned interest to each member country that has deposited SDRs into the account.[62] This system not only diversifies reserve currencies but also promotes further development of the SDR system. On the one hand, countries can reduce their exposure to US dollar volatility by using SDRs when they have sufficient foreign exchange reserves. This increases the stability of foreign exchange reserves and allows countries to redeem them whenever they need to use them. On the other hand, SDRs are only supplementary reserve assets in the international monetary system and do not change the basic structure of the system. The US dollar remains the major international currency, and its dominant position has not changed. Moreover, SDRs do not affect global reserve levels or the world's currency supply.

As early as the early 1970s, the stability of the US dollar as the major international currency had been questioned by many experts and organizations. Some proposed the establishment of SDR accounts to replace the previous quota accounts in the IMF. In 1979, the IMF first proposed the establishment of SDR substitution accounts to centralize the excessive accumulation of foreign reserves and enhance the role of SDRs as international reserves.

Bergsten believes that the above approach can achieve mutual benefits. However, it should be acknowledged that the substitution account for SDRs is a compromise within the existing system, and its implementation requires addressing the financial risks and costs of the account. Member countries can exchange their international reserve currencies, such as the US dollar, for SDRs through the substitution account. The US dollar mainly refers to short-term US Treasury bonds, which the IMF then converts into long-term bonds, and the interest differential is credited to the SDR holders' accounts. However, this approach leads to significant differences in the risk costs that member countries need to bear, damaging the interests of most IMF member countries. Additionally, the substitution account creates significant moral hazards, as account holders continually seek to expand their reserves while being unable to escape the inherent asymmetry of the system. Whether it is the gold standard, the Bretton Woods system, or the current international monetary system, these experiences have taught us the need to strengthen regulatory and supervisory mechanisms.[63] The substitution account for SDRs increases the role and liquidity of SDRs to some extent, and it can move SDRs toward becoming a complete currency. However, because it does not align with the interests of many member countries, it has not been recognized or implemented.

(4) Euro Plan

Since its inception, the euro has possessed a unique characteristic of a supersovereign currency due to its establishment through a collective decision of numerous European Union (hereafter referred to as the "EU") member states. As an international

---

[62] See footnote 12.

[63] See footnote 19.

currency, it can be freely used and exchanged within the framework of agreements and conventions, making the euro inherently possess the most typical features of a supersovereign reserve currency.

The euro was created in 1999 and officially replaced the national currencies of eurozone countries on July 1, 2002, marking its transition into a true supersovereign currency. Non-EU member countries have also gradually joined the eurozone and adopted the euro. As of 2009, the euro had replaced the national currencies of 19 EU countries, including Ireland, Austria, Belgium, Germany, France, Finland, the Netherlands, Luxembourg, Portugal, Spain, Greece, Italy, Slovenia, Cyprus, Malta, Slovakia, Estonia, Lithuania, and Latvia. Additionally, the euro serves as the currency of six non-EU countries and regions, namely, Monaco, San Marino, Vatican City, Andorra, Montenegro, and the Kosovo region.

The creation of the euro signaled a potential threat to the US dollar's international currency hegemony, as noted by Frankel. Despite facing several economic and political challenges, the euro has established itself as a prominent currency in the global financial system, serving as a reserve currency and a means of exchange in international trade.[64]

The euro is widely recognized as possessing the characteristics of a supersovereign currency, but whether it can truly play the role of a supersovereign reserve currency on the international stage remains uncertain. While the euro has the potential to promote economic development, this effect has yet to be fully validated. Moreover, the euro's policy consistency and flexibility still need to be addressed, particularly in terms of how to coordinate the monetary and fiscal policies of member countries when they differ. The European debt crisis was a clear example of the consequences of failing to resolve these issues. Without fundamental solutions, the likelihood of future crises cannot be ruled out, as demonstrated by Brexit. To address these challenges, some scholars argue that the eurozone's financial market needs further improvement and that the current fragmentation in the bond market may lead to a decline in the euro's position among international currencies, thereby jeopardizing its stability.

Before the euro was introduced, the US used its absolute economic, military, and political advantages to make the US dollar the major international currency. Although at that time, the US Federal Reserve essentially acted as the World Central Bank, the US continued to benefit from the dominance of the US dollar by collecting international seigniorage taxes, among other benefits. However, the US also maintained the unity of the international monetary system and international trade, avoiding chaos in the international trade system and promoting the development of the world economy and trade.

With the birth of the euro, it is likely that the unity of the international monetary system has been disrupted, ushering in an unstable era of "dual-core currencies."[65] Therefore, the euro project does not solve the current problems in the international

---

[64] Jeffrey. A Frankel, What's In and Out in Global Money, Finance & Development 2009(9), pp. 13–17.

[65] See footnote 29.

monetary system but instead exacerbates the instability of the international monetary system.

(5) Single World Currency

Charles P. Kindleberger proposed the idea of a single world currency as early as 1969 in a meeting of the US Federal Reserve. In the 1980s, the American economist Richard Cooper also proposed a plan to establish a single currency mechanism among modern industrialized democratic countries, which he published in his article "The Future Monetary System." Cooper suggested creating currency target zones among modern industrialized democratic countries, followed by the formation of a single currency system among the US, Japan, and European Community countries. Eventually, this system could be gradually implemented worldwide, leading to the establishment of a global single currency system.[66]

Mundell was also one of the main advocates of a single currency system and has been dedicated to the research and promotion of regional currencies. In 2005, he proposed a plan to create a single world currency unit, called the DEY, consisting of the US dollar, euro, and Japanese yen, which would be managed and supervised by the IMF. Following the global economic crisis at the beginning of the twenty-first century, the international economic structure underwent significant changes, and the international monetary system was adjusted accordingly. Mundell then proposed the idea of establishing a diversified world currency, which would consist of five currencies—the US dollar, British pound, euro, Japanese yen, and Chinese yuan—according to a certain weight ratio and would adjust the functions of the IMF to include currency issuance, making it a central bank of the world.[67]

According to the currency development goals established by the Single Global Currency Association (hereafter referred to as the "SGCA"), it is planned to complete the unification of international currency and the establishment of a World Central Bank by 2024. John Pompas was the first to propose the 3-G Plan, which refers to the Global Monetary Union (hereafter referred to as the "GMU") consisting of the Global Central Bank (hereafter referred to as the "GCB") and the SGCA. Pompas believes that one of the tasks of the GMU is to discover its own development direction and future. Before establishing a single international currency, it is necessary to establish a globally unified central bank and regulatory mechanism to strictly control inflation. The location of the headquarters of the global central bank also needs to be comprehensively considered, with a preference for Basel, Geneva, or Zurich, which have a good currency reputation. In the plan, the future major international currencies will no longer be based on the gold credit foundation but more on the credit of international organizations and governments and eventually transition to a single world currency. There are many ways to transition: the first is from regional currency unions to gradually transition to a single international currency; the second is to implement a fixed exchange rate and settle major currencies with a single currency at a fixed exchange rate to achieve the transition; the third is to achieve currency

[66] Richard. N Cooper, A Monetary System for the Future, Foreign Affairs 1984(63), pp. 25–42.

[67] Mundell, R. The Idea of a World Currency [J]. Economic Reform, 2010(2), pp. 20–24.

unification through political alliances; and the fourth is to allow small economies to pilot the direct replacement of their sovereign currency with a single international currency, gradually achieving the transition to a single international currency such as the US dollar or the euro.[68] However, the above schemes have some feasibility but are still not perfect.

(6) Bitcoin Plan

The concept of "supersovereign currency" proposed by Zhou Xiaochuan, the former governor of the Central Bank of China, can be understood as the creation of a currency form that is detached from national sovereignty, ensuring the stability of international reserve currencies and effectively overcoming the inherent flaws of sovereign currencies as international reserve currencies. The establishment of a supersovereign currency can be considered an ideal path for reforming the international monetary system. In addition, some scholars have suggested adding Bitcoin to the composition of the basket of currencies to achieve the goal of perfecting the international monetary system. The reasons for this concept include the following. First, since Bitcoin is not issued by any specific country or institution, it can serve as a nearly neutral international payment method. Second, from the value exchange process of Bitcoin, it can be seen that when major sovereign currencies depreciate or fluctuate, Bitcoin often appreciates or fluctuates in the opposite direction, effectively hedging the impact of currency devaluation. Third, when the value of Bitcoin is recognized worldwide, it has fulfilled its function as a "measure of value" and compared to the exchange rate fluctuations of sovereign currencies, it will become increasingly stable, thus better fulfilling its function as a "store of value." At that time, Bitcoin could legitimately serve as a regular international payment method, allowing it to occupy a place in currency settlements in international trade and financial markets and may to some extent compensate for the inherent flaws of sovereign currencies as international currencies. This concept of a "supersovereign currency" system can help alleviate the "Triffin Dilemma" of sovereign currencies serving as the major international currencies and reserve assets.[69]

Bitcoin differs from traditional electronic currency in several ways. First, the issuance method is different. Traditional electronic currency is usually issued by a specific platform or organization, and its usage is limited to within that entity. However, Bitcoin is not issued by a specific entity; it is created through mining on the network. Second, the supervision and management mechanisms are different. The Chinese government has already legalized traditional electronic currency and included it in a third-party regulatory mechanism. Related activities must strictly follow the legal provisions. On the other hand, Bitcoin is managed by its own system and is not monitored by the government or individuals, making it difficult to track transactions and activities and to control related tax activities. Third, the anonymity

[68] See footnote 29.

[69] Lu Yibin. Exploration of Advancing World Monetary System by Referring to the Efficiency of Supersovereign Currency: A Case Study of the Pros and Cons of Bitcoin. Finance World (Academic Edition), 2014(7), pp. 24–26.

level is different. In the process of traditional electronic currency transactions, real account information must be used every time. Bitcoin transactions, on the other hand, do not require registration of an account, and the primary tools for its transactions are public and private keys, which provide a very high level of anonymity. Fourth, the underlying value is different. The value of traditional electronic currencies, such as "Q coins" and in-game currency, is not uniform and is determined by each network company. The value of network payments, such as payments via Alipay and WeChat, is linked to Chinese yuan and serves as a digital form of Chinese yuan. However, Bitcoin's value is not restricted and does not have a fixed exchange rate with any sovereign currency. Currently, it is more like a highly liquid electronic financial asset.[70]

As a reserve currency, Bitcoin has special advantages. The key point to solving the "Triffin Dilemma" lies in the issue of currency ownership and the determination of its legal status, thus requiring exploration and establishment of nonsovereign currency. Bitcoin is an ideal model actively explored in the field of nonsovereign currency. As a reserve currency, Bitcoin has several advantages. First, as a distributed and decentralized issuance model, the total amount of Bitcoin issued is determined in the initial stage, making the currency value stability relatively high throughout the entire circulation process. Second, Bitcoin can be used as an asset for reserves and is not affected by the country's monetary policies and related economic reform measures. Therefore, the currency value system is relatively stable in transactions based on Bitcoin as a payment basis. Third, using Bitcoin as an international reserve currency can effectively avoid the risk of currency devaluation, thereby safeguarding the security of the currency value system.[71]

As Bitcoin holding and storage can only rely on the promotion of national public power institutions, each country has absolute autonomy in the amount of Bitcoin storage. It will not be affected by the economic policies and currency values of other countries in the world. Therefore, even under the background of the world economy being influenced by the economic crisis of hegemonic countries, the value of Bitcoin will not be negatively affected, and it has value stability and sustainable development. Since most transactions using Bitcoin as a payment method are conducted online and Bitcoin is issued and circulated as a virtual currency, it does not require traditional physical carriers for value transmission, thus reducing the issuance, circulation, and reserve costs of currency to a large extent. Moreover, since the information transparency level of Bitcoin trading platforms is relatively high, it can effectively avoid security vulnerabilities caused by data asymmetry, thereby safeguarding the effective rights and interests of both parties in transactions and the fairness and rationality of transactions.

Although Bitcoin has certain advantages over traditional currencies as a modern international reserve currency, it still has some vulnerabilities and shortcomings. Despite being held as a reserve currency at the national level, many countries rarely

---

[70] See footnote 45.

[71] Lou Yaoxiong, Wu Jun. Legal Analysis of Bitcoin Issues. Journal of Beijing University of Posts and Telecommunications (Social Sciences Edition), 2013(4), pp. 25–31.

use Bitcoin as a means of payment in actual transactions and settlement payments. In most cases, Bitcoin is first exchanged as a virtual commodity for fiat currency and then used for settlement transactions. Moreover, Bitcoin cannot generate interest like traditional currencies when held as a reserve and instead requires payment of storage fees to the corresponding management organizations, increasing the management costs of currency reserves and transactions.

Furthermore, while Bitcoin as a storage currency can ensure the stability of its value, there is still a certain degree of transaction risk in economic development. The limited total supply of Bitcoin inevitably leads to insufficient currency supply, which can have negative impacts on the construction and development of the global economy and the international monetary system as a whole. Therefore, while Bitcoin has potential as a reserve currency, it also faces practical and structural challenges that must be carefully considered before widespread adoption.[72]

It is evident that Bitcoin still has many shortcomings and faces significant obstacles, which is why it cannot become a true currency within the world's mainstream trading sphere. However, various countries are developing their own sovereign cryptocurrencies and supersovereign cryptocurrencies based on blockchain technology, which have overcome many of Bitcoin's shortcomings while retaining its convenience and functionality. One such example of a supersovereign cryptocurrencies is cryptoSDRs, which have gained recognition from most national governments and market participants.

Therefore, the author believes that using SDRs as the credit carrier for currency and utilizing the blockchain technology of Bitcoin to create a supersovereign currency is a more forward-looking and feasible solution for international monetary system reform than the other proposals mentioned above.

1.2.2 Reform Options for SDRs

SDRs were created in the late 1960s as a means of reducing the impact of the US dollar on international trade and finance. Unlike traditional currencies, SDRs are not intended to be used as a medium of exchange but rather represent the right of member countries to use a certain amount of funds.

Currently, SDRs cannot be used in private transactions as a currency. Governments must first convert SDRs into directly tradable currencies, such as the US dollar, euro, pound, yen, or yuan, before using them in international transactions. The IMF issued regulations in 2011 and 2016 that highlight two primary functions of SDRs. First, SDRs serve as a special currency asset issued and supervised by the IMF and can be used as official international reserves held by member countries. Second, SDRs can be used as a unit of measurement for currency, including pricing international

[72] See footnote 45.

investments, trade, financial assets, and commodities, as well as serving as an official exchange rate anchor unit.[73]

Many scholars have provided arguments in support of the reform of SDRs and have proposed several practical suggestions. Rossi is an advocate for developing and expanding SDRs. He pointed out that the exacerbation of global economic imbalances has increased the volatility of the international monetary system and that expanding the use of SDRs is highly feasible within this system.[74] Mateosy Lago and others believe that SDRs have existed in the international monetary system for a long time and are currently in a period of revival. To improve the effectiveness of SDRs as a comprehensive currency for asset diversification and value stability, it is necessary to increase their liquidity. Therefore, many countries around the world should take various measures to increase their support for SDRs, such as issuing bonds priced in SDRs in the name of nations or individuals, linking major international currencies to SDRs, and using SDRs as accounting units for trade settlements.[75] Carney believes that the most effective way to expand the use of SDRs is to promote the development of reserve assets that include SDR-priced assets, allowing holders of reserve assets to convert their assets in US dollars or other currencies into assets priced in SDRs, increasing the diversity of investments and asset portfolios, and thereby promoting a more stable international monetary system.[76] The United Nations Reform Commission, represented by Nobel Prize-winning economist Stiglitz, also acknowledges the important role of SDRs in the international monetary system and has published a report entitled "International Monetary and Financial System Reform in a Time of Crisis," which proposes to increase the weight of SDRs in the existing international monetary system and issue them countercyclically. In the implementation process, the distribution mechanism of SDRs should be continuously improved to promote stability in the international financial market.[77] Zhou Xiaochuan, the former governor of the Central Bank of China, proposed in his paper "Reflections on the Reform of the International Monetary System" that SDRs have the characteristics of a supersovereign currency and have tremendous potential in the international monetary system. He believes that by improving the distribution mechanism of SDRs, increasing the proportion of SDR issuance, and expanding their scope of use, the needs of all member countries for international reserve currencies can be met. He also proposed the concept of a supersovereign currency, suggesting that a currency from independent of sovereign states could be created to ensure the stability of international reserve currencies. He suggested gradually expanding the functions of SDRs

[73] Shi Jianxun, Wang Panpan. Does Expanding the Use of SDR Help the Internationalization of Renminbi? [J]. World Economic Research, 2018(10), pp. 3–17 + 64 + 135.

[74] See footnote 10.

[75] Mateo. Y. Lago & R. Duttagupta Isablle & Goyal Abd R. Goyal, The Debate On The International Monetary System, Imf Staff Position Note, 2009, spn/09/26.

[76] M. Caryney, The Evolution of the International Monetary System, New York City: Foreign Policy Association, pp. 40–58.

[77] P. Alessandrini & M. Fratianni, International Monies, Special Drawing Rights and Supranational Money, Rome: Prepared for the 2009 Pre-G8 Summit Conference on "Global Financial Crises: National Economic Solutions, Geopolitical Impacts," 2009.

and establishing a clearing relationship with other sovereign currencies, creating a pricing system in international trade and investment, and gradually replacing the US dollar as the international reserve currency.[78] Clark and Polak pointed out that if the expanded use of SDRs were to form a new international monetary system, it would need to have the following characteristics. The new SDR system should be diversified, with more stable value returns that can effectively avoid the instability of a single reserve currency. However, this stability is not fixed and is constrained by the stability of a basket of currencies, with the weights of different currencies in the basket automatically updated and adjusted based on real-time exchange rates. At the same time, the components of the currency basket must be subject to rigorous evaluation and selection criteria, and the selection process must be transparent and open to ensure the credibility of the system. The second is account balanced. The SDR system will distribute the so-called exorbitant privilege to the currencies in the basket, resulting in a more rapid and widespread expansion than the previously discussed multiple currency system. Third, developing SDRs is expected to enhance international cooperation by enabling countries to use them as a bridge to connect with each other, thus facilitating trade and financial exchanges between nations. Additionally, it is hoped that this will encourage closer cooperation in financial regulation and the fight against international financial crimes.[79]

In addition, expanding the recognized and accepted scope of SDRs means increasing the international use and proportion of SDRs as reserve assets and units of account. In the current international monetary system, enhancing the reserve currency role of SDRs can reduce the negative impact of the US dollar as the major international currency and alleviate the difficulties caused by the "Triffin Dilemma." Expanding its role as a financial settlement unit can also reduce economic risks caused by fluctuations in the US dollar, promote the anchoring of SDRs to the official exchange rates of various countries, and help noninternational currency issuing countries regain their monetary policy independence, which is lost due to a single currency peg. Therefore, continually expanding the functions of SDRs as a currency can further improve the international monetary system and enhance its stability and resilience.[80]

In summary, the limitations of sovereign currencies as international reserves and major international currencies have predetermined the creation of an international currency that transcends national sovereignty and circulates worldwide as an inevitable trend.[81] However, as mentioned earlier, returning to the gold standard is a backward institutional approach. Using scarce gold as the major international currency would inevitably lead to deflation and a repeat of the history of Bad Money Drives Good Money out of Circulation, which is not conducive to the development of modern economies. Similarly, Triffin's "internationalization of foreign exchange

---

[78] See footnote 55.

[79] P. B. CLARK & J. J POLAK, International Liquidity and the Role of the SDR in the International Monetary System, IMF Staff Position Note 2002 WP/02/217.

[80] See footnote 73.

[81] Cheng Enfu, Wang Cui. Possibility and Implementation Path of Creating a "Shiyuan" Currency. Haipai Economics, 2013(1), pp. 1–16.

reserves" proposal is also difficult to implement because it attempts to transfer the foreign exchange balances of various countries to the IMF to obtain credit balances. However, governments of various countries are unlikely to accept the conversion of freely convertible foreign exchange into credit balances that the IMF cannot directly circulate. This proposal was difficult to adopt several decades ago, and it is still challenging to be adopted by governments of various countries. The substitution account of SDRs has some feasibility but is still not perfect. The substitution account of SDRs can relieve the pressure of insufficient US dollar international reserves to some extent. However, liquidity shortages may also exist, causing countries to reduce their willingness to store foreign exchange reserves in substitution accounts. Therefore, it cannot be accepted by countries around the world. The euro has been weakened due to the financial crisis within the EU and Brexit. In addition, the primary use of the euro is limited to the European continent, making it unable to rival the US dollar. It may even lead the current international monetary system into a more chaotic "bipolar" system, so the euro proposal is not a good reform plan for the international monetary system. The proposal of a single world currency currently has no feasible plan that can be accepted by countries around the world, and it is only a utopia of a small group. Although it has a similar goal as the proposed cryptoSDRs, the approach is different, and they can learn from each other. The Bitcoin proposal cannot become the mainstream payment method worldwide due to significant price fluctuations, technical limitations, and insufficient credit. Currently, it is only a niche financial product. Even if Bitcoin gains recognition from countries worldwide in the future, the fixed total number of Bitcoins means that it will serve more as a tool for storing value, and its impact on the reform of the current international monetary system is limited.

Although Bitcoin may not be a viable solution for reforming the current international monetary system, there is potential for its underlying technology to be combined with SDRs to create a more feasible reform approach. The author suggests utilizing the supersovereign credit of the IMF, which is inherent in SDRs, for monetary reform. By combining this with blockchain technology as a new generation of currency carriers, a new supersovereign cryptocurrency, named cryptoSDRs, can be formed.

CryptoSDRs can address the shortcomings of current SDRs and possess many advantages that are not present in other reform proposals. Legal and technological reforms can help to further enhance cryptoSDRs, making them a more stable and feasible solution to address the inherent defects of the current international monetary system. The creation of a supersovereign currency through cryptoSDRs can bring greater stability to the international monetary system and provide a more reliable foundation for global financial transactions.

In summary, although Bitcoin is not a viable solution for international monetary reform, the combination of its underlying technology and SDRs can create a new cryptocurrency that is capable of addressing the shortcomings of the current international monetary system. With legal and technological reforms, cryptoSDRs can provide a more stable foundation for global financial transactions and help to resolve the inherent defects of the current international monetary system.

1.3 Encrypted Currency Reform of SDRs

Digitalizing SDRs refers to the reform and improvement of SDRs and their related systems, combining blockchain technology and cryptocurrencies with the current international monetary system. Therefore, to understand what cryptoSDRs are, one must first understand their underlying technology, blockchain, as well as the basic principles of cryptocurrency.

Blockchain technology is a combination of Internet protocols and new data structures. Similar to the most important application protocol HTTP in the Internet application layer, blockchain is also a protocol for point-to-point value transfer in the Internet application layer. Based on the protocol, blockchain has defined a distributed ledger with "blocks" and "chains." With the help of encryption algorithm technology, blockchain has added anonymity, decentralization, and other functions to electronic currencies. Cryptocurrencies exist in various electronic devices in a distributed accounting manner and are protected by encryption in the network to facilitate their transaction circulation. This cryptocurrency satisfies both the requirement of the currency value scale and the value requirement as a medium of exchange. The Financial Action Task Force on Money Laundering (hereafter referred to as the "FATF") defines cryptocurrency as a currency form that is traded on the network in electronic data form and has the functions of exchange medium, currency pricing, and value storage.[82]

Now, Bitcoin has been around for more than a decade, and we can increasingly feel the atmosphere of the widespread use of cryptocurrencies. The China central bank has already tested and promoted the Digital Currency Electronic Payment (hereafter referred to as the "DC/EP") in many cities. American financial giants such as JPMorgan have also completed their layout in the field of cryptocurrencies. An increasing number of people hold cryptocurrencies and push their market value to new heights. The news of Facebook's launch of cryptocurrency "Libra" pushed the global attention of cryptocurrencies to historic heights. In December 2020, the company decided to change "Libra" from a basket of currencies to a programmable stablecoin called "Diem" backed by the US dollar. From this development process, it can be seen that cryptocurrencies are not declining but rather flourishing in their winding development.

[82] The Financial Action Task Force (FATF). Virtual Currencies: Key Definitions and Potential AML/CFT Risks. At https://www.fatf-gafi.org/media/fatf/documents/reports/Virtual-currency-key-definitions-and-potential-aml-cft-risks.pdf. Accessed 6 May 2022.

1.3.1 The Concept of Cryptocurrency and Blockchain Technology

Blockchain technology serves as the fundamental infrastructure for cryptocurrencies. To fully comprehend the intricacies of cryptocurrency, it is essential to have a comprehensive understanding of blockchain technology.

(1) Blockchain Technology

The foundation of Bitcoin is built upon blockchain technology. In the early twenty-first century, Satoshi Nakamoto published an article about the principles of Bitcoin on a website dedicated to discussing encryption information on the Internet.[83] In 2009, Nakamoto established an open-source project for the system and developed the first 50 Bitcoins, known as the "genesis block," on a small server located in Helsinki, Finland. This official birth of Bitcoin marked the beginning of a new era for the development of blockchain technology. As research and application of blockchain technology progressed and evolved, it became clear that this technology and cryptocurrencies were complementary, leading to explosive growth in both areas. Blockchain technology is considered to be the fifth paradigmatic innovation in the history of technological development, following large-scale computers, personal computers, the Internet, and mobile/social networks. Meanwhile, the credit of cryptocurrencies is viewed as the fourth credit milestone in the evolution of human credit after blood relationship credit, precious metal credit, and central bank paper currency credit.

In 2016, the Ministry of Industry and Information Technology released the "White Paper on the Development of China's Blockchain Technology and Applications," providing narrow and broad definitions of blockchain technology from a technical perspective. It defines it as a new type of immutable and tamperproof distributed infrastructure and computing paradigm.[84]

Blockchain technology is a novel way of recording, storing, exchanging, transmitting, and displaying data by combining a variety of technologies and mechanisms, including time-stamping, asymmetric cryptography, token economics, Byzantine fault tolerance, psychology, peer-to-peer file transfer technology, and databases.

Unlike traditional data storage methods that rely on designated platform institutions, blockchain technology is a distributed storage network formed by everyone who participates in the system. Through the participation of everyone in the recording and storage of data, a peer-to-peer network system is established, and a consensus is reached through complex multiverification mechanisms, such as Byzantine fault tolerance, to maintain the consistency, integrity, and continuity of financial ledgers and database data on the blockchain.

[83] Nakamoto S. Bitcoin: A Peer-To-Peer Electronic Cash System. At https://bitcoin.org/bitcoin.pdf. Accessed 6 May 2022.

[84] China Blockchain Technology and Industry Development Forum. "2016 China Blockchain Technology and Application Development White Paper." [EB/OL]. Available at: http://chainb.com/download/工信部-中国区块链技术和应用发展白皮书1014.pdf. Accessed 6 May 2022.

In addition, blockchain technology professionals define and interpret it from different perspectives. From the perspective of management systems, blockchain technology is a complete and secure asset and data management system that transfers and registers asset ownership during equal intervals of time and links database data changes in chronological order. From the perspective of the underlying technical structure, blockchain technology is a data structure that records information in chronological order, forms blocks, and links them according to time relationships. It can store simple data with sequential relationships that can be verified within the system and cleverly set up a secure and stable system that cannot be falsified or tampered with using principles of cryptography, economics, and other disciplines. The open-source code allows for a consensus mechanism to be formed for information and transaction records throughout the network.

From the perspective of the underlying protocol, blockchain technology is an open-source consensus protocol and one of the many applications that run databases on the blockchain. It follows an open-source consensus mechanism that stores data records, changes, and other information on data blocks that are commonly accepted. From the perspective of financial systems, blockchain technology is a distributed ledger and database application technology that encrypts real and effective financial transaction information and database data records and changes and uses distributed storage to allow all network users to verify, store, process, and maintain all financial and data information, thereby constructing a new type of financial and data application management system.[85]

Overall, blockchain technology has created a chronological record of transactions and data that is tamperproof, secure, and stable. In cryptocurrency systems that use blockchain technology as a fundamental technology, users do not need to know the background information of other users, nor do they need to rely on the credit and guarantee of third-party financial institutions such as banks and Alipay. They can trust the accuracy of the value records, transfers, and storage of cryptocurrency and use them with confidence.

(2) Cryptocurrency

The FATF has not only explained the meaning of cryptocurrency but has also distinguished between cryptocurrency and electronic currency, recognizing that these types of currency have fundamental differences from popular payment methods such as Apple Pay, Paypal, Alipay, and WeChat Pay.[86]

The difference between cryptocurrency and electronic currency is that cryptocurrency can be considered a virtual currency based on a distributed storage network and asymmetric encryption algorithm, while electronic currency is the result of digitizing paper currency issued by a country's legal system through banks or financial institutions. Electronic currency can be stored and used for payment online. Its circulation

[85] Zhou Ruijue. Legal Regulation of Blockchain Technology. Journal of Beijing University of Posts and Telecommunications (Social Sciences Edition), 2017(3), pp. 39–45.

[86] Shi Xiuxia. Research on Money Laundering Crimes Using Virtual Currency [J]. Journal of the People's Public Security University of China (Social Science Edition), 2017(33), pp. 32–41.

and use depend on the recognition of national laws and the stable operation of the banking and financial system, giving users a high level of security. When funds are transferred between users, only the information about the funds is transmitted. Users typically store electronic currency through bank cards or accounts, making daily economic transactions more convenient and fast. The economic value represented by electronic currency is equivalent to that of ordinary currency in circulation. Each issuing institution has its own savings forms, such as debit cards, credit cards, stored value cards, shopping cards, and more convenient electronic payment methods such as PayPal, Alipay, and WeChat Pay.

Cryptocurrency, on the other hand, is a virtual currency based on a distributed storage network and asymmetric encryption algorithm. Its biggest difference from electronic currency is that it is a representation of wealth itself, without relying on any physical assets, while electronic currency is a mapping of physical currency in the digital world. Cryptocurrencies like Bitcoin have three core features: (1) they are open-source code, with no issuing entity directly controlling their issuance and operation; (2) they have a fixed total amount to counteract the inflation and depreciation that paper currency is inevitably subject to; and (3) the transaction process requires verification by countless node servers on the network, providing extremely high security.[87]

Among the numerous cryptocurrencies, Bitcoin is currently the most widely used and successful one. Based on Bitcoin, a large number of decentralized cryptocurrencies have emerged, collectively known as "altcoins" or "copycats." Some well-known altcoins include IXCoin, Litecoin, Dogecoin, Butterflycoin, and Ripple. There have been thousands of cryptocurrencies created around the world, and currently, there are still over 800 operational altcoins, with more than half of them cloned from Litecoin.[88]

However, after the emergence of Ethereum, creating cryptocurrencies became exceptionally simple through smart contract programming. As a result, from 2015 to 2018, in less than three years, more than a thousand cryptocurrencies were created, and the market capitalization of cryptocurrencies peaked at over $590 billion in January 2018.[89] With the development of cryptocurrencies, stablecoins, represented by USTD (Tether), GUSD (Gemini Dollar), and PAX (Paxos Standard), have also emerged and rapidly gained popularity among investors. They are often backed by a sovereign currency, such as USTD, which promises to be equivalent to one US dollar. In addition, many countries have issued sovereign cryptocurrencies with the same legal status and value as their own fiat currency.[90]

---

[87] Zou Jun. "Will Blockchain be the Protagonist in the Second Half of the Internet?" [EB/OL]. https://www.jianshu.com/p/635e95e09bd0?utm_campaign=maleskine&utm_content=note&utm_medium=seo_notes&utm_source=recommendation. Accessed 6 May 2022.

[88] Cheng Hua, Yang Yunzhi. Research on the Development Trend of Blockchain and the Response Strategies of Commercial Banks. Financial Regulatory Research, 2016(1), pp. 73–91.

[89] Data Source. Coin World Website Data [EB/OL]. https://bishijie.com/hangqing. Accessed 6 May 2022.

[90] C. Calcaterra & W. A. Kaal & V. Rao, Stable Cryptocurrencies, *Washington University Journal of Law & Policy* 2020(61), pp. 193–228.

1.3.2 The Creation of CryptoSDRs

Currently, the US dollar still holds its dominant position as the world's primary international currency for international trade and reserve currency. The US holds significant influence in international organizations such as the IMF and the World Bank, even possessing veto power. Maintaining the global hegemony of the US dollar remains a top priority and a feasible strategic goal for the US. However, the world order today is vastly different from the postWorld War II era, where the US held unparalleled economic, military, technological, and political power. Today, the trend of China's rise and America's decline is becoming increasingly evident. Therefore, this book explores the future of highly developed financial technology, the decline of the US dollar, and the already high level of global integration. By reforming the IMF, expanding the scope of SDRs, and increasing their supply, SDRs could gain liquidity similar to major international currencies such as the US dollar and the euro. Based on this foundation, a new type of supersovereign cryptocurrency—cryptoSDRs—could be created by leveraging the supersovereign credit of SDRs after they are monetized, combined with a blockchain-based cryptocurrency carrier. This is the basic concept behind the creation of cryptoSDRs. Therefore, as the most likely supersovereign cryptocurrency in the author's opinion, cryptoSDRs could be issued and circulated by the IMF using blockchain technology to transform and strengthen the existing SDRs. It could serve as a cryptocurrency for transaction and value storage on a global scale and, after expanding its circulation and increasing its supply, could become a supersovereign currency that can be used in government and private domains. Currently, SDRs are merely accounting units issued by the IMF and can only be circulated between governments. They can only serve as a unit of account in international bulk transactions or cross-border financial fields and cannot circulate freely in the private sector. Therefore, they are not yet a currency and do not possess the basic attributes of currency. There are many debates among scholars on whether they can become a supersovereign currency, but they have already been held by most governments worldwide, allocated by the IMF, and recognized by these governments. The monetization of SDRs still has a long way to go, including reforms and improvements in legal, political, and technical aspects of issuance and circulation.

(1) CryptoSDRs Plan

The cryptoSDR plan is a proposal to create encrypted SDRs that can circulate globally in both the public and private sectors. This will be achieved through the reform and improvement of the SDR system by the IMF. The goal is to establish a supersovereign currency that can reform the existing international monetary system.

Many researchers have recognized the drawbacks of sovereign currency serving as an international currency. From the perspective of Alessandrini and Fratianni, it is becoming increasingly difficult for sovereign currency to become a world currency. Different countries prioritize domestic policies such as unemployment and inflation over the stability of sovereign currency value, which results in inherent defects in sovereign currency as an international currency.[91] Rossi's article "Global Imbalances and International Monetary Disorder: Supranational" highlights the increasingly obvious economic disparities among countries worldwide, which are a crucial factor leading to the instability of the world monetary system. While using SDRs as a reserve currency is theoretically feasible, it is also certain to reduce the status of the US dollar to some extent. Once foreign investment entities holding US dollars experience a loss of purchasing power, they will opt for other international currencies as their primary holding currency. Therefore, SDRs as an international currency can solve the inherent defects of the current international monetary system, and they have the potential to become a supersovereign currency.[92] Bergsen proposes one approach to promoting the development of a supersovereign currency: national decision-makers should convert the surplus of foreign exchange reserves into bonds denominated in SDRs. This approach would benefit all parties. In contrast, the issuance of a supersovereign currency replaces one currency with another.[93]

Scholars such as Mateosy Lago hold the view that SDRs, which have had foreign exchange reserves as their core function for several decades, are increasingly revealing their importance today. To promote SDRs as an artificial currency that has both diversity of assets and stability of value, it is necessary to increase their usage in various industries. Therefore, countries that bear international responsibility must support and encourage the circulation and development of SDRs. One basic method to achieve this goal is to issue bonds denominated in SDRs and adopt the SDRs as the currency unit for international trade settlement, among other measures.[94]

In his book "The Evolution of the International Monetary System," Carney suggests that the diversification of reserve assets can be achieved by expanding the usage and scope of the SDRs, allowing more countries to convert their reserves into SDRs.[95] Meanwhile, Williamson argues in his article "The Future of the Reserve System" that the expansion of SDR usage depends on its recognition by private companies and individuals. He believes that SDRs have a series of drawbacks from the perspective of noninternational currency issuing countries, but their monetary function can be enhanced only by integrating them into the private sector and improving their flexibility.[96]

Clark and Polak, in their article "International Liquidity and the Role of the SDRs in the International Monetary System," point out that the new SDRs as an international currency and reserve will have the following characteristics. First, their value will not fluctuate excessively. By including more sovereign currencies in the currency basket and imposing constraints on the issuance of sovereign currencies, the value

---

[91] See footnote 77.

[92] See footnote 10.

[93] FRED BERGSTEN. How to Solve the Problem of the Dollar? [EB/OL]. https://www.ft.com/content/75cb5f2e-a729-11dc-a25a-0000779fd2ac. Accessed 6 May 2022.

[94] See footnote 75.

[95] See footnote 76.

[96] John Williamson, The Future of the Reserve System, *Journal of Globalization and Development* 2010(2), Article 15.

of the SDRs can be stabilized. Second, SDR account balances should be balanced. A system based on the SDRs needs to be redistributed throughout the entire monetary system to provide emerging economies and developing countries with a reasonable amount of SDRs to maintain the balance of the entire system. Third, it can promote international cooperation and development. The further development and prosperity of SDRs can promote more exchanges and cooperation between countries, which is beneficial to the global economy.[97]

In "The Cryptocurrency Conundrum: Regulating an Uncertain Future," Howden analyzes the development and regulatory history of cryptocurrencies, arguing that cryptocurrencies can only be better developed if they are brought under the regulatory framework of the IMF, the Financial Stability Board, and the World Trade Organization.[98] In "Regulating Digital Currencies: Bringing Bitcoin within the Reach of the IMF," Plassaras analyzes the development and attacks on cryptocurrencies and suggests that the IMF should strengthen its ability to stabilize the international foreign exchange market and intervene in attacks on cryptocurrencies.[99]

Alexander proposes two solutions for combining SDRs with blockchain technology to form eSDRs: the first is to create a brand new cryptocurrency from SDRs, and the second is to create a new cryptocurrency that joins a basket of currencies that make up SDRs.[100] The author prefers the first solution, which is in line with Tobias Adrian's view that eSDRs or dSDRs can be issued using the characteristics of eMoney and stablecoins based on cryptocurrencies, as expressed at the 2019 IMF and Swiss National Bank conference.[101] Similarly, Zhou Xiaochuan suggested at the Boao Forum for Asia's second "Asia-Europe Dialog" held in Chongqing in 2019 that global cooperation and active responses from the financial sector are necessary to address new issues such as digital economy tax, digital currency, and electronic payments. He also believed that the world is indeed facing an opportunity to promote global cryptocurrencies such as eSDRs and synthetic hegemony currencies (SHCs).

Meanwhile, Li Bo suggested that a global cryptocurrency can be created through a public–private partnership (hereafter referred to as the "PPP") between an international organization and private sector entities. Examples include partnering with Facebook to link Libra with SDRs, accepting BIS regulation, and paying reserves to the BIS.[102]

---

[97] See footnote 79.

[98] Howden E., The Cryptocurrency Conundrum: Regulating an Uncertain Future, 29 *Emory International Law Review* 2015(4), pp. 741–798.

[99] Plassaras Nicholas A., Regulating Digital Currencies: Bringing Bitcoin within the Reach of the IMF, *Chicago Journal of International Law* 2013(14), pp. 377–390.

[100] Alexander M. Heideman, Can IMFcoin Be Scaruffi's Moneta Immaginaria, *Marquette Intellectual Property Law Review* 2019(23), pp. 137–150.

[101] Tobias Adrian. Stablecoins, Central Bank Digital Currencies, and Cross-Border Payments: A New Look at the International Monetary System. At https://www.imf.org/en/News/Articles/2019/05/13/sp051419-stablecoins-central-bank-digital-currencies-and-cross-border-payments. Accessed 6 May 2022.

[102] Xie Juan. The Next Step for Financial Globalization: Opportunities for eSDR and SHC [EB/OL]. https://www.yicai.com/news/100426479.html. Accessed 6 May 2022.

As a supersovereign cryptocurrency, cryptoSDRs possess not only a credit rating superior to sovereign currencies but also the advantages of a new generation of currency with low issuance and circulation costs and fast usability. It can adapt to the current trend of globalization and meet people's expectations for the next generation of currency. Since its inception, it has had the potential to replace the US dollar as the primary international reserve currency or even the major international currency, thereby addressing the inherent flaws of the existing international monetary system dominated by sovereign currencies and resolving the "Triffin Dilemma." The emergence of cryptoSDRs also signifies a substantive change for the IMF and SDRs, whose organizational structure and legal mechanisms have been recognized by major countries around the world. The current shortcomings and deficiencies of the IMF and SDRs can also receive more attention, encouraging more countries to participate in the reform and improvement of the rules and systems of the IMF. Furthermore, with the development of technology and transportation industries and the increasing closeness of interaction among countries, the demand for a unified global currency is becoming increasingly strong. Although existing sovereign or supersovereign currencies such as the US dollar, Chinese yuan, and euro can serve as an international currency, the "Triffin Dilemma" and the continuous decline in the creditworthiness of the US dollar due to the long-term trade deficit and loose monetary policy have resulted in international trade companies and non-US citizens enduring exchange rate risks and exchange costs caused by fluctuations in the US dollar. If the world continues to rely on sovereign currencies as the international currency, the inherent flaws of the existing international monetary system and the periodicity of financial crises will not change, and the current situation of major international trade and private transactions bearing exchange risks and costs will not be alleviated. Although the euro is issued by the regional international organization of the EU, its rules and main circulation areas exist only in Europe, making it unable to gain global recognition and participation. In addition, negative impacts such as Brexit and the Greek debt crisis have led to a continuous decline in the creditworthiness and value of the euro, and the dual international monetary system formed by the euro and the US dollar has instead made the entire international financial order more unstable.

International economic experts have noted that currency diversification is an essential part of the process of establishing a supersovereign currency. This crucial stage is not a transitional phase from the internationalization and regionalization of multiple currencies to a supersovereign currency but rather a proactive exploration by countries around the world to establish a supersovereign currency after fully recognizing the defects of sovereign currencies as the international main currency and the instability of a multipolar international monetary system.[103] Therefore, only an international unified currency issued by a super international organization that surpasses sovereign states and has supersovereign credit and credibility can ultimately change the chaotic situation of the existing international monetary system.

---

[103] Sun Yexia. The Disadvantages of Sovereign Currency as a World Currency from the Perspective of Marx's International Currency Function [J]. Economist, 2019(1), pp. 94–101.

The euro, as a product of currency cooperation among European countries, was born and operated stably, which proves that as currency cooperation among countries around the world crystallizes, the issuance of cryptoSDRs by the IMF is entirely feasible.

At present, many scholars believe that some cryptocurrencies may become the prototype of supersovereign cryptocurrencies. For example, in 2019, Facebook started to create a new cryptocurrency "Libra" based on blockchain technology and composed of a basket of currencies within its ecosystem and planned to have its 2.7 billion users hold and use it. However, due to the questioning and opposition from the US government and the Federal Reserve, "Libra" has been shelved.[104] This shows that even for the world's leading companies with billions of users, it is extremely difficult to launch a legal currency without the government's permission or official organizational credit authorization.

Many nonsovereign cryptocurrencies, including Bitcoin and others issued by small companies without any official background, can only operate in a gray area and are even explicitly prohibited in some countries. However, many countries are already researching and issuing sovereign cryptocurrencies as upgrades and substitutes for their national currencies. Regarding this, the author believes that sovereign cryptocurrencies are ultimately only a country's sovereign currency, and their circulation will inevitably involve international games and conflicts with other countries' national currencies, making it impossible for most countries in the world to accept and popularize them.

Creating a supersovereign currency beyond sovereign states from scratch is also undoubtedly challenging. Therefore, only a quasicurrency issued by the IMF—the SDRs—combined with blockchain technology to become cryptoSDRs is most likely to become a supersovereign cryptocurrency that can be realized and become a good way to reform the current international monetary system.

SDRs themselves are a product of compromise among major powers after World War II. To expand its scope of use and make it play a major role in reforming the international monetary system, consensus needs to be reached among major powers to overcome the difficulties of world political struggles, build the infrastructure needed for the development of SDRs, and resolve the obstacles that hinder their growth. Indeed, it is not easy for SDRs to become a supersovereign currency at present, but the trend of globalization is increasingly evident today. SDRs, with cryptocurrency as its technical carrier for monetization, have a certain feasibility of becoming a supersovereign cryptocurrency. At the same time, cryptoSDRs not only have stronger advantages than nonsovereign cryptocurrencies and sovereign cryptocurrencies in terms of currency and legal attributes but can also fundamentally solve the inherent defects of the current international monetary system.

First, the circulation scope of cryptoSDRs is bound to be broader than that of sovereign cryptocurrencies. SDRs are issued by the IMF, and as of 2023, there are

---

[104] Du Huitang, Huoxing Finance. Breaking News! The Wall Street Journal reveals that Facebook's cryptocurrency has the support of seven major companies including VISA, PayPal, and Uber [EB/OL]. https://mp.weixin.qq.com/s/ya1gj1sY-bTu6WUUIYl2Lw. Accessed 6 May.

190 IMF member countries and 9 regional members, with only 27 countries and regions not having joined.[105] Therefore, the circulation and trust of cryptoSDRs must be greater than that of any sovereign currency. Although SDRs currently exist only as national reserves and are mainly used by countries to regulate their foreign exchange balances, many scholars believe that to fully utilize the role of SDRs, they can be used as currency units for international trade and financial product pricing.[106] Additionally, as SDRs have already become the reserves of most countries in the world, cryptoSDRs are more likely to gain the support and recognition of these countries. In relevant conventions, recognition of the currency status of cryptoSDRs can be regarded as an obligation of IMF member countries, requiring each member country to appropriately reference and integrate relevant provisions of the legitimacy of cryptoSDRs into their domestic laws and to allow their residents to hold and use cryptoSDRs. In this way, cryptoSDRs may become a new major international currency and legally circulate worldwide.

Second, the currency value risk of cryptoSDRs will be reduced due to the endorsement of multiple countries and authoritative international organizations, which is more favorable for international trade and global prosperity. Although the IMF cannot endorse currencies like a country does through taxes or other sources of wealth, because SDRs are priced in a basket of currencies, their value fluctuations are relatively small, which is incomparable to any sovereign currency. At the same time, the IMF can require member countries to provide corresponding assets or wealth as collateral and guarantee when exchanging for cryptoSDRs, ensuring that cryptoSDRs have legal solvency. Moreover, as their credit is backed by the credit and assets of multiple governments, their credit risk is smaller than that of a single country's government and assets, which means their currency value risk is bound to be smaller than that of any sovereign currency. Therefore, ordinary people may prefer to choose cryptoSDRs for value storage and trade payment rather than sovereign currencies.

Third, SDR itself is a type of bookkeeping asset, similar to the distributed ledger form of blockchain technology. It will not have the conflict and substitution relationship that may arise between sovereign cryptocurrencies and fiat currencies. As mentioned earlier, when a country issues a sovereign cryptocurrency, it will inevitably form a substitution relationship with its existing fiat currency system, sometimes even encountering certain conflicts. Furthermore, when a country wants to issue and promote sovereign cryptocurrency, it will also need to overturn people's habits of using paper currency and existing monetary policies and thus encounter resistance and policy conflicts that are difficult to reconcile with the fiat currency system. In contrast, cryptoSDRs will continue to use the existing SDR bookkeeping system and even make it more perfect and convenient by adding properties that facilitate circulation. It will not conflict with its existing attributes and architecture and will be easier to promote and popularize.

---

[105] IMF. IMF COUNTRY INFORMATION [EB/OL]. https://www.imf.org/en/countries. Accessed 6 May 2022.

[106] See footnote 76.

Finally, the promotion of cryptoSDRs could easily trigger momentum for it to replace the US dollar as the new major international currency. This would lead to its widespread use in the pricing of international trade and financial products, creating a new international currency and financial system that reduces the probability of a global financial crisis caused by systemic risks passed on by the US to other countries. It could even force the US to change its loose monetary policy and long-standing economic structure of trade deficits and become a tool for promoting the benign development of the world economy. The resulting new international currency and financial system will also be more in line with the current international situation, fairer to emerging economies, and more stable in structure. The IMF is an international organization that does not represent the interests of any individual country. Its currency policies are based on the interests of the majority of countries in the world. Countries will also allocate benefits such as "coinage tax" in a relatively fair proportion based on economic strength, political influence, and other factors, which can better represent the interests and demands of all countries.

(2) Advantages of CryptoSDRs

After digitalizing SDRs on the blockchain, cryptoSDRs can have the same convenient storage and divisibility features as cryptocurrency. Anyone can freely trade and use cryptoSDRs on their mobile phone, computer, or other devices. Additionally, the high transparency feature of cryptoSDRs allows everyone to see the total amount of cryptoSDRs, which can be monitored and restricted to prevent phenomena such as overissuance of US dollars and subsequent collapse of the system and depreciation of the dollar under the Bretton Woods system. For regulation, cryptoSDRs can fully implement real-name registration for accounts, allowing for anonymous transactions for small amounts and mandatory real-name registration for large transactions to prevent illegal activities such as money laundering and tax evasion. This allows governments to better monitor large transactions while allowing people to choose small anonymous transactions to protect their privacy without violating the law.

When cryptoSDRs are used as a payment method for international bulk trades, it becomes very easy to carry out large transactions and receive payments in real time without having to pay high transfer fees or wait for several days for traditional remittance methods. Financial products issued in the international financial market or cryptoSDR debt will no longer bear exchange rate risks and exchange costs, making it more convenient to finance and issue financial products such as stocks and bonds worldwide. Developing countries and regions can also enjoy financial services from developed countries or regions, promoting the development of global integration and upgrading and improving the international financial system. When the barriers of exchange rate differences between countries disappear, the circulation of goods will be faster, the price differences of goods in different countries will be reduced, and the gap between rich and poor will gradually narrow. The walls built by different laws and currencies between countries will also gradually disappear, greatly improving the efficiency of global resource allocation.

In regard to storing and transferring value in the private sector using cryptoSDRs, many citizens of various countries may prefer to use cryptoSDRs instead of precious metals such as gold or sovereign currencies such as the US dollar due to their greater stability. This is especially true for citizens of countries that participate in cryptoSDRs. Additionally, using cryptoSDRs for cross-border travel, shopping, studying abroad and immigrating is more convenient and can avoid exchange rate risks and costs. Furthermore, cryptoSDRs do not require a physical carrier, making them more efficient and convenient when passing through border customs. These benefits will undoubtedly further stimulate cross-border communication, encouraging people to allocate their assets around the world. International consumer markets, such as the tourism, aviation, and entertainment industries, will experience significant growth, driving the global economy forward.

For developing countries, selling their dollar reserves and purchasing cryptoSDRs as national reserve assets can reduce the risk of currency depreciation caused by the US dollar. This can also promote the upgrading of their domestic monetary systems and financial systems, allowing their citizens to use mobile payments instead of cash payments and making transactions more convenient and quick. Additionally, during global pandemics such as COVID-19, the use of paper currency as a transmission medium can be effectively avoided. Without exchange rate differences, developing countries will have a more obvious advantage in attracting consumers with their low-cost labor and goods, which will attract purchasing power to flow into these price-competitive areas, promoting the export of goods and the development of industry in developing countries and accelerating the narrowing of the gap between them and developed countries.

For developed countries, selling their dollar and other sovereign currency reserves and buying more cryptoSDRs as national reserve assets can make their currency reserves more stable. Additionally, developed countries' advantages in technology products, education, entertainment, healthcare, and services will be more attractive to consumers from other countries. At the same time, tourism and cross-border shopping, which are popular among citizens of developed countries, will become more convenient and quick, significantly improving their quality of life.

(3) Opportunities

Once known as the "Empire on which the sun never sets," the UK established an international monetary system supported by the gold standard during its global domination in the nineteenth century. After World War II, the UK's strength had greatly weakened, and the US, the most powerful country after the war, took over the UK's world leadership role and established the postwar international monetary system centered on the US dollar, the Bretton Woods system, to consolidate its position as the world's dominant power. Currently, the US's economic, political, and military power has declined significantly, while China has become the world's second-largest economy and has achieved world-class levels in technology, politics, and military affairs, as well as consecutive successes in industrial upgrading while maintaining its position as the world's factory. China's "Belt and Road Initiative," led by China, has gained recognition and support from many countries and has achieved regional dominance in international relations. Despite the COVID-19 pandemic in 2020, China was able to maintain positive GDP growth. In contrast, the US GDP severely declined due to improper pandemic control, and China has already surpassed the US in fields such as information technology and financial payments, making it likely that China will replace the US as the world leader in various fields in the future. According to the prediction of the UK institution "Centre for Economics and Business Research," by 2030, China will surpass the US to become the world's largest economy. By then, China may become a creator and maintainer of the new international order.[107] Therefore, China needs to establish a new international monetary system to maintain and consolidate its dominant position within that system. As a sovereign currency, Chinese yuan, acting as a major international currency, will inevitably have various drawbacks similar to the current US dollar system and may even evolve into a more chaotic multipolar monetary system dominated by Chinese yuan, with the US dollar and the euro as supplementary currencies. This result will undoubtedly be detrimental to the development of globalization and the maintenance of China's dominant position. By actively participating in and leading the creation of cryptoSDRs, China will have the opportunity to use a supersovereign currency recognized by countries around the world to establish a more stable international monetary system, thereby constructing and maintaining a new international order to safeguard China's stable dominant position in the world. At the same time, by creating cryptoSDRs, China can reform the IMF and SDRs and tilt the balance of the system slightly toward China and other developing countries, making the international system fairer, reducing global conflicts and contradictions, and stabilizing the international order.

As previously mentioned, the core element for the monetization of the SDRs is to obtain the support of a superpolitical entity. China's rise represents the emergence of a responsible major power and the construction of a new international order, making it a perfect opportunity for the birth of cryptoSDRs. On the one hand, in the near future, when China becomes a leader in various aspects compared to the US, it will be easier to persuade other countries to support the reform of the existing international monetary system to gain dominance. Compared with completely denying the original international monetary system and establishing a brand new one, reforming the existing system is easier to achieve. It is similar to the Jamaica system, which is not a complete denial of the Bretton Woods system but rather a reform and improvement on its basis.

On the other hand, the international nature of cryptoSDRs and their public service characteristics are consistent with the spirit of "the world is for everyone" in Chinese culture and in line with the connotation of China's financial system, which provides high-quality services to customers. The design principles should follow the following four principles.

The first is the principle of "global village." With the help of transportation tools such as cars and airplanes, people can easily reach most areas of the world, and energy, time, and space can be easily exchanged with the help of technology. For human

---

[107] Jimu News. UK research agency predicts China will surpass the US and become the world's largest economy in 2030 [EB/OL]. https://baijiahao.baidu.com/s?id=1720194822613589762&wfr=spider&for=pc. Accessed 6 May 2022.

beings, it is an indisputable fact that the earth has become a "global village." Super-sovereign international currency is a product of the trend of "global village" development. It should serve the "community of human destiny," provide public financial services for the globalization of human beings, and construct an international monetary system that is more in line with the principle of "global village."

The second is the principle of equality and universality. The international cryptocurrency jointly participated and operated by the IMF and its member countries should adhere to the principles of mutual benefit, equality, cooperation, and win–win and abandon factors that may cause discrimination based on differences in race, religion, wealth, territory, and other aspects. It should provide universal financial services to people all over the world and realize the true "community of human destiny."

The third is the principle of efficient management. CryptoSDRs issued by the IMF and managed by its member countries should be effectively controlled and efficiently regulated to prevent financial crises from occurring and to prevent individuals, organizations, or countries from infringing on the common interests of people around the world for their own interests. Therefore, the international monetary system constructed by cryptoSDRs should be a regulated, constrained, and protected system.

The fourth is the principle of freedom. The international monetary system constructed by cryptoSDRs should be subject to strict regulation and effective control at the level of international organizations, governments, and legal frameworks, but at the same time, users of cryptoSDRs should be given full freedom to maximize the efficiency of the entire system.[108] At the same time, according to Article 13(1) of the IMF Agreement, "the headquarters of the IMF shall be located in the territory of the member having the largest quota, and agencies or branches may be established in the territories of other members." When China obtains the largest or a significant quota of the IMF, the headquarters of the IMF could be relocated to China or a branch office could be established in China, and the creation, operation, and management of cryptoSDRs could be conducted by the headquarters or branch office. Since China has world-leading electronic payment systems and blockchain technology, it is well positioned to implement the creation and operation of the cryptoSDR system.

[108] Yu Zhonghua, Yu Wenshan. Blockchain Concept, Financial Meta-Logic and Reconstruction of the International Monetary System [J]. Regional Financial Research, 2020(7), pp. 5–13.

Chapter 2
The Realization Path of CryptoSDRs Monetization

After analyzing the previous chapter, it is evident that the birth of cryptoSDRs, which serve as a prototype for a unified global currency, offers an opportunity to address the inherent flaws and various drawbacks of the current international monetary system. Therefore, how will cryptoSDRs be created? What technological and legal paths need to be followed for their creation? Does the creation of the euro offer any inspiration or lessons for the creation of cryptoSDRs?

2.1 The Practice of the Euro and Enlightenment

Against the backdrop of economic globalization, the regionalization and globalization of currency and finance have become increasingly apparent trends. Currency regionalization refers to the coordination and integration of related countries and regions in specific areas such as currency and finance, gradually forming a unified economic and political community and ultimately achieving a unified monetary system. To date, there have been two different paths to currency regionalization. The first is the unified use of the euro in the European region, which has already been achieved. The second is the unified use of the US dollar in Latin America. However, these two paths have fundamental differences in nature. The euro was formed through cooperation agreements among multiple countries with similar economic development levels, ultimately achieving a form of currency regionalization. In contrast, the dollarization of Latin America reflects the control of a strong currency over weak countries. This occurs as the dollar infiltrates weak countries such as those in Latin America and partially or completely suppresses weak currencies, thus forming a form of currency regionalization within the region. In other words, dollarization can only occur between countries with significant economic disparities, and the ultimate form of this currency regionalization is the gradual replacement of weak currencies by

L. Zeng, *A Study on the Creation, Impact and Legal Issues of Crypto Special Drawing Rights*, Modern China and International Economic Law,
https://doi.org/10.1007/978-981-99-9975-0_2

strong international currency in certain countries and regions.[1] This chapter mainly focuses on the successful case of the optimal currency area, which is the process of the European Currency Unit (hereafter referred to as the "ECU") evolving into the euro as a form of currency regionalization.

2.1.1 Optimal Currency Area and Digital Currency Area

In the 1960s and 1970s, Robert Mundell first proposed the theory of "optimal currency area," which elaborated on how to unify currencies within a region and put forward economic indicators for optimizing the formation of currency areas. He believed that in the optimal form of a currency area, factors required for production within the same region could flow freely, while there would be obstacles to circulation outside this region. Economic development among countries within the same region could be adjusted through the free flow of production factors, particularly labor, whereas the economic development of countries outside this currency area could only be regulated through monetary policy in international trade to stabilize the micro- and macroeconomics of that region. Thus, he concluded that countries or regions with high fluidity of production factors, especially labor, were the optimal currency areas that made up a unified currency.[2]

In the 1970s, scholars such as Corden, Mundell, Ishiyama, Tower, and Willet shifted their research focus from determining the optimal currency area to analyzing the cost–benefit of a country participating in a currency union, resulting in deeper research into the theory of the optimal currency area. They analyzed the cost of forming a currency union, including the loss of regulatory capacity and independence of exchange rate policy, the loss of revenue from currency issuance, and the cost of joining the currency area. At the same time, they also analyzed the benefits of establishing a currency union, such as reducing losses from currency conversion between countries, accelerating trade within the region, reducing the cost of capital flow, avoiding policy protection measures, and reducing investment risk. Krugman even conducted research on the benefits of Norway's accession to the EU and proposed a famous theoretical model, providing a powerful reference for countries to determine whether to join a currency union.[3] With the trend of globalization, cross-border exchanges, and trade continuing to grow, currency regional integration or even global currency unification will increasingly highlight its benefits and eventually be recognized and implemented worldwide.

---

[1] Li Yang, Huang Jinlao. Research on Dollarization Issues. Financial Research, 1999(9), pp. 56–62 + 81.

[2] ROBERT A. MUNDELL. A Theory of Optimum Currency Areas [J]. American Economic Review, 1961(4), pp. 657–665.

[3] PAUL R. KRUGMAN. A Model of Balance of Payment Crisis [J]. Journal of Money Cridet and Banking, 1979(11), pp. 311–325.

Based on the foundation of an optimal currency area, Markus Brunnermeier, a professor at Princeton University, and others proposed the concept of a "digital currency area" (hereafter referred to as the "DCA") as the digital economy and electronic payments rapidly developed. A DCA is defined as a network where transactions and payments are made using the same digital currency. A DCA differs significantly from an optimal currency area, which is primarily characterized by geographically close countries or regions that can achieve an optimal currency arrangement by adjusting exchange rates. Participants in this region are affected similarly by macroeconomic shocks, and factors of production such as labor and goods can flow relatively freely within the area.[4] In contrast, participants in a DCA can be closely connected by using the same digital currency, regardless of distance, with the main driving force being the widespread use of mobile payments. The common goal of both currency areas is to reduce transaction obstacles and make the economy more liquid.

Brunnermeier and others believe that the future international monetary system will be constructed in the form of a DCA. Even if this does not occur, the competition among future currencies will reshape the international monetary system through the digitization of existing currencies. Furthermore, a DCA can use social connections provided by digital networks to create stronger cohesion than traditional optimal currency areas, which could increase the chance of nurturing an international currency.[5] CryptoSDRs issued in a digital form are consistent with the concept of a DCA and may thus become a pioneer of the future international monetary system.

To become a supersovereign digital currency, cryptoSDRs issued in a digital form first need to draw on the theoretical foundation of an optimal currency area, such as the euro. They also need to combine the principles and advantages of a DCA to achieve their global layout.

2.1.2 *European Union Currency Practice*

Unlike sovereign currencies that arise from geopolitical or natural processes within a country's history, artificial currencies are created by people to achieve economic or political goals through a commonly agreed-upon convention. The cryptocurrency known as cryptoSDRs that this book explores is not a currency that naturally arises in historical processes, but rather, like the euro, it is an artificial currency designed to achieve economic and political goals. The two artificial currency units that have emerged in history are the ECU, which preceded the euro, and the SDRs. Currently, the ECU has been successfully created through a series of treaties and legal arrangements and has evolved into the euro, which has become the second-largest international reserve currency after the US dollar. Its level of acceptance and circulation

---

[4] FRANKEL, ROSE. The Endogeneity of The Optimum currency Area Criteria [J]. The Economic Journal, 1998(108), pp. 1009–1025.

[5] MARKUS BRUNNERMEIER, HAROLD JAMES, JEAN-PIERRE LANDAU. The Digitalization Of Money [EB/OL]. https://www.nber.org/papers/w26300. Accessed 6 May 2022.

worldwide is second only to the US dollar as a major international currency. The success of the euro demonstrates that an artificial supersovereign currency unit can emerge in a certain region of the world. Therefore, whether a currency can circulate as a general equivalent in different countries and regions which depends not on whether it is backed by gold or has physical value but on whether there are a series of treaties and legal arrangements that are recognized by the countries accepting its circulation.[6] Therefore, in the process of monetarization, the design of legal systems and the evolution of the ECU into the euro can be used as a reference for the development of cryptoSDRs.

(1) Creation of the European Currency Unit

The core of the Bretton Woods system was the establishment of the dominance of the US dollar, which put an end to the competitive devaluation of currencies that occurred among countries after the World War II. However, there existed an inherent contradiction that made it difficult to resolve the "Triffin Dilemma." The US dollar was both the currency of a sovereign nation and an international currency, and this inherent contradiction led to frequent financial crises on a global scale, making it difficult for the international monetary system to maintain stability.

Faced with the difficulties brought about by the US dollar and the Bretton Woods system, various European countries believed that they could only overcome these challenges through unity and cooperation. Thus, with the help of the Marshall Plan implemented by the US, European countries assisted one another and established the "Organization for European Economic Cooperation" in 1948.[7] In 1950, the European Payment Union (hereafter referred to as the "EPU") was formed by 17 European member countries of the Organization for European Economic Cooperation in response to the crisis caused by the exhaustion of bilateral trade credit limits in Europe's internal payment system, taking the first step toward European currency integration.

In August 1955, the member countries of the Organization for European Economic Cooperation signed the "European Monetary Agreement" to further develop the convertibility of internal currencies. In 1957, the European Coal and Steel Community was formed by six European countries, including the Federal Republic of Germany and France, to establish a common market for European agriculture, and the Treaty of Rome was jointly signed. At the end of the same year, these countries signed additional agreements based on the monetary agreement and adjusted the fluctuations of their national currencies against the US dollar, reducing the fluctuation range between countries by 0.5% and the overall fluctuation range by at least 1%.

Subsequently, France adjusted its monetary policy to reduce its financial pressure, and the UK began to implement the free exchange of pounds. Other signatory countries also began to adopt similar monetary policies. Thus, the "European Monetary

[6] Li Xiang. The Establishment of Asian Monetary Unit from the Development of Artificial Currency SDR and European Currency Unit. Shanghai: Fudan University, 2008, p. 23.

[7] EICHENGREEN, BARRY. Globalizing Capital: A History of the International Monetary System [M]. Princeton: Princeton University Press, 1996, pp. 62–105.

Agreement" replaced the EPU.[8] The "European Monetary Agreement" was established by European countries to overcome internal currency payment problems, and the crisis at the time was somewhat similar to the current foreign exchange problem of the international monetary system.

At the beginning of the establishment of the European Economic Community (hereafter referred to as the "EEC"), the operation of the Bretton Woods system was stable, which promoted the economic development of the currency area. The stable economic development of the member countries of the EEC kept their unemployment rates at a low level, achieved net profits in their fiscal revenue, and maintained the stability of their currency value. Therefore, during this period, European countries did not deliberately develop currency cooperation plans, nor did they have a strong need to establish an independent monetary system.[9] This is similar to the current stage of the international monetary system, which still relies mainly on the US dollar as the major international currency, and developed countries, including the US, do not have a strong desire to promote the unity of international currencies and the creation of a supersovereign currency. However, the "dollar system" is already faltering, and the current monetary system is at the end of its life cycle.

The following events have important reference significance for promoting European currency cooperation. The signing of the Treaty of Rome in 1958 made the economic and trade relations between member states of the EEC more closely integrated, and countries began to focus on advancing currency cooperation plans. At the Hague Conference in late 1969, which was attended by European countries, Germany took the lead in proposing a currency cooperation plan to reduce the influence of the US dollar on member countries' currencies.

In June 1970, the EEC adopted the famous Werner Report, which was the first complete theoretical conception for the creation of a European Economic and Monetary Union and was the first important report in the history of the euro. In this report, the EEC stated the main purpose of establishing the union, which was to ensure the economic interests of the EEC and maintain its steady economic growth. The plan first called for the establishment of a political entity that was completely independent of each country and accountable only to the EEC parliament to ensure that the currency and economic policies formulated by it had unique authority. At the same time, an independent European Central Bank was to be established to formulate monetary policy. The European Economic and Monetary Union is similar to the IMF today, but the IMF's functions have not been fully realized, and since SDRs are not yet a currency, the IMF does not have a similar central bank function and system structure.[10] The text below will mention that IMF can establish currency expert group, but as to whether IMF will eventually become a World Central Bank similar to the

[8] DUTTA M. Seminar on the EU and the Euro Revolution: The Theory of Optimum Currency Area Revisited [M]. Colorado: Colorado University Press, 2001, pp. 352–375.

[9] BARRY EICHENGREEN. Global Imbalance and the Lessons of Bretton Woods [N]. NBER Working Paper, NO. 10497, 2004.

[10] Rahbari Beck. Optimal Reserve Composition in the Presence of Sudden Stops: The Euro and the Dollar as Safe Haven Currencies [N]. ECB Working Paper, NO. 916, 2008.

European Central Bank, the author believes that it can develop into a World Central Bank with all or part of the functions through compromise and cooperation from multiple parties and member countries.

The Werner Report clearly outlined the work content and completion node servers for the implementation of the currency cooperation plan, which was to be implemented in stages, with each stage lasting for a period of three years, starting from 1971. The first stage was from January 1, 1971, to December 31, 1973. The main plan content of this stage was to adjust monetary policy to reduce currency exchange rate fluctuations among member countries, establish a currency exchange rate system for the EEC that included the currencies of all member countries, and establish a currency reserve fund to stabilize the currency exchange rates of various countries. The second stage was from 1974 to the end of 1976. Its main objective was to concentrate part of the foreign exchange reserves of each member country to build a currency reserve fund, strengthen the EEC's influence on foreign exchange transactions, minimize foreign exchange fluctuations among member countries, and further accelerate capital flows among various countries. The third stage was from 1977 to the end of 1979, and the main work content of this stage was to ensure that all the factors needed for production could flow freely within the EEC, achieve currency unification among member countries, and thus achieve the goal of currency unification. However, because the Werner Report was based on the temporary stability of the Bretton Woods system, its theoretical support was lost with the collapse of the Bretton Woods system. In addition, the ensuing chaos in the currency market ultimately led to the shelving of the Werner Report. At the same time, there were also major problems in the global economy, with two global economic crises occurring in the 1970s, and the economic gap and uneven development within the European Community intensified, resulting in even the first-stage goals not being achieved.[11] Although there were various reasons for the delay in the launch of the euro, it is still worthwhile to plan and prepare ahead of time. Therefore, it is necessary to advance the implementation plan for the introduction of cryptoSDRs, and the author will present specific plans and proposals in the following text.

On February 9, 1971, the European Community created a new currency unit called the ECU as a response to currency fluctuations. The ECU was equivalent to the US dollar and aimed to provide a stable and reliable alternative to the US currency.

Due to two devaluations of the US dollar in the 1970s, the ECU's value was no longer equal to the US dollar but instead was equivalent to the SDRs. Thus, the SDRs to some extent were considered to have monetary value, and the ECU's value was tied to it.

In 1971, the SDRs were decoupled from gold and pegged to a basket of 16 currencies, including the US dollar, the West German mark, the Japanese yen, the British pound, the French franc, the Canadian dollar, the Italian lira, the Dutch guilder, the Belgian franc, the Swedish krona, the Australian dollar, the Norwegian krone, the Danish krone, the Spanish peseta, the South African rand, and the Austrian schilling. The European Community then created a new ECU in 1979, which was

[11] See footnote 7.

jointly determined by the currencies of the nine member countries of the European Community.

The share of each currency in the basket depends on the ratio of the member countries' GDP and trade volume, and the ECU was mainly used for pricing purposes. However, the US dollar still had a significant impact on the European Community's foreign exchange reserves and exchange rate fluctuations.[12] The composition and attributes of the ECU and the SDRs are very similar, and the ECU was later upgraded to the euro. This demonstrates the feasibility of monetizing the SDRs.

(2) Evolution of the European Currency Unit into the Euro

Under the Bretton Woods system, the frequent financial crises caused by the US dollar as the major international currency seriously affected the stability of the exchange rates of the EEC's currency. To address the increasingly severe international monetary pressure and exchange rate fluctuations, the EEC adjusted its internal monetary policies and changed its economic development trends. The chairman of the EEC Commission, Roy, once again declared the significance of establishing the European Economic and Monetary Union, and the member countries of the EEC gained more support in jointly establishing a European Monetary System. As seen from the laws of global economic development, the fluctuation of the European currency exchange rate is largely influenced by the fluctuation of the US dollar; that is, the fluctuation of the US dollar determines the fluctuation of the European currency exchange rate. Therefore, the member states of the EEC reached a consensus that before a more suitable international monetary system is established, it is necessary to establish a regional international monetary system that meets the conditions and actual needs of the EEC to cope with the frequent impact of the US dollar crisis on the European currency.[13] Similar to the EEC, facing the frequent outbreak of the US dollar crisis, the current international monetary system also needs to be reformed. Only by establishing a monetary system that adapts to the new international economic situation can the adverse effects of financial crises on the global economic market be alleviated.

In December 1978, the Brussels European Community Summit decided to officially use the European Monetary System from January 1, 1979. At that time, there were seven member countries, and the UK, which was a member of the European Community at the time, did not join the European Monetary System because it refused to participate in the European Exchange Rate Mechanism. Ireland and Italy requested increased assistance from the European Community. France's condition for joining was to cancel the currency compensation policy for agriculture in the agreement, but this requirement would harm Germany's interests. After multiple coordinations

[12] LANDAU DOOLEY, GARBER DOOLEY. Management on Interest Rates and Exchange Rates in Center Countried [N]. NBER Working Paper, NO. 10332, 2004.

[13] BARRY EICHENGREEN, MARC FLANDREAU. The Rise and Fall of the Dollar, or When did the Dollar Replace Sterling as the Leading Reserve Currency? [N]. NBER Working Paper, NO. 14154, 2008.

on the different requirements of these countries, the European Monetary System officially came into effect on March 13, 1979.[14]

The purpose of creating the European Monetary System was to ensure that the international exchange rates of European countries were not affected by the US dollar, to improve the status and role of these countries' currencies in international transactions, to further unify the European economy, to promote long-term stable economic integration and development, and to inject new vitality into the construction of the European Community. There are three elements that make up the European Monetary System: the ECU, the European Monetary Cooperation Fund (hereafter referred to as the "EMCF"), and the Exchange Rate Stability Mechanism (hereafter referred to as the "ERM").[15] The new international monetary system based on cryptoSDRs can also learn from the composition of the European Monetary System and establish a Currency Cooperation Fund and an Exchange Rate Stability Mechanism.

One important component of the European Monetary System is the ECU, which was the new form of the European Monetary Unit of Account (hereafter referred to as the "EMUA"). The ECU itself is not a currency but rather a unit of account based on a weighted calculation of the shares of each member country's currency in a basket system.[16] Its main functions are threefold: first, to establish the central exchange rate and deviation standards for each member country's currency based on different circumstances; second, to serve as the value scale and calculation unit for official credit in the European Community; and third, to serve as the reserve asset and intervention measure of the European Community.

The European Council calculates each country's currency share in the ECU by averaging its GDP over the past five years, its share of intracommunity trade, and its original share of the short-term currency support fund of the European Community. Based on these evaluation principles, Germany's currency had a one-third share in the European Monetary Mechanism at the beginning, while France, the Netherlands, and the UK had 10% each. These percentages can be adjusted in the first six months after the system takes effect based on actual circumstances. The European Community Commission (hereafter referred to as the "ECC") reviews and adjusts each country's currency share every five years, and if a country's currency share changes by more than 25%, a review and adjustment can be requested.

Because of the different economic development situations of each member country, the currency shares in the EMU were adjusted on September 15, 1984,

[14] BARRY EICHENGREEN. The Euro as a Reserve Currency, Journal of the Japanese and International [J]. Economies, 1998(12), pp. 8–24.

[15] GREENWALD, STIGLITZ. A Long Term Perspective On The Euro [N]. NBER Working Papers, NO. 13815, 2008.

[16] While the United Kingdom did not participate in the European Exchange Rate Mechanism, the pound was included in a basket of currencies. As a result, the basket of currencies that formed the European currency system at its inception included the West German mark, the French franc, the Pound sterling, the Dutch guilder, the Belgian franc, the Italian lira, the Danish krone, the Irish pound, and the Luxembourg franc.

September 15, 1989, and March 6, 1995.[17] These rules for the ECU are similar to those for SDRs, but the latter cannot adequately reflect the current economic weight of each country in the world, and the basket of currencies is not diverse enough. We should learn from the ECU's practice and include as many member countries' currencies as possible in the currency basket in the later stage.

The European Monetary System operates the foreign exchange intervention mechanism through the currency basket system and the Parity Network System to stabilize the exchange rates of each country's currency. The Parity Network System means that in the same exchange rate system, the central exchange rate of any two member countries' currencies can be determined, and the ECU serves as the value standard. The exchange rate fluctuation of each currency in the currency basket system must be less than the specified limit; otherwise, any participating country can intervene in foreign exchange transactions to keep the bilateral exchange rate within the allowed limit. The ECU can be used as a standard for exchange rate deviation to calculate exchange rate fluctuations.[18] In the process of monetizing SDRs, we can learn from the Parity Network System in the European Monetary System to intervene in exchange rates for countries requesting to use cryptoSDRs, gradually stabilize the exchange rate between the member country's currency and cryptoSDRs, and then achieve currency substitution, gradually promoting the use of cryptoSDRs in the member country and eventually replacing its sovereign currency.

The ECU serves as a pricing tool and value standard for clearing and settlement, trade, and all official credit transactions between member countries of the European Community. All financial and accounting activities related to trade within the European Community are based on the ECU as a pricing unit and measurement benchmark. Additionally, the financial and technical aid provided by the Lomé Convention[19] is also accounted for in the ECU. Furthermore, the SDR is used as a pricing unit in international trade, financial investment, and cross-border settlement to better fulfill its functions and become a major international currency.

Since its establishment in April 1973, the EMCF has issued the ECU, which is based on 20% of the central banks' gold holdings and foreign exchange reserves of the participating countries. For each member state, the ECU has become the most important reserve currency, and its importance is on par with that of the US dollar and the Deutsche mark. The role of the central banks of the member states of the European Community is also changing, as they can adjust the volatility of their currencies by

[17] ELIAS PAPAIOANNOUA, RICHARD PORTES, GREGORIOS SIOUROUNISE. Optimal Currency Shares in International Reserves: The Impact of the Euro and the Prospects for the Dollar [N]. CEPR Discussion Paper, NO. 5734, 2006.

[18] BORDO, FLNADREAU. Core, Periphery, Exchange Rate Regimes, and Globalization [N]. NBER Working Paper, NO. 8584, 2001.

[19] The Lomé Convention, also known as the "Europe Agreement on Economic Cooperation with African, Caribbean, and Pacific (ACP) States," was signed on February 28, 1975. Representatives from 46 developing countries in the ACP region and 9 countries in the European Economic Community have gathered in Lomé, the capital of Togo, to sign a 5-year trade and economic agreement. The convention officially came into effect on April 1, 1976, and has since been renewed several times.

issuing money. When the central bank of a single country is unable to intervene effectively, the EMCF can provide financial support and encourage all countries to use the ECU for loan repayment. Therefore, the role of the ECU is highlighted.[20] This operating model of the ECU also provides a good reference for cryptoSDRs. If a member country faces currency runs or other disruptions during the process of replacing its sovereign currency with cryptoSDRs, it can establish a corresponding monetary cooperation fund within the IMF and use cryptoSDRs as a settlement unit and repayment currency. This can help cryptoSDRs gain more recognition as a major reserve asset by international funds and governments.

Among them, the EMCF collects 20% of the foreign exchange reserves and gold reserves of each member country as the funding basis for providing credit and improves the institutional support for credit. It can provide very-short-term financing, short-term monetary support, and medium-term financial assistance to each member country. To strengthen the foreign exchange anti-interference ability of each member country, the EMCF provides very-short-term loans to each member country. When the bilateral exchange rate fluctuations between any two member countries are too large or exceed the limit, any member country can apply for an unlimited ECU-denominated very-short-term loan to adjust the fluctuation of the bilateral exchange rate and enhance the effectiveness of intervention. The main purpose of short-term monetary support is to provide loans to member countries that need to balance their international trade deficits within three or nine months. The amount of such loans is directly affected by the amount of bond issuance by the borrowing country. The main object of medium-term financial assistance is countries with severe government fiscal deficits, with a credit term of 2–5 years. Since it is generally impossible for all member countries to have serious international trade deficits at the same time, the upper limit of the loan amount for this type of loan has not been clearly stipulated. However, according to the usual operating rules, the amount of loans applied for by any member country cannot exceed half of the maximum amount of such loans. The source of funds for loans is provided on average by each member country.[21] The various details of the above funds can serve as a reference for currency funds that use cryptoSDRs as reserves and settlement units.

The European Monetary System adopts a fixed exchange rate mechanism within the European Community, but the exchange rates of the currencies of each participating country can be adjusted within the prescribed range. For countries outside the European Community, a joint floating exchange rate mechanism is used. Within the European Community, the foreign exchange rates between member countries are fixed, and the central exchange rate and fluctuation limit are clearly defined in terms of the euro, while corresponding foreign exchange intervention measures are also stipulated. If the intervention measures cannot achieve the desired effect, the ultimate measure of adjusting the central exchange rate is used to adjust the

[20] MENZIE CHIN, JEFFREY FRANKEL. Why the Euro Will Rival the Dollar [J]. International Finance, 2008(1), pp. 49–73.

[21] See footnote 20.

exchange rate.[22] This is also a measure that member countries using cryptoSDRs as the circulating currency can adopt. After joining cryptoSDRs, the exchange between the currencies of each member country and cryptoSDRs, as well as the exchange between the currencies of member countries and nonmember countries, all adopt a fixed exchange rate mechanism, while a joint floating exchange rate mechanism is used for nonmember countries.

(3) Birth of the Euro

As the role of the European Monetary System continued to emerge, it attracted more European countries to join. In the 1990s, the UK's entry into the European exchange rate mechanism made the economic development and foreign exchange markets of the European Community more stable. The vast majority of countries have adopted the euro as their foreign exchange currency unit, creating a clearing system based on the euro as the unit and enacting corresponding laws to protect it. Since the 1970s and 1980s, global economic development has been rapid, and international economic trade and cooperation have increased rapidly. In December 1985, the ECC proposed the establishment of a unified European market plan and the "European Economic and Monetary Policy Cooperation Alliance" by the end of 1992, enabling labor, goods, and capital to flow freely without borders within the alliance.[23]

However, the economic development speed of the European Community was far lower than that of the US and Japan. Faced with fierce external competition and the close connection of the domestic economy of each member country, the call to accelerate the establishment of the European Economic and Monetary Union grew louder. As the then President of the ECC, Delors was authorized to establish a special committee to study the strategy for European monetary unification and implement it at the European Council meeting held in June 1988. On April 17, 1989, after in-depth research by the Economic and Monetary Union Committee,[24] the report "On Economic and Monetary Union" was compiled. This report is the famous "Delors Report." The specific content proposed in the report was unanimously agreed upon by the ECC and was passed at the European Community Summit in June of the same year. The report pointed out that the future monetary union must be able to ensure the free flow of capital, the free exchange of currencies, and the monetary system of member countries that implement fixed exchange rate systems must be consistent with the monetary system established by the union. Based on this report, the "Charter of the European Central Bank (Draft)" and the "Treaty on Economic and Monetary Union (Draft)" were formulated. The 46th European Community Summit was held in Maastricht, the Netherlands, in December 1991, and the "Maastricht Treaty" was passed at the meeting, including the "Treaty on Economic and Monetary Union" and the "Political Union Treaty," which stipulated the specific process of establishing

[22] BORDO. Exchange Rate Regime Choice in Historical Perspective [N]. NBER Working Paper, NO. 9654, 2003.

[23] See footnote 8.

[24] The committee was established during the June 1988 European Community Summit, with the main task of researching and drafting specific plans to establish an economic and monetary union.

an economic, political, and monetary union within the European Community and laid a solid foundation for the establishment of the EU.[25] This can also serve as a reference for the monetarization and promotion of the universal use of cryptoSDRs. The IMF will form an "economic and monetary community" consisting of countries willing to use cryptoSDRs as circulation currencies and formulate the "Charter of World Central Bank" and the "Treaty on Economic and Monetary Union" to ensure the free flow of capital, the free exchange of currencies, and the currency policies of countries implementing fixed exchange rate systems.

The Maastricht Treaty stipulates that after the establishment of the Economic and Monetary Union, member countries must use a unified currency to maintain price and exchange rate stability and prohibit the occurrence of large amounts of debt and national fiscal deficits. At the same time, the treaty also makes clear provisions for the period and work content of the Economic and Monetary Union's creation.

The first stage is from July 1, 1990, to the end of 1993. Member countries should, if necessary, develop appropriate methods and measures to fulfill the prohibitive obligations stipulated in Articles 56, 101, and 102 (1) of the Maastricht Treaty. The main task of this stage is to eliminate barriers to financial integration, which includes promoting the participation of all EU member states in the European currency exchange rate system, reducing the impact of foreign exchange fluctuations, requiring internal foreign exchange controls to be lifted, strengthening the mobility of production factors among member states, and promoting consistency and coordination of economic and monetary policies among member states to create a unified economic market within the EU.

The second stage starts on January 1, 1994, and lasts for five years. This stage can be called the transitional stage, during which the European Monetary Authority is established. The prerequisite for forming the European Central Bank system is that the central banks of each member country must have independent operational capabilities. The main work of this stage is to further promote economic consistency among member states on the basis of the first stage, develop policies that are more suitable for each country's currency and exchange rate, and require each member country to formulate its own budget in accordance with the relevant provisions of the Maastricht Treaty, ensuring that its fiscal deficit does not exceed 3% of the GDP for that year and government debt does not exceed 60% of the GDP for that year. Suitable fiscal policies must also be established to maintain the independent operational functions of central banks in each country and ensure the normal operation of their stable price functions, establish a European unified financial system department, and promote the normal operation of the European currency mechanism. The third stage involves creating the European Central Bank, issuing a unified circulating currency, and ensuring the legal status of the euro by legislation. It also specifies the exchange rates between the currencies of EU countries and the euro and determines the foreign

[25] COHEN, BENJAMINJ. The Geography of Money [M]. Cornell: Cornell University Press, 1998, pp. 27–47.

exchange rates between non-EU countries and EU countries, as well as the position of the euro as the valuation unit for national debt issuance in each member state.[26]

As the euro is highly popular among European countries, people have shown support for the policy of monetary unification in Europe. The euro is widely valued in international economic exchanges, and many private banks issue bonds in euro in the European market. In the 1990s, euro-denominated bonds were highly anticipated internationally.[27]

The sign of the European Economic and Monetary Union entering the third stage is the official launch of the euro on January 1, 1999. The union stipulates that from July 1, 2002, the own currencies of all euro area countries will be phased out of circulation, and EU countries must exchange their currencies for the unified currency within the EU at the prescribed exchange rate by June 30 of that year.[28] Thus, the euro finally came into being.

(4) Guaranteeing the Legal Status of the Euro Through Conventions

The legal status of the euro is primarily guarded through conventions, and eurozone member states are required to incorporate the relevant conventions into their domestic legislation as a legal guarantee of the legitimacy of the euro's introduction, the legal status of its use, and the exclusivity of its issuance.

1. Legitimacy of the Euro's Introduction

Article 2 of the Treaty on European Union stipulates that the monetary policy objective of the EU is to adopt a single currency throughout the union. Article 4 of the Treaty of Rome also specifies the name of the single currency as the ECU. At the European Council meeting held in Madrid in 1995, the 15 member states of the EU changed the name of the single currency to "euro."

2. Legal Status of the Euro's Use

Several provisions of the Treaty on European Union define the status of the euro as the only legal tender currency in the eurozone and confer upon it the status of legal tender. Some provisions also clarify the legal status of euro coins. Although both euro banknotes and coins are legal tender, there are some differences in their legal status. For example, there are no restrictions on the legal currency status of banknotes, but coins are subject to certain limitations, such as the obligation of no one to accept more than 50 coins in a transaction unless otherwise provided by law.

3. Exclusivity of the Euro Issuance

The European Central Bank is the sole institution responsible for issuing the euro, with exclusive rights. The euro can be issued by the European Central Bank or the

---

[26] See footnote 8.

[27] See footnote 6.

[28] DUTTA M. Theory of Optimum Currency Area Revisited: Lessons From the Euro/Dollar Competitive Currency Regimes [J]. Journal of Asian Economics, 2005(16), pp. 352–375.

central banks of the member states. Member states still have the power to issue coins, but the total amount of issuance must be approved in advance by the European Central Bank. Within the approved limit for coin issuance, the number of coins issued is determined by the eurozone member states themselves, allowing them to collect a certain amount of seigniorage.

The legitimacy of the euro's introduction, the legal status of its use, and the exclusivity of its issuance are the legal basis and guarantee of the euro's currency attributes. Similarly, the monetarization of SDRs also requires that the legitimacy of their introduction, the legal status of their use, and the exclusivity of their issuance by the IMF and its member states can be clearly stipulated in international treaties and regulations to legally protect the currency attributes of cryptoSDRs and their legal status for circulation in the international market.

The euro is the first regional artificial supersovereign currency, and prior to its creation, there had never been a case where an independent country gave up its sovereign currency and adopted another single currency. Therefore, the birth of the euro is a milestone in the history of artificial currencies and holds great significance. From its creation process to the establishment of its legal framework, the birth of the euro is worth studying for the full guidance of the monetarization and promotion of cryptoSDRs.

2.2 Legal Paths to Monetize CryptoSDRs

The underlying reason for the instability in the current international monetary system is that the issuance and management of sovereign currencies are determined by a single country. To address the various issues in the international monetary system, a structural reform of the global credit system is needed. This reform should transform the system from being managed by a single country to one that is characterized by mutual restraint and joint management among nations. This approach would be an effective way to solve the problems of the current international monetary system, especially during the unregulated expansion of global credit, which necessitates the establishment of a global organization with a role similar to that of national central banks.

Before the emergence of national central banks, private banks within countries issued their own banknotes to facilitate business. The issuance of these banknotes lacked order and regulation, resulting in credit crises in many countries by the end of the nineteenth century. This led to political and social turmoil, which prompted governments to enact laws governing currency issuance and establish central banks to take on the responsibility of issuing currency. The establishment of central banks helped to resolve national monetary crises.

The current international monetary system is facing similar challenges. The global economy is growing rapidly, and countries are cooperating more closely than ever before. The world is moving toward becoming a unified whole, and the flow of international trade and large amounts of capital are promoting the globalization of strong economies, which in turn are expanding the scope of credit economies. The existing global monetary rules are insufficient to constrain the expansion of this credit globalization and the dominance of strong currencies in the market, leading to instability in the global credit system. To maximize their benefits, central banks of various countries are not adhering to the regulations of international currency issuance but are instead gradually increasing the amount of international currencies they issue.[29]

To address the inherent flaws of the current international monetary system, it is necessary to establish a new system based on the creation of a global cryptocurrency, cryptoSDRs. This cryptocurrency would be issued and managed by the IMF, which would act as a "World Central Bank" responsible for the unified management of global credit. This approach would help to solve the root causes of the issues in the international monetary system.

As mentioned earlier, the euro and SDRs have many similarities as the two most successful artificial currencies in human history. This is why the development of SDRs toward a supersovereign cryptocurrency can benefit from the euro's experience. The process of SDR monetization requires the following safeguard. First, it needs the leadership of a politically strong international organization and the support of major member countries. This is an important prerequisite for the reform of SDRs to be put on the agenda and for the design of cryptoSDRs to be continuously promoted. Second, it needs to be legally established through a convention, i.e., by modifying or adding provisions to the IMF's role and application scope of cryptoSDRs to give them the status of an international currency that can flow freely in the international community and to require all member countries to incorporate the relevant convention into domestic legislation to ensure that cryptoSDRs are legal, lawful, and enforceable. Third, it needs to learn from the European Monetary System and establish a Currency Cooperation Fund, exchange rate stabilization mechanism, and Parity Network System to facilitate the transition from national sovereign currencies to supersovereign currencies. Fourth, the use of cryptoSDRs in the private sector needs to be expanded. Fifth, at the technical level, a blockchain payment network needs to be designed that can meet the payment needs of frequent daily and international bulk transactions worldwide while also meeting the requirements of ultrahigh frequency, superfast speed, security, and stability.

First, the development of the European single currency unit and its eventual conversion to the euro is an inevitable result of EU countries' firm commitment to promoting European integration. The fundamental reason why the euro can ultimately be accepted by various countries is that it can bring more abundant benefits to their economies. These benefits are not only the increase in labor rates brought about by expanding the trade scope but also the cost reduction of the circulation of production factors due to more convenient and faster transportation and transactions. Moreover, in terms of political stance, cooperation between countries can bring more

[29] Qiao Yide, Xu Mingqi. Strengthening the Status and Role of the SDR in the International Monetary System [J]. International Economic Review, 2011(1), pp. 52–65 + 4.

favorable policies. Therefore, all member countries have expressed a unified willingness to adopt the euro. It can be seen that the creation and development of a currency cannot be separated from the support of relevant countries.[30] The establishment and development of cryptoSDRs also depend on the leadership of powerful countries and the cooperation and support of the major member countries of the IMF.

Second, to make cryptoSDRs obtain international legal currency status and legal tender, they not only need to be authorized by the IMF Charter but also require member states of the IMF to stipulate the legal currency status and legal tender of cryptoSDRs as an obligation to bind the member governments in relevant international conventions. At the same time, it requires each member state to make explicit provisions on this obligation in domestic laws and regulations.

Finally, the European Currency Unit guarantees the smooth transition of member states' currencies from sovereign currencies to the euro by establishing a Currency Cooperation Fund, Exchange Rate Stability Mechanism, and Parity Network System. CryptoSDRs also need to establish corresponding Currency Cooperation Funds, Exchange Rate Stability Mechanisms, and Parity Network Systems to ensure exchange rate stability before the currency transition and to obtain support during the currency transition. In addition, through the above discussion and analysis of the euro and SDRs, it can be seen that the role of the basket currency form in achieving the stability of artificial supersovereign currency value is very obvious, and it can be designed in combination with the actual situation and currency acceptance of each country.[31] However, SDRs cannot be directly used in market transactions, and when used, they must go through a cumbersome licensing process. That is, only within the scope permitted by the IMF can they exchange foreign currency. This has led to a very limited private market for SDRs. The reason why the euro is widely popular in the international financial market is closely related to the circulation and development of the euro in the private market. It can be seen that the promotion and circulation of a currency are directly affected by its development in the private market to a large extent. Therefore, in the process of issuing a currency, it is necessary to pay great attention to the development trend of the currency in the private market. This is the important reason why it is necessary to expand the application of SDRs in the private sector of international trade, financial investment, and other fields.

In summary, the IMF should gradually elevate the status and role of SDRs in the international monetary system and turn them into a supersovereign international currency by combining them with blockchain technology to create a supersovereign cryptocurrency—cryptoSDRs. At the same time, reforming the IMF to become the "World Central Bank" is the most ideal progressive reform path and the fundamental solution to the current instability of the international monetary system and the "Triffin Dilemma."

Figure 2.1 is the author's proposed roadmap for the reform of the international monetary system, and the analysis in the following sections mainly focuses on the

[30] See footnote 6.

[31] See footnote 6.

enhancement of the international status and role of SDRs, including the transformation of SDRs through blockchain technology and the reform of the governance structure of the IMF.

2.2.1 *Strengthening the Role of SDRs*

Improving the status of SDRs in the international economic market, particularly strengthening their role in the financial market, can reduce the currency reserve costs of countries and expand the range of their currency reserves, thus reducing the potential losses caused by fluctuations in reserve currency exchange rates.[32] Although several major economic powers are not very willing to accept SDRs as the new major international currency, they still believe that the IMF should serve as the World Central Bank.[33] Therefore, in the current period, it should be easier to enhance the role and international status of SDRs. This book divides the reform of cryptoSDRs into the following three main stages.

(1) Preparation for the Birth of CryptoSDRs

To smoothly create cryptoSDRs, it is first necessary to reform SDRs, especially in terms of issuing and distributing SDRs, making them more reasonable and possessing the basic attributes of currency, thus preparing for the creation of cryptoSDRs.

1. Develop legal rules for the issuance cycle of cryptoSDRs.

To increase the effectiveness and international status of SDRs, the first step is to increase the amount and distribution of SDRs. Since its creation, SDRs have only been issued five times, with the most recent issuance totaling approximately 456 billion SDRs (equivalent to approximately $650 billion USD).[34] To date, SDRs only account for 4% of global reserves, which is too small to act as an international currency in the world financial market. Therefore, it is necessary to significantly increase the issuance and frequency of cryptoSDRs under appropriate conditions to ensure that their status and effectiveness steadily improve.

By increasing the issuance of SDRs, it can gradually replace the US dollar as the major international reserve currency, reduce the dependence of various countries on the US dollar, and ease the imbalance in their international accounts.[35] Many scholars

[32] INTERNATIONAL MONETARY FUND. International Monies, IMF Executive Board Concludes the Meeting on Enhancing International Monetary Stability—A Role for the SDR? Washington D.C.: Prepared by the Strategy, Policy, and Review Department, 2011 [EB/OL]. https://www.imf.org/en/News/Articles/2015/09/28/04/53/pn1122. Accessed 6 May 2022.

[33] ROBERT ZOELLICK. The IMS Must be Reformed [EB/OL]. http://www.finance.sina.com.cn/roll/20101227/00053560431.shtml. Accessed 6 May 2022.

[34] IMF, 2021 General SDR Allocation [EB/OL]. https://www.imf.org/en/Topics/special-drawing-right/2021-SDR-Allocation. Accessed 6 May 2022.

[35] See footnote 33.

Reform Roadmap for CryptoSDRs			
Period	Short-term (preparation for the birth of cryptoSDRs)	Medium-term (early stage of the birth of cryptoSDRs)	Long-term (maturity of cryptoSDRs)
Duration	Year 1～5	Year 6～10	Year 11～15
Annual Sequence	1 | 2 | 3 | 4	5 | 6 | 8 | 9 | 10	11 | 12 | 13 | 14 | 15
Strengthening the role of SDRs and monetization	Establishing legal rules for the issuance cycle of cryptoSDRs		
	Establishing standards for the issuance amount of cryptoSDRs		
	Establishing rules for the issuance of cryptoSDRs		
	Establishing legal rules for the allocation standards of cryptoSDRs		
	Adding a fixed value clause for cryptoSDRs		
	Adding currencies of emerging market countries to the SDRs basket		
	Establishing SDR alternative account		
		Establishing a currency cooperation fund, exchange rate stability mechanism, and parity network system	
		Establishing cryptoSDRs	
		Expanding the scope of use of cryptoSDRs	
			Assisting member countries in transitioning from sovereign currencies to cryptoSDRs
			Promoting private use of cryptoSDRs in international financial markets
	Establishing a currency expert group and a management department for cryptoSDRs		

Fig. 2.1 Roadmap for the monetarization reform of cryptoSDRs

	Establishing a monetary policy committee						
	Clarifying the role of the IMF in international financial regulation and global currency management						
	Reforming the mechanism for issuing cryptoSDRs to meet the requirements of global economic balance						
	Adjusting the selection of the Executive Board to reflect the status of emerging market countries in the world economy						
	Strengthening the coordination and regulatory capacity of the IMF in international reserves and international currency operations						

Fig. 2.1 (continued)

have studied the issue of SDR issuance, and Stiglitz and others have proposed that the amount of each SDR issuance should be a fixed value between $150 billion and $300 billion based on the annual increase in international reserves.[36] Williamson has further calculated a more accurate value of $457 billion based on this method.[37] Although this method of calculating the SDR issuance amount based on the annual increase in international reserves is relatively accurate, the amount of the international reserve increase is not a fixed value due to different economic development situations and market demands each year. Therefore, it is not very reasonable to stipulate a fixed amount as the SDR issuance amount for a long period. After the birth of cryptoSDRs, their issuance calculation method should be determined based on the method of calculating the annual increase in international reserves, and the calculation method should be adjusted according to the actual situation within an appropriate period, such as five years.[38] In addition to the regular issuance cycle, the issuance cycle can also be adjusted based on the actual situation, especially during financial crises. Concentrated issuance of cryptoSDRs can play a role in crisis alleviation and regulation. These two methods can be used in combination, where established plans and emergency mechanisms are developed based on prevention mechanisms, and concentrated issuance of cryptoSDRs can be carried out during financial crises.[39]

[36] Stiglitz, Joseph E. Global Financial Regulation and Financial Structure Reform: Research Report of the International Commission on Reform of the International Financial and Economic System. Shanghai Economic Review, 2010(Z1), pp. 26–27.

[37] JOHN WILLIAMSON. The Future of the Reserve System [J]. Journal of Globalization and Development, 2010(2), Article 15.

[38] See footnote 29.

[39] JOSE ANTONIO OCAMPO. Building an SDR-Based Global Reserve System [J]. Journal of Globalization and Development, 2010(2), pp. 11–12.

This approach can avoid liquidity flooding during financial market booms and solve liquidity shortages during financial crises.[40]

2. Establish standards for the issuance of cryptoSDRs

Regarding the issue of the annual issuance limit of cryptoSDRs, scholars have begun to conduct research. The research viewpoints mentioned earlier have also been recognized by many economic researchers. Since the annual growth rate of international reserves varies each year, the resulting amounts calculated for different years are bound to be different. Therefore, the author suggests setting a period for the issuance of cryptoSDRs and using the average increase in world reserves every five years as the basis for calculating the issuance limit for each cycle, with adjustments made every five years. The premise for this calculation method is to replace the US dollar as the primary international reserve currency with cryptoSDRs. Therefore, in the current environment, a transitional plan should be established first, and the current issuance of cryptoSDRs should only serve as a small part of the total reserve increase, gradually expanding the issuance limit of cryptoSDRs to ensure their future role as the major international reserve currency.

After cryptoSDRs replace the US dollar as the major international reserve currency, their issuance limit should be calculated based on the annual growth rate of international reserves. However, in the actual financial market, whether cryptoSDRs can replace the US dollar as the major international reserve currency still needs to be tested in practice. During the process of SDRs becoming the major international reserve currency, their issuance will not suddenly increase, and often the amount of SDRs issued is much lower than the annual increase in international reserves. At present, cryptoSDRs have not yet emerged, and SDRs can only serve as international reserves. The annual issuance limit of 200 billion US dollars of SDRs can meet their proportion in international reserves. Of course, even if the current amount of SDRs is not "totally neutral," it can change the situation of international reserves relying solely on US deficit and increasing US dollar reserves on a large scale.[41] However, blindly increasing the issuance amount of SDRs may lead to an oversupply problem and exacerbate the problem of liquidity. Therefore, this book suggests conducting scientific and prudent research before increasing the issuance of SDRs at the current stage, gradually expanding their issuance limit based on the small proportion of SDRs in the issuance amount. When cryptoSDRs emerge and enter the circulation field as a supersovereign currency, a large-scale issuance based on the currency usage demands of member countries and international trade is needed to meet the currency usage requirements of all member countries and international trade.

[40] Li Renzhen, Xiang Yaping. Analysis of Legal Paths to Strengthen the Role of SDR. Journal of Wuhan University (Philosophy & Social Sciences Edition), 2012(3), pp. 59–64.

[41] See footnote 37.

3. Develop rules for the issuance of cryptoSDRs

Before the birth of cryptoSDRs, scholars suggested that the simplest method of issuing SDRs as international reserves was through regular issuance.[42] These scholars also have calculated the quantity of SDRs issued based on their research and analysis using the periodic issuance method. Although periodic issuance is the simplest method, it is not necessarily the best. The best method for issuing SDRs should be countercyclical issuance,[43] which not only satisfies the demand for increasing global reserves but also mitigates the impact of economic cycle fluctuations. However, after the birth of cryptoSDRs, as they can function as a supersovereign currency for circulation both internationally and within member countries, they are required to replace the total amount of current US dollars and member state sovereign currencies, thereby demanding a larger and more flexible issuance to meet the exchange needs of gold and currency held by governments and individuals.

4. Develop legal rules for the distribution standards of cryptoSDRs

Under the current international monetary system, economically strong countries receive significantly more SDR allocations than economically underdeveloped countries. However, investigations have revealed that developing countries actually require more currency reserves due to their economic development needs. Therefore, Stiglitz proposed the principle of demand-based allocation. One method for resolving the impact of economic fluctuations on trade management and foreign exchange accounts is for developing countries to equally distribute all quotas.[44] Some scholars have proposed the "inverted hook system," which configures the allocation of SDR quotas and the proportion of each country's fund shares in inverse proportion. The higher the theoretical allocation amount calculated, the lower the actual allocation amount obtained. Similarly, the lower the calculated allocation amount, the higher the obtained allocation amount.[45] However, this arrangement is certain to face strong opposition from the world's economic powers. Therefore, scholars have proposed a slow transition suggestion, which is to take out 20% of the allotted quotas for special distribution arrangements within a determined annual issuance amount, while the remaining quotas are still distributed according to the normal allocation method. At the same time, scholar Li Renzhen also agrees with Williamson's opinion, which is

[42] Stiglitz, Joseph E. Global Financial Regulation and Financial Structure Reform: Research Report of the International Commission on Reform of the International Financial and Economic System. Shanghai Economic Review, 2010(Z1), pp. 26–27; JOSE ANTONIO OCAMPO. Building an SDR-Based Global Reserve System [J]. Journal of Globalization and Development, 2010(2), pp. 11–12.

[43] Stiglitz, Joseph E. Global Financial Regulation and Financial Structure Reform: Research Report of the International Commission on Reform of the International Financial and Economic System. Shanghai Economic Review, 2010(Z1), pp. 26–27; United Nations, Toward a New International Financial Architecture [R]. New York: Report of the Task Force of the Executive Committee on Economic and Social Affairs of the United Nations, 2001: 2–14. JOSEANTONIO OCAMPO. Recasting the International Financial Agenda//International Capital Markets: Systems in Transition [M]. New York: Oxford University Press, 2002.

[44] See footnote 42.

[45] See footnote 37.

to classify member countries of the IMF into two types: developed and developing countries, based on their economic development situation, and allocate quotas based on the different needs of the two types. This allocation system can reflect the demand of each country for SDRs and consider the correlation with the IMF's shares.[46] I also believe that the suggestions of Li Renzhen and Williamson are more feasible, and further consideration should be given to the future trend of the monetarization and circulation of cryptoSDRs on a global scale, requiring further development of the rules for their issuance and exchange.

5. Add fixed clauses for cryptoSDRs

As the IMF Chapter has not clearly explained or stipulated the customary rules and calculation methods for SDRs, it is up to the executive board of IMF to review the currency composition and confirm the role of SDRs in the international financial market during the routine five-year review cycle. In November 2010, during the periodic review and evaluation, the IMF made a reservation decision on the four currencies that make up the SDR basket architecture and made corresponding adjustments to their proportions. Currently, the US dollar still has the largest proportion, and the status quo of the US dollar as the main reserve currency has not fundamentally changed.[47] However, in the current stage, the economic growth rate of many developing countries is significantly higher than that of developed countries, and they play an increasingly important role in the global economy.[48] Therefore, the IMF should adjust the proportion of the basket currency appropriately based on this situation and increase the types of currencies in the SDR basket to enhance its international acceptance. In addition, it is necessary to clearly define and divide the entry conditions of the basket monetary system, such as the GDP ranking of the currency issuing country, the degree of capital project control, and the freedom of currency exchange.[49]

6. Add the currency of emerging market countries to the SDR basket

In today's international economy, the position of emerging economies in economic market competition is becoming increasingly important, and the economic growth rate of developing countries actually determines the growth rate of the world economy.[50] Therefore, it is necessary to add the sovereign currencies of emerging economies to the basket currency of SDRs and make reasonable adjustments to the proportion of basket currencies based on the current economic development of each country. Even if the monetary system of emerging economies is not yet perfect, their currencies can be added to the SDR basket before cryptoSDRs are widely used in

---

[46] See footnote 40.

[47] Huang Meibo, Xiong Aizong. Special Drawing Rights and the Reform of the International Monetary System [J]. International Financial Research, 2009(8), pp. 47–54.

[48] ROBERT ZOELLICK. A Monetary Regime for A Multipolar World [J]. Financial Times, 2010(2), p. 9.

[49] See footnote 40.

[50] See footnote 48.

private transactions so that emerging economies can play a role in the global financial system while accelerating their financial and monetary policy reforms.

7. Establishment of a legal framework for alternative accounts

Establishment of an alternative account system can effectively increase the issuance of SDRs. The idea of creating an alternative account system was proposed in the 1970s, and its main content includes the following: each member country of the IMF sets up an account within the IMF that can be flexibly handled according to each country's needs. The main approach is as follows: each country deposits excess US dollar assets into an alternative account and exchanges them for bonds denominated in SDRs issued by the IMF. This alternative account is managed uniformly by the IMF. After a member country deposits its US dollar assets into the account, its debt relationship with the US is transformed into a debt relationship with the IMF. From the 1970s onward, the IMF conducted two internal discussions over the next decade regarding the establishment of the alternative account system but ultimately failed to reach a consensus. The main reason was that after the US dollar crisis in the 1970s, the US no longer supported the establishment of an alternative account system. In addition, due to technological limitations, the alternative account system could not fully meet the needs of the time.[51] After the US dollar crisis of the 1970s, the US government also recognized the dual pressures brought by the "twin deficits" to the development of the US economy. Therefore, the US intentionally lowered the role of the US dollar in foreign exchange reserves. Countries that use the US dollar as a foreign exchange reserve also realized the huge impact of US dollar fluctuations on their economies. Against this background, economists Bergsten and Truman once again proposed establishing an alternative account mechanism.

Through analysis of the current international economic development situation, it can be seen that the benefits brought about by the establishment of an alternative account mechanism are manifold.[52] First, this mechanism is beneficial to the debtor countries of the US, as they can convert a portion of their foreign exchange reserves into SDRs, thereby reducing the impact of US dollar fluctuations on their economic development. Second, this mechanism is also beneficial to the US itself, as the alternative account system can ensure that foreign exchange transactions can be handled without any pressure while also avoiding the economic pressures brought about by US dollar fluctuations. Third, for countries holding other forms of foreign exchange currency, the establishment of an alternative account system can reduce the direct benefits of countries holding euro or yen, thereby achieving the effect of controlling global trade balance.[53] Finally, this mechanism can to a certain extent solve the imbalance in the global financial system, ensure its stability, and achieve

---

[51] Zhang Yiping, Huang Shengbin. Alternative Accounts and International Monetary System Reform. International Trade Issues, 2011(1), p. 130.

[52] Fred Bergsten. We should Listen to Beijing's Currency Idea [EB/OL]. [2022-09-27]. https://www.ft.com/content/7372bbd0-2470-11de-9a01-00144feabdc0. Accessed 6 May 2022.

[53] Zhang Ming. International Monetary System Reform: Background, Reasons, Measures and China's Participation. International Economic Review, 2010(1), pp. 114–137.

effective regulation of currency liquidity through centralized management of foreign exchange reserves.

Thus far, the biggest obstacle to establishing alternative accounts is how to solve the technical problem of alternative accounts, which involves who will foot the bill for the losses incurred by the depreciation of the US dollar in the alternative accounts. Establishing an alternative account system may face dual risks of interest rate risk and exchange rate risk, resulting in loss of benefits. Based on current international reserve information, taking out 20% of the funds from the international reserves of emerging and developing countries to deposit into alternative accounts would amount to trillions of dollars. If this huge amount of funds incurs losses due to the depreciation of the US dollar, it would be difficult for any organization to bear. Moreover, countries capable of maintaining a balance of payments view it as unfair for member countries of the IMF to jointly bear the exchange losses incurred in the alternative accounts. Kenen used data from nearly 30 years of simulations to propose that the IMF could establish a management fee for alternative accounts, which could be provided by member countries of the fund at a rate of 1%, and the fund could use this management fee for daily management and to bear losses from failed investments. If the funds in the alternative accounts cannot repay the losses, they can seek assistance from the IMF, and the funds received can be repaid using future management fees.[54] Although this approach solves the problem of loss-bearing, it adds costs to investing countries and reduces the cohesion of the alternative account mechanism. Therefore, the most practical solution at present is to bear the losses according to the principle of "who benefits, who shares."

The above analysis shows that the IMF should formulate relevant rules for establishing an alternative account mechanism in the near future. These rules should specify the IMF's work in establishing the alternative account mechanism, as well as the rights and responsibilities of investing countries in the mechanism. The rules should also establish the form of returns, profit distribution, and loss sharing in the alternative account system.[55]

In summary, the SDR alternative account can serve as a transitional product before the birth of cryptoSDRs, allowing the SDRs to expand their functions and circulation range through the alternative account and eventually smoothly upgrade and evolve into cryptoSDRs.

The deepening reform of the global financial system is facing not only technical difficulties but also political competition among various countries. In particular, due to the dominance of the US, which has the largest say in the IMF, the promotion of cryptoSDRs will also depend on the attitude of the US. In terms of expanding the issuance of cryptoSDRs, the US is not against it but also not fully supportive. Increasing the status of SDRs in the international monetary and financial system is also beneficial to the US. The US is more supportive of the establishment of an alternative account system, as this system can alleviate the economic pressure on the

[54] PETER B. KENEN. The Substitution Account as a First Step Toward Reform of the International Monetary System [J]. Peterson Institute for International Economics, 2010, pp. 5–10.

[55] See footnote 40.

US while ensuring the international status of the US dollar. Countries that hold the US dollar as their primary international reserve welcome the creation and promotion of cryptoSDRs because it can reduce their dependence on the US dollar and mitigate the impact of US dollar depreciation on their economies. However, as the interests of these countries vary, it remains uncertain whether a consensus can be reached on promoting cryptoSDRs.[56]

(2) Initial Stage of the Birth of CryptoSDRs

After the successful evolution of SDRs into cryptoSDRs, the latter became a super-sovereign currency with the ability to circulate globally. However, during its early stages, although many countries had become members of cryptoSDRs, there were still some countries that had not yet joined. Therefore, during this phase, a phenomenon of coexistence between cryptoSDRs and sovereign currencies will emerge, with both having a relationship of mutual competition and substitution. This requires strengthening and refining the monetary attributes and competitiveness of cryptoSDRs to accelerate their process of becoming an international currency.

1. Establishing a Currency Cooperation Fund, Exchange Rate Stability Mechanism, and Parity Network System

Drawing from the process of the European Currency Unit evolving into the euro, cryptoSDRs also need to establish a Currency Cooperation Fund, Exchange Rate Stability Mechanism, and Parity Network System. The European Currency Cooperation Fund helps member countries intervene in exchange rate fluctuations when the central bank of a single country is unable to stabilize them. The ERM and Parity Network System are also used to maintain exchange rate stability among EU member states, ensuring that the birth and transition of the euro is more stable. The IMF can also establish a Currency Cooperation Fund by concentrating 20% of member countries' gold holdings and foreign exchange reserves, providing very-short-term credit, short-term currency support credit, and medium-term financial aid credit to help member countries maintain exchange rate stability. In addition, through the Parity Network System, member countries are required to use cryptoSDRs as the value standard to determine the central exchange rate between two member countries, establish Exchange Rate Stability Mechanisms, achieve fixed exchange rates among member countries, and implement joint floating exchange rates among nonmember countries, ensuring exchange rate stability among member countries and a smooth creation and transition of cryptoSDRs.

2. Establishing cryptoSDRs

On the basis of the SDR alternative account, cryptoSDRs are created through the combination of SDRs and blockchain technology, giving SDRs a freely circulating technical carrier. A country's government, institutions, enterprises, and individuals

[56] Shi Jing. SDR and the Reform of the International Monetary System [J]. Economic Research Guide, 2012(33), pp. 56–58 + 134.

can use cryptoSDRs as a payment tool in international financial bond markets, cross-border payments, bulk commodity trading, and daily consumption transactions, achieving the goal of truly becoming a supersovereign international currency. At the same time, through conventions and other means, the international reserve currency and legal status of international circulation of cryptoSDRs are determined, and member countries are required to legalize cryptoSDRs through legislation, allowing central banks to exchange gold and assets with cryptoSDRs at a certain exchange rate to ensure that cryptoSDRs have a monetary status in member countries and can freely circulate legally. The IMF also needs to establish the Currency Cooperation Fund, Exchange Rate Stability Mechanism, and Parity Network System mentioned earlier to help cryptoSDRs circulate in member countries and requires member countries to sign the "World Central Bank Charter" and the "Economic and Monetary Union Treaty" to ensure the free flow of capital among member countries, free currency exchange, and the implementation of fixed exchange rate policies, as well as to formulate rules for increasing and exchanging cryptoSDRs to meet member countries' demand for supersovereign cryptocurrency use.

3. Expanding the use of cryptoSDRs

Despite having been in existence for over 40 years, the SDRs have not developed as expected due to their limited application and incomplete monetary function. To establish SDRs as a major international currency and international reserve, it is necessary to continuously expand their scope of use and international recognition with guidance and promotion from the international monetary system and relevant international laws.

(1) Borrowing and lending cryptoSDRs positions. To fully leverage the SDRs' potential in the existing international monetary system without the need to expand their issuance, the IMF needs to coordinate this effort. For instance, on the basis of the IMF's existing assistance mechanism for member countries, member countries should be encouraged to lend their surplus SDRs to countries in need. However, the lending of SDRs is not without interest, as the lending country can earn a certain amount of interest income, while the borrowing country can exchange their own currency by borrowing other countries' shares to solve their own financial difficulties.
(2) Daily calculation of cryptoSDRs interest rates. Currently, the SDR's interest rate calculation method is updated daily, based on a certain proportion of the short-term interest rates of the five currencies that make up the SDRs. The SDR exchange rate is also published on the IMF's official website every day, along with the exchange rate of the member countries' sovereign currencies. This calculation method not only provides convenience for SDR reserves but also promotes the development of bond markets, thereby increasing the appeal of cryptoSDRs in the international monetary system. However, for cryptoSDRs to become widely accepted in the private market, it is necessary to require central banks and even commercial banks in each member country to publish the SDR exchange rate on their websites.

(3) Issuance of bonds denominated in cryptoSDRs. In the process of becoming the major international currency and international reserve, it is necessary to issue bonds denominated in cryptoSDRs. Initially, although the cryptoSDR bond is priced in cryptoSDRs, it can be settled in other sovereign currencies. However, the stability of cryptoSDRs will continuously expand the scope of bond use, gradually increase the settlement ratio of cryptoSDRs in the bond market, and promote the continuous prosperity of the cryptoSDR bond market. When cryptoSDRs occupy a more important position in international reserve currencies, it will also encourage the international bond market to use cryptoSDRs more for settlement. The bond issuer can be the IMF, sovereign countries, or other institutions. Overall, cryptoSDRs with stable value undoubtedly have stronger appeal to countries with unstable currency values.

In the development process of the cryptoSDR bond market, the IMF will play an important driving role that cannot be ignored. First, as the issuer of cryptoSDRs, the IMF has the power to set the yield curve of cryptoSDR bonds and price the bonds issued for countries or other institutions based on this. Compared with other institutions, the cryptoSDR bonds issued by the IMF are more secure due to the support of its member countries. In addition, the IMF can also obtain certain economic benefits by issuing cryptoSDR bonds by charging member countries for contributions.

Moreover, if it can obtain support from other sovereign countries and jointly issue or invest in cryptoSDR bonds, it can promote further development and deepening of the bond market. At the same time, after cryptoSDR bonds issued by official institutions gain market-wide recognition, they can also promote the issuance of cryptoSDR bonds in the private sector. Compared with national debt, the stability of cryptoSDR bonds increases their inherent safety and can effectively avoid exchange rate risk. With the development and deepening of the cryptoSDR bond market, its liquidity will also be effectively demonstrated. However, there will still be relatively high pricing costs due to market imperfections during the initial issuance. To improve liquidity and reduce pricing costs, a feasible approach is to increase the number of institutions participating in the issuance, that is, jointly issued by multiple countries or institutions.

(4) Valuing international economic trade in terms of cryptoSDRs. While valuing in domestic currency can be used to determine the final profit directly in international trade, this method is highly inefficient and carries significant exchange rate risk. Valuing in cryptoSDRs can mitigate exchange rate risk to a certain extent. Furthermore, increasing the use of cryptoSDRs can effectively promote the development of the bond market, enhance the liquidity of cryptoSDRs, and provide a solid foundation for pricing and valuing in international trade. In the practice of promoting widespread use of cryptoSDRs, companies engaged in cross-border trade may choose to use cryptoSDRs for accounting purposes to facilitate comparisons between different countries. The IMF may also use cryptoSDRs as the accounting unit for international balance of payments. Moreover, due to their higher stability, multinational organizations may also try to use

cryptoSDRs as the accounting unit and eventually use them for payments and settlements in international trade and cross-border payments.

(3) Maturity Stage of CryptoSDRs

After the birth of cryptoSDRs, it is necessary to continue promoting their development and popularization, making them to obtain a larger circulation market, expanding their scope of use, and making them a true supersovereign cryptocurrency.

1. Promote the use of cryptoSDRs by individuals in the international market

Both the share of cryptoSDRs in international currency reserves and their scope of use have increased significantly. Therefore, from the perspective of its development trend, there are now conditions to use cryptoSDRs in the private sector, such as allowing individuals to open cryptoSDR accounts or increasing their scope of use and usage rights in international settlements.[57] Furthermore, the thriving cryptoSDR bond market, coupled with its characteristics of value stability and strong liquidity, will undoubtedly become increasingly attractive to individuals and institutions in the future. However, cryptoSDRs can only become a real currency if they are widely authorized and recognized for use. International pricing and settlement are the two functions that cryptoSDRs must have as a currency, and they are interdependent and mutually reinforcing. Moreover, when cryptoSDRs are widely used in the private sector, governments can intervene and adjust economic activities by controlling cryptoSDRs. Since it does not involve the exchange of other countries' reserve currencies, this can greatly improve efficiency and make cryptoSDRs more attractive in the international reserve monetary system, thereby promoting the further development of the cryptoSDR bond market.[58] However, some problems have arisen as a result. For example, the use of cryptoSDRs in international settlements will inevitably increase the transaction costs of the US, so it will inevitably encounter obstacles from the US.[59] Therefore, from a legal perspective, only when the IMF Agreement adds provisions to open up cryptoSDRs can it provide legal space and policy conditions for the future development of cryptoSDRs.[60]

2. Help member countries' transition from sovereign currencies to cryptoSDRs

Looking back at the process of the birth of the euro, especially when the euro was officially launched on January 1, 1999, the EU also stipulated that from July 1, 2002, all countries in the eurozone would withdraw their own currencies from circulation and would need to exchange their own currencies for the unified currency of the EU at the prescribed exchange rate before June 30 of the same year. This also requires member countries of IMF to complete the procedures for cryptoSDRs replacing

[57] PETER B. KENEN. Use of SDR to Supplement or Substitute for Other Means of Finance [J]. International Money and Credit: The Policy Roles, 1984, ch. 7.

[58] See footnote 29.

[59] See footnote 39.

[60] See footnote 40.

their sovereign currencies at the exchange rate prescribed by the IMF within the prescribed period. At the same time, to help member countries smoothly transition to cryptoSDRs, the IMF needs to dispatch experts and provide corresponding financial support.

2.2.2 *Reforming the Structure of the IMF*

SDRs have gradually evolved into a true international reserve currency, and their managing institution, the IMF, needs to undergo adaptive reforms to meet the needs of current world development. Specifically, it needs to transform its functions and assume the responsibility of a "World Central Bank" to play a more prominent role in the new international monetary system. This book divides IMF reform into three stages: short term, medium term, and long term. The author believes that the difference between SDR reform and IMF reform is that the medium term of IMF reform includes both the short term and medium term, while the long term refers to the entire process of implementation from beginning to end. This setting is mainly because IMF reform needs continuity, and many reforms have a relatively long process. The proposed reform steps start from the same period, but some reform measures need to continue to be carried out with the changes in the world's situation, while others can be ended after achieving their goals.

(1) Short-Term IMF Reforms

In the short term, the IMF's reform mainly prepares for the birth of cryptoSDRs, including the establishment of a currency expert group, a cryptoSDR management department, and a Monetary Policy Committee.

1. Establishing a currency expert group and a cryptoSDR management department

By establishing a currency expert group, the rationality of cryptoSDRs can be continuously improved. The main members of the currency expert group are currency experts and central bank governors of the countries that issue international reserve currencies. The authority of the currency expert group includes providing opinions and suggestions on the IMF's relevant policies and regulations, solving global currency liquidity issues, and the issuance and cancelation conditions of cryptoSDRs. In short, the establishment of the currency expert group improves the issuance mechanism of cryptoSDRs. At the same time, other technical and management institutions need to be established to achieve the operation and management of cryptoSDRs, such as establishing a blockchain technology and cryptocurrency research center responsible for researching the application of blockchain technology to the carrier of the SDRs to achieve the issuance and circulation of cryptoSDRs; establishing a cryptoSDR management department responsible for implementing the resolutions of the Monetary Policy Committee set up under the IMF; and establishing node verification agencies responsible for managing node servers, verifying the accuracy of information, and ensuring the continuous and secure operation of cryptoSDRs system.

2. Establishing a Monetary Policy Committee

The Monetary Policy Committee is composed of representatives appointed by member countries and is responsible for formulating the monetary policy of cryptoSDRs. It meets once a year to mainly study issues such as the allocation, issuance method, total issuance, node server allocation, distribution of "coinage taxes," and asset management of cryptoSDRs. At the same time, it adjusts the total amount of cryptoSDRs and cooperates with corresponding monetary policies according to changes in the world economy to ensure the stability of the world currency and financial system and provide more effective global financial governance through the monitoring data provided by blockchain technology to prevent and solve global financial crises and ensure the safe and stable operation of the new international monetary system centered on cryptoSDRs.

(2) Medium-Term Reforms of the IMF

The midterm reform of the IMF is mainly aimed at preparing for the creation of cryptoSDRs and making corresponding reforms to ensure the stable operation of cryptoSDRs during their initial stages.

1. Clarifying the role of the IMF in international financial regulation and global monetary management

Optimizing the structure of the IMF and transforming its functions into a "central bank" that plays a role in global credit management. The first step is to clarify the responsibilities and obligations of the IMF in the international financial market and strengthen its role in international monetary management. In a narrow sense, central banks are government-based, and without an international government, there can be no international central bank and hence no international currency. However, in a broad sense, through the cooperation of various major economies, it is possible to establish an organizational structure with the functions of a global central bank, playing a role in global credit and monetary management.

2. Reforming the mechanism of cryptoSDR issuance to meet the requirements of global economic balance

Currently, although SDRs have been applied to a certain extent, the corresponding issuance mechanism remains imperfect and cannot meet the different needs of different member countries. Therefore, when reforming the current international monetary system, the first step should be to strengthen the perfection of the SDR issuance mechanism, which should be coordinated and regulated by the IMF, mobilizing multiple resources and forces to initially establish the framework for the issuance of cryptoSDRs and continuously demonstrate the role of cryptoSDRs in stabilizing the international financial market.

(3) Long-Term Reforms of the IMF

The long-term reform of the IMF refers to the continuous adjustments and reforms required from the birth of cryptoSDRs to their maturity in response to changes in the global economic landscape.

1. Adjustments to the executive board's constituencies to reflect the position of emerging market countries in the world economy

The IMF sets specific functions for the executive board's constituencies but currently faces similar problems to those encountered with SDRs. With the rapid development of developing countries and emerging market countries, their economic strength has increased rapidly, and the existing method of setting executive board constituencies can no longer meet the needs of the current international financial situation, making it difficult to mobilize the enthusiasm of emerging market countries. Therefore, it is necessary to adjust the existing method of setting executive board constituencies to match the position of emerging market countries in the international economy with their economic strength. Even after cryptoSDRs have reached maturity, ongoing adjustments and reforms are still required to reflect changes in the global economy and the strength of various countries.

2. Strengthen the IMF's coordination and regulatory capabilities for international reserves and international currency operations

Issuing countries and holding countries of international reserve currencies have common interests but also hope that the other side will take on more responsibility. For example, issuing countries hope that holding countries will maintain a stable reserve currency holding volume and avoid large-scale sell-offs to maintain currency stability, while holding countries hope that issuing countries and the IMF will take into account the needs of all member countries when formulating monetary policies and strive to maintain currency stability. Against this background of practical needs, the IMF needs to play its due role in intervening in and coordinating between issuing and holding countries of reserve currencies and continuously monitoring the operation of international reserve currencies and assets. When cryptoSDRs become more popular, the IMF is also required to manage and supervise them continuously.

As Hayek once said in "The Denationalization of Money," "...the inevitability of current politics should not be the concern of economists. The task of economists should be, as I have tediously repeated, to make policies that are currently politically impossible politically possible. What should be done at this moment is the task of politicians, not economists...." Since there is a clear boundary between economics and politics, economists and political scientists can reasonably distinguish and define their respective roles in these two areas.[61] However, if coordination and collaboration between politics, economics, and law are required to achieve comprehensive development, with economic growth as the foundation, and fully consider the issues and feasibility of legal and political aspects, it may be possible to accelerate the

[61] See footnote 29.

birth of cryptoSDRs, which is the underlying logic behind our proposal to reform the international monetary system.

Meanwhile, for member countries of the IMF, such transitional arrangements are advantageous in achieving fairer treatment for all nations, and gradual reform can better help each member country adapt to the changes brought about by cryptoSDRs. The acceleration of globalization and the emergence of supersovereign currencies are predictable future trends, where convergence among countries, similar to the formation of the EEC, will create a common destiny through currency, and with the intensification of economic exchanges, culture, ideas, technology, finance, and politics will also blend with one another. Therefore, cryptoSDRs will promote the stability of the global economy and finance, reduce the losses caused by exchange rate differentials, lower the risk of global financial crises, facilitate international trade, and contribute to the rapid development of the global economy. Moreover, giving member countries of the IMF the choice to participate or not in cryptoSDRs and allowing countries with a shared aspiration for global integration to join freely can better meet the needs of different countries and reflect the interests of countries at different levels of development.

2.3 Technical Issues on the Monetization of CryptoSDRs

To successfully create a low-cost, convenient, and globally accessible supersovereign cryptocurrency, cryptoSDRs need to be combined with blockchain technology. There are still some differences between cryptoSDRs and nonsovereign cryptocurrencies in terms of issuance and design, requiring corresponding adjustments and changes in technology to cater to the unique characteristics of cryptoSDRs.

This section first analyzes the characteristics of blockchain technology and cryptocurrencies and then proposes improvements and developments based on the specific attributes and requirements of cryptoSDRs. The resulting technical solution can adapt to cryptoSDRs and serves as a reference for the creation of cryptoSDRs, providing a technical research foundation for subsequent chapters.

2.3.1 Technical Characteristics of Blockchain Technology and Cryptocurrency

CryptoSDRs, cryptocurrency, and blockchain technology are closely intertwined, and this section provides a detailed analysis of their technical commonalities and differences to enhance the reader's understanding of cryptoSDRs and their legal implications.

(1) Characteristics of Blockchain Technology

The main characteristic of blockchain technology is its ability to reasonably record relevant data information at specific time intervals, using time as nodes. It is a widely applicable distributed data information processing technology that maintains and organizes distributed information data based on corresponding decentralized node servers. This technology involves associating data blocks using cryptographic hash algorithms and measuring and recording relevant system information and transaction data at the same time interval for each data module. Using the asymmetric encryption method, the data blocks are connected from head to tail in chronological order to form a data chain using pointers and timestamps.

In short, blockchain technology is a decentralized online information recording system that ensures the security and reliability of information data, making it difficult to modify. It also supports online communication and sharing of data information, provides corresponding ledger recording services through information encryption and asymmetric encryption methods, and ensures the security and accuracy of users' financial account information. It can also ensure the traceability of transaction data information, enhancing users' privacy and security experience. The main features of blockchain technology include the following aspects.

1. Distributed storage

Distributed storage fundamentally relies on various data node servers within a network, regardless of their location or affiliation, to ensure open and transparent access to data information in the information repository. Each node server is able to backup and update the database in real time within a few seconds or minutes, ensuring comprehensive data sharing and dynamic processing.

Because each node server can equally store and record system information, the robustness of a blockchain-based information recording system is stronger than that of a centralized storage information system. The distributed recording and storage of accounting information give the corresponding data processing system strong stability, improving the system's fault tolerance during operation. If a few node servers encounter errors or lack certain functions, it will not affect the overall functionality of the system, nor will it cause damage or loss to existing data and information in the system.

Meanwhile, the user information data network built on blockchain technology is a huge information data storage center established through countless node servers. It can fully record and store the transaction information and user data involved in the system while reasonably and effectively supervising the behavior of each node server's recorded transactions, ensuring the accuracy and security of user data. This gives the data information module strong inclusiveness.

2. Consensus mechanism

Consensus refers to data synchronization among node servers based on predetermined rules through data interaction of transaction activities. The definition of a consensus mechanism is a compilation of computer algorithms based on the consensus process, a common agreement, and basic rules. The consensus mechanism of blockchain conforms to the characteristics of "minority obeys majority" and "node equality." However, the "minority obeys majority" principle does not refer to the number of node servers but rather to the computing power of computers and other measurable indicators. "Node equality" means that all node servers have the right to propose their computed consensus result, which becomes the final consensus result after obtaining the joint recognition of other node servers.[62] The blockchain consensus mechanism ensures that all information in the system database is truly open and shared during user usage and transaction processes through existing network interaction protocols. Due to the strong independence of each node server in the blockchain, it can guarantee the authenticity, effectiveness, and accuracy of blockchain system data information, and there is no need for further data verification between node servers, effectively improving operational efficiency.

In the process of running the blockchain system, since it adopts a decentralized mode, there is no need for centralized management of each management module. Each data interaction node server has equal rights and responsibilities, and information maintenance needs to be implemented through all node servers in the entire system. Due to the high degree of integration, the functions of each node server are the same. The loss or intentional or unintentional error of a small number of node servers will not affect the normal operation of the entire system. Based on this, when data node servers interact and transfer information, user transactions can be automatically identified, effectively improving the system's information processing efficiency while significantly reducing operating management costs and ensuring the security and effectiveness of data information transfer and interaction.

3. Tamper Proof

Some network systems currently have strong continuity, and each data node server carries different functions and responsibilities. Therefore, when a node server or data storage center in the information storage system is damaged, it will affect the normal operation of the entire system and even lead to the collapse of the entire data system. However, using blockchain technology for accounting records and information storage through distributed node server settings can largely ensure the normal operation of the system. Even if some node servers are damaged, it will not have a significant impact on the overall system operation. In an information system based on blockchain technology, each node server has the immutability of information and timely storage and double backup functions. Therefore, for some network attackers, the probability of breaking into a system node server and committing illegal activities is very low. Even if a node server is successfully compromised, it will not have an impact on the normal operation of the entire system. If network hackers want to completely control the system, they need to control 51% or more of the computing power in the entire system and at the same time control all the node servers they control to broadcast the same erroneous data to the entire network, achieving malicious tampering of newly generated block contents. However, this behavior is highly

[62] Li Jun. Technology and Law: Dual Tracks of Blockchain Financial Development [J]. Journal of Shanghai Lixin Accounting and Finance College, 2017(3), pp. 54–59.

costly and has minimal benefits, so no one will do this kind of unprofitable business. Moreover, in a blockchain system with many node servers, it is almost impossible to control at least 51% of the computing power.[63]

4. Open, Transparent, and Anonymous

In the entire information data recording system based on blockchain technology, the information interaction and transmission between each node server do not require traditional trust foundations. In the operation of the entire system, all information and data transmission and usage are open and transparent. Due to the high degree of data sharing within the system, the trust between each node server is also strongly guaranteed. To ensure fairness and increase the trust of users in the system's interactive data, almost all blockchain technologies adopt open-source codes to facilitate users checking system rules and source codes at any time. Since the trust foundation of blockchain is established through pure mathematical algorithm endorsement, each node server does not need to establish corresponding trust foundations, which ensures the security and confidentiality of the identity information of each node server. For the entire information data transmission system based on blockchain technology, replacing users' specific information data with public keys can largely ensure the privacy of user transaction information. Additionally, due to its high degree of anonymity, it ensures that users can maintain their information security while using Internet services normally. In summary, in the system where blockchain technology is applied, although all data information and transaction records are shared and open, users' personal information can be effectively protected. The transaction information is public, but the personal privacy of the transaction parties can be effectively hidden, thereby achieving highly transparent transaction activities and strong protection of personal information data privacy. The specific implementation process is to encrypt the information with one of the keys in the public–private key pair, and only the other key can unlock it. In addition, even if the public key is made public, it is impossible to deduce the corresponding private key based on the public key alone.[64]

5. Programmable Scripts

The main building block of blockchain technology is a programmable on-chain system that works in conjunction with computer scripts. This technology's principles ensure that user transactions based on this technology can be more efficient and convenient and that an intelligent programmable module system can be implemented. For example, in the case of the use of donation funds, the donor can make personalized settings and restrictions. This transaction mode and the associated limitation conditions can be embedded into the system's program script through effective program editing, creating a highly intelligent information transaction system. Based on the intelligent contract's various characteristics and strong operability and high degree

[63] Zhang Rui. Traditional Finance Innovation and Reform Based on Blockchain. Southwest Finance, 2016(10), pp. 18–23.

[64] See footnote 62.

of automation in program compilation, the sustainable operation of the information transaction record system in the blockchain can be greatly guaranteed.

6. Blockchain Database Models

Due to the constant development of computer databases and different requirements for database formats and styles, the diversified development mode of blockchain has gradually expanded. After long-term research and optimization, blockchain technology has been continuously developed and optimized in various industries and fields. To date, blockchain technology has developed public blockchains, side chains, alliance chains, and private chains, which have lower degrees of decentralization.[65]

These features of blockchain have also laid the technological foundation for the emergence of cryptoSDRs. Some of their underlying attributes are similar, and they are technically related. Therefore, understanding the basic attributes of blockchain technology can help us to understand the technical features and legal attributes of cryptoSDRs.

(2) Characteristics of Cryptocurrency Technology

Blockchain technology employs a distributed management model that continuously improves the authenticity and security of data. The data stored in each node server are tamper-proof, ensuring the security of users' personal information and transaction data. In addition, blockchain technology provides advantages such as intelligent transaction programming. This makes it clear that cryptocurrencies based on blockchain technology have significant advantages over traditional physical currencies.

Studying the changes and development of currency from ancient times to the present day reveals that every change in the form of currency has occurred during a period of high scientific and technological development and economic and cultural advancement. From physical forms of currency in the past, such as those made from precious metals, to modern-day paper currency and now to cryptocurrency, each stage of currency evolution and development represents a significant social transformation and shows that society's economic and cultural development has reached a new stage.

Cryptocurrency is significantly different from paper currency, not only in terms of its physical form, transaction efficiency, and corresponding financial regulatory agencies but also in terms of the lower cost of currency issuance, increased online payment channels, and expanded payment scope compared to paper currency. Moreover, the unique algorithm compilation of cryptocurrency can effectively prevent counterfeit currency while also enhancing the quality and security of transactions. Additionally, the decentralized nature of cryptocurrency greatly simplifies the user's transaction process, and the distributed accounting record processing system ensures the operability and efficiency of transaction management, which is beneficial for

[65] Lin Xiaochi, Hu Yeqianwen. A Review of Research on Blockchain Technology. Financial Market Research, 2016(2), pp. 97–109.

timely supervision and management. With the continuous improvement and optimization of network technology, the form of currency will gradually become more digitized.

1. Effectively reducing costs and improving payment efficiency

During the currency issuance phase, cryptocurrency largely reduces the cost of currency issuance. Compared to physical currencies such as paper money, it can greatly improve the efficiency of transactions and value storage. The transformation of currency from a physical form to a virtualized encrypted digital form is more conducive to the inventory and counting of currency, simplifies transaction steps, and improves transaction efficiency. Meanwhile, in the process of related transaction activities, this type of cryptocurrency usually uses electronic ledgers for accounting and processing, eliminating the need for users to establish private accounts. This account has a wide range of uses and features decentralization, only requiring participation from the two parties involved in the transaction, without the intervention of third-party institutions. This simplifies the transaction process, facilitates the circulation and settlement of funds, and has the characteristics of making transactions more transparent and secure, which can help to achieve information symmetry between the two parties and effectively improve user efficiency.

2. Improved security, reduced possibility of counterfeiting

Unlike centralized management in the past, cryptocurrency can record and store detailed information about the trader's various transaction activities and behaviors simply through the data information of the two trading parties and various node servers in the system. Each node server is independent and has consistent responsibilities, so even if one node server has a functional failure or information error broadcast, it will not affect the normal operation of other node servers. Since the transmission and sharing of information data usually use one-way encryption algorithms, it can not only ensure the accuracy of information transmission and improve system security to a large extent but also effectively prevent data from being maliciously modified, reducing the risk of counterfeiting currency or creating false transaction information.

3. Comprehensive and effective provision of financial services, promoting inclusive financial development

Cryptocurrency transactions only require the participation of the trading parties, without the intervention of third-party financial institutions. They not only support remote transaction operations but also support the docking and matching of various advanced network technologies. With the rapid advancement of Internet technology, this type of cryptocurrency can continue to evolve and develop with the improvement of Internet technology, keep pace with the times, and effectively expand the scope of related financial industry businesses, achieving the goal of strengthening the financial industry. In addition, using cryptocurrency as the transaction basis can simplify the steps of financial services, improve business efficiency, and effectively reduce the cost of business transactions, with significant advantages and development prospects.

Moreover, the global circulation characteristics of cryptocurrencies help to achieve and popularize inclusive finance in remote areas.

4. Facilitating Effective Regulation and Building an Efficient and Stable Financial System

Cryptocurrencies have distributed characteristics that can ensure that users' transaction activities and information are effectively recorded and stored in the system. This allows for effective supervision of transaction information and provides effective solutions and approaches for conflicts and problems that may arise during the transaction process. It also ensures the traceability of data and the integrity of information.

The complete recording of data can also provide a corresponding information basis for the adjustment of national monetary policies. By analyzing and predicting various complete data in the system, it can timely track and manage the current situation and trends of various industries, which is conducive to the continuous development and optimization of the economy and society. Since cryptocurrencies have tamper-proof features and the authenticity of currency value can be effectively protected by technology, they can help to establish a national financial information security system and credit system based on open and transparent information systems and build an efficient, fast, and stable social and economic development system.[66]

(1) The technical characteristics of nonsovereign cryptocurrencies.

First, as the "king of cryptocurrency" that opened the blockchain era, Bitcoin and thousands of different cryptocurrencies that exist now have a significant feature: strong liquidity and transaction convenience. Before the birth of Bitcoin, although electronic currency could help realize traditional international monetary transactions and settlements, it still required the involvement of third-party financial institutions and complex checks on the personal account information of the transaction parties, leading to increased transaction costs and making each transaction step more complex and cumbersome. However, for cryptocurrencies, because they only require the participation of the transaction parties, transactions can be conducted in the system through computers or mobile terminals without the participation of third-party intermediaries. This can greatly reduce transaction costs and achieve the immediacy of currency circulation.[67]

Second, nonsovereign cryptocurrencies have a certain level of privacy, which comes from their unique operating mechanism in the compilation process. Since the core control system of cryptocurrency is independent, it can ensure that only two parties need to participate in the transaction to a large extent. For example, in the process of using Bitcoin, by downloading and installing the corresponding system software, very brief personal information input and storage can be carried

[66] Liu Wei. Exploration and Risk Prevention of Digital Currency Issuance Mechanism Based on International Experience. Southwest Finance, 2017(11), pp. 51–58.

[67] Lin Liangchun. Research on the Legal Issues of Bitcoin. Citizen and Law (Law Edition), 2015(10), pp. 8–11.

out within the software, while creating public and private keys that can meet the transaction requirements, which can effectively protect and hide personal information before the transaction occurs. Through the blockchain system, the two parties in the Bitcoin transaction can freely record and trade information node servers. The two parties in the transaction only need to confirm the transaction amount through the seller's account and the public key address of the buyer, and the seller can sign the transaction agreement with a private key. The transaction is then broadcast throughout the network, completing the transaction. After the transaction is successful, the two parties only know a seemingly random string of the other party's public key and cannot confirm the other party's personal information. Therefore, both parties can remain anonymous, and this type of transaction is difficult to trace, ensuring the security and privacy of the transaction.[68]

Finally, nonsovereign cryptocurrencies are robust. Robustness refers to the stability and strength of the network state in which the currency is located. With the continuous updating and development of Internet technology, as well as the increasing diversity of social, economic, and cultural forms, currency can be transmitted and circulated not only through physical carriers but also through digital information. However, as electronic currency continues to develop, there are corresponding security risks in financial services. Some financial transaction institutions have caused information leakage due to malicious intrusion, causing a crisis of trust among users and posing a risk to the security of user data and information in the entire financial industry. However, because nonsovereign cryptocurrencies mainly rely on the peer-to-peer network mode and do not have corresponding issuing institutions and organizations, they are less affected by external factors. In addition, network hackers cannot invade the system through technical means. Even if hackers intend to manipulate node servers that account for 51% or more of the total computing power of the entire cryptocurrency network, it is currently impossible to achieve.[69] Even if they are capable of doing so, the profits they can gain from manipulating a few transactions will be much lower than the returns gained from normal accounting by controlling 51% of the computing power. This makes it almost irrational for anyone to attempt to control 51% of the computing power. Therefore, the system of nonsovereign cryptocurrency is highly robust.

(2) The technical characteristics of sovereign cryptocurrency.

Currently, government-issued paper currency has advantages and disadvantages. While it can promote economic development, especially in times of financial crisis and global pandemics, it can also lead to serious inflation and affect currency stability. The emergence and development of sovereign cryptocurrency can effectively solve this problem. Sovereign cryptocurrency can reasonably adjust and allocate effective control over the currency, achieving balance and stability of the issuance and

[68] See footnote 67.

[69] Zhang Chen. Research on the Realistic Risks of Bitcoin and the Legal Regulation in China [J]. Journal of Chongqing University of Posts and Telecommunications (Social Science Edition), 2014(5), pp. 27–31.

control of currency between the government and the people. If cryptocurrency based on blockchain technology is designated a legal tender, namely, sovereign cryptocurrency, the quantity and value of the currency can be determined at the outset, and the public can supervise it through the transparency mechanism of sovereign cryptocurrency. The government will not have unrestricted issuance and absolute control over sovereign cryptocurrency, which can form a safe and effective monetary value credit system that is beneficial to preventing inflation. In countries with high inflation rates, where the constraint on the government's currency issuance is low, using decentralized management of sovereign cryptocurrency as the country's legal tender can technically prevent the possibility of arbitrary issuance of currency and eliminate public expectations of inflation.[70]

In addition, sovereign cryptocurrency can provide stable and specific information data support for the country's overall macroeconomic policies and monetary policies, guaranteeing relevant departments' timely supervision and tracking of transaction activities and behaviors, thus ensuring that the central bank can use corresponding economic stimulus measures and policies more accurately. At the same time, cryptocurrency can continuously trace the transaction funds within the system, providing a data basis for relevant supervisory and management departments, which is advantageous for their understanding of the current financial market dynamics and analysis of market risks. The introduction of blockchain technology can enable the entire cryptocurrency system to conduct transactions openly and transparently, share all data information, and prevent modification and forgery, effectively combating illegal activities such as tax evasion and fraud.

China's sovereign cryptocurrency, DC/EP, which has already been widely adopted nationwide, has some similarities with nonsovereign cryptocurrencies, such as using blockchain technology as the underlying technical architecture and having traceability features. In addition, it also has some technical settings consistent with national legal paper currency features, such as dual offline payment, unlimited legal tender, and dual-layer operation settings.

First, the operational model adopted for sovereign cryptocurrency in China is a dual-layer structure. Operators are required to deposit sufficient reserves with the central bank before engaging in sovereign cryptocurrency and cash equivalent exchanges with the public. Sovereign cryptocurrency is the liability of the central bank and is backed by its credit guarantee, with unlimited legal tender status.

Second, China's sovereign cryptocurrency will not affect the current binary account processing system and can largely ensure the transmission mechanism and implementation mode of current monetary policy.

Third, the central bank is currently primarily focused on replacing M0, gradually reducing the use of M1 and M2 substitutes.

Fourth, the sovereign cryptocurrency issued by the Central Bank of China can largely guarantee the essential characteristics and attributes of currency while

[70] Wang Sheng. Research on Blockchain-based Legal Currency System [J]. Economist, 2016(9), pp. 77–85.

possessing strong confidentiality and high flexibility and can effectively replace cash as an equivalent for exchange.

Fifth, to ensure that sovereign cryptocurrency has effective legal tender status, the Central Bank of China can only allow it to have the four basic functions of currency and cannot undertake any other social functions. Therefore, China's sovereign cryptocurrency will not include features such as smart contracts.

Sixth, the Central Bank of China can also use effective competition between commercial banks to promote the continuous optimization and renewal of the monetary and financial markets, thereby improving the innovation and development capabilities of the industry.

In addition, China's sovereign cryptocurrency has some special technical arrangements. For example, during cash transactions, sovereign cryptocurrency can ensure the confidentiality of the transaction activity and maintain the security of user personal information and transaction activity data. When the technology of sovereign cryptocurrency cannot guarantee the security of transaction activities, it will not be able to form core competitiveness in the user market, which will affect the expansion of the market to some extent. Therefore, sovereign cryptocurrency needs to be managed by regulatory agencies through internal real-name operations while allowing small amounts of anonymous transactions on user clients, similar to cash. During the transaction and currency payment process, transaction data can be set to include transaction codes, sender public keys, cryptocurrency information, payment amounts, and receiver public keys. Hash algorithms can be used to process and simplify the data information, and user private keys can be authenticated for specific transaction information, which is then introduced into the bank's internal information processing system.

Finally, China's sovereign cryptocurrency has a dual offline payment function. Compared with domestic third-party payments, sovereign cryptocurrency has a notable feature, namely, the ability to conduct offline payments. As DC/EP is the digital form of cash, it must have the basic functions of cash. In extreme adverse situations or when the network is abnormal, DC/EP can still be used normally to ensure the stable development of social life and economics.

The development of blockchain technology and cryptocurrencies marks a milestone in the evolution of decentralized systems, which contrasts with centralized organizations that were originally created as intermediaries for information exchange. Communication is a crucial aspect of human expression in daily life, and it relies heavily on information as its main basis. As such, intermediary institutions arose to analyze and search for people's information needs and facilitate the exchange of data with information seekers while collecting corresponding fees for their services to generate profits. However, this traditional mode of transaction involves high costs and low efficiency in information exchange.

Centralized organizations, as a highly concentrated information market trading system, have existed and operated for a long time, but they have many vulnerabilities. First, in this type of trading system, because information is widely distributed, each information exchange is centralized in different systems, which increases the cost of data flow between them. Second, some centralized information intermediaries can obtain considerable information data through certain means, and due to the limited flow and interaction of the traded object's value, the operational cost of the entire system increases while the execution efficiency decreases. Third, in such systems, information data are in a centralized management state, which greatly increases the probability of network hacker attacks.

As Internet information technology continues to develop and optimize, the cost of credit value system-based transactions that require third-party institutional intervention has become increasingly high. Therefore, related researchers have gradually begun to explore new network technologies. Blockchain technology allows value exchange and other transactions without the need for a corresponding credit system, achieving true decentralized management and a peer-to-peer trading network, thereby transforming the Internet from an information-based system to a value-based system.[71]

In 2008, the global financial crisis triggered by the US subprime mortgage crisis prompted countries worldwide to adopt a loose monetary policy to stimulate domestic consumption. In this economic environment, Satoshi Nakamoto published a paper on a peer-to-peer electronic payment system—Bitcoin, ushering in the era of cryptocurrencies and blockchain. In January 2009, Bitcoin officially began operating on the Internet. In May 2010, Bitcoin was first used as a payment currency to purchase two pizzas in the real world. That same year, the world's first Bitcoin trading platform, Mt. Gox, was established. In 2011, Bitcoin exchange platforms with the British pound and the Brazilian peso were established, and the market value of Bitcoin has continued to rise. In 2013, its value skyrocketed, reaching US$300 at one point. However, due to the potential risks of Bitcoin analyzed and publicized by the People's Bank of China, its market price plummeted. However, from 2016, the price of Bitcoin started to rise again. By early 2017, its price had reached and surpassed its previous high in 2013, reaching US$1242 per coin. At the end of 2017, the price of Bitcoin reached a new high of US$20,000 per coin. By 2021, the price of Bitcoin had risen to over US$50,000 per coin.

After the birth of Ethereum in 2015, blockchain technology truly became independent from the concept of Bitcoin and gained market recognition. To date, the market's attention to blockchain technology has been far greater than that to Bitcoin. According to Melanie Swan's theory, the development process of blockchain technology can be divided into the following three stages.

The first stage is Blockchain 1.0: Programmable Currency. The emergence of programmable currency can greatly facilitate the circulation and transactions of value in the network. The construction of blockchain technology ensures the decentralized management of the cryptocurrency payment system, improves the convenience and frequency of transactions, and even for international payment transactions, there are no obstacles, and the operating costs of the entire system can be kept to a minimum. In the first stage of blockchain development, this technology was first applied to the field of cryptocurrency. Although this technology is often mentioned in the same breath as Bitcoin, the two concepts do not belong to the same field nor do they have

[71] See footnote 65.

a dependent relationship. The scope of application of blockchain technology is very wide, and cryptocurrency is just one application scope of blockchain technology, but it was the first to be developed, followed by the separate classification of blockchain technology. The relationship between them is rather subtle.

The second stage is Blockchain 2.0: Programmable Finance. Due to the continuous development and optimization of cryptocurrencies, their applicable scope and involved fields have gradually expanded. Based on the ability of blockchain technology to be compiled, this technology is combined with smart contracts to form a programmable technology in the financial field. On this basis, the technology can be effectively used in various transaction activities in the financial market. Currently, many financial institutions have begun to devote themselves to the development of blockchain technology and incorporate it into practice.

The third stage is Blockchain 3.0: Programmable Society. With the continuous update and iteration of blockchain technology, the decentralized management and nonfalsifiable functions of information data have also begun to be applied in nonfinancial fields. Researchers in related fields have begun to devote themselves to developing blockchain technology in various industries and integrating it with the underlying needs of each field. Therefore, blockchain technology has also been applied in fields such as law, logistics, and postal services. In the third stage of blockchain technology development, its users have even begun to try to replace and modify the underlying protocols of the Internet through blockchain technology, aiming to transform the entire economy and society into a giant information Internet and achieve the programmability of the entire society. In this stage, the technology will be applied to more extensive fields, connect various mobile terminal users effectively and organically by building information schemes suitable for the global Internet, enhance the intelligence of data prospect prediction, and operate and develop various services efficiently and at low cost based on decentralized management.[72]

In 2015, large financial trading enterprises and platforms such as the New York Stock Exchange and Goldman Sachs Group devoted themselves to exploring investment opportunities in the Bitcoin field. At the same time, the NASDAQ Stock Exchange announced a partnership agreement with Bitcoin Technology Company Chain in June of the same year, becoming the first stock market exchange to venture into blockchain technology management and research.

The agreement reached between Nasdaq and Chain aimed to achieve the function of securities free trading based on distributed management without the involvement of third-party financial intermediaries. Normally, completing a securities transaction on Nasdaq requires a multilayer review system. However, with the support of relevant technology, blockchain perfectly replaces the physical form of transaction certificates. By incorporating the specific business information of each enterprise into the corresponding blockchain module, the specific situation of each enterprise can be clearly assessed, ensuring fair and reasonable, secure, and effective trading

[72] Zhou Ruijue. Legal Regulation of Blockchain Technology. Journal of Beijing University of Posts and Telecommunications (Social Sciences Edition), 2017(3), pp. 39–45.

activities. This effectively solves the contradiction of information asymmetry and helps investors make investment decisions.

In early 2016, the blockchain group R3 CEV created the first decentralized ledger processing experiment, combining and matching with eleven member banks using Ethereum and Microsoft's blockchain services. According to the group's announcement, the eleven member banks are conducting cross-border settlement experiments through decentralized ledgers.

In 2019, Facebook and Uber, among other companies, collaborated to discuss the creation of "LIBRA" and released a white paper. By using a basket of currencies as a pricing standard for creating and circulating cryptocurrencies, such currencies can be used in all Facebook programs. The current total number of Facebook users is close to three billion.

The Central Bank of China had already established a research and development team for cryptocurrency in 2014. Currently, significant progress has been made in the research of both technology and legal regulations in this field. In early 2016, a research conference on cryptocurrency was successfully held, which mainly included a reasonable reference to the research achievements in relevant fields abroad, breakthroughs in technology, and the formulation of corresponding development plans and goals for the issuance of cryptocurrency. In August 2019, the People's Bank of China announced the issuance of sovereign cryptocurrency. In April 2020, China's sovereign cryptocurrency DC/EP was piloted in Shenzhen, Suzhou, Xiongan New Area, Chengdu, and the Winter Olympics scenarios. It was tested at Shanghai Tongren Hospital in January 2021,[73] and in February of the same year, it reached a strategic partnership with the cross-border payment platform CBP.[74] From this, it can be seen that China has always maintained a positive and optimistic attitude toward the continuous advancement of sovereign cryptocurrency and has always expressed its determination to develop it through practical actions.

However, relying solely on the efforts and promotion of national government departments is far from sufficient. We also need researchers and organizations to work together and provide technical support and market space to jointly plan and strategize for the development of this field. The market should also play an active leading role in promoting the development and promotion of such products and advancing the internationalization of Chinese yuan.

The birth of cryptoSDRs also requires blockchain technology supported by private innovation capabilities to promote the technological development of supersovereign cryptocurrency to better solve the technical problems in the process of monetization. Encouraging more scholars to participate in the discussion and thinking of cryptoSDRs is also conducive to breaking through political and legal barriers and jointly setting up a reasonable and effective development plan for cryptoSDRs.

[73] Tencent. Pilot Process of Central Bank's Digital Currency DC/EP—We Need to Learn to Adapt Quickly [EB/OL]. https://new.qq.com/rain/a/20210113A0785N00. Accessed 6 May 2022.

[74] Tencent. Breaking News: Cross-border Payment Platform CBP Officially Forms Strategic Partnership with Central Bank's Digital Currency DC/EP [EB/OL]. https://new.qq.com/rain/a/20210204A0BEI500. Accessed 6 May 2022.

2.3.2 *Technical Settings for CryptoSDRs*

The technical architecture of cryptoSDRs can be based on the nonsovereign blockchain technology of Bitcoin while also borrowing the advantages of offline payment and the dual-layer issuance structure of sovereign cryptocurrencies such as China's sovereign cryptocurrency DC/EP. Based on this, both cryptoSDRs and sovereign cryptocurrencies have a two-tiered issuance structure: One is the wholesale issuance structure between the IMF and central banks of various countries, and the other is the retail issuance structure between central banks and private sectors of each country.

(1) Technical Features and Advantages of CryptoSDRs

First, cryptoSDRs can replace the original SDRs as a balance sheet asset. CryptoSDRs can be obtained through exchange with gold or assets of various countries, just as SDR alternative accounts. This achieves the replacement of M0 of various countries' currencies, that is, the replacement of cash. Countries transfer their corresponding assets to cryptoSDRs as credit endorsements, enhancing their credit and stabilizing the value of cryptoSDRs, maintaining their exchange rate stability, and providing legal status and legal liability for their currency circulation domestically.

Second, cryptoSDRs are issued using a two-tier operating model. CryptoSDRs and China's sovereign cryptocurrency should adopt the same two-tier operating model, with the upper layer being the World Central Bank formed by the IMF and the lower layer being the central banks of various countries. According to the agreed cryptoSDRs share, each central bank of member countries delivers 100% of gold or assets to the IMF, and then the IMF gives each member country an equal amount of cryptoSDRs, which users can exchange for an equivalent amount of cash or bank deposits. Through this process, the government and the people of member countries can hold and use cryptoSDRs universally, which helps to promote and popularize cryptoSDRs.

Third, cryptoSDRs use distributed storage to ensure their security. The accounting method of cryptoSDRs should not use the public blockchain system of nonsovereign cryptocurrencies but should use the alliance blockchain. Because the public blockchain is slow and unable to be modified, it cannot be used normally in the more developed payment field. Therefore, using the alliance blockchain, only institutions with specific permits have the right to query and verify accounting information. The IMF can authorize the central banks of member countries to become node servers of the cryptoSDR blockchain, allowing them to set up and manage the corresponding account. The IMF has node servers and super node servers, and node servers, similar to other member countries' node servers, are responsible for storing and recording transaction information, while super node servers can be used to review the record status and error information of node servers in real time. Different countries apply to the IMF for a moderate number of node servers to store and record transaction data according to their own needs. Each member country's node server adopts distributed storage and a Byzantine fault tolerance mechanism, which is responsible for maintenance and management by the governments and central banks of each country. At the same time, hacking the IMF and the node servers of member countries is defined as a crime, which technically and legally guarantees the secure operation of the cryptoSDR system. Each member country can also receive corresponding coin casting tax revenue based on its contribution to providing computational power.

Fourth, cryptoSDRs have controllable anonymity. The cryptoSDR system adopts a front-end anonymous and back-end real-name system, that is, each member country can use a real-name system to supervise its own citizens' accounts, but merchants and users cannot trace the circulation of cryptoSDRs. Even if banks and users cooperate, they have no right to view or trace the flow of cryptoSDRs. Except for the governments and central banks of member countries, no institution or organization can query specific information about various transaction activities on the platform. Even between countries, information cannot be directly exchanged, and it is necessary to apply to the IMF to query the accounts of other countries to obtain information about their citizens. However, the global total and basic information of cryptoSDRs can be monitored by the IMF to avoid illegal activities.

Fifth, cryptoSDRs have unforgeability. Physical anti-counterfeiting measures must be used for cash, which are limited and can result in counterfeit currency being found worldwide. CryptoSDRs, on the other hand, must be signed with a private key by the IMF and are thus unforgeable. Each member country is responsible for managing its own node server within the system, and each node server is independent and equal in rights and responsibilities. The data and information generated by each node server can be transmitted throughout the entire system, and even if one node server is compromised, it will not have a significant impact on other parts of the system, and the system will continue to operate normally. In addition, the transmission of data and information is unidirectional and asymmetric, and the corresponding algorithm compilation is encrypted to ensure the accuracy and security of the transmission results. If a government or central bank of a country or several countries collude to modify node server ledgers, the IMF can initiate its own super node server to conduct an investigation and sanction these member countries.

Sixth, cryptoSDRs have controllable total quantity, which is advantageous for regulatory authorities to develop corresponding monetary policies. The IMF's Monetary Policy Committee can convene meetings of committee members and representatives from each member country to adjust the total quantity of cryptoSDRs and formulate corresponding monetary policies based on the actual situation of each member country and the global economic situation. According to the results of the meetings, adjustments can be made to the cryptoSDR system, and the effects and impacts of monetary policy can be observed in real time. In the event of a crisis, emergency meetings on monetary policy can be held to discuss and develop corresponding response strategies, adjust the system, and eliminate inflation and currency depreciation expectations, thus maintaining the stability and sustainable development of the global monetary and financial system. In addition, cryptoSDRs can provide technical and informational support for a country's economic policies and macro measures, optimize the accuracy and flexibility of government monetary policy use while ensuring the authenticity and accuracy of government information, and conduct real-time monitoring and management of the circulation of monetary funds to analyze potential risks in the current financial sector. Furthermore, through peer-to-peer network transactions, cryptoSDRs can ensure the free circulation of user funds and promote the stability and sustainability of interest rate term structures.

Seventh, cryptoSDRs have low issuance costs and are easy to circulate globally. In the process of currency issuance, cryptoSDRs can effectively reduce issuance costs compared to physical cash and facilitate currency circulation and storage while enhancing transaction flexibility. During transactions, cryptoSDRs are electronically recorded on the unique transaction ledger of the entire network, free from time and space limitations, and as long as both parties use computers or mobile devices, they can directly transfer and trade cryptoSDRs in their respective accounts. Direct transactions between users on the network can thus maximize the convenience of circulation, facilitating the low-cost and rapid flow of assets globally.

Eighth, cryptoSDR systems can effectively prevent and combat transnational crimes. With the support of blockchain technology, the entire transaction process can be publicly transparent and secure. Additionally, the information on each node server is immutable and cannot be tampered with or forged, thereby ensuring the fairness, reasonableness, and security of transactions to a large extent. In the event of transnational crimes such as money laundering, tax evasion, and fraud, regulatory authorities can easily request information from the IMF to obtain more accurate and transparent flows of criminal funds, enabling them to effectively prevent and combat such crimes.

(2) Specific Technologies and Application Scenarios for CryptoSDRs

The following text intends to provide a feasible solution for the monetization of cryptoSDRs under current technological capabilities by analyzing the issuance and trading techniques and scenarios, helping readers to understand its technical essence and imagine the future financial world constructed by cryptoSDRs, and laying a foundation for readers to better understand the legal issues of cryptoSDRs.

First, the issuance of cryptoSDRs. Compared with the printing and issuance of banknotes, the issuance of cryptoSDRs requires digital signatures from the super node servers of the IMF. First, the cryptoSDR management department of the IMF creates and sets unified standards for passwords and denominations. Different passwords are used in cryptoSDRs with different denominations. Second, the system's random numbers are compiled and converted through a hash value, and then the numbers are randomly attached to cryptoSDRs. Finally, the node servers of the cryptoSDR management department digitally sign the encrypted codes to generate cryptoSDRs.

Second, user login. Users need to connect and authenticate through the node servers of the central bank or commercial bank of their respective countries and the cryptoSDR institution. During the login process, users need to download the electronic wallet of their respective governments, register and log in their personal information in the program, and use their mobile phone numbers as public keys for login registration and information registration. After completing user authentication and setting personal private keys and user logins, the specific data of the keys will be recorded and stored by the data system.

Third, cryptoSDRs are extracted. First, users need to use the electronic wallet and log in. After selecting specific bank information, the legitimacy of the transaction is verified through the bank's data information. During this process, the node server of the commercial bank will audit the stock of cryptoSDRs to ensure that the quantity is always correct. After passing the verification, the node server of the commercial bank can enter the exchange process between cryptoSDRs and fiat currency and conduct transactions according to the exchange rate specified by the IMF. At the same time, all transaction data information will be published to the database of the IMF node server through blockchain technology. After verification by the super node servers of the IMF, the ownership authentication and conversion of cryptoSDRs will be conducted on the cryptoSDR blockchain, and detailed records and storage of trading activities on the platform will be made. Finally, the node server of the commercial bank sends cryptoSDRs through the mobile client to complete the attribution and confirmation of the ownership of cryptoSDRs.

Another solution is to destroy the existing cryptoSDRs and generate new cryptoSDRs instead of changing ownership during the transaction process mentioned above. After cryptoSDRs pass the verification process on the IMF's super node server, they are directly destroyed, and new cryptoSDRs of equivalent value are generated. The main advantage of this solution is that it only requires confirmation of the legality of the transaction through digital information, without the need to disclose detailed transaction records. This solution ensures the security and confidentiality of both transaction activities and user information while also meeting the regulatory requirements of governments and central banks around the world.

Both of these solutions have their own advantages and disadvantages, and with the development of technology, there may be better solutions in the future.

Fourth, the payment of cryptoSDRs involves online payments between the two parties using cryptoSDRs as the payment method. The payment process involves logging in to the wallet software, selecting the function mode, inputting relevant information such as the payee and payment amount, and then sending a certain amount of cryptoSDRs information to the node server of the commercial bank. The node server of the commercial bank verifies the legality of the transaction and other information to ensure the rationality and accuracy of the transaction. After the transaction is approved, the information is sent to cryptoSDRs node server under the IMF. The node server modifies and confirms the ownership of the corresponding value of cryptoSDRs and then returns the information to the node server of the commercial bank to complete the payment activity of cryptoSDRs.

2.4 The Dilemma of Blockchain Technology and CryptoSDRs

To address the challenges facing cryptoSDRs, we must explore solutions starting from the underlying blockchain technology. A comprehensive understanding and analysis of the challenges faced by SDRs from the inside out are necessary to find a breakthrough.

2.4.1 The Dilemma Faced by Blockchain Technology

From the creation to the development of blockchain technology, as it is increasingly integrated into practical applications, people have gradually discovered doubts and technical vulnerabilities in blockchain technology. Therefore, to apply blockchain technology to more industries and fields, corresponding solutions and countermeasures must be formulated from the perspective of energy consumption, information storage, transaction scale, and transaction security to ensure the continuous optimization and sustainable development of blockchain technology.

(1) Deficiencies of Blockchain Technology

In the early stages of blockchain technology development, the technology itself was still in its infancy, such as early products in the Industrial and Information Technology Revolutions, and there were many flaws that needed to be improved. These urgent shortcomings mainly include the following aspects.

First, there is the issue of high energy consumption. According to the "impossible triangle" theory in cryptocurrency economic studies, it is impossible to achieve low energy consumption, decentralized management, and security and confidentiality simultaneously in the practical application of blockchain technology. Therefore, performance optimization is the only way to achieve overall maximization of benefits. As of 2016, Bitcoin's computing power was 8 × 10^18 operations/second, which is 28,571 times faster than the computing power of the world's most powerful and fastest computer, the Blue Gene supercomputer in the US. However, because the computing power of computers on the Internet cannot match that of cloud computing, the characteristics of blockchain technology require that the right to bookkeeping can only be processed singularly, and the acquisition of the right to bookkeeping is unique. Moreover, because the computing power of blockchain technology cannot meet the standard of cloud computing, it inevitably causes huge energy consumption. Additionally, because blockchain technology has high requirements for infrastructure construction, a large amount of network bandwidth is consumed in the underlying information data transmission mechanism network, and with the rate limit of data interaction, it will inevitably result in broadcast storms in the queued messages during the data processing process, causing energy consumption and a slowdown in the overall network operation speed.[75]

Second, the storage space for information is too large. Because the information database of blockchain technology stores all transaction activity information since the platform was established, each additional data node server requires downloading and dynamically updating historical data information. It requires a powerful and complete information storage space for all node server information on the entire blockchain to be dynamically updated and fully synchronized. If the storage capacity is not sufficient, it will be a major obstacle to the development of the entire blockchain technology.

Third, there is an issue with the system's ability to withstand pressure. For projects or activities with larger transaction volumes, the entire data system needs to have strong pressure resistance. The transaction volume generated or carried out on a transaction platform established based on blockchain technology is relatively small, and the current blockchain transaction system can still support its normal operation. However, if blockchain technology is introduced into a more extensive transaction field, the pressure resistance of the entire system will be a major test, which may cause the collapse or even paralysis of the data system.

Fourth, transaction speed is slow. Taking Bitcoin as an example, the generation cycle of a blockchain is 10 min, which means that each transaction activity or transaction business will be recorded in the entire data system 10 min after its completion, which results in low operating efficiency of the system. Moreover, the storage space of the module is only 1 MB, which is much lower in terms of transaction volume and operating speed compared to widely used third-party payment systems on the market.

Fifth, regulatory policies are still in a state of ambiguity, posing a significant challenge to financial regulation. The formulation of laws and regulations by relevant government departments and market supervision have a significant impact on the sustainable development of blockchain technology. The creation and issuance of Blockchain 1.0 as a currency pioneered new avenues for supervision and management mechanisms and had a significant impact on the national currency issuance system. Additionally, due to the distributed ledger processing characteristics of blockchain technology, it will have a considerable impact on the construction of the national tax collection system. With the emergence and application of Blockchain 2.0 and 3.0, the use of decentralized management models continues to expand, resulting in a constant decline in the government's influence in market management and policy-making. Furthermore, since blockchain technology mainly automates business processing through machines, it may result in the reduction of some government departments and personnel, hindering the implementation of blockchain technology in such government departments. Additionally, because blockchain technology is still in its early stages, the legal and regulatory policy systems in this field are not yet mature and cannot be effectively unified, resulting in numerous conflicts in practice.

[75] Mei Haitao, Liu Jie. Current Status, Existing Problems, and Policy Suggestions of the Blockchain Industry [J]. Telecommunications Science, 2016(11), pp. 134–138.

In the financial transaction industry, market regulatory agencies can effectively safeguard the confidentiality of the entire financial transaction market and all transaction information data. However, the Internet financial transaction service system established on the basis of blockchain technology, due to its decentralized management characteristics, causes the entire transaction platform business module to have a low concentration and a radiative distribution, resulting in the lack of a complete system architecture for market supervision and management and the inability to carry out a systematic construction of professional supervision measures. Moreover, because blockchain technology is a new and emerging technology with a limited scope of popularity, users and investors have little understanding of the concept of blockchain technology, resulting in blockchain technology's inability to obtain stable customer traffic in the consumer market, leading to a weak market foundation. Therefore, in addition to being widely used in the currency payment field, the promotion of blockchain technology in other fields still requires considerable time and effort.[76]

Sixth, there are significant challenges in the development of blockchain technology. First, the technical scope of blockchain technology research and development is relatively wide, making it a highly comprehensive Internet technology. This has led to high research and development costs and many difficulties in promoting the development of blockchain technology, increasing the difficulty of blockchain technology research and development. Second, blockchain technology has poor flexibility. As each node server of blockchain technology is tamper-proof, even if an error is discovered during the entry of information data into various node servers, it cannot be corrected in a timely manner, resulting in irreversible transactions and the inability to ensure the orderly progress of subsequent services. This reduces the flexibility of various transaction activities on the trading platform and cannot guarantee the legitimate rights and interests of users. Third, there is a lack of an ecosystem for blockchain technology. Currently, the blockchain operating system lacks a unified technical application standard, and various cryptocurrencies continue to emerge on the market. The construction of the entire blockchain ecosystem is still in its infancy. In addition, problems such as data information security, distributed information storage, and data interaction in the field of blockchain technology have not formed a unified and integrated technical solution. Some businesses are still in the experimental stage of research and development, with a lack of practical data and information as research samples, resulting in a relatively weak overall business operation model. Last, blockchain technology lacks cross-technology integration. Under current technical conditions, it is necessary to quickly establish certain restriction standards for various transaction activities on the blockchain and the operating performance of smart contracts. At the same time, corresponding rules should be enacted for the speed of the entire system's operation to impose reasonable limitations.

[76] Zhang Xiuguang, Li Zhengdao. Prospects, Analysis, and Challenges of "Blockchain + Internet" in the Financial Field. Modern Management, 2016(6), pp. 4–6.

(2) Risks of Blockchain Technology

As part of the Internet system, blockchain technology inherently carries many security risks that have been identified in the field of computers and the Internet or are similar to them. Furthermore, since it is still in the early stages of development, it faces many system risks. The main risks include the following:

First, there is algorithmic security risk. While the security of blockchain technology in algorithm compilation is strong, there is a risk of vulnerabilities and hacking as Internet and cryptographic technologies continue to evolve. The information security foundation of blockchain technology is based on asymmetric encryption algorithms, which may already have the risk of being decrypted. For example, the emergence of quantum computers poses a significant threat to the security of the information system of blockchain technology. If an information data processing system built on blockchain technology is compromised, it can result in the leakage of transaction records and users' personal identity information, which in turn can cause the credit system of the entire data platform to collapse, posing a significant threat and impact on users' financial security and even life safety.[77]

Second, protocol security risk. This type of risk mainly covers security risks at two levels: fork and computational power attacks. The former mainly refers to a single blockchain being split into two or more new blockchains, mainly due to changes in the underlying protocol of each node server that affect the cohesiveness of the blockchain operating mechanism, resulting in inconsistent tasks in the information data system, obstructing the immutability of each node server and causing the credit system of the entire blockchain to collapse. The latter refers to the possibility that some consensus mechanisms of the blockchain may be vulnerable to manipulation under certain conditions, which may result in the entire data network being controlled by external attacks. Once the attacker controls more than 51% of the computational power of the node server, they can broadcast incorrect information and add it to the newly generated blocks, causing errors in the information on the blockchain and leading to the collapse of the blockchain's credibility.

Third, there is data security risk. When the blockchain data information system cannot achieve completely anonymous transactions, it still needs to use the corresponding user IP address to exchange information and complete transactions. Even if the user's network address does not match their actual identity information, with all the information being shared and transparent on the blockchain system and various anti-anonymity technologies constantly improving and advancing, it is possible to identify user identities through network testing. In addition, in a public data network based on blockchain, since all users on the platform can access complete information data in the database and all transaction activities conducted on the platform are public, if user identity information is leaked, it will pose a threat to financial security and violate users' privacy rights.

Fourth, user security risks. As blockchain technology operates on cryptographic techniques, potential security risks and vulnerabilities may still exist within the

[77] See footnote 65.

blockchain system. In traditional centralized platforms, if an account password is lost, it can be retrieved through the platform's services. However, in blockchain technology, personal keys are managed independently by platform users without the intervention of a third-party intermediary. When a user loses their private key, there is no other effective way to retrieve it, and the user cannot effectively control the funds in their personal account. This means that losing a private key directly results in the loss of the user's personal assets. Additionally, due to the broad scope of the Internet finance industry and low entry barriers, all transaction activities and users' personal data on the trading platform are shared and publicly available, increasing the risk and threat of online fraud and privacy invasion. When the entire Internet blockchain system is attacked by hackers or malicious software, it affects the basic operation of the network system and can result in the leakage or loss of users' personal identity information. Moreover, because all information data on blockchain technology are irreversible, if a user's rights are violated, the system cannot provide effective relief and solutions. When a user's personal account data are lost or leaked, it can affect the security of the user's funds on the platform, leading to irreversible asset losses.

Fifth, system security risks. The development of blockchain technology requires a combination of related advanced technologies in cryptography, resulting in a high degree of algorithm concentration during the research process. This can easily lead to algorithmic data compilation errors. As blockchain technology lacks a physical carrier as a tool to enhance security performance, all node servers on the blockchain can independently add information data that cannot be modified. If the data added by each node server contain a virus or Trojan, it can lead to malicious attacks on the information system. When the blockchain system is compromised, the security of users' personal assets in the system is at risk.

In addition, as smart contracts continue to evolve, systems related to blockchain technology will be combined with smart contract technology. However, due to vulnerabilities in the algorithmic compilation of smart contracts themselves, the collapse of the smart contract credit system can lead to significant threats and risks to the funds and properties involved in transactions under the system. Additionally, the difficulty of updating smart contracts means that existing vulnerabilities may persist, increasing the likelihood of system attacks and invasions.

Shared blockchain technology allows for free data entry by various node servers on the Internet, while user information cannot be displayed on the blockchain network layer. This may lead to many uncontrollable factors and increase security risks for sectors with high data security standards. Since blockchain technology implements dynamic updates of information data through peer-to-peer interaction, when network hackers attack a specific node server, it may cause communication barriers between that node server and other node servers, resulting in it being isolated. If the attacker manipulates the view of that node server, they may directly obtain the victim's displayed information module.[78]

[78] Zhang Bin. Research on Blockchain Security Risks [J]. Telecommunications Engineering Technology and Standardization, 2017(11), pp. 1–5.

(3) New Problems Arising from Blockchain Technology

As blockchain technology continues to evolve, new problems continue to arise, mainly in the following aspects.

First, there is the issue of system centralization. Although blockchain technology can achieve a distributed mode of operation during the operation process, it strengthens the centralization degree in the design process. Taking Bitcoin's core algorithm code as an example, it can be found that since Satoshi Nakamoto handed over the control of the entire Bitcoin business to Gavin Andresen in 2010, the core code output of Bitcoin has been concentrated in six foreign programmers. Due to the high degree of centralization in the code design process, if the blockchain algorithm compilation and the core code coverage range expand and even become the evaluation standard for the entire Internet blockchain technology, it will form a centralized organization in system optimization and development.[79]

Second, there is the problem of circular execution in smart contracts. Since smart contracts have autonomous feedback loop features, they constantly amplify the impact of commodity price fluctuations. Continuously executing incorrect code will not only cause problems in the system but also consume many resources, resulting in error amplification effects for users and the system, leading to significant negative feedback.

Third, the node server number is stable. Based on the peer-to-peer network structure, it can be observed that the stability of the existing Internet operating system is based on the participation of a large number of node servers. Therefore, when external environmental changes cause various node servers in blockchain technology to constantly drop out, the stability and security of the entire network system's transaction platform and operating system become difficult to guarantee, resulting in security and operational vulnerabilities.

In summary, although there are still many obstacles to the development of blockchain technology, its progress in this field will not be hindered by the aforementioned issues. With the continuous deepening and development of Internet technology, blockchain technology will gradually enter people's field of vision, and investors will also see the development prospects of this field. Funds and various social wealth resources will continue to flow into the research on blockchain technology. The challenges faced by blockchain are also similar to those faced by cryptoSDRs. Currently, most of these issues have been resolved: slow transaction speed has been addressed by technical capacity expansion, the difficulty of development has been solved by unified blockchain development technology standards, financial regulation issues have also been addressed through on-chain warnings and smart contract supervision, and system security risks can be prevented by increasing the support of security software and hardware. The issues of high energy consumption, resistance capacity, and unstable node server numbers can also be addressed through the use of alliance chains. Therefore, with the development of blockchain technology, cloud computing, artificial intelligence, the arrival of 5G technology, and

[79] Mei Haitao, Liu Jie. Current Status, Existing Problems, and Policy Suggestions of the Blockchain Industry [J]. Telecommunications Science, 2016(11), pp. 134–138.

the upgrading of hardware devices, many early issues of blockchain technology can be easily solved. However, while solving the problems of blockchain technology, nonsovereign cryptocurrencies such as Bitcoin and the creation of cryptoSDRs also face many new problems and challenges.

2.4.2 The Dilemma Faced by Bitcoin and Other Cryptocurrencies

After Bitcoin ushered in the blockchain era, tens of thousands of nonsovereign cryptocurrencies were issued unofficially, but their influence was not as great as Bitcoin and is thus more valuable and significant for discussion. Currently, the advantages and obstacles of Bitcoin represent the entire cryptocurrency industry, and the more widely it is accepted, the more popular other cryptocurrencies will become. However, the greater the resistance it faces, the greater the obstacles faced by the entire cryptocurrency industry.

First, there is resistance to reform from developed countries. In the current international monetary and economic structure, the US is the biggest beneficiary of the current economic system. By implementing loose monetary policies domestically to stimulate domestic economic growth, the US has shifted the problems and threats arising from economic crises onto the world economy, hindering the normal development and construction of the global economy. The issuance and circulation of nonsovereign cryptocurrencies such as Bitcoin pose a certain degree of threat to the dominant position of the US dollar, affecting the US's world economic domination status and causing a certain degree of impact on the interests of other developed countries. Therefore, in the development process of cryptocurrencies led by Bitcoin, it will certainly face obstacles from these developed countries.

Second, there are security issues with Bitcoin. On the Bitcoin trading platform, the large flow of participants and transaction projects, as well as the continuous expansion of transaction volume, will seriously affect the normal operation of the entire cryptocurrency trading system and the construction of the entire operational system. At the same time, the continuous influx of traffic will also affect the security of the entire operational system, leading to information and data security loopholes. In addition, Internet trading activities conducted on a network are constantly threatened or even attacked by Internet hackers, posing serious threats to the personal information of users and the safety of their transaction activities. Performance issues of operational equipment and the limitations of Internet technology development will also lead to the impact of various transaction activities and hinder the development of Internet trading platforms, causing losses to users and leading to an increase in overall operating costs.

Third, Bitcoin has an ambiguous legal status. Although Bitcoin has a certain position in the international circulation field and has been permitted by policies in most countries as a virtual asset, the related laws and regulations for classifying and supervising Bitcoin still have significant loopholes, resulting in ambiguous concept definitions and limitations. Therefore, many criminals in various countries like to use Bitcoin as a tool for money laundering. Germany was the first country in the world to recognize the legal status of Bitcoin and stipulate that it must be taxed. Japan believes that policy management and restrictions on Bitcoin need to be strengthened, and reasonable adjustments and avoidance of potential risks and crises need to be made from a policy perspective. In 2013, China issued a notice stating that Bitcoin can only be regarded as a virtual commodity and is not recognized as a legal currency status in the law and stipulated that it cannot be used as a medium for transactions and payments.

Fourth, Bitcoin has a credit problem. In terms of building a credit system, Bitcoin lacks government-backed credit and does not have physical assets to provide effective credit endorsement, which leads to its low credit rating in the transaction process. Moreover, with the continuous development and update of Internet technology, Bitcoin, which is based on algorithm compilation, is likely to be replaced at any time, resulting in poor stability of its issuance basis.

Fifth, there is the problem of Bitcoin block storage expansion. Bitcoin has the characteristic of decentralization, and each node server needs to record a complete ledger, so the storage capacity of the entire system is relatively high. In the actual application process, there may be a phenomenon of continuous expansion of data storage capacity. To date, Bitcoin has established more than 700,000 running blocks, and the data capacity has reached 478 GB.[80] In practice, to effectively ensure the traceability and authenticity of transactions, new blocks will be continuously generated during the transaction process, further increasing the expansion speed of Bitcoin storage space capacity and resulting in a decline in the operating efficiency of the Bitcoin system.

Sixth, the proliferation of nonsovereign cryptocurrencies. As the issuance of Bitcoin is limited, various new types of cryptocurrencies continue to flood into the cryptocurrency market, resulting in a continuous increase in the types and quantities of nonsovereign cryptocurrencies on the Internet. At the same time, many cryptocurrencies involve financial fraud, such as Ponzi schemes, which greatly hinder the development of nonsovereign cryptocurrencies, including Bitcoin.

2.4.3 The Dilemma of Monetizing CryptoSDRs

CryptoSDRs face not only the same challenges as blockchain technology and most cryptocurrencies but also various obstacles in the process of expanding their use to become a supersovereign currency. In theory, SDRs are a reserve asset beyond sovereignty. Since the issuance of SDRs is not closely tied to the interests of any individual country, they can avoid the disadvantages of credit currency as a reserve asset. However, in practical applications, SDRs still have significant vulnerabilities that need to be addressed and fixed.

---

[80] Blockchair, https://blockchair.com/zh/bitcoin. Accessed 4 May 2023.

According to Karl Marx's definition of the nature of money in "capital," for SDRs to become money, first, they must be a general equivalent; second, they must have the function of measuring value and be convenient for circulation, payment, transportation, and storage.[81] To become a supersovereign currency, SDRs also need market appeal, support from a superpolitical entity, technical and financial support for issuance and circulation, authorization from the IMF, and legal currency status and legal tender status granted by member countries.

(1) The Dilemma of SDRs Becoming Supersovereign Currencies

Whether SDRs have sufficient monetary attributes, and even whether they have the foundation to become a supersovereign currency, depends on their ability to overcome the following challenges.

First, value. The value of the SDRs is more stable compared to the US dollar. SDRs' value is accurately measured using a basket of currencies, which makes it less susceptible to external influences than individual country currencies. However, the value of the SDRs is mainly determined by five currencies, with the US dollar having the highest influence at 41.73%. The Chinese yuan is the only sovereign currency of a developing country among the five, while the remaining four are sovereign currencies of developed countries that cannot effectively measure and adapt to emerging economies and developing countries. Therefore, it lacks typicality and representativeness for the construction and optimization of the entire emerging financial market system.

Second, there is supply. The supply of SDRs refers to their distribution. SDRs are distributed to member countries as credit lines without conditions. Based on the principle of double-entry bookkeeping, the use of SDRs increases the assets and liabilities of central banks simultaneously. SDRs are recorded as assets, while the corresponding liabilities are contingent liabilities. These liabilities are only required to be repaid when a member country no longer participates in the IMF or recognizes the SDR's legal status. However, as the probability of this happening is small, this liability is almost negligible and does not require international fund flows or compensation.

The distribution of SDRs needs to be reviewed by the IMF periodically, with a review cycle of five years. However, this process is inflexible and can have a significant impact on the legal policies related to SDRs. Due to the small supply and low flexibility of SDRs, they cannot achieve the goal of replenishing reserve assets for member countries. Moreover, as the distribution of SDRs requires the approval of more than 85% of the votes, it is greatly influenced by major countries. Meanwhile, the distribution standard of SDRs is based on the proportion of the subscribed shares of member countries in the IMF. Therefore, developed countries will receive more SDRs than developing countries, which lead to resources not flowing to countries that truly need funds and contribute to lower international reserves of other emerging economies and developing countries.

[81] Jia Liping. Theory, Practice, and Impact of Bitcoin [J]. International Financial Research, 2013(12), pp. 14–25.

Third, there is attractiveness. Attractiveness is a major factor that determines the willingness of member countries to hold reserves of a certain asset. The attractiveness of an asset is mainly determined by its functionality. SDRs have a strong impact due to their ability to diversify member countries' international reserve resources, reduce their dependence on sovereign currencies, and effectively mitigate currency storage risks. In addition, for some emerging market countries with nascent markets, if their corresponding foreign reserves can function as a risk control mechanism and have better credit conditions than sovereign currencies such as the US dollar, then the reserve currency will have a greater impact and appeal to these countries. However, due to the limited supply of SDRs, their impact on the foreign exchange market is relatively low. Furthermore, SDRs cannot be used as a payment medium for international market transactions due to their mechanisms and characteristics. Therefore, if SDRs are to be used as the basis for a currency and financial system in international trade activities, it is necessary to continuously expand their coverage and enhance their impact on emerging market countries.[82]

Fourth, SDRs are lacking in currency attributes. Researchers in related fields believe that SDRs lack the basic characteristics of a currency. Some scholars argue that SDRs can only be used and stored as derivative currencies of the five sovereign currencies and do not possess the essential features and properties of a currency. The credit system of international sovereign currencies such as the US dollar is based on national credit and production capacity, while the issuing institution of SDRs is the IMF, which has no authority to levy taxes and has no national production capacity. Therefore, SDRs do not have the conditions to issue currencies. Moreover, even if the governments of the EU and the US allow SDRs to be issued and used as currency, they will never give the issuing power of currency to the IMF.[83] Scholars Alessandriniand and Fratianni also believe that SDRs have two fundamental flaws: first, they are not sovereign currencies and do not constitute claims on the IMF; second, history has shown that SDRs are insufficient as a supplementary reserve currency.[84] Scholars Clark and Polak acknowledge that SDRs have many shortcomings: first, they lack the basic functions of a currency, are not legally tender, and have no physical carrier; second, there are technical difficulties that prevent them from being monetized.[85]

Fifth, the support of a super political entity is necessary. The construction of the Bretton Woods system shows that governments are the key factors that determine whether a currency and financial system can be successful on a global scale. Throughout the process of constructing the entire system, the most critical factors affecting success are the interests of various groups and the economic strength of member countries. Therefore, the most important and decisive factor in constructing

---

[82] See footnote 56.

[83] SSAAIYA, An International Monetary Fund Currency to Rival the Dollar? [M]. Washington DC: Cato Institute 2009(10), pp. 1–15.

[84] P. ALESSANDRINI, M. FRATIANNI. International Monies, Special Drawing Rights and Supranational Money [M]. Rome: Prepared for the 2009 Pre-G8 Summit Conference on "Global Financial Crises: National Economic Solutions, Geopolitical Impacts", 2009.

[85] P. B. CLARK, J. J. POLAK. International Liquidity and the Role of the SDR in the International Monetary System [R]. IMF Staff Position Note, 2002WP/02/217.

an international currency and financial system is the economic and political strength of various interest groups.

The evolution of the international monetary system reveals some key factors that have driven institutional changes. These factors not only played decisive roles in the establishment and collapse of the previous international monetary systems but also continue to have a major influence on the future formation and development of the international monetary system. Under the gold standard, the natural value of gold maintained the entire system without intervention from national governments. However, with the formation of the gold exchange standard, governments began to intervene in the international monetary system. In this system, as long as a few countries committed to gold exchange, there was no need for multiple countries to sign a common agreement. The operation and maintenance of this international monetary system were primarily based on the value of gold, with government power as a secondary factor. The Bretton Woods system was an international monetary system in which the value of gold served as an auxiliary credit endorsement for powerful economic, military, and political countries. This system was established and maintained through mutual agreements among various countries. After the Jamaica Agreement, the international monetary system shifted from the US dollar standard to a multicurrency standard, in which the value of gold was essentially excluded from the monetary system. The normal operation of the international monetary system has since relied almost entirely on the power of national governments and mutual agreements among countries. Therefore, government power has gradually become a key factor in the evolution and maintenance of the international monetary system.

However, the main problem and key influencing factor in the creation and maintenance of the international monetary system are whether sovereign countries with currency control authority allow such a situation to arise. Additionally, corresponding solutions and policy measures need to be developed to limit the actions of powerful countries and protect the legitimate rights and interests of weaker economies. Economically powerful countries have the strength to destroy any international monetary and financial system, and they will never allow their fundamental interests to be infringed upon or damaged. Although the SDRs in the past largely maintained the fundamental interests of the US dollar, the value that the US dollar provides cannot be compared with what SDRs offer. Therefore, even if there were to be a new form of cryptoSDRs, it would not have a positive impact on the interests of the US dollar. The creation of cryptoSDRs is not intended to be controlled by economically powerful countries but to be established on top of sovereign countries, to serve countries more fairly and equally and to form a new supersovereign monetary and financial system.

The key to establishing a supersovereign currency lies in how to create a monetary system that transcends the sovereignty of each country. The policy activities and economic behaviors of various economically powerful countries are all aimed at safeguarding their fundamental interests. Therefore, relying solely on agreements or contracts cannot effectively achieve this goal. However, some researchers believe that the continuous expansion of the issuance scope of supersovereign currencies has caused the level of confusion in the world economic system to continue to rise and that SDRs cannot effectively replace the US dollar or euro as the major international currency.

Meanwhile, the development and optimization of the international monetary and financial system cannot be carried out only at the technical level. The formulation of related laws and regulations requires negotiation among various interest groups to achieve consensus. As the US has veto power in the IMF, the issuance and subsequent development of cryptoSDRs will inevitably be subject to the political agenda of the US. However, the expanding coverage of cryptoSDRs can reduce the dependence of other countries on the US dollar, thereby easing the pressure on US dollar reserves and effectively guaranteeing the status and value of the US dollar in the international monetary and financial system. Obviously, if the development and optimization of cryptoSDRs affect the status and value of the US dollar's international currency sovereignty and interests, the US will obstruct its further development. For other countries in the world, as their dependence on the US dollar continues to increase, they hope that a new supersovereign currency can emerge, forming a new international monetary and financial system to reduce their dependence on the US dollar and lower the impact of US dollar exchange rate fluctuations on their economy.[86]

Sixth, there are other difficulties. According to relevant researchers, there are still many obstacles to sustainably expanding the coverage of cryptoSDRs in practical applications. First, this measure will lead to a rise in operating costs. Currently, the US dollar and the euro already bear the function of payment media in international trade. Therefore, for cryptoSDRs to enter and occupy the market, significant costs are needed to maintain the normal operation and development of the market. Second, there is also an issue of uneven demand at the demand level. Meanwhile, due to the limited power of the IMF, it is difficult for the IMF to make all countries take unified action on power issues in the international market.[87] Therefore, the currency properties and free circulation of cryptoSDRs cannot be guaranteed. As the US dollar is the most valuable sovereign currency in the world, some scholars believe that cryptoSDRs cannot replace the US dollar as an international reserve currency.[88] However, other scholars believe that a supersovereign currency can exist and that the associated problems and loopholes can be effectively resolved through effective means. The premise is that the IMF and member countries reach consensus in various aspects and make a joint decision on the issuance and circulation of cryptoSDRs.

Currently, the internal mechanisms of the IMF involve a reassessment of the allocation of SDRs every five years and a decision on whether the US and the EU, among others, have veto power. This mechanism may make member countries feel unfair. Therefore, it is still very difficult to achieve a consensus among all member

---

[86] See footnote 56.

[87] BARRY EICHENGREEN. The Dollar Dilemma: The World's Top Currency Faces Competition [J]. Foreign Affairs, 2009(5), pp. 47–49.

[88] HUMPAGE O. F. Will Special Drawing Rights Supplant the Dollar? [EB/OL]. https://wallstreetpit.com/4204-will-special-drawing-rights-supplant-the-dollar/. Accessed 6 May 2022.

countries.[89] Some researchers believe that expanding the coverage and performance of SDRs has a positive effect, but SDRs cannot be developed into a supersovereign currency. The use of SDRs can effectively address the issue of some countries' abuse of power in currency and foreign exchange reserves, but due to limitations in scientific and technological development, it still takes a long time for SDRs to become a supersovereign currency. If restrictions are to be imposed on countries with privileges in currency reserve competition, such as limiting their currency usage and surplus, it is not enough to just focus on the centralization of SDRs. The scale of a basket of currencies needs to be constantly expanded, and the currencies of various countries need to be included in the basket to effectively promote the circulation and exchange of SDRs. The promotion of a diversified mode of a basket of currencies can ensure that the currency sovereignty of developed countries is not abused. However, if SDRs are reformed into a supersovereign currency in the international market, it will also have a significant impact on the existing foreign exchange market.[90]

(2) The Challenges of Implementing CryptoSDRs

The popularization and implementation of cryptoSDRs as a supersovereign currency require not only the support of a superpolitical entity and the empowerment of the IMF but also the combination of blockchain technology with SDRs. However, this process will inevitably face many obstacles.

First, there is a technological challenge. Apart from overcoming the technical difficulties that blockchain technology has yet to solve, cryptoSDRs would require solving their unique technical issues. As discussed earlier, cryptoSDRs need to adopt an alliance chain and a dual-layer structure, with node servers established in the IMF and each member country, to ensure transaction speed, stability, and coverage. At the same time, further research and testing need to be conducted on anonymity, system security, regulatory technology, and other aspects to ensure the feasibility of the cryptoSDR system.

Second, legal obstacles need to be overcome. As mentioned earlier, the currency status, legal validity, and regulatory issues of cryptoSDRs still require extensive discussions among experts and scholars worldwide before they can have a chance to be put into practice. Moreover, there is still much disagreement around the world regarding the legal status of nonsovereign cryptocurrencies and sovereign cryptocurrencies. Therefore, reaching a consensus on the legal status and regulatory issues of supersovereign cryptocurrency worldwide will take a very long time.

Third, there is the issue of circulation cost. When cryptoSDRs are issued and circulated using alliance chain technology, they cannot rely on individuals' spontaneous purchase of accounting equipment to support the entire system's operation, as with nonsovereign cryptocurrencies such as Bitcoin. Therefore, in the early stages of cryptoSDR implementation, a large number of node servers and various devices

---

[89] RICHARD N. COOPER. Necessary reform? The IMF and international financial architecture [J]. Harvard International Review, 2009(04), pp. 52–55.

[90] Li Lingyun. Formation and Influence of the "Dual Standard" International Monetary System [D]. Tianjin: Nankai University, 2010, pp. 186–189.

need to be purchased to support its operation. Moreover, during the operation phase of cryptoSDRs, a significant amount of funds is needed to support system maintenance, upgrades, operation and promotion, and dispute resolution. The sources of these funds need to be explored, and solutions need to be proposed by governments and industry experts. Therefore, issues related to operation cost, funding sources, and distribution are all obstacles that are currently hindering the implementation of cryptoSDRs.

Finally, there is the usage challenge. For cryptoSDRs to truly land and become a supersovereign cryptocurrency that can shake the position of the US dollar, they also need to become a major pricing tool in critical global fields such as bulk commodity trading, financial product pricing, and energy trading. Currently, the US dollar still firmly holds the pricing power of various important trades internationally, and breaking through this challenge would require the support of powerful economic entities.

2.4.4 The Possibility of Implementation of CryptoSDRs

From the previous discussion, it can be seen that the implementation of cryptoSDRs requires overcoming numerous difficulties. However, these obstacles are not insurmountable, and with the development of technology and the maturation of timing, these difficulties can be easily overcome.

First, there is a trend. The author believes that emerging market countries have a demand to eliminate the US dollar system and support a supersovereign currency. With the development of technology, combining blockchain technology with existing international organizations' credit-empowered currency units can make them supersovereign cryptocurrencies. This will promote greater stability in the international monetary system and reduce the risk of financial crisis outbreaks, and it is an inevitable trend. Moreover, with the development of technology and the continuous growth of emerging market countries, especially China, which has become the world's second-largest economy, it will likely lead the global reform process and formulate new global cooperation systems and policies, promote the emergence and implementation of supersovereign currency, create a new international monetary system, and gain a new dominant position in world politics and the economy, better maintaining the balance of the world pattern and serving all countries equally and fairly. This is also in the interest of the vast majority of countries in the world.

Second, there are advantages to supersovereign currencies. Rosensweig (2009) proposed that the emergence of supersovereign currency has a positive effect on the construction of the world economic system based on the nature of currency globalization. He believed that there was a certain degree of misunderstanding in the absence of a tax base and other defects of supersovereign currencies, as the key to currency lies in the establishment of a trust system, and the collection of taxes and fees only serve as a means and measure for establishing a trust system.[91] He also believed that in past international economic crises, the problems reflected the flaws and loopholes in government departments' management and issuance of currency, and the creation of cryptoSDRs could form organic connections between various economic entities worldwide and promote economic globalization and trade among all countries. At the same time, if cryptoSDRs are used as the main currency for foreign exchange reserves and major international currency, it can improve the trading efficiency of all parties in the international market, effectively enhancing the convenience and flexibility of business procedures. Additionally, since cryptoSDRs have the characteristics of a mixed currency, running them through a basket of currencies can effectively reduce exchange rate risks and ensure the stable development of world trade and investment in all countries.

CryptoSDRs will have a certain degree of impact on countries that are currently issuing international reserve currency. During the initial currency issuance and circulation phase of cryptoSDRs, these countries can receive some compensation through the allocation of cryptoSDRs to make up for the partial loss of revenue. Typically, countries that provide reserve currencies also receive a higher proportion of SDR allocations. The flow of cryptoSDRs can also effectively increase the purchasing power of member countries in the IMF. However, due to the dynamic fluctuations in the currency indicators of reserve currency issuing countries, the stability of the domestic economy may decrease. If the monetary reserve ratio of the central bank continues to be lowered, it will directly lead to inflation and further economic decline. China has a relatively positive attitude toward using SDRs as foreign exchange reserve currency. If cryptoSDRs can be successfully converted into China's foreign exchange reserve currency, it can reduce China's dependence on the US dollar and alleviate the impact of US dollar value fluctuations on the domestic economy. In the long run, Chinese yuan is also one of the currencies that make up the SDR basket, and the rise in the status of cryptoSDRs can effectively increase the status and influence of Chinese yuan in the world trade system.

Third, there is the upgrading of the currency carrier. Currently, SDRs cannot be used in the private market or international circulation, partly because the IMF does not have enough budget to print paper currency and transport it to various parts of the world for use by governments, residents, and enterprises. Another reason is that some countries may face physical and legal resistance. CryptoSDRs, through blockchain technology, have become a supersovereign currency that can circulate worldwide, and they do not require the high printing and transportation costs associated with traditional paper currency. As long as there is an Internet connection, cryptoSDRs can be used conveniently. Meanwhile, even if some countries resist cryptoSDRs, by legislating to prohibit the use of cryptoSDRs domestically, their citizens can still hold and use them in the online world. This allows cryptoSDRs to be used and circulated worldwide, greatly increasing the possibility of their adoption and popularity.

---

[91] J. A. ROSENSWEIG. Single Reserve Currency: An Analysis Of The Benefits And Challenges With Implementing A Single Reserve Currency [J]. Global Macroseconomic Perspectives, 2009, pp. 25–86.

Fourth, there is support from a super political entity. China is currently the world's second-largest economy country and has achieved world-leading positions in areas such as technology, military, politics, and finance. Especially during the COVID-19 pandemic, China became the only country in the world to have positive economic growth in the second half of 2020. The pandemic has reshaped the entire world and changed the positions of major countries to some extent. After the pandemic, China's comprehensive strength is closer to that of the US, bringing it closer to the center of the world stage and playing an important role in the establishment of a new international monetary system based on cryptoSDRs. The Russo-Ukrainian War, US interest rate hikes, and events such as the bankruptcy of Silicon Valley Bank have strengthened the global movement toward reducing dependence on the US dollar. At the same time, a new international monetary system is needed in the postpandemic era to replace the US dollar and the current international monetary system. The birth of cryptoSDRs and the establishment of a new international monetary system may in turn rapidly increase China's voice in the international monetary order, achieving a win–win situation between the construction of a new international monetary system and China's position elevation in the international monetary system.

Fifth, there is the power to price international major trades. As mentioned earlier, with China's support, cryptoSDRs have the opportunity to serve as a pricing unit in the international trade of rare minerals. In China's "A Belt and a Road" initiative, the use of Chinese yuan can be expanded in China's economic and trade exchanges with neighboring countries while promoting the use of cryptoSDRs. By using the supersovereign currency attributes of cryptoSDRs, some countries that do not yet trust Chinese yuan can also be brought into the "A Belt and a Road" scope, thus expanding China's economic and trade scope under the "A Belt and a Road" initiative.

To increase the usage rate of local currencies in trade and strengthen currency cooperation between China and neighboring countries to ensure smooth trade, the Chinese government, the China-Africa Development Fund Limited, and the China Development Bank signed the "Framework Agreement on Jointly Promoting the Establishment of a Fund and Actively Participating in the Strategic Cooperation of the Construction of the twenty-first Century Maritime Silk Road" in 2014,[92] and in 2015, the State Council released the "Vision and Actions on Jointly Building Silk Road Economic Belt and twenty-first-Century Maritime Silk Road." These international economic, trade, and currency cooperation initiatives led by China not only help improve the internationalization level of Chinese yuan but also support the promotion and popularization of cryptoSDRs. Meanwhile, the forms of economic, trade, and currency cooperation led by China, such as the Asian Infrastructure Investment Bank (hereafter referred to as the "AIIB") established in 2015, can also provide more channels for the circulation and investment of Chinese yuan and cryptoSDRs, effectively promoting the harmonious development of the internationalization of Chinese yuan and the monetization of cryptoSDRs.

[92] Website of the China State Council Information Office. Signing of the Strategic Cooperation Framework Agreement for the "Maritime Silk Road" Fund [EB/OL]. http://www.scio.gov.cn/ztk/wh/slxy/htws/Document/1379029/1379029.htm. Accessed 6 May 2022.

Chapter 3
Risks and Regulations in the Early Stage of the Birth of CryptoSDRs

Based on the introduction provided in the previous chapters, we can see that the birth of cryptoSDRs was a gradual process, and the reform of the IMF and SDRs followed a step-by-step approach. The order in which IMF member countries accepted and popularized cryptoSDRs also varied. Therefore, in the early stages of the birth of cryptoSDRs, different countries may have experienced different situations: some member countries of the IMF recognized and accepted cryptoSDRs first and allowed their citizens to exchange and use them domestically. Some of these countries may have quickly and fully adopted the use of cryptoSDRs, while others may have used cryptoSDRs alongside their sovereign currency. Some countries may have only allowed the use of cryptoSDRs in certain fields initially while continuing to use their sovereign currency in other areas. In addition, some member countries of the IMF may be unwilling to accept cryptoSDRs. They may restrict the flow of cryptoSDRs within their own country and even regard the use and trading of cryptoSDRs as illegal activities. In non-IMF member countries, some may not accept cryptoSDRs, but there may be countries that do not oppose their citizens using cryptoSDRs for transactions and may only define them as a new payment tool or financial asset.

Once cryptoSDRs are circulating in the market, there may be legal issues, including anti-money laundering, cross-border asset recovery, regulation, and currency substitution.

3.1 Supervision in the Early Stage of CryptoSDRs

At the beginning of the birth of cryptoSDRs, the international monetary system was in a state of multiple currencies coexisting and competing with each other. Some countries joined the IMF, while others did not. Some accepted cryptoSDRs as a currency, while others did not recognize their currency status and only treated them as financial assets. Some even prohibit their citizens from holding and using cryptoSDRs

L. Zeng, *A Study on the Creation, Impact and Legal Issues of Crypto Special Drawing Rights*, Modern China and International Economic Law,
https://doi.org/10.1007/978-981-99-9975-0_3

within their own country. Different countries have different legal definitions for cryptoSDRs, and their regulations on them are bound to differ.

To facilitate discussion, the author categorizes cryptocurrencies into three main forms based on the issuing authority: nonsovereign cryptocurrencies, sovereign cryptocurrencies, and supersovereign cryptocurrencies. By discussing the advantages and disadvantages of different cryptocurrencies and their regulations, the author provides reference and guidance for the legal positioning and regulation of cryptoSDRs.

3.1.1 Nonsovereign Cryptocurrencies and Their Regulatory Reference

(1) Nonsovereign Cryptocurrency

Nonsovereign cryptocurrency refers to cryptocurrency issued by private or nongovernmental organizations such as individuals or private companies, institutions, etc., using blockchain as the underlying technology, with decentralized, distributed storage, difficult attack, traceability, and other characteristics. The most typical representative is Bitcoin.

Since the birth of Bitcoin in 2009, thousands of nonsovereign cryptocurrencies with different functions and features have emerged in the blockchain world. Among them are powerful and Turing-complete Ethereum, as well as stablecoins such as USDT anchored to the US dollar. The reason why Bitcoin, as a nonsovereign cryptocurrency, can be held and circulated by many people mainly lies in trust. The value of sovereign currency comes from trust. Holding and circulation are based on trust in sovereign currency's value, so trust is the first element. From the perspective of ultimate value and purchasing power, Bitcoin is very similar to sovereign currency, and its value depends entirely on people's trust in it. "In God We Trust" written on the US dollar also applies to Bitcoin.[1]

In the early twentieth century, Austrian economist Hayek fully discussed the concept of nonsovereign currency in "Denationalization of Money": abolishing the central bank system, allowing individuals and private companies to issue currency and compete freely, and the competitive process will unearth the best currency.[2] Nonsovereign cryptocurrencies such as Bitcoin meet Hayek's requirements for nonsovereign currency, with the characteristic of being free from strong government intervention. Therefore, they have been sought after by most people for some time. However, it is worth mentioning that because nonsovereign cryptocurrencies do not have the endorsement of government credit, their monetary attributes are relatively poor, so they are prohibited from circulation and use in some countries. Nonsovereign cryptocurrencies have many shortcomings in terms of compliance,

[1] Jiang Liwen, Hu Yue. The Legal Nature and Challenges of Bitcoin [J]. Journal of Fujian Financial Management Cadre Institute, 2013 (4), pp. 12–17.

[2] FRIEDRICHA. VON HAYEK. Denationalization of Money [M]. London: Institute of Economic Affairs,1976, pp. 40–55.

legal scope of use, and liquidity. Currently, their credit value has not been widely recognized by the world, so they are not truly currencies but commodities that act as currencies in specific situations. In practice, the drastic fluctuations in the value of Bitcoin are due to its limited scope of use and influence, which makes it vulnerable to manipulation and speculation by speculators, and its inherent constraints are not fully demonstrated.[3]

(2) Legal positioning and regulation of Bitcoin in various countries for reference

To explore the legal positioning and regulation of cryptoSDRs, it is necessary to discuss the "king of nonsovereign cryptocurrency"—Bitcoin. Over the past decade, as the influence of Bitcoin has continued to expand, it has had varying degrees of impact on the economic environment and financial systems of countries around the world, and different countries have different attitudes toward it. While cryptoSDRs have not yet been universally recognized by all countries, they may be deemed illegal in some countries and subject to the same status and regulation as nonsovereign cryptocurrencies such as Bitcoin. Therefore, exploring nonsovereign cryptocurrencies such as Bitcoin can help us understand the regulatory scenarios of cryptoSDRs in non-IMF member countries.

At the end of 2013, the Central Bank of China issued a relevant announcement on the risks of Bitcoin, defining the concept and nature of Bitcoin as a virtual trading commodity, which does not enjoy the same status as legal tenders such as the Chinese yuan under the law. Bitcoin is not issued by the Central Bank of China, so the Chinese government cannot determine the specific issuance and circulation volume of this cryptocurrency, leading to Bitcoin not having legal debt obligations, being unable to be bound by law, lacking enforceability, and not being used as a currency for transactions and payments. It can only be traded as a network commodity. The Chinese government holds a skeptical attitude toward the security of Bitcoin and considers it to have certain transaction risks that cannot effectively guarantee the security and reliability of transactions. Therefore, Bitcoin is not considered a legal payment method in China.

Initially, Thailand had restrictions on the circulation and use of Bitcoin, but with the advancement of Internet technology and the development of fintech, the status of Bitcoin in Thailand has improved and has received policy support and encouragement from the Thai government. For example, in 2013, the Central Bank of Thailand believed that the legal status of Bitcoin was inconsistent with domestic laws in Thailand and therefore forcibly restricted any transaction activity involving Bitcoin. However, in 2014, the issuance and trading of Bitcoin received recognition from the Thai government, and the trading platform involving Bitcoin was allowed to resume operation.[4]

Just as China and Thailand have issued prohibitive regulations on Bitcoin, if in the future some countries do not recognize cryptoSDRs and the trading and circulation

[3] Jia Liping. Theory, Practice, and Impact of Bitcoin [J]. International Financial Research, 2013 (12), pp. 14–25.

[4] Zhou Ruijue. Legal Regulation of Blockchain Technology. Journal of Beijing University of Posts and Telecommunications (Social Sciences Edition), 2017(3), pp. 39–45.

of cryptoSDRs are restricted, then the supervision of cryptoSDRs in these countries will be weak. People in these countries can only hold and trade cryptoSDRs through illegal channels, and after converting their assets into cryptoSDRs, their assets may not be protected by the laws in these countries. Such results not only hinder the government's effective supervision of illegal activities but also indirectly encourage people to engage in illegal activities that are beyond supervision through cryptoSDRs, Bitcoin, and other cryptocurrencies.

In contrast, cryptocurrencies such as Bitcoin have been greatly accommodated and recognized in Malta. In February 2018, the Maltese government established the Malta Digital Innovation Authority and began providing a deep legislative framework for the cryptocurrency industry. This agency can provide user authentication for cryptocurrency platforms and support the application of blockchain technology in enterprises. The Maltese Prime Minister highly values Bitcoin and blockchain technology, proposing to turn Malta into a "legislative pioneer for global blockchain technology companies and the quality choice of world-class technology financial companies." He also proposed at an EU meeting to increase investment in cryptocurrencies and blockchain technology. That same year, the Maltese financial services agency began preparing for investments in compliant cryptocurrencies and authorized initial cryptocurrency offerings (hereafter referred to as the "ICOs").[5]

In 2017, the Bermuda government proposed supporting cryptocurrencies in the hope of attracting the cryptocurrency and blockchain industry and formulated corresponding policies to curb-related crimes. The Bermuda Monetary Authority released a proposal on "Regulating the Digital Asset Business" in April 2018, which aimed to implement anti-money laundering measures and provide a reasonable and friendly framework for cryptocurrency companies and start-ups. At the same time, the Bermuda government paid special attention to ICOs, and Bermuda banks also maintained an open attitude toward cryptocurrencies in accordance with government regulations.

Bitcoin and other cryptocurrencies are also quite popular in Estonia, and the government has been considering developing its own sovereign cryptocurrency called Estcoin. Compared to other Baltic countries, Estonia is considered the most convenient country for setting up cryptocurrency enterprises, with simple procedures and lower costs. However, cryptocurrency companies still need to apply for specific licenses, reflecting the country's clear and standardized legislative framework. In 2017, the Estonian government also proposed establishing a sovereign fund based on Bitcoin.[6]

Gibraltar's main industries are online gambling and financial services, attracting numerous banks, brokers, and headquarters of investment and insurance companies. It has also attracted many cryptocurrency and blockchain enterprises. In January 2018, Gibraltar established regulations for distributed ledger technology that can

[5] Blockchain Industry Service Platform. 12 Countries Supporting Bitcoin Globally in 2018 [EB/OL]. https://www.greendeco.com.cn/29604.html. Accessed 6 May 2022.

[6] Pencil Path. Understanding the Central Bank's Digital Currency with One Article [EB/OL]. http://m.sohu.com/a/345381277_649045/. Accessed 6 May 2022.

grant legal operating certificates to local cryptocurrency companies. In addition, the Gibraltar Financial Services Commission became the first regulatory agency in Europe to draft regulations for ICOs. Given that ICOs are still in legal gray areas in most countries, these regulations are undoubtedly very attractive to many groups or companies planning to conduct ICOs. On July 25, 2016, the Gibraltar Stock Exchange issued BitcoinETI, the first cryptocurrency-based security in Europe, officially incorporating cryptocurrency into its financial projects.[7]

Small countries that support Bitcoin, such as Malta, Bermuda, Estonia, and Gibraltar, hope to gain opportunities for technological and financial innovation through a shortcut, so they are more willing to actively participate in the emergence of cryptoSDRs and incorporate relevant regulatory requirements into their domestic laws. In this way, the regulation of cryptoSDRs will be more effective. Moreover, since the gambling industry and other industries in these countries are relatively open and developed, integrating cryptoSDRs will be more conducive to the government's anti-money laundering supervision and taxation of the gambling industry.

The Swiss city of Zug is home to several major cryptocurrency companies, such as Shapeshift and XAPO, earning it the nickname "Crypto Valley." It has passed several laws promoting cryptocurrency and related businesses, even accepting Bitcoin as a major payment method in daily life. Other regions of Switzerland, such as Chiasso, have also followed suit in supporting cryptocurrency policies. The Swiss national railway company also accepts Bitcoin as a payment method for purchasing train tickets.[8] In January 2018, the Swiss Minister of Economic Affairs announced at a private meeting on cryptocurrencies that Switzerland intends to become a major player in the cryptocurrency industry to maintain its status as a financial privacy country. In February 2018, a regulatory measure passed by the Swiss Financial Market Supervisory Authority stated that ICOs are considered securities in Switzerland. According to the news of February 2018, while sending and receiving Bitcoin does not require any identification, cryptocurrency companies must comply with Switzerland's anti-money laundering laws.[9]

Developed European countries such as Switzerland have sufficient financial confidence to acknowledge that cryptoSDRs have a specific currency status while using cryptocurrency to maintain their financial leadership position. This has a positive effect on the promotion and development of cryptoSDRs.

Belarus has already legalized cryptocurrency and blockchain technology nationwide. However, it does not grant cryptocurrency legal currency status and does not force individuals or businesses to use cryptocurrency instead of the Belarusian ruble. At the same time, Belarus allows foreign IT experts to stay in the country for up to 180 days without a visa. The Central Bank of Belarus announced that it will apply

[7] Ostrich Blockchain. Gibraltar Launches Regulation to Protect Cryptocurrency Value and Reputation [EB/OL]. http://dy.163.com/v2/article/detail/D780A1PQ0511QUF7.html. Accessed 6 May 2022.

[8] Chen Minxuan. Official issues first ICO license, can Bermuda become the next digital currency center? [EB/OL]. https://www.walian.cn/news/9454.html. Accessed 6 May 2022.

[9] Btctq.com. Swiss Economy Minister: Switzerland wants to become a "crypto-nation" [EB/OL]. http://www.btctq.com/a/01/569.html. Accessed 6 May 2022.

blockchain technology to the management of the Belarusian currency and stock market. In July 2017, the National Bank of the Republic of Belarus used blockchain technology for the first time to transfer bank guarantees.[10]

Developing countries such as Belarus want to benefit from the technological innovation brought by cryptocurrency, but they are hesitant to grant nonsovereign cryptocurrency such as Bitcoin legal currency status. They may be willing to actively develop and accept cryptoSDRs to a certain extent when they arrive, but they may need to consider joining international treaties that monetize cryptoSDRs. Overall, they will cooperate with the regulation of cryptoSDRs, which will be conducive to the experimentation and development of cryptoSDRs in these countries.

The Monetary Authority of Singapore (hereafter referred to as the "MAS") has maintained a neutral stance toward Bitcoin. In February 2018, the Deputy Prime Minister and Minister for Finance of Singapore stated that MAS would strengthen its regulation of cryptocurrencies and provide timely risk warnings. The MAS hopes to categorize the services of Bitcoin and other cryptocurrencies under a single regulation. However, the Deputy Prime Minister also noted that there is currently no foreseeable reason to ban Bitcoin, and Singapore is open to the application of cryptocurrencies.

International financial centers such as Singapore place greater emphasis on the financial attributes of nonsovereign cryptocurrencies such as Bitcoin and are more tolerant of technological financial innovation. They also have more experience in regulation. Therefore, after the creation of cryptoSDRs, they were able to more quickly and effectively accept cryptoSDRs, provide more effective advice and standards for regulation, and their relevant legislation can also serve as a reference for other member countries.

Japan is also at the forefront of international support for Bitcoin. For example, the location of the world's first Bitcoin exchange, Mt. Gox, was in Tokyo. The inventor of Bitcoin, Satoshi Nakamoto, is also a pseudonym for a Japanese person. Japan is one of the earliest countries to accept, legalize, and integrate Bitcoin. For instance, Japan is the first country in the world to approve Bitcoin as a legal currency, and it is also the first country to approve the establishment of more than 32 cryptocurrency exchanges. According to data from the first quarter of 2018, Japan has the world's largest trading volume for cryptocurrency assets, and many cryptocurrency exchanges in Japan do not charge transaction fees. In the first quarter of 2016, the Cabinet of Japan officially recognized Bitcoin's currency status in Japan. In Japan, Bitcoin is legal, and to avoid suppressing the development of Bitcoin, Japan's regulations on Bitcoin are not very strict. On April 1, 2017, Japan's cryptocurrency law officially came into effect, mainly managing capital requirements and the safe operation of exchanges. The Accounting Standards Board of Japan formulated a handling method for cryptocurrency in the first quarter of 2017. Japan's largest bank, MUFG, plans to issue its own cryptocurrency and separate Bitcoin accounts from other transactions. Japan's Ministry of Finance and regulatory agencies have proposed that the

[10] IT Xiaobai Ge. Belarus signs new law, giving blockchain technology protection [EB/OL]. http://m.sohu.com/a/212408220_100035093. Accessed 6 May 2022.

legal status of cryptocurrencies, represented by Bitcoin, should be recognized from a policy perspective, and relevant implementation rules and legal schemes have been formulated. If the enacted bill can be smoothly implemented, according to relevant institutional regulations, a series of transaction activities and behaviors related to cryptocurrencies such as Bitcoin should be registered with the Financial Bureau in advance. In addition, Japan legally stipulates that the trading value of Bitcoin can be equivalent to the US dollar, which can effectively guarantee the security of Bitcoin transactions while implementing efficient management and supervision of relevant transaction activities.[11]

Germany's attitude toward Bitcoin is both supportive and restrictive. While Germany recognizes Bitcoin as a form of currency, it has also attempted to impose further regulatory restrictions on cryptocurrencies such as Bitcoin. In February 2018, at the G20 summit, Germany and France jointly called for a more serious investigation and stricter restrictions on Bitcoin and other cryptocurrencies. That same year, Deutsche Bank proposed stringent regulations on cryptocurrencies. However, overall, Germany's restrictions on cryptocurrencies are relatively minor.[12]

Japan and Germany are both representatives of developed countries, and they are very mature in terms of technology and finance. They not only recognize the currency status of cryptocurrencies such as Bitcoin but also have relatively few restrictions and constraints on them. As financial powerhouses, Germany and Japan have more experience and ability to bear the risks of financial innovation and obtain the benefits of technological progress and financial innovation. Therefore, after the creation of cryptoSDRs, they and other developed countries are more capable of participating in the monetization of cryptoSDRs and formulating complete financial regulatory rules to cope with their operation and circulation.

As early as 2013, the US formulated relevant policies and laws and regulations on the use of personal accounts for cryptocurrencies. Among them, regulations in the state of New York define currency as the US dollar or any other country's coins and banknotes that can circulate and be widely used and accepted. As a medium of exchange, different from cash banknotes, "virtual" currency is another medium of exchange that operates like currency in certain environments but does not have all the attributes of real currency. In particular, virtual currencies do not have legal currency status in any jurisdiction. The "convertible" virtual currency mentioned in the regulations either has the same value as real currency or can be used instead of real currency. The US Department of the Treasury has stated that the only currency that can have legal payment status in the US and can flow and be used normally in transactions is coins or banknotes that are circulated domestically or internationally, issued by the state and can circulate and be used as a medium of exchange in daily transaction activities. However, compared with physical currencies, cryptocurrencies

---

[11] Nikkei. Japan eyes treating bitcoins the same as real money [EB/OL]. https://asia.nikkei.com/Politics-Economy/Policy-Politics/Japan-eyes-treating-bitcoins-the-same-as-real-money. Accessed 6 May 2022.

[12] Qiu Bijun. 2018 Global Currency Circle Regulatory Trends: Different Attitudes from Various Countries, However, You Need to Know! [EB/OL]. https://www.qqbite.com/bitcoin/3196.html. Accessed 6 May 2022.

can also be used as a medium of exchange in certain internal and external transaction environments and can circulate and be used as legal physical media, but they do not have all the basic characteristics of physical currencies and cannot obtain the same legal status as physical currencies.

In August 2015, the state of New York in the US issued policies related to the Bitcoin market, which stipulated that both parties involved in any transaction and trading activities related to Bitcoin must be registered with the government and obtain a transaction license (hereafter referred to as the "BitLicense") issued by the government. This ensures that the transaction is legally allowed and protects the basic rights of both parties. The policy also recognizes two types of transactions that do not require government authorization: first, transactions and trading activities that occur and are conducted under the New York banking law system and are regulated by the government; second, activities related to using Bitcoin for the purchase, sale, or investment of goods or services. In the practical implementation of the policy, the government must continuously promote its regulatory role in the Bitcoin market. When registering for government records, relevant personal identity information must be carefully investigated and recorded, and relevant data must be backed up and saved. Cryptocurrency start-ups can obtain conditional government authorization when they do not yet meet the requirements of relevant policies. At the same time, the government will conduct stricter and more comprehensive audits and investigations on related enterprises and continuously monitor their actual development status during normal operation. The validity period of the government license is generally only two years. The registration and storage period for application information for BitLicense has been reduced from ten years to seven years.[13] At a macrolevel, BitLicense adjusts the concept and essential features of cryptocurrency, recognizes the legal status of cryptocurrency through policy, optimizes policies and restructures systems based on the different actual situations of cryptocurrency enterprises.[14]

The US is the most proactive in researching and legislating nonsovereign cryptocurrencies such as Bitcoin. As the most powerful country in the current international monetary system, the US has gained many benefits from the international currency status of the US dollar, and its technology and military power are world-class. Currently, many financial innovations internationally originate from the US, and it will not easily give up any opportunities for technology and financial innovation. However, whether a nonsovereign cryptocurrency threatens the status of the US dollar is another matter. If the US can dominate the creation of cryptoSDRs, the birth of cryptoSDRs is imminent, relying on the US's powerful military and technological strength. However, this premise must be that the US continues to maintain its existing dominant position in the international monetary system. Controlling cryptoSDRs will ensure that the US continues to receive excess income, such as a "seigniorage tax," and the regulation of cryptoSDRs and the development of related regulatory rules

---

[13] New York State Department of Financial Services (NYSDFS). BitLicense [EB/OL]. https://www.dfs.ny.gov/reports_and_publications/press_releases/pr1509221. Accessed 6 May 2022.

[14] Zhou Ruijue. Legal Regulation of Blockchain Technology. Journal of Beijing University of Posts and Telecommunications (Social Sciences Edition), 2017(3), pp. 39–45.

will also be dominated by the US and centered on US interests. In addition, if the US is concerned about losing its benefits and attempts to continue to maintain the dominant position of the US dollar, it will continuously restrict and obstruct the creation of cryptoSDRs. At this point, there needs to be a country with sufficient strength to lead and unite the forces of many countries and international organizations to promote cryptoSDRs, and the rules and regulations for cryptoSDRs will be the result of balancing the interests of multiple countries and will be more reasonable and fair.

From the various countries' regulations on nonsovereign cryptocurrencies, led by Bitcoin, we can see different attitudes toward the new form of fintech in each country. The listed regulations on the issuance and trading of cryptocurrencies demonstrate a more positive attitude and active embrace of cryptocurrencies. This relatively open policy and practice are worth considering and learning from in China, especially the "BitLicense" enacted by the state of New York in the US, which provides certain access and operational constraints for enterprises engaged in blockchain fintech experiments without completely banning it and allowing for controllable regulation, which is conducive to innovation and development in blockchain finance. At the same time, based on the different attitudes of different countries toward cryptocurrencies, China can also infer and explore regulatory issues after the birth of cryptoSDRs and actively participate and pursue the creation of cryptoSDRs and the formulation of regulatory rules.

3.1.2 *Sovereign Cryptocurrencies and Legal Status*

(1) Sovereign Cryptocurrency

Sovereign cryptocurrencies are cryptocurrencies issued by the government or central bank of a sovereign state, with the same legal status and attributes as the fiat currency issued in the country. Jacob Goldsmith (2020) defined sovereign cryptocurrencies as cryptocurrencies backed by national credit in the book "The IMF Must Develop Best Practices before Government-Backed Cryptocurrencies Destabilize the International Monetary System."[15] The digital currency issued by China is a sovereign cryptocurrency. Sovereign cryptocurrencies complement and replace fiat currency issued by the government in different scenarios. For example, in terms of value storage and online transactions, sovereign cryptocurrencies complement the shortcomings of cash, while in most offline payment scenarios, they are substitutes. More importantly, sovereign cryptocurrencies have better compliance, a wider range of use and circulation, and more comprehensive monetary attributes than nonsovereign cryptocurrencies. As cryptocurrencies not only reduce the cost of currency issuance and increase convenience but also make financial services more accessible to remote

[15] JACOB GOLDSMITH. The IMF Must Develop Best Practices Before Government-Backed Cryptocurrencies Destabilize the International Monetary System [J]. Emory International Law Review, 2020(2), pp. 595–638.

areas not easily covered by bank financial resources, many central banks and financial institutions in various countries have expressed recognition of the positive role of cryptocurrencies. According to a survey by the Bank for International Settlements (hereafter referred to as the "BIS"), approximately 80% of central banks in the world are currently researching sovereign cryptocurrencies, more than 40% of central banks have entered the experimental stage, and 10% of central banks are in the research and development stage of sovereign cryptocurrencies. China is in a leading position in the world in the research of sovereign cryptocurrencies.

The People's Bank of China released a development strategy for the digital currency of Chinese yuan in 2016, and at the meeting, it first explicitly defined the name of China's digital currency as DC/EP. In 2017, the People's Bank of China established the Digital Currency Research Institute, and in 2019, it piloted DC/EP mobile payments in Shenzhen. In August 2020, China's Ministry of Commerce issued a notice on the comprehensive deepening of pilot schemes for innovative development of trade in services, proposing that DC/EP would first be piloted in regions including Beijing-Tianjin-Hebei, Yangtze River Delta, Guangdong-Hong Kong-Macao Greater Bay Area, and central and western regions, as well as the location of the 2022 Winter Olympics for testing, and eventually expanded to other areas of China, including major cities such as Beijing, Shanghai, and Hong Kong. Currently, DC/EP has been used nationwide in China.[16]

To catch up with China's research progress in sovereign cryptocurrency, countries such as the US, Switzerland, the UK, and Japan have begun to negotiate the design standards for sovereign cryptocurrency. At the same time, the US has also accelerated the process of sovereign cryptocurrency at the legislative level. In March 2020, the US Congress included a plan to issue cryptocurrency of the US dollar in three proposals to stimulate the economy during the COVID-19 pandemic. In April of the same year, some members of the House of Representatives proposed issuing US dollar cryptocurrency to provide relief to the American people. Although the final version of the proposal did not include information about US dollar cryptocurrency, it can be seen that the US government is making efforts to promote it. In May 2020, the US government published a white paper entitled "The Digital Dollar Project: Exploring a US Central Bank Digital Currency (hereafter referred to as the "CBDC")," which proposed a framework for creating a US CBDC and set out its promotion plan.[17]

The Bank of England and the University of London jointly developed the sovereign cryptocurrency RScoin in March 2016. According to the plan, individuals, companies, and commercial banks can open accounts on a central bank-controlled sovereign cryptocurrency trading platform and settle funds directly with the central bank. In

[16] Shi Jianxun, Liu Yu. The Significance and Countermeasures of the Legal Digital RMB on the Internationalization Strategy of RMB [EB/OL]. https://doi.org/10.14100/j.cnki.65-1039/g4.20201102.001. Accessed 6 May 2022.

[17] Bai Jinfu, Bai Xi. New Patterns of Currency Competition and Central Bank Digital Currency. Financial Theory and Practice Exploration, 2020(3), pp. 3–9.

March 2020, the Bank of England also issued an opinion paper on the issuance of a sovereign cryptocurrency, CBDC.[18]

Furthermore, Canada began developing its own cryptocurrency called CADcoin in 2016. The project, named JASPER, was jointly formed by the Canadian payment institution PAYMENTS, the Distributed Ledger Alliance R3, and several commercial banks.[19] In addition, the MAS launched the sovereign cryptocurrency project Ubin in June 2017, releasing the digital currency SGD. Ubin was created by several commercial banks in Singapore, the Distributed Ledger Alliance R3, and Deloitte Accounting Company.[20]

Tunisia allows its citizens to use its own sovereign cryptocurrency to conduct commodity transactions and even to pay for utilities such as water and electricity.[21] Sweden also published a report on its sovereign cryptocurrency, the e-krona, in September 2017 and tested its use in a pilot environment in 2020.[22] In December 2017, the National Bank of Denmark released an analytical report on CBDC, which emphasized that the decision to issue CBDC was essential for Denmark and needed to be treated with great caution.[23]

Christine Lagarde, the President of the European Central Bank, stated in an interview that the European Central Bank organized experts to discuss and explore various forms of the euro CBDC and analyze the pros and cons, further promoting the development of the euro CBDC at the end of 2019.[24]

Compared with nonsovereign cryptocurrencies, sovereign cryptocurrencies have many unique features beyond the adoption of blockchain technology, such as distributed storage and peer-to-peer transaction settlements. First, due to the need for regulated monetary policies and prevention of financial market volatility risks, the issuance of cryptocurrency by countries still needs to be centralized. Sovereign cryptocurrencies will be uniformly issued and controlled by the currency issuing institutions of each country, which have national credit endorsements and enforceability. This is conducive to government regulatory supervision, strengthens the transparency

[18] Bank of England. Central Bank Digital Currency Opportunities, Challenges and Design, Bank of England [EB/OL]. https://www.bankofengland.co.uk/paper/2020/central-bank-digital-currency-opportunities-challenges-and-design-discussion-paper. Accessed 6 May 2022.

[19] Babite. Bank of Canada unveils digital currency experiment, using blockchain to create CAD-Coin [EB/OL]. https://www.8btc.com/article/93547. Accessed 6 May 2022.

[20] He Dexu, Yao Bo. Practice, Influence and Countermeasures of Legalizing RMB Digital Currency. Financial Review, 2019(5), pp. 116–117.

[21] Sohu. Tunisia to Replace its National Digital Currency eDinar with Monetas Currency Driven by Blockchain [EB/OL]. https://www.sohu.com/a/235535833_100180465. Accessed 6 May 2022.

[22] RIKSBANK. The Riksbank to Test Technical Solution for the E-Krona, Riksbank [EB/OL]. https://www.riksbank.se/en-gb/press-and-published/notices-and-press-releases/notices/2020/the-riksbank-to-test-technical-solution-for-the-e-krona/. Accessed 6 May 2022.

[23] Danmarks National Bank. Central Bank Digital Currency in Denmark? [EB/OL]. https://www.nationalbanken.dk/en/publications/Documents/2017/12/Analysis%20-%20Central%20bank%20digital%20currency%20in%20Denmark.pdf#search=CBDC. Accessed 6 May 2022.

[24] PIERRE-HENRI DE MENTHON, SABINE SYFUSS-ARNAUD. Interview with Christine Lagarde, President of the ECB. [EB/OL]. https://www.ecb.europa.eu/press/inter/date/2020/html/ecb.in200108~f3ba434000.en.html. Accessed 6 May 2022.

of circulation, and even implements real-name authentication to ensure the stability of the transparency and legal ownership of cryptocurrencies.

Second, to maintain the system stability of sovereign cryptocurrencies, improve transaction speed and security, and meet the daily transaction needs of millions of transactions within a country or even globally, the currency issuing institutions of each country will not adopt the same "mining" mechanism as Bitcoin but only allow specific banks or institutions to have accounting rights and are not fully open to everyone.

Third, due to the changes in national production and the need to maintain value stability, sovereign cryptocurrencies need to be adjusted according to market and policy total demand. In general, the increase in the issuance of currency should be as close as possible to the inflation rate, which can ensure the value stability of cryptocurrencies and reduce the currency depreciation caused by loose monetary policies.[25]

Last, due to the deep-rooted use of paper currency and the long process of market education for cryptocurrencies, sovereign cryptocurrencies will coexist with paper currency for a certain period of time. However, with policy guidance and the formation of people's habits of using cryptocurrencies, sovereign cryptocurrencies will eventually replace paper currency. Similar to the gradual maturity of China's third-party payment market, such as WeChat and Alipay, cash payments have gradually decreased, and some developed countries are conducting research on paperless transactions. The circulation of cryptocurrencies has become inevitable.[26]

(2) Legal Positioning and Advantages of Sovereign Cryptocurrency

Currently, the development and experimentation stages of sovereign cryptocurrencies are ongoing in various countries, and many specific regulations have yet to be established. Discussions are also underway regarding the legal and technical regulations for the supervision of sovereign cryptocurrencies.

Although sovereign cryptocurrencies are issued by a government's central bank or its monetary authority, the laws of sovereign states often only specify the legal status and legal tender of paper currency. Therefore, governments of sovereign states also need to modify corresponding laws and regulations to give sovereign cryptocurrencies legal status. For example, Article 16 of the People's Bank of China Law states, "The legal currency of the People's Republic of China is Chinese yuan. All public and private debts within the territory of the People's Republic of China shall be paid in Chinese yuan." Article 20 specifies: "No organizations or individuals may produce or sell tokens or digital tokens to replace Chinese yuan in circulation in the market." In October 2020, China issued a draft amendment to the People's Bank of China Law and an explanation of the draft amendment, which included Article 19 stating: "Chinese yuan includes physical and digital forms," and Article 22 stating:

---

[25] Zhang Rui. Traditional Finance Innovation and Reform Based on Blockchain. Southwest Finance, 2016(10), pp. 18–23.

[26] Zeng Jinhai. Legal Analysis and Enlightenment of Cryptocurrency. Information Security and Communications Privacy, 2019(11), pp. 71–79.

"No organizations or individuals may create or sell tokens or digital tokens to replace Chinese yuan in circulation in the market."[27] However, these legal provisions only establish that digital currency has the same legal status as paper currency, and the specific legal status of DC/EP needs to be more clearly defined in relevant laws and regulations, such as the People's Bank of China Law, the Commercial Bank Law, and the Regulations on the Administration of Chinese yuan, to ensure the legal currency status and mandatory circulation of China's sovereign cryptocurrency.[28] In addition, future legislation needs to specify the characteristics, styles, and production methods of DC/EP, which are not currently included in the provisions of the People's Bank of China Law regarding the denominations, patterns, and styles of Chinese yuan. The legal effectiveness of DC/EP also requires unanimous approval by the National People's Congress or its Standing Committee to have sufficient national credibility support.

Moreover, while sovereign cryptocurrencies are similar in form to traditional bank accounts, Alipay, WeChat, and other electronic payments, they focus more on M0 replacement. According to traditional currency theory, M0 refers to cash in circulation. Correspondingly, M1 refers to M0 plus demand deposits, M2 refers to M1 plus personal deposits, time deposits of units, foreign currency deposits, margin deposits of securities companies, and other deposits, and M3 refers to M2 plus financial bonds, commercial bills, large negotiable certificates of deposit, and other financial assets.[29] For the most basic currency M0 replacement, the currency authority places greater emphasis on ensuring the legal currency status and cash management and anti-money laundering requirements of M0. For example, in the current design of DC/EP in China, it is stated that it focuses more on M0 replacement than M1 or M2 replacement. Commercial banks, as the second-level distribution institution, need to deposit full reserves with the Central Bank of China in exchange for DC/EP. For the Central Bank of China, DC/EP is its liability, which is guaranteed by its credit and has unlimited legal tender.[30]

The struggle for control of sovereign cryptocurrencies in the Internet space has become a major point of competition among countries at the international level. The reason why increasingly more countries are constantly emphasizing investment and research and development in sovereign cryptocurrencies is because they have many advantages.

---

[27] People's Bank of China. "Notice of the People's Bank of China on Publicly Soliciting Opinions on the Draft Amendments to the Law of the People's Republic of China on the People's Bank of China." [EB/OL]. Available at: http://www.gov.cn/zhengce/zhengceku/2020-10/24/content_5553847.htm. Accessed 6 May 2022.

[28] Duan Jinyu. Legal Barriers and Solutions for China's Digital Currency—A Case Study of Bitcoin. Northern Economy and Trade, 2020(3), pp. 62–64.

[29] People's Bank of China. "Interim Measures for Statistics and Publication of Monetary Supply." [EB/OL]. Available at: https://www.pinlue.com/article/2018/09/1809/017273406401.html. Accessed 6 May 2022.

[30] Zhang Qian, Zhang Hongxu. The Role of DC/EP in the Internationalization of RMB. Financial Observer, 2020(10), pp. 52–53.

First, sovereign cryptocurrencies can reduce the problem of lags in monetary policy transmission. The circulation of sovereign cryptocurrencies can allow monetary policy to be directly reflected in the regulation of wallets for sovereign cryptocurrencies. This enables central banks' monetary policies to directly adjust the demand for funds in the market, transmit interest rate effects directly to the private market, and guide the direction of commercial bank loans, which helps to improve the effectiveness of monetary policy tools.

Second, sovereign cryptocurrencies can promote innovation in central bank monetary policy tools. Since sovereign cryptocurrencies are in electronic form, unlike traditional paper cash, they can implement monetary policies that were impossible during the paper currency era. For example, by increasing or decreasing corresponding funds in the electronic wallets of sovereign cryptocurrencies proportionally, the degree of inflation can be controlled.

Third, information is more transparent. Through the sovereign cryptocurrency system, central banks can have a clearer understanding of real-time information on individual and corporate consumption and lending. This is conducive to the accurate understanding of the macro and microeconomic situations of the country's economic growth, inflation level, and international balance of payments and thus to making accurate judgments.

Fourth, maintain financial stability. Sovereign cryptocurrencies can effectively reduce market risks such as anti-money laundering and anti-terrorism financing, reduce the rollover risk and transition period conversion of the financial market, and thus help enhance financial stability.

Fifth, maintain a competitive payment system. In the COVID-19 pandemic, the use of cash has significantly decreased in the market, and electronic payments are gradually occupying the private payment market. Monetary authorities in various countries need a new means of payment to maintain the healthy and stable operation of their economic and financial systems and to continue to gain the trust of the people to guarantee the soundness of the official payment system.

Sixth, enhance the potential of cross-border payments and occupy the international payment market. Governments can tap into the cross-border payment potential of their sovereign cryptocurrencies by promoting their circulation domestically and internationally, thus enabling their financial systems to expand into other countries and promoting the development of financial products and services in financially underdeveloped areas.

Although sovereign cryptocurrencies have various advantages compared to paper currency, there may be some conflicts between the two before sovereign cryptocurrencies completely replace paper currency. To reduce the impact of sovereign cryptocurrencies on the existing financial system, central and commercial banks in various countries need to take appropriate risk prevention measures in advance. For example, after the popularization of sovereign cryptocurrencies, most of the deposits of commercial banks will be transformed into sovereign cryptocurrencies as a new value storage method, which may cause the traditional operating model of commercial banks to be unable to survive and a crisis in the traditional financial system, and the traditional deposit and loan model may undergo substantial changes. Therefore, central banks of various countries need to balance the relationship between sovereign cryptocurrency, paper currency, and deposits.

Moreover, the promotion of sovereign cryptocurrencies does not mean the disappearance of nonsovereign cryptocurrencies, but the latter may be marginalized. However, nonsovereign cryptocurrency may still exist as an asset and be priced in sovereign cryptocurrency units, similar to the valuation method of stocks and real estate today. It is even possible that some countries may establish a special cryptocurrency market for various nonsovereign cryptocurrencies to be traded, similar to today's stock trading market, where the market discovers and evaluates their true value.[31]

3.1.3 The Legal Status and Supervision of CryptoSDRs

Supersovereign cryptocurrency and supersovereign currency have some similar characteristics, as they are both issued by authoritative international organizations or multiple governments and can legally circulate in multiple countries and regions. Supersovereign credit and international cryptocurrency have a natural fit; that is, supersovereign credit is attached to the blockchain value carrier, thus creating supersovereign cryptocurrency. Currently, the most likely candidate for a supersovereign currency is the SDR issued by the IMF with the joint recognition of most countries in the world. Before the G20 summit in 2009, Zhou Xiaochuan, the former governor of the Central Bank of China, suggested that the role of the SDRs should be fully utilized to create an international reserve currency that is decoupled from sovereign states and can maintain long-term currency stability, and the SDRs have the characteristics and potential of a supersovereign currency.[32] Joseph Stiglitz, the Nobel laureate in economics, proposed reforming the current US dollar-centered international monetary system by increasing the role of SDRs.[33] At the same time, by drawing on the path and practice of the EMU becoming the euro and promoting the combination of SDRs and blockchain technology, it will greatly improve transparency, convenience, and scope of use and may become a supersovereign cryptocurrency, cryptoSDRs.

As the SDRs are issued by the IMF, their legal status requires authorization from the IMF's Articles of Agreement during their monetization process. Additionally, member countries accepting cryptoSDRs must incorporate appropriate provisions into the corresponding conventions, recognizing the legal status and legal tender of cryptoSDRs as their responsibility and obligation. They must also legislate and ensure the legal currency status of cryptoSDRs in their domestic laws. Therefore,

[31] Zhang Rui. Traditional Finance Innovation and Reform Based on Blockchain. Southwest Finance, 2016(10), pp. 18–23.

[32] Zhou Xiaochuan. Thoughts on Reforming the International Monetary System. Theoretical Reference, 2009(10), pp. 4–5.

[33] Stiglitz, et al. Stiglitz Report: Reforming the International Monetary and Financial Systems in the Aftermath of the Global Crisis [M]. Translated by Jiang Shu. Beijing: Xinhua Press, 2011, p. 4.

cryptoSDRs will have different legal statuses in the domestic laws of both IMF member and nonmember countries.

First, for member countries, the legal currency status of cryptoSDRs can be obtained by following the example of sovereign cryptocurrencies. CryptoSDRs can only be considered the currency of member countries if they join the IMF, sign the corresponding international treaties and accept cryptoSDRs as a supersovereign currency. This means that member countries must allow cryptoSDRs to have the same legal tender and legal status as their sovereign currencies, allowing free circulation within their borders.

The legal currency status of cryptoSDRs stems from the fact that the IMF has the right to issue supersovereign currency. However, there are three important issues that need to be addressed to acquire this right:

First, there is the legal basis for issuing supersovereign currency. The issuance of supersovereign currency is an international public power that requires agreement between the IMF and its member countries to determine the specific currency value form of expression, amount, total quantity, distribution, and circulation methods of cryptoSDRs. "No authorization, no exercise of power" is one of the basic principles of exercising public power. Therefore, the issuance of cryptoSDRs requires the IMF to amend its Articles of Agreement to grant cryptoSDRs legal currency status and to require all member countries to transfer their monetary power to the IMF's currency issuing institution. At the same time, an international convention must be drafted to grant the IMF the power to issue supersovereign currency and commit member countries to grant legal currency status and legal tender status to cryptoSDRs in their domestic laws.

The second is the establishment of the legal status of cryptoSDRs as legal tender. Granting a currency legal currency status involves issues of national currency sovereignty for each country and requires each member country to establish the legal status of legal tender currency in its corresponding domestic laws and regulations. Therefore, for cryptoSDRs to circulate legally and have legal currency status and currency enforcement power in each member country, each member country needs to modify its relevant currency laws through national-level legislative means and grant them legal currency status and legal currency status.

The third is the relationship between cryptoSDRs and the sovereign currencies of each member country. The sovereign currencies issued by each member country may be ordinary paper currency, sovereign cryptocurrencies, or both paper currency and sovereign cryptocurrencies issued by a country at the same time. When cryptoSDRs also obtain the same currency status and legal currency status as the sovereign currency or sovereign cryptocurrencies in member countries, they may create conflicts and substitution issues. Member countries need to clarify the legal currency status and currency relationship of cryptoSDRs with the sovereign paper currency or sovereign cryptocurrencies in their relevant currency laws. Member countries can allow their sovereign currencies to have a higher circulation right than cryptoSDRs for a certain period of time. After cryptoSDRs gradually become popular, the circulation rights of cryptoSDRs should be increased. Here, the circulation right refers to the priority of receiving a certain currency without legal punishment when users receive transaction payments. Although cryptoSDRs and other forms of sovereign currencies have the same legal currency status, it takes time and education for them to become the main currency within a member country, as there are exchange rate differences. Therefore, it is necessary to have a transitional period where citizens can convert prices or display prices of the same product in two currencies until cryptoSDRs become popular. Before cryptoSDRs became popular, it was impossible to force everyone to quickly accept them as payment tools in all transactions and financial fields. Citizens should be allowed to accept sovereign currencies while allowing some people to try to accept cryptoSDRs.

Currently, the regulations of currencies in countries around the world are mainly based on paper money and coins, and the design of currency issuance systems is also based on the characteristics of paper money and coins. For example, the legal status of the euro is stipulated in Article 128(1) of the Treaty on the Functioning of the European Union (hereafter referred to as the "TFEU"): "Bank notes issued by the European Central Bank and the central banks of the Member States shall be the only legal tender currency of the Union." Therefore, to establish the legal currency status of cryptoSDRs, it is necessary for the EU to modify relevant laws to enable cryptoSDRs to circulate within the EU.

Similarly, Section 31 of the Coinage Act of 1965 in the US stipulates that "coinage and currency of the US (including circulating notes of Federal Reserve banks and national banks) is legal tender for all debts, public charges, taxes, and dues." This provision clearly establishes the property of paper money and coins as legal tender currencies. If cryptoSDRs are to circulate within the US, the US will need to modify the Coinage Act to include cryptoSDRs in the legal tender currency.

Although China has already implemented the sovereign digital currency DC/EP in cities such as Shenzhen, the relevant laws in China have not yet paved the way for the formal issuance of DC/EP. For example, according to Article 4, paragraph 1, item 3 of the Law of the People's Bank of China, the People's Bank of China has the right to issue Chinese yuan and manage its issuance and circulation on behalf of the state. However, according to Article 2 of the Regulations on the Administration of Chinese yuan, the currency that the People's Bank of China can legally issue currently only includes physical currencies such as paper money and coins and does not include intangible digital currencies such as DC/EP. Therefore, if cryptoSDRs are to circulate within China, similar to DC/EP, relevant laws and regulations will need to be modified to give them legal currency status.[34]

Meanwhile, the relationship between cryptoSDRs and the sovereign currencies of member countries is a topic that deserves careful consideration. The circulation of cryptoSDRs relies on electronic devices and networks, making it susceptible to objective situations where these necessary conditions are not available. Furthermore, some users may encounter difficulties in operating cryptoSDRs due to factors such as

[34] Yu Pinxian. Analysis of Legal Issues of Central Bank Digital Currency [J]. Journal of Shanghai University of International Business and Economics, 2020(2), pp. 88–102.

their education level, age, and habits. This may lead to a situation where cryptoSDRs and a country's sovereign currency coexist for an extended period of time when circulating within that country.

In addition, while cryptoSDRs share certain features with paper money and coins, such as anonymity and universality, they may require an interest rate advantage to gradually replace bank deposits as a substitute. Without such an advantage, a country's bank deposits may also coexist with cryptoSDR accounts for a period of time and form a competitive relationship.

Taking into account the factors mentioned above, during the initial period of the birth of cryptoSDRs, they will coexist with sovereign currencies. However, corresponding legal modifications are necessary to recognize the coexistence between them, prevent major conflicts and clarify the obligations of citizens and businesses to receive certain legal tender currencies and the order in which they will receive different types of currencies. Each enterprise also needs to know which currency to choose as the unit of account for its balance sheet, income statement, and commodity prices and to understand the legal restrictions associated with these currencies.[35]

Article IV, Section 5(a) of the IMF Articles of Agreement stipulates that "actions taken by a member in accordance with this Article with respect to its own currency shall be considered by the Fund as applying to all currencies of other members accepted by that member under Article XXXI, Section 3.2(g), unless the member declares that its action applies only to the currency of the metropolitan area or to certain other currencies, or to the currency of the metropolitan area and certain other currencies." Paragraph (b) of the same section stipulates that "actions taken by the Fund under this section shall be considered as relating to all currencies of the member referred to in (a) above, unless the Fund otherwise specifies." This provision indicates that, unless there are special reasons, IMF member countries should also accept the currencies of other member countries. CryptoSDRs have monetary attributes and, as a supersovereign currency issued by the IMF, should have the same currency status as the member country's currency.

For non-IMF member countries, the legal positioning and regulatory issues of cryptoSDRs can be referred to the practices of various countries in the world regarding the legal positioning and regulation of nonsovereign cryptocurrencies such as Bitcoin. Currently, after Bitcoin opened the era of cryptocurrencies and blockchain, it is considered the most influential and penetrative killer application of cryptocurrencies and blockchain, and regulatory authorities in different countries still have different attitudes toward it. Drawing on the regulatory experience of these countries with regard to cryptocurrencies such as Bitcoin, it is beneficial for academia to study and explore the regulatory issues that cryptoSDRs may face in nonmember countries after their creation.

[35] M. Kumhof, C. Noone. Central Bank Digital Currencies——Design Principles and Balance Sheet Implications [EB/OL]. https://www.bankofengland.co.uk/-/media/boe/files/working-paper/2018/central-bank-digital-currencies-designprinciples-and-balance-sheet-implications. Accessed 6 May 2022.

Different countries have different attitudes toward Bitcoin, leading to varying legal and regulatory frameworks. Therefore, nonmember countries can be divided into two categories based on their attitudes toward the use of cryptocurrencies: the first category of nonmember countries accepts the circulation of cryptoSDRs domestically, allowing their citizens and companies to hold and use them, but they do not recognize their legal currency status, nor do they join international agreements to monetize cryptoSDRs, and therefore they do not have corresponding rights and obligations. These countries will define cryptoSDRs as financial products and regulate them by extending laws and regulations related to financial products. The attitude of these countries is similar to that of Singapore at present.

The second category of nonmember countries prohibits the circulation of cryptoSDRs domestically, does not recognize the legal currency status of cryptoSDRs, and even does not define them as financial products. They also prohibit their citizens and companies from holding and using cryptoSDRs, resulting in no specific regulatory issues regarding SDRs in these countries. The attitude of these countries is similar to that of China and Thailand, which ban Bitcoin.

Article 11 of the IMF Agreement sets out the relationship between member and nonmember countries, the most important of which is that member countries must not violate the interests and objectives of the IMF and the IMF Agreement in transactions or activities with nonmember countries. The global circulation of cryptoSDRs issued by the IMF certainly complies with the interests and objectives of the IMF and the IMF Agreement. Therefore, the circulation of cryptoSDRs in nonmember countries should also be encouraged and supported by the IMF and member countries.

Finally, for the IMF, cryptoSDRs need to obtain the status of a supersovereign currency, which requires the IMF to reform and empower its board of directors to establish a corresponding monetary authority, with member countries ceding their currency issuance rights to the IMF and providing detailed regulations and empowerment regarding cryptoSDRs and corresponding currency issuance institutions in its articles of agreement. Article 15, Paragraph 2 of the IMF Agreement stipulates that the method of determining the value of SDRs is determined by a majority vote of 70% of the total voting rights of the Fund. However, changing the principle of fixed value or fundamentally changing the application of existing principles requires a majority of 85% of the total voting rights to pass. Therefore, as long as more than 85% of the voting rights are obtained, the fixed value method and principles of SDRs can be changed.

Currently, Article 17, Paragraph 3 of the IMF Agreement does not specify the holdings of individuals and companies other than member states. Therefore, adding nonofficial holders such as individuals and companies to this paragraph is necessary to promote the use of cryptoSDRs. At the same time, it is also necessary to change or abolish the principle of "necessity" in Article 19, Paragraph 3 of the IMF Agreement, to support private sector transactions using SDRs and support the monetization of cryptoSDRs. According to Article 28(a) of the IMF Agreement, if more than 85% of the total voting rights of member states accept amendments, the IMF Agreement can be amended. Appendix B, Article 7 of the IMF Agreement specifies the price of SDRs, which means that SDRs have value and can be circulated in encrypted form.

3.2 Research on Anti-money Laundering of CryptoSDRs

In the early days of the emergence of cryptoSDRs, only some countries were likely to accept and recognize them, while others would not participate in them, and some even banned their circulation. This was because cryptoSDRs and other cryptocurrencies were technically highly mobile, distributed, and, to some extent, anonymous, making it possible for them to circulate without relying on any traditional banking system of any country. Furthermore, governments cannot prevent the circulation of cryptoSDRs by using traditional methods such as blocking IP addresses on the Internet.

These features also made cryptoSDRs susceptible to being used for money laundering. In countries that participated in cryptoSDRs, authorities could prevent and track money laundering by viewing real-name system information. However, countries that did not participate in cryptoSDRs did not have this authority. Therefore, it was likely that in countries that did not accept cryptoSDRs, they would be used for money laundering by criminals.

Compared to traditional currency money laundering, the use of cryptoSDRs for money laundering occurred in countries that did not participate in cryptoSDRs. This made it faster and more challenging to track, increasing the difficulty of anti-money laundering work in these countries.

To effectively curb the spread of criminal activities such as money laundering and terrorist financing on the Internet, it was necessary for financial crime law enforcement agencies in countries that did not participate in cryptoSDRs to further strengthen cooperation with the IMF, share information, and develop specialized anti-money laundering regulations for cryptoSDRs.[36]

3.2.1 *Money Laundering Models of CryptoSDRs*

During the early stages of the emergence of cryptoSDRs, compared to traditional money laundering crimes, money laundering crimes using cryptoSDRs were less likely to be detected and traced. Steven David Brown believes that the characteristics of cryptocurrency can be utilized by money launderers and can play different roles in the three stages of money laundering: placement, layering, and integration.[37] Moreover, cryptoSDRs and cryptocurrencies share similar properties, and their use in money laundering is the same. In the placement stage of money laundering, the criminal can exchange illicitly obtained funds into cryptoSDRs through decentralized cryptoSDR providers or decentralized cryptoSDR exchanges. These cryptoSDR providers and exchanges can offer exchange and transaction services for cryptoSDRs.

---

[36] MOHAMMED AHMAD NAHEEM. China's dirty laundry-international organizations posing a risk to China's AML systems [J]. Journal of Money Laundering Control, 2018(2), pp. 189–202.

[37] STEVEN DAVID BROWN. Cryptocurrency and criminality: The Bitcoin opportunity [J].The Police Journal: Theory, Practice and Principles, 2016(89), pp. 327–339.

In the layering stage, the criminal can convert purchased cryptocurrency and cryptoSDRs back and forth between different accounts and different cryptocurrencies, making it difficult to trace illegally obtained funds. Finally, in the integration stage, the criminal can typically use cryptoSDRs to cash out in casinos or purchase real estate, insurance, high-value items, etc., to legitimize their proceeds.[38] In practice, criminals use several methods to launder money, including.[39]

(1) Money Laundering through CryptoSDR Exchanges

After cryptoSDRs are launched and begin to circulate, their purchase and usage are similar to most cryptocurrencies. Currently, there are many ways to purchase cryptocurrency, and compared to buying with cash at a Bitcoin ATM, money launderers prefer to buy cryptoSDRs through cryptoSDR exchanges. This is because ATM operators usually need to comply with anti-money laundering requirements set by financial regulatory authorities, while many exchanges may passively apply regulation or deliberately ignore anti-money laundering procedures to cater to user demand. Some centralized exchange service providers may require identity verification, but money launderers can still evade identity verification by using false identities or stealing others' identities or using straw men or agents while combining anonymous electronic wallets, untraceable VPN networks, and even dedicated networks to achieve transaction anonymity. The European Council's Cybercrime Global Project and the Committee of Experts on the Evaluation of Anti-Money Laundering and Countering the Financing of Terrorism Measures (hereafter referred to as the "MONEYVAL") pointed out that money launderers often use the irreversible and immediate settlement services provided by the cryptocurrency system to achieve the confidentiality of their cryptocurrency transactions.[40] These characteristics are also possessed by cryptoSDRs, and in nonmember states where they are not recognized as currency, they will become tools for money laundering, similar to cryptocurrencies.

(2) Person-to-person Money Laundering

After the emergence of cryptoSDRs, peer-to-peer transactions can also be conducted, similar to cryptocurrencies. Through direct online or offline transactions between individuals using cryptoSDRs, exchange between cryptoSDRs and legal tenders as well as exchange between different cryptocurrencies can be realized to inject funds into the accounts of criminals of cryptoSDRs without the intervention of third parties. One typical method employed by money launderers is to hire "money mules" to

[38] NORMAH OMAR ZAITONHAMIN, WAN ROSALILI WAN ROSLI. Airing Dirty Laundry: Reforming the Anti-Money Laundering and Anti-Terrorism Financing Regime in Malaysia [J]. Global Jurist, 2016(16), p. 128.

[39] Shi Xiuxia. Prevention and Control Strategies for Money Laundering Crimes Using Virtual Currency [J]. Journal of the People's Public Security University of China (Social Science Edition), 2016(1), pp. 1–11.

[40] Council of Europe Global Project on Cybercrime and MONEYVAL. Criminal Money Flows on the Internet: Methods, Trends and Multistakeholder Counteraction [EB/OL]. http://www.coe.int/t/dghl/monitoring/moneyval/Typologies/MONEYVAL(2013)6_Reptyp_flows_en.pdf. Accessed 6 May 2022.

help them carry out their online money laundering crimes. For example, "money mules" use bank accounts or other electronic cash accounts (such as Alipay and PayPal) to transfer fiat currency funds received from other bank accounts or electronic cash accounts to other accounts or to withdraw the funds in cash. Then, they can use cryptoSDRs of the same value to transfer these funds to the accounts of money laundering criminals. Finally, criminals use cryptoSDRs in different countries or regions to exchange legal tenders. In short, the transfer of funds between different accounts can directly or indirectly interrupt the flow of funds of money launderers, thereby achieving the effect of blocking tracking. During this process, the "money mules" earn commissions, and the criminals achieve their money laundering purposes. Individuals who act as third parties may either be accomplices in money laundering crimes or unwittingly act as "money mules." Regarding how to recruit unsuspecting "money mules," criminal actors often use false recruitment information, for example, posting job positions such as "financial managers" or "remote workers" on job recruitment websites.[41]

(3) Money Laundering Using the Vulnerability of Cryptocurrency Accounts to Cyber Attacks

Using blockchain technology, the utilization of cryptoSDRs is highly secure. However, cryptoSDR holders are at risk of having their account passwords for their cryptocurrency wallets stolen by traditional phishing or hacking methods, resulting in losses. As most cryptoSDR transactions in the future are expected to be conducted without face-to-face interactions, individuals may abuse legitimate accounts they control to launder cryptoSDRs. As described by the FATF in their report, online payment methods are often used to launder proceeds from identity theft, fraud, hacking, phishing, and other illicit activities, and the anonymity of cryptocurrencies enables the transfer of these funds to untraceable locations.[42]

Money launderers may also crack the identities of legitimate users to open cryptoSDR accounts and use them as intermediaries to obscure the trail of criminal proceeds, impeding regulatory oversight. To avoid leaving traces of cryptoSDR purchases, launderers often use mixing services to exchange transaction addresses of their primary currency with temporary addresses in mixing service pools or use more anonymous cryptocurrencies such as Monero Token to evade exchange analysis. This completely severs the audit trail of cryptoSDRs, forex, and wallet addresses, preparing the way for the reintegration of illegal gains into traditional financial systems.

Moreover, individuals frequently combine cryptoSDRs with other payment technologies to incorporate multiple laundering techniques into the process of cleaning

[41] Council of Europe Global Project on Cybercrime and MONEYVAL. Criminal Money Flows on the Internet: Methods, Trends and Multistakeholder Counteraction [EB/OL]. http://www.coe.int/t/dghl/monitoring/moneyval/Typologies/MONEYVAL(2013)6_Reptyp_flows_en.pdf. Accessed 6 May 2022.

[42] The Financial Action Task Force (FATF). Money Laundering Using New Payment Methods [EB/OL]. http://www.fatf-gafi.org/media/fatf/documents/reports/ML%20using%20New%20Payment%20Methods.pdf. Accessed 6 May 2022.

illicit proceeds, such as with laundering software "Quick Launder," bank transfers, cash withdrawals, digital currencies, "money mules," and fund remittance services. This renders the illicit gains untraceable code that can be anonymously transferred to other countries or converted into digital currencies.[43] Therefore, for law enforcement agencies, monitoring and tracing the flow and destination of criminal cryptoSDR funds becomes exceedingly difficult.

However, for member countries that recognize the status of cryptoSDRs as a currency and use it as their national currency, it is a supersovereign cryptocurrency issued by the IMF and differs significantly from nonsovereign cryptocurrencies in terms of legal attributes and technical settings. Especially in terms of real-name authentication, it will require member country governments to authenticate relevant accounts through real-name authentication, effectively identifying the account holder, thereby avoiding regulatory loopholes and preventing it from becoming a breeding ground for money laundering such as nonsovereign cryptocurrencies. Moreover, it can better utilize the global transparent cryptoSDR information network for anti-money laundering supervision and positioning, even setting up corresponding anti-money laundering mechanism codes in advance on the cryptoSDR blockchain and controlling and cracking down on anti-money laundering behavior through smart contracts and other means.

Money laundering crimes often occur between different countries, and it is often difficult to trace the evidence chain of money laundering. However, member countries of cryptoSDRs typically keep financial data and digital assets of their own citizens, and therefore, the country where the money laundering crime occurs can obtain the entire evidence chain by applying to the IMF for access to financial information of other member countries, thus better carrying out anti-money laundering activities. On the other hand, nonmember countries that do not recognize cryptoSDRs as a currency and have not joined the corresponding agreement cannot reach an information sharing agreement with the IMF to trace the flow of funds, and their citizens can only register and use cryptoSDRs privately without the knowledge of the government. Therefore, money laundering crimes in these countries will continue to occur, and the emergence of cryptoSDRs may even exacerbate money laundering crimes in these countries.

3.2.2 The Anti-money Laundering Dilemma of CryptoSDRs

Due to the anonymity and other characteristics of cryptoSDRs, there are many difficulties in tracking and enforcing them when they are used for cross-border money laundering crimes.

[43] DORAN, MICHAEL DENNIS. A Forensic Look at Bitcoin Cryptocurrency [M]. Ann Arbor: ProQuest LLC, 2014, p. 19.

(1) Jurisdictional Ambiguity and Difficulties in the Application of Evidence Rules

Due to the anonymity and other characteristics of cryptoSDRs, there are many difficulties in tracking and enforcing them when they are used for cross-border money laundering crimes.

Determining jurisdiction and applicable law are two major challenges in judicial practice after a cross-border infringement of cryptoSDRs occurs. The determination of jurisdiction and applicable law will directly affect the litigation costs and rights protection results of the victims.

First, due to the distributed storage of cryptoSDRs, all data and applications are deployed on the blockchain and stored in node servers of the IMF or member countries. These node servers can be distributed in any corner of the world to some extent, which means that jurisdiction can be distinguished. However, nonmember state governments do not have jurisdiction over these node servers. When nonmember state residents use cryptoSDRs for cross-border money laundering in nonmember state territories, the nonmember state will encounter difficulties in combating money laundering. Moreover, cryptoSDRs have anonymity features for nonmember countries. Therefore, there is currently no clear and uniform standard or regulation for determining the jurisdictional court based on the location of the money laundering activity (usually the location of the launderer's computer), the place where the infringement occurred (usually the server location of the cryptoSDR trading platform), the defendant's domicile, or the plaintiff's domicile.

When cryptoSDRs cause cross-border legal disputes, the reasonable determination of jurisdiction is still a thorny problem with unpredictable outcomes. Although there are some international treaties for cross-border cybercrime, countries still lack corresponding domestic legislation, and there is a lack of uniform international rules or treaties to regulate money laundering crimes using cryptoSDRs.[44]

Currently, Article 15 of the United Nations Convention against Transnational Organized Crime and Article 42 of the United Nations Convention against Corruption establish the jurisdictional principles for international money laundering crimes, including territorial jurisdiction, personal jurisdiction, passive personality jurisdiction, protective jurisdiction, universal jurisdiction, and the "extradite or prosecute" principle for cases where extradition is refused on the grounds of nationality. With the exception of territorial jurisdiction and the "extradite or prosecute" principle, which are mandatory obligations, the other forms of jurisdiction are optional obligations, meaning that contracting states can choose the jurisdictional standards that best serve their interests. Of course, these conventions do not prevent contracting states from exercising any form of jurisdiction under their domestic law as long as they do not violate general international legal principles, which to some extent provides a useful solution for jurisdictional disputes regarding cryptocurrencies. However, since the jurisdictional powers stipulated by the above conventions are mostly optional,

[44] Lin Liangchun. Research on the Legal Issues of Bitcoin. Citizen and Law (Law Edition), 2015 (10), pp. 8-11.

different countries may apply different jurisdictional standards based on their own interests, which may lead to a lack of cooperation agreements.[45]

Furthermore, Article 6(2)(c) of the United Nations Convention against Transnational Organized Crime and Article 23(2)(c) of the United Nations Convention against Corruption set out jurisdictional standards for transnational money laundering crimes, requiring that contracting states must satisfy the dual criminality principle before exercising jurisdiction over such crimes. However, the upstream crimes of transnational money laundering may also include various forms of cybercrime, which further complicates the determination of jurisdictional authority.[46]

In addition, due to significant differences in the integration and social impact of cryptoSDRs in different nonmember countries, the legal provisions of different countries vary greatly.[47] This can lead to completely different litigation results for the same cryptoSDR transaction depending on the applicable law. Determining the governing law in cross-border cryptoSDRs litigation is both a matter of great concern to the parties involved and a very difficult problem in cross-border judicial practice. The practice of cryptoSDRs in nonmember countries can be compared to the case of Bitcoin.[48] For example, in 2014, the FBI shuts down a black market shopping website that used anonymous technology Tor as its operating tool, which mainly traded in prohibited items such as drugs and weapons. For people who purchased drugs online, cryptocurrencies such as Bitcoin were necessary. From February 2011 to July 2013, the website's transaction volume reached more than $1.2 billion. When the FBI arrested the website's controllers, they also confiscated 30,000 Bitcoins, which were later sold at an auction for nearly $17.7 million. Due to the anonymity of the website and Bitcoins, users involved in money laundering were spread across different countries. In addition, the unclear jurisdiction and difficulty in tracing funds made it difficult to impose sanctions on users of the money laundering website.[49] The emergence of cryptoSDRs will also lead to different results in the same case due to differences in applicable laws and regulations between member and nonmember countries.

(2) Difficulties in Obtaining Evidence

Undoubtedly, difficulty in obtaining evidence is another difficult problem faced by nonmember countries in dealing with anti-money laundering of cryptoSDRs. On

---

[45] Shi Xiuxia. Prevention and Control Strategies for Money Laundering Crimes Using Virtual Currency [J]. Journal of the People's Public Security University of China (Social Science Edition), 2016(1), pp. 1–11.

[46] Yu Zhigang. The Era of "Transnational Information Crime" and China's Choice of the <Cybercrime Convention>—Additionally, on the Reshaping of the Idea and Rules of Criminal Jurisdiction over Cybercrime [J]. Law Forum, 2013(2), pp. 94–104.

[47] Lou Yaoxiong, Wu Jun. Legal Analysis of Bitcoin Issues. Journal of Beijing University of Posts and Telecommunications (Social Sciences Edition), 2013 (4), pp. 25–31.

[48] Shu Shuang. A Brief Discussion on the Nature of Currency [J]. Economic Research Guide, 2012(3), pp. 97–98.

[49] 51CTO. The fall of the online black market "Silk Road" [EB/OL]. http://netsecurity.51cto.com/art/201311/415727.htm. Accessed 6 May 2022.

the one hand, since cryptoSDRs are essentially a set of computer character codes, ownership acquired through transactions or gifts is completed online. Therefore, when there is a legal dispute or criminal activity, the relevant evidence that the parties can provide and that the court can review and use mostly consists of electronic evidence. Considering that electronic evidence is highly susceptible to illegal network attacks, without sound computer security protection measures, electronic evidence is vulnerable to tampering and damage, leading to loss of its value as evidence or even complete loss.[50] Taking China as an example, although China's laws regulate electronic evidence, there are still shortcomings such as unclear concept definitions, lack of a complete regulatory system, ambiguous evidence classification, and incomplete evidence rules.[51]

On the other hand, the anonymity of cryptoSDRs determines the difficulty in obtaining evidence when proving money laundering crimes. Currently, most cryptocurrency service and transaction providers do not perform real-name authentication on users or adopt rules of "one-time use, anytime replacement." This greatly exacerbates the difficulty in proving money laundering and terrorist financing crimes. As one type of cryptocurrency, cryptoSDRs face the same problem. Even if relevant departments of non-IMF member countries track the network path of the flow of cryptoSDRs, it is still difficult to identify the specific actors in the real world.[52] More importantly, money launderers can use the characteristics of cryptoSDRs to innovate their money laundering methods, making it impossible for regulatory agencies to predict and prevent.

Money laundering criminals often evade capture by exploiting the difficulty of obtaining evidence in a timely manner. With the emergence of cryptoSDRs, these criminals may find it even more convenient to launder money. For instance, in March 2018, a hacker used a phishing attack to take control of numerous accounts on a popular cryptocurrency exchange. Within just 30 min, the hacker sold a significant amount of Bitcoin from these accounts and used the proceeds to purchase a lesser-known cryptocurrency, artificially inflating its price. The hacker then sold this currency at a higher price on other exchanges, making a tidy profit and eluding law enforcement. This type of innovative financial technology-based crime poses a dual challenge for regulatory agencies: not only is it increasingly difficult to prevent such crimes, but it is also challenging to collect evidence that can be used to prosecute the perpetrators.[53] Moreover, the fact that cryptoSDRs are backed by international organizations could lead to the emergence of even more sophisticated financial technology crimes.

[50] Shi Danlin, Li Xiuping. Monetary and Banking Studies [M]. Beijing: Tsinghua University Press, 2012, p. 11.

[51] Lou Yaoxiong, Wu Jun. Legal Analysis of Bitcoin Issues. Journal of Beijing University of Posts and Telecommunications (Social Sciences Edition), 2013 (4), pp. 25–31.

[52] Lin Liangchun. Research on the Legal Issues of Bitcoin. Citizen and Law (Law Edition), 2015 (10), pp. 8–11.

[53] Sina Finance. Binance Suspected to Have Been Attacked, Causing Failure and a Sudden 10,000% Surge in VIA Price [EB/OL]. http://finance.sina.com.cn/stock/usstock/c/2018-03-08/doc-ifxpwyhv7094818.shtml. Accessed 6 May 2022.

(3) Enforcement Difficulties

From the characteristics of cryptoSDRs, it can be inferred that money laundering using cryptoSDRs can easily involve different countries, including member and nonmember countries that have adopted the use of cryptoSDRs. The nationality of the money launderer, the location of the crime, the country of detention, or the country of escape may all be different. If there is no extradition agreement between these countries, the enforcement of the judgment may be interrupted even if there is sufficient evidence. Meanwhile, because funds laundered using cryptoSDRs can easily flow across national borders, it may be difficult to determine the illegality of the laundered funds in a country where the source of the funds is confirmed to be illegal. This is because the funds may have already been laundered through channels such as entering a foreign casino or investing in real estate using cryptoSDRs, and as a result, it may be impossible to enforce the judgment on illegally obtained assets outside of the jurisdiction where the judgment was issued.

Taking Bitcoin as an example, the final civil judgment of Heilongjiang Provincial Higher People's Court [2016] Hei Min Zhong No. 274 showed that the suspect obtained 12 million Chinese yuan through fraud. Afterward, the suspect recharged 2 million Chinese yuan to the OKCOIN Bitcoin trading platform using someone else's identity information, and within one and a half hours, he made 34 purchases of 553.0346 Bitcoins worth approximately 2 million Chinese yuan in total. The suspect then transferred all the Bitcoins in four transactions within one hour to their own Bitcoin wallet and sold them through an underground money market in Macau, thus achieving the transfer and laundering of illegal funds. The judgment stated that because the platform did not fulfill its review and regulatory obligations in a timely manner, the suspect was able to complete the money laundering crime smoothly, resulting in the huge financial loss of the victim and the inability to recover the funds.[54]

3.2.3 Current International Anti-Money Laundering Laws and Regulations

The FATF, one of the most important global anti-money laundering international organizations, has released the "Guidance for a Risk-Based Approach to Virtual Currencies" (2015) and "Recommendations of the Financial Action Task Force" (hereinafter referred to as "FATF Recommendations"). These international rules apply a risk-based approach to combating money laundering and terrorist financing using cryptocurrencies. The recommendations and reports published by the FATF are recognized by the international community, and these rules and standards have

[54] Jinli International. Bitcoin platform was once used by criminals to launder money: daily trading reached over 40,000 coins [EB/OL]. http://max232.net/btb/kuangye/6252.html. Accessed 6 May 2022.

been determined to some extent by most countries as their international obligations to address anti-money laundering and terrorist financing.

According to the "FATF Recommendations," the FATF mainly proposes the following standards and obligations for combating money laundering using cryptocurrencies[55]:

(1) They clearly require countries to ensure that financial institutions and specific nonfinancial industries identify and assess the sources and flow of funds and take effective measures to reduce the risk of money laundering and terrorist financing, including the relevant risks of cryptocurrencies in the payment process ("FATF Recommendations" Article 1).
(2) The FATF requires countries to use independent and reliable source documents, information, or data to conduct due diligence on customers when establishing business relationships or conducting transactional activities with cryptocurrency trading providers.
(3) Regarding the anonymity feature of cryptocurrency in the transaction process, the country should require the transaction providers of cryptocurrency to follow the best practices suggested in the "Risk-based Approach Guidelines for Prepaid Cards, Mobile Payments, and Internet-based Payment Services" (2013), including verifying customer identity information (ID number) through information from third-party databases or other reliable sources, collecting relevant data from the network to verify consistency with customer transaction information, and tracking and locating customer IP addresses while complying with relevant privacy protection legislation in each country.
(4) Analysis and evaluation of the source of funds.
(5) At present, multisignature technology can be used in cryptocurrency transactions to limit their value or speed, thereby mitigating the critical risk of "transaction monitoring." However, cryptocurrency still lacks effective means to impose geographical restrictions to prevent peer-to-peer transfers or to restrict its use to specific products and services.
(6) The government should encourage the monitoring of transaction risks related to blockchain transactions. Decentralized cryptocurrency transactions cannot authenticate users, making it difficult to monitor transactions and identify suspicious activities. Therefore, there is a high risk of money laundering and terrorist financing. Countries should strengthen the application of transaction monitoring technology to eliminate these risks.
(7) Article 20 of the FATF Recommendations stipulates that when cryptocurrency transactions involve proceeds of crime or terrorist financing, the following transaction records should be kept: public key, private key, address, username, identity information of both parties, transaction nature and date, and amount. Article 15 of the FATF Recommendations requires that financial institutions and certain nonfinancial institutions registered or operating within a country implement

[55] Shi Xiuxia. Legal Regulation of the Risk of Money Laundering Using Virtual Currency [J]. Southern Finance, 2016(6), pp. 81–88.

necessary risk control and risk management measures when using new products, new business models, or new technologies related to cryptocurrency.

The Budapest Convention on Cybercrime (hereafter referred to as the "Budapest Convention") is the first international convention on cybercrime worldwide.[56] Its main objective is to strengthen international cooperation on the basis of relatively unified cybercrime policies to prevent harm and abuse to confidentiality, integrity, and availability of computer systems, networks, and computer data. Articles 2.2 (illegal access), 2.3 (illegal interception), 2.6 (misuse of devices), and 2.8 (computer-related fraud) of the Budapest Convention are related to the use of cryptocurrencies and cryptoSDRs for money laundering. Although the Budapest Convention came into effect in 2004, before the emergence of blockchain technology and the advent of cryptoSDRs, it seeks to respond to the development of new information technologies based on the standards and values of the Council of Europe, as stated in its preamble. Therefore, it can be understood that the Budapest Convention is equally applicable to cryptoSDRs based on new information technologies. In particular, the act of laundering cryptoSDRs through improper means such as network attacks and fraudulently obtaining personal cryptoSDR accounts can be deemed a crime in cyberspace under the Budapest Convention. Member states can prosecute this type of cryptoSDR money laundering based on relevant provisions and reach international cooperation on this basis. As cryptoSDRs are a type of cryptocurrency, they will also be subject to international conventions such as the FATF Recommendations and the Budapest Convention on anti-money laundering regulations and supervision.

3.3 Research on the Cross-Border Recovery Mechanism of CryptoSDRs as Corrupt Assets

The anonymity, distributed storage, and global convenience of cryptoSDRs in nonmember countries make them an easy tool for cross-border criminal and illegal activities. This has facilitated illegal activities to a certain extent. In the future, corrupt individuals may prefer to transfer their illegal gains to other countries in the form of cryptoSDRs, increasing the invisibility of their illegal assets and making cross border recovery more difficult.

[56] Council of Europe. Convention on Cybercrime [EB/OL]. https://www.coe.int/en/web/conventions/full-list/-/conventions/treaty/185. Accessed 6 May 2022.

Currently, there is much research on the cross-border recovery of general corrupt assets[57] and legal issues related to cryptocurrencies,[58] but there is no literature on how to recover corrupt assets in the form of cryptoSDRs. This section discusses the characteristics and challenges of the cross-border recovery of cryptoSDRs as corrupt assets and argues that the IMF and the entire international community should strengthen legislation and judicial cooperation to facilitate the cross-border recovery of corrupt assets. In addition, the traceability and real-name sharing features of cryptoSDRs' international flow will help member countries recover corrupt assets transferred in the form of cryptoSDRs.

3.3.1 Features of Cross-Border Recovery of CryptoSDRs as Corrupt Assets

Due to the anonymity and easy transfer of cryptoSDRs in nonmember countries, it will become a preferred way for corrupt individuals to transfer their corrupt assets. However, since it is difficult to establish a unified international legal standard for cryptoSDRs in nonmember countries, they will not be easily recognized and recovered. As cryptoSDRs become more popular, more corrupt assets may be transferred in this form, making cryptoSDRs a target for cross-border pursuit.

In the cross-border recovery of corrupt assets, "corrupt property" is defined as "criminal proceeds" in Article 2(e) of the United Nations Convention against Corruption, which refers to assets obtained from criminal activities. In China's current legal system, "corrupt property" mainly refers to the assets involved in the case, including criminal proceeds and their interests, assets involved in the case and their interests, and prohibited items illegally held.[59] "Border" not only refers to the physical borders or national borders but also includes the boundaries of different legal systems. The United Nations has pointed out in its Implementation Guide to the United Nations Convention against Corruption that many corrupt criminals can find shelter in other "legal domains."[60]

[57] For example, Zheng Hongguang. The Impact of the United Nations Convention against Corruption on Improving China's Overseas Asset Recovery Mechanism. Liaoning Rule of Law Research, 2007(3), pp. 59–62. Li Zongli. Study on the Cross-border Recovery of Corruption Crimes. Journal of Hebei University of Science and Technology (Social Sciences Edition), 2010 (3), pp. 41–46. Many articles have suggested ways to improve China's cross-border recovery of corrupt assets through interpretation and study of the United Nations Convention against Corruption.

[58] TREVOR I KIVIAT. Beyond Bitcoin: Issues in Regulating Blockchain Transactions [J]. Duke Law Journal, 2015(65), pp. 569–608.

[59] People's Republic of China. "Provisions on the Management of Property Involved in Criminal Proceedings by the People's Procuratorates," Article 2. [EB/OL]. Available at: http://politics.people.com.cn/n/2015/0309/c70731-26662761.html. Accessed 6 May 2022.

[60] United Nations Office on Drugs and Crime. Legislative Guide for the Implementation of the United Nations Convention against Corruption [M]. Vienna: United Nations Office at Vienna English, Publishing and Library Section, 2012, pp. 194–196.

As cryptoSDRs, a special type of "corrupt property," the cross-border recovery of corrupt assets in this form is also unique.

(1) Unique Characteristics of Corrupt Assets in the Form of CryptoSDRs

The cross-border pursuit of cryptoSDRs refers to the recovery of illegally obtained funds and assets by corrupt individuals through criminal acts such as corruption, which have been transferred abroad in the form of cryptoSDRs. The goal is to recover SDRs that have been used as corrupt assets and to surrender the recovered funds and assets to the National Treasury or return them to the victims.

In Chap. 1, Section 3.2 of the United Nations Convention against Corruption, "proceeds of crime" is defined as "any property derived from or obtained, directly or indirectly, through the commission of an offense," and "property" is defined as "assets of every kind, whether corporeal or incorporeal, movable or immovable, tangible or intangible, and legal documents or instruments evidencing title to, or interest in, such assets."[61] In accordance with Article 74 of the German Criminal Code, seized objects include "property obtained intentionally through criminal activity, or objects used for or intended to be used for criminal activity, that is, objects resulting from criminal activity and criminal tools."[62] According to Article 64 of China's Criminal Law, assets obtained through corrupt activities include three forms: illegally obtained assets, prohibited items, and the perpetrator's own assets used for criminal purposes, including movable and immovable property, tangible and intangible assets. Therefore, as an asset of corruption, cryptoSDRs can be recovered, and they are also a special type of corrupt asset.

CryptoSDRs, as corrupt assets, have unique properties. In terms of physical attributes, cryptoSDRs are defined as intangible assets, similar to cryptocurrencies, in nonmember countries and can be identified as proceeds of crime and recovered. In terms of location, cryptoSDRs exist wherever there is a network, both domestically and abroad. However, from a jurisdictional perspective, the actual controller of the private key or electronic wallet for cryptoSDRs can be used as the location of the recovered assets and further distinguished as follows: (1) the private key is kept by the individual or family member; (2) it is entrusted to a third party for safekeeping; (3) it is stored in a financial institution, such as a bank safe deposit box; and (4) it is stored in a third-party service provider, such as a cryptoSDR exchange. In terms of the difficulty of recovery, intangible assets are more complex than tangible assets, and recovering assets related to cryptoSDRs is even more difficult. Moreover, in terms of evidence in recovery cases, the burden of proof for private keys of cryptoSDRs that are not kept by the individual or family member is higher than for those that are self-managed.[63]

[61] China Central Commission for Discipline Inspection and National Supervision Commission website. "Full Text of the United Nations Convention Against Corruption." [EB/OL]. http://www.ccdi.gov.cn/special/lygz/flfg/201310/t20131008_11282.html. Accessed 6 May.

[62] Federal Republic of Germany. German Criminal Code [M]. Translated by Xu Jiusheng and Zhuang Jinghua. Beijing: China Fangzheng Publishing House, 2004, pp. 40–43.

[63] Li Zongli. Study on the Cross-border Recovery of Corruption Crimes. Journal of Hebei University of Science and Technology (Social Sciences Edition), 2010 (3), pp. 41–46.

(2) Eligibility of Corrupt Assets in the Form of CryptoSDRs as Objects of Cross-Border Recovery

Because the cross-border pursuit of cryptoSDRs is conducted globally, especially when cryptoSDRs are pursued across nonmember countries, the legal basis involved includes international conventions, regional international conventions, and relevant domestic laws and regulations. According to these conventions and domestic laws, cryptoSDRs can be the object of cross-border pursuit as corrupt assets.

(1) Objects of cross-border pursuit under global and regional international conventions

The international conventions applicable to the cross-border recovery of corrupt assets mainly include the United Nations Convention against Corruption, which has been in force since 2005. CryptoSDRs, as a form of corruption, also fall under the provisions of this convention regarding corrupt assets. Meanwhile, the cross-border pursuit methods stipulated in the convention can be applied according to the special nature of cryptoSDRs.[64] Therefore, when pursuing the recovery of stolen funds or property related to cryptoSDRs across borders, contracting parties of the convention can be requested to engage in international judicial cooperation based on the relevant provisions of the convention.

Regional international conventions include the Inter-American Convention on Mutual Assistance in Criminal Matters, adopted by the Organization of American States in 1992, and the Inter-American Convention against Corruption, adopted on March 29, 1996. These conventions provide detailed provisions on the conditions, standards, scope, basis of cross-border recovery, necessary actions at each stage, handling of stolen funds, etc.[65] They also provide a corresponding legal basis for the cross-border recovery of cryptoSDRs, which are treated as corrupt assets.

The EU is committed to coordinating cross-border recovery efforts within Europe and has played a leading role in the adoption of many regional treaties that also serve as references for international judicial cooperation. Examples include the European Convention on Mutual Assistance in Criminal Matters, adopted by the EU in 1959; the Additional Protocol to the European Convention on Mutual Assistance in Criminal Matters, adopted in 1978; the Criminal Law Convention on Corruption, adopted in 1999; and the Council Framework Decision 2003/577/JHA of 22 July 2003 on the Execution in the EU of Orders Freezing Property or Evidence, adopted in 2003. These treaties provide specific provisions for dealing with recovered assets, enforcing fines, and requiring contracting states to amend their domestic legislation according to the conventions to provide a legal basis for international judicial assistance.[66] They

[64] Treaty and Law Department of the Ministry of Foreign Affairs of the People's Republic of China. The United Nations Convention Against Corruption and Relevant Legal Documents [M]. Beijing: Law Press, 2004, p. 36.

[65] Inter-American Convention Against Corruption, Art13.15.16.

[66] Council Framework Decision2003/577/JHA of 22July2003 on the Execution in the European Union of Orders Freezing Property or Evidence, Art5.6.20. & European Convention on the International Validity of Criminal Judgments, Art6. & European Convention on Mutual Assistance in

also apply to the cross-border recovery of cryptoSDRs, especially those related to corruption.

(2) Cross-border fugitives subject to domestic laws

In accordance with international conventions such as the UN Convention against Corruption, each country is required to legislate for cross-border recovery of confiscated assets, including provisions for identification, disposal, and enforcement of confiscated assets, recognition and enforcement of decisions made by signatory countries, and inclusion of corresponding clauses in criminal laws for countries in the continental legal system. For example, France has made specific provisions for cross-border judicial assistance in the "Special Proceedings" section of the fourth volume of the French Code of Criminal Procedure.[67] Germany has established procedural matters for the recovery and confiscation of illegal gains in the Code of Criminal Procedure, with substantive matters addressed in the seventh section of the German Criminal Code.[68] Japan has also made corresponding provisions in the International Cooperation in Criminal Investigations Act. The common law systems of England and the US tend to favor independent legislation. For example, the US passed the Civil Asset Forfeiture Reform Act in 2000 and included recovery-related laws in the US Code, while the UK's independent legislation for cross-border recovery includes the Criminal Justice (International Cooperation) Act 1990, the Proceeds of Crime Act 2002, and the Criminal Justice (International Cooperation) Act 2003.

In the domestic laws of various countries, whether cryptoSDRs can be subject to recovery is provided in Article 73 of Chap. 3, Section 7 "Recovery and Confiscation" of the General Provisions of the German Criminal Code: "(1) Where the principal offender or accomplice has obtained a property interest due to illegal acts or based on the illegal acts themselves, the court shall order recovery. "(2) The effectiveness of the recovery order is based on the benefit obtained. It also applies to property obtained by the principal offender or accomplice by relinquishing the acquired property, or property compensated for by others for the destruction, damage or deprivation of the property, or property obtained based on the right to claim compensation." "(4) If the property to be recovered belongs to a third party or the third party has the disposal right, the recovery order shall also apply to that property." Therefore, when cryptoSDRs have a legal currency status in member countries, they are inevitably the object of recovery. In nonmember countries where cryptoSDR circulation is

Criminal Matters, Art2. & Additional Protocol to the European Convention on Mutual Assistance in Criminal Matters, Art2.

[67] French Code of Criminal Procedure [M]. Translated by Yu Shutong and Xie Chaohua. Beijing: China University of Political Science and Law Press, 1998, pp. 232–235. See Article 696, Chap. 10 of Volume 4 of the French Code of Criminal Procedure: "The judicial authorities seeking urgent mutual judicial assistance may submit the matter to the competent authorities of the requested state within the scope of the existing convention, in order to promptly return the documents related to the requested act.".

[68] German Criminal Code [M]. Translated by Xu Jiusheng and Zhuang Jinghua. Beijing: China Fangzheng Press, 2004, pp. 38–44. See Section 7 of Chap. 3 of the German Criminal Code: "If the perpetrator or accomplice has obtained pecuniary advantage from the criminal offense or from the offense itself, the court shall order its forfeiture...".

not prohibited, they can still be recognized as financial products or commodities rather than currency, as in Singapore and the US, and can still be recovered. In nonmember countries where cryptoSDR circulation is prohibited, they can also be punished for relevant crimes, and the property involved can be recovered, as in countries that restrict the circulation of cryptocurrencies such as China and Thailand. For example, in August 2019, the Hangzhou Internet Court recognized the property rights of Bitcoin as a virtual commodity in the case of Wu suing a Shanghai technology company and Taobao company for a Bitcoin property dispute.[69] In the future, when there is a dispute over cryptoSDRs in China, the legal characterization of Bitcoin can be referred to for judgment.

In addition, according to Article 73a of the German Criminal Code, "If the nature of the acquired item or other reasons make it impossible to recover a particular item or the substitute item provided for in the second sentence of paragraph 2 of Article 73, the court may order that the acquired item be offset for an appropriate amount to be recovered. If the value of the item being recovered is lower than the value of the original acquired item, the court may not only order the recovery of the item but also the recovery of the difference."[70] When cryptoSDRs cannot be recovered as corrupt property, they can be auctioned off to obtain the corresponding value and returned. The provisions of domestic laws in most countries, represented by the German Criminal Code, can be applied to the cross-border recovery of cryptoSDRs as corrupt assets. Combined with the aforementioned global and regional international conventions on judicial assistance, both international conventions and domestic laws can be applied to the cross-border recovery of cryptoSDRs as corrupt assets.

(3) Special Characteristics of Cross-Border Recovery of CryptoSDRs as Corrupt Assets

According to the provisions of the United Nations Convention against Corruption, cross-border asset recovery can be classified into direct and indirect mechanisms. The direct mechanisms include three ways: simplified return, civil action for damages, and civil action for ownership confirmation. The indirect mechanism is mainly the confiscation system for illegal assets, including confiscation of illegal gains through foreign civil confiscation systems, recognition and enforcement of foreign judgments for confiscation of illegal gains, and confiscation of illegal gains through foreign criminal proceedings. Due to the unique nature of cryptoSDRs, not all cross-border recovery methods are suitable for cryptoSDRs. The following is a description of each method:

[69] Legal Daily. The first bitcoin network property rights infringement dispute is pronounced [EB/OL]. http://www.pkulaw.cn/fulltext_form.aspx?Db=news&Gid=c6403738c43b014dbdfb&from=singlemessage&isappinstalled=0#10006-weixin-1-52626-6b3bffd01fdde4900130bc5a2751b6d1. Accessed 6 May 2022.

[70] Federal Republic of Germany. German Criminal Code [M]. Translated by Xu Jiusheng and Zhuang Jinghua. Beijing: China Fangzheng Publishing House, 2004, pp. 38–42.

1. Simplified Return

Simplified return refers to the direct recovery of corrupt assets by participating in the litigation process in the country where the assets have flowed into, based on proof of ownership of corrupt assets that have flowed out of the country. Because of its simplicity, it is called simplified return.[71] The United Nations Convention against Corruption requires all signatory countries to recognize and cooperate with other countries' requests for simplified returns, and many countries have accordingly adjusted their corresponding legislation.[72] However, due to the anonymity of nonsovereign cryptocurrencies, the difficulty in proving the origin and ownership of criminal proceeds, and the easy disconnection of the evidence chain through money laundering, it may be difficult to apply simplified returns to the recovery of nonsovereign cryptocurrencies. On the other hand, cryptoSDRs are different from nonsovereign cryptocurrencies. As they are managed by the IMF, the underlying transparency and flow of funds are relatively easy to grasp. CryptoSDRs can obtain a complete chain of evidence to prove their criminal origin and ownership under the application of member countries and nonmember countries. Therefore, unless nonmember countries do not cooperate, simplified returns can be applied to cryptoSDRs. However, if the crime occurs between nonmember countries and does not meet the conditions for requesting relevant cryptoSDR ownership information from the IMF, a simplified return cannot be applied.

2. Cross-border Civil Action for Ownership Confirmation Recovery

Cross-border civil action for ownership confirmation recovery refers to a civil lawsuit filed by the owner of corrupt assets to confirm their ownership in the court of the country into which the assets have flowed.[73] According to the United Nations Convention against Corruption, the conditions for realizing cross-border civil action for ownership confirmation recovery are (1) sufficient evidence of ownership of the corrupt assets and (2) acceptance of the final judgment by the country into which the assets have flowed, and the judgment is limited to civil judgment only.[74] The proof

[71] See Article 53 of the United Nations Convention against Corruption: "3. Each State Party shall adopt such measures as may be necessary to enable its courts or competent authorities to give effect to an order of confiscation issued by a court of another State Party concerning proceeds of crime, property, instrumentalities or other things for which confiscation is ordered in accordance with the provisions of this Convention."; Treaty and Law Department of the Ministry of Foreign Affairs of the People's Republic of China. The United Nations Convention against Corruption and Relevant Legal Documents [M]. Beijing: Law Press, 2004, p. 38.

[72] United Kingdom of Great Britain and Northern Ireland. Proceeds of Crime Act 2002 [M]. Translated by Huang Feng and Zhao Linna. Beijing: China University of Political Science and Law Press, 2010, pp. 185–187.

[73] Zhao Bingzhi, et al. The United Nations Convention against Corruption and Relevant Important Documents [M]. Beijing: People's Public Security University of China Press, 2004, p. 56.

[74] See Article 53(1) of the United Nations Convention against Corruption: "Take necessary measures to allow another State Party to initiate civil action in its courts to establish its ownership of or right to property acquired through the commission of an offense established in accordance with this Convention.".

of ownership of cryptocurrency mainly lies in the actual control of the private key, and after money laundering operations such as buying, selling, and transferring the corrupt cryptocurrency, it is difficult to prove its transfer path. Therefore, it is relatively difficult to obtain proof of ownership. Although cryptoSDRs are also a type of cryptocurrency, they can prove their ownership by applying to the IMF to obtain the underlying flow of funds. Therefore, cross-border civil action for ownership confirmation recovery can be applied to the cross-border recovery of cryptoSDRs.

3. Cross-border Civil Tort Litigation Recovery

Cross-border civil tort litigation recovery refers to filing a tort lawsuit in the court of the country where the corrupt property has flowed into, in the name of the victim, to claim compensation or restitution. Article 53(2) of the United Nations Convention against Corruption provides that each contracting state shall determine whether compensation or reparation for cross-border civil tort litigation shall be attached to criminal or civil proceedings.[75] When it is not possible to directly seize the private key of cryptoSDRs or prove its illegal origin, cross-border civil tort litigation can be used to request compensation or restitution for the corresponding losses.[76] It should be noted that cross-border civil litigation is convenient for property preservation. When the plaintiff initiates a civil lawsuit, they can generally request prelitigation preservation of the property. Many countries' civil litigation laws allow judges to immediately freeze and seize relevant property based solely on the consideration of maintaining the status quo after accepting requests for prelitigation preservation. Prelitigation property preservation can immediately freeze highly liquid cryptoSDRs, effectively preventing the transfer and concealment of corrupt funds.

4. Cross-border Criminal Litigation Recovery

Cross-border criminal litigation recovery refers to the process of confiscating and seizing corrupt property in the country where the property has flowed into according to its own criminal litigation procedures and then making a request to the country where the property has flowed out to return the corrupt property in accordance with the law.[77] Article 54(1) of the United Nations Convention against Corruption also makes corresponding provisions.[78] In fact, this is a criminal punishment for criminals, which is based on the premise that the offender has committed a crime and requires

[75] See Article 53(2) of the United Nations Convention Against Corruption: "Take necessary measures to enable a court or competent authority when having to decide on confiscation, to recognize another State Party's claim as a legitimate owner of property acquired through the commission of an offense established in accordance with this Convention.".

[76] MARK V VLASIC, JENAE N NOELL. Fighting Corruption to Improve Global Security: An Analysis of International Asset Recovery Systems [J]. Yale Journal of International Affairs, 2010(106), p. 111.

[77] Yang Yuguan, Wu Gaoqing. Interpretation of the United Nations Convention against Corruption [M]. Beijing: People's Public Security University of China Press, 2004, p. 460.

[78] See Article 54, paragraph 1, item 2 of the United Nations Convention against Corruption: "Take necessary measures to enable competent authorities having jurisdiction over such offenses to seize, freeze and confiscate the proceeds of crime derived from offenses established in accordance with this Convention or property the value of which corresponds to such proceeds.".

a sufficient degree of correlation between the corrupt property and the illegal acts.[79] When it is not possible to directly determine the origin of cryptoSDRs, but it can be confirmed that there is sufficient correlation between it and the criminal acts of the offender, this cross-border recovery method can be adopted.

5. Nonconviction-Based Confiscation

Nonconviction-based confiscation, also known as civil confiscation, is essentially "confiscation of property."[80] This method is commonly used in maritime law, where law enforcement agencies directly prosecute the ship itself when a ship is involved in a criminal case rather than prosecuting the people on board. Article 54(1)(3) of the United Nations Convention against Corruption also has relevant provisions for this.[81] Nonconviction-based confiscation has six characteristics: (1) The primary purpose is to recover corrupt property, the recovery action is independent of criminal litigation, and it does not require a crime to have occurred. (2) The separation of individuals and property applies when the court has jurisdiction over the property involved in the case, especially in special circumstances such as the absence, absconding, or death of the defendant. (3) The jurisdictional country of the property involved in the case has the discretion to choose whether to use evidence and information from foreign law enforcement agencies as a basis. (4) When there is a substantive connection between the illegal act and the corrupt property, judicial measures can be taken; that is, the civil law "preponderance of evidence" standard can be applied.[82] (5) The confiscation objects cover all corrupt property involved in the case, including tools used in the crime. (6) According to domestic law, the proportion of recovered funds to be returned can be determined independently, without consulting the victim country. Therefore, as long as cryptoSDRs related to money laundering, corruption, and other illegal acts are discovered, nonconviction-based confiscation can be carried out under the premise of obtaining corresponding control to improve recovery efficiency.[83]

6. Recognition and Enforcement of Overseas Confiscation Decisions

Recognition and enforcement of overseas confiscation decisions refers to the direct or indirect recognition and enforcement of confiscation orders issued by the country from which the proceeds of crime have been transferred, based on international

---

79 Fan Chongyi. "Exclusion of Reasonable Doubt: New Standards for Criminal Evidence." [N]. Procuratorial Daily, May 16, 2012.

80 Morishita Tadashi. Introduction to International Criminal Law [M]. Translated by Ruan Qilin. Beijing: People's Public Security University of China Press, 2004, pp. 183–185.

81 See Article 54(1)(3) of the UN Convention against Corruption: "Consider taking necessary measures to enable confiscation of such property without criminal conviction in cases where the alleged offender cannot be prosecuted by reason of death, flight or absence or in other appropriate cases.".

82 EMILE VAN DER DOES DE WILLEBOIS, JEAN-PIERRE BRUN. Using Civil Remedies in Corruption and Asset Recovery Cases [J]. Case Western Reserve Journal of International Law, 2013(45), p. 620.

83 MARK V VLASIC, JENAE N NOELL. Fighting Corruption to Improve Global Security: An Analysis of International Asset Recovery Systems [J]. Yale Journal of International Affairs, 2010(106), p. 111.

conventions or bilateral agreements, by the country that has actual control over the crime property.[84] According to Article 55(1)(2) of the United Nations Convention against Corruption,[85] all contracting states have an obligation to cooperate in the enforcement of confiscation orders issued by other countries. This method can effectively encourage countries that have actual control over corrupt property to provide cooperation and improve enforcement efficiency when faced with confiscation decisions involving cryptoSDRs.

3.3.2 *Difficulties in Cross-Border Recovery of Cryptocurrency as Corrupt Assets*

Due to the inherent characteristics of cryptoSDRs, differences in laws and regulations among different countries, and the imperfect legal provisions related to judicial assistance in China, the cross-border recovery of cryptoSDRs is extremely challenging.

(1) Difficulties in Locating Cryptocurrency

The search for and recovery of corrupt property is the foundation of cross-border recovery. When cryptoSDRs are used for illegal activities, their anonymity in nonmember countries and global circulation make it very difficult to track and recover them.

First, the anonymity of cryptoSDRs in nonmember countries conceals the identity of their owners. When suspects flee to foreign countries, they will inevitably carry their private keys with them or hand them over to trusted persons for safekeeping, making it very difficult to locate and seize the private keys.

Second, cryptoSDR transfer is complex and secretive. They can be exchanged between different accounts and different types of cryptocurrencies, combined with anonymous electronic wallets, untraceable VPN networks, and even dedicated networks, making it difficult to track and locate them. It is worth mentioning that cryptoSDRs are more likely to be used for fraudulent contracts, investment and shareholding, anonymous custody, purchase of real estate, and large insurance policies to hide the illegality of corrupt money, conceal the transfer of illegal funds, and sever the connection between corrupt property and suspects' illegal activities.

Finally, the confidentiality system of financial institutions in countries where corrupt funds flow, the exclusion of overseas investigative powers and judicial

---

[84] Chen Lei. Legal Basis and Main Ways of International Cooperation in Tracing Stolen Assets in China. Rule of Law Research, 2013(12), pp. 32–39.

[85] See Article 55(1)(ii) of the United Nations Convention against Corruption: "Submit the confiscation order issued by the courts in the territory of the requesting State pursuant to Article 31, paragraph 1, or Article 54, paragraph 1 (a), for enforcement to the competent authorities of the requested State, provided that the confiscation order relates to proceeds, property, equipment or other instrumentalities referred to in Article 31, paragraph 1, located in the territory of the requested State.".

powers, and the lack of international judicial assistance all further increase the difficulty of searching for and recovering corrupt property involving cryptoSDRs.[86]

(2) Difficulties in Obtaining Evidence

Similar to all other cryptocurrencies, the recovery of cryptoSDRs requires a complete chain of evidence to support cross-border retrieval, which often requires cooperation between two or more countries. Due to the distributed nature of cryptoSDRs and the possibility that the location of criminal activity, the country of the perpetrator, and the location of the private key may not be the same, different legal systems may be involved, and different requirements for evidence may apply. Developed countries such as the UK, the US, and Canada, which are major recipients of asset flows, have relatively well-established legal systems and higher requirements for evidence.[87] Therefore, when submitting evidence to these developed countries, there is a possibility that the evidence may not be accepted because it does not meet the domestic legal standards of the country.

CryptoSDRs are just a string of electronic codes in a distributed ledger, and most of their activities occur in the network, including ownership obtained through transactions and gifts. Therefore, when there is a legal dispute or illegal activity, the evidence that the parties can provide and the court can use for review are similar to those for anti-money laundering crimes, mostly consisting of electronic evidence. If electronic evidence is not protected by adequate computer security measures, it is vulnerable to tampering, damage, and even complete loss.[88]

(3) Legal Barriers Arising from Differences in National Legal Regulations

In both member and nonmember countries of the IMF, there are countries that allow unrestricted use of cryptoSDRs and those that restrict their use. The legal classification of cryptoSDRs and the laws required for their recovery vary among these countries. For example, in China, there are currently no laws explicitly defining the nature of cryptocurrencies, but there are regulatory documents such as the "Notice on Preventing Bitcoin Risks"[89] jointly issued by five government departments in December 2013 and the "Announcement on Preventing Token Issuance and Financing Risks" issued by seven departments, including the People's Bank of China, in September 2017.[90] These regulatory documents are not considered legal regulations or laws of higher authority.

[86] Li Zongli. Study on the Cross-border Recovery of Corruption Crimes. Journal of Hebei University of Science and Technology (Social Sciences Edition), 2010(3), pp. 41–46.

[87] Zhang Mao. US International Civil Litigation Law [M]. Beijing: China University of Political Science and Law Press, 1999, p. 14.

[88] Shi Danlin, Li Xiuping. Monetary and Banking Studies [M]. Beijing: Tsinghua University Press, 2012, p. 11.

[89] China Securities Regulatory Commission. "Notice on Preventing Risks of Bitcoin." [EB/OL]. Available at: http://www.csrc.gov.cn/pub/newsite/flb/flfg/bmgf/zh/gfxwjfxq/201401/t20140122_242972.html. Accessed 6 May 2022.

[90] People's Bank of China. "Announcement by the People's Bank of China and 7 Other Departments on Preventing Risks of Token Issuance and Financing." [EB/OL]. Available at: http://www.sohu.com/a/169507895_523492. Accessed 6 May 2022.

Germany and Japan recognize that Bitcoin has monetary attributes. Therefore, in these two countries, laws related to currency can be used to convict criminal activities related to cryptocurrencies. However, in countries such as the US and Singapore that consider cryptocurrencies to be financial products, laws related to securities are used to determine illegal activities related to cryptocurrencies. Due to the general requirement of dual criminality for cross-border judicial assistance, if the laws regarding upstream crimes are different or not considered crimes in certain countries, cross-border recovery may not be possible.

In addition, according to Chinese law, investigating agencies can query and seize corrupt money and goods without the authorization of judicial institutions. However, most countries around the world strictly protect the property rights of citizens and require court review and authorization before taking compulsory measures. Therefore, the freeze and seizure documents issued by Chinese investigating agencies may not be recognized and enforced in many countries.[91]

(4) Inadequate Cross-Border Judicial Cooperation

As of September 2018, China had concluded judicial assistance treaties with 76 countries, including 159 agreements on asset recovery and sharing, extradition, transfer of convicted persons, and other treaties. Among them, there were 54 extradition treaties, 37 of which were in effect; 44 criminal judicial assistance treaties, 35 of which were in effect; 19 civil and criminal judicial assistance treaties, all of which were in effect; 20 civil and commercial judicial assistance treaties, 18 of which were in effect; and one agreement on asset recovery and sharing, which has not yet taken effect. There were also 14 treaties on the transfer of convicted persons, 12 of which were in effect.[92] The contracting countries for these judicial assistance treaties include major asset inflow countries such as the UK, the US, and Canada. Although China issued the "Criminal Judicial Assistance Law of the People's Republic of China" in October 2018, there are still no clear provisions for investigation measures such as customer information query orders and account monitoring orders, which may result in the inability of judicial assistance treaties concluded between China and other countries to achieve the expected results. Therefore, this law still needs further improvement in practice.

The system of sharing criminal assets has become an important international mechanism for disposing of criminal assets, but such a system has yet to be established in China. The system of sharing criminal assets refers to the system by which the criminal assets that flow out of a country are divided and received in proportion by the country that controls the assets after necessary expenses are deducted, in accordance with international conventions and bilateral agreements.[93] This system

---

[91] Li Zongli. Study on the Cross-border Recovery of Corruption Crimes. Journal of Hebei University of Science and Technology (Social Sciences Edition), 2010 (3), pp. 41–46.

[92] Ministry of Foreign Affairs. List of Signatory Countries for Judicial Assistance Treaties [EB/OL]. https://www.fmprc.gov.cn/web/ziliao_674904/tytj_674911/tyfg_674913/t1215630.shtml. Accessed 6 May 2022.

[93] Gao Junyi. A Preliminary Study on the Issue of "Sharing Criminal Assets" in International Criminal Judicial Assistance. Public Security Research, 2005(12), pp. 72–78.

can materially incentivize the country that controls criminal assets to actively participate in international judicial assistance for the search, seizure, confiscation, and transfer of criminal assets, especially in regard to the difficult task of locating, identifying, seizing, and confiscating cryptoSDRs. The sharing of criminal assets was first established in an international convention in 1988, the United Nations Convention against Illicit Traffic in Narcotic Drugs and Psychotropic Substances. In China, the 57th article of the Anti-Drug Law of 2008 stipulates that "if a drug crime case is solved through international anti-drug cooperation, the government of the People's Republic of China may share the illegal gains confiscated, the proceeds obtained from the illegal gains, and the funds obtained from the sale of property used for drug crimes with the relevant countries."[94] However, in regard to transnational crimes involving corruption and the use of cryptoSDRs, the system of sharing criminal assets has not been formally established in relevant laws and regulations. The agreement between the government of the People's Republic of China and the government of Canada on sharing and returning confiscated assets, also known as the "China-Canada Asset Recovery Agreement," signed on September 22, 2016, has yet to come into effect. This agreement divides confiscated criminal assets into "assets that should be returned in full" and "assets that can be shared." "Assets that should be returned in full" mainly include state-owned assets embezzled or misappropriated or assets of enterprises or individuals obtained through fraud, which apply to cryptoSDRs involved in the case. "Assets that can be shared" refer to criminal proceeds whose rightful owners cannot be determined, such as proceeds from smuggling and drug trafficking. These assets will be shared by the contracting parties according to their respective contributions after the proportion is determined.[95] After the birth of cryptoSDRs, many smuggling and drug trafficking transactions will begin to use cryptoSDRs to increase their concealment and value, and these proceeds will belong to the "assets that can be shared."

3.4 Legal Regulation of Illegal and Criminal Activities of CryptoSDRs

As a future unified supersovereign currency, cryptoSDRs will be a crucial anti-money laundering tool for both member and nonmember countries of the IMF, especially given their technical characteristics. Nonmember countries, in particular, need a clear legal framework to effectively implement their anti-money laundering mechanisms. In the event that cryptoSDRs become involved in corrupt activities, improving relevant legal regulations and enhancing judicial cooperation will be necessary to increase the success rate and efficiency of cross-border asset recovery.

---

[94] Huang Yan. Research on Legal Systems of Cross-border Asset Recovery between China and Canada [J]. Times Law, 2016 (1), pp. 90–98.

[95] Huang Yan. Research on Legal Systems of Cross-border Asset Recovery between China and Canada [J]. Times Law, 2016 (1), pp. 90–98.

(1) Establish an Inclusive Regulatory "Sandbox Mechanism"

China has achieved remarkable success in the Internet field, which is closely related to the government's early policy guidance and an open and inclusive regulatory environment.[96] The "regulatory sandbox" concept was first introduced by the FCA of the UK, which defined it as a way for financial innovation institutions to conduct limited testing within the FCA's specific approval process, after which the FCA evaluates the results to decide whether to grant formal regulatory authorization and promote it outside the regulatory sandbox.[97] Its purpose is to allow innovative businesses to develop relatively freely in a noninterventionist environment until they reach a certain size, at which point regulatory oversight gradually increases. The original intention of the sandbox mechanism is to encourage financial service innovation by reducing entry barriers.

The main functions of the "regulatory sandbox" include (1) improving communication effectiveness between financial innovation enterprises or institutions and regulatory agencies; (2) sending signals to the market that encourage financial innovation, lowering regulatory barriers to provide space for financial innovation, identifying valuable financial innovation and promoting competition among traditional financial institutions; and (3) providing scientific evaluation methods and procedures for assessing the risks and benefits of financial innovation, including testing processes, testing schedules, key node servers, testing structure evaluation criteria, testing parameters, risk assessments, consumer protection measures, and testing exit methods.[98]

Regulating innovative financial services should not be a "one-size-fits-all" approach but rather should adopt "graded supervision" and "open and inclusive supervision." Currently, the MAS has used the "sandbox mechanism" to strongly support the development of financial technology, including blockchain technology.[99] If China could establish a "sandbox mechanism" for regulating cryptocurrencies, it would be beneficial for China to prepare for the birth and regulation of cryptoSDRs and accumulate research and practical experience for the development of cryptoSDRs and their anti-money laundering mechanism. It could even create a special "simulation sandbox" for cryptoSDRs, fully simulating the best response and regulation under the environment of financial liberalization and the free circulation of super-sovereign currency. The IMF should also use the "sandbox mechanism" to simulate the operation and regulation of cryptoSDRs before they are officially circulated globally.

[96] Huang Rui. Regulatory Research on Financial Blockchain Technology [J]. Academic Forum, 2016 (10), pp. 53–59.

[97] FCA, Regulatory sandbox [EB/OL]. https://www.fca.org.uk/firms/innovation/regulatory-sandbox. Accessed 6 May 2022.

[98] China News Network. "Guangzhou Financial 'Regulatory Sandbox' Pilot Lands." [EB/OL]. Available at: https://baijiahao.baidu.com/s?id=1668653511174163928&wfr=spider&for=pc. Accessed 6 May 2022.

[99] Huang Rui. Regulatory Research on Financial Blockchain Technology [J]. Academic Forum, 2016 (10), pp. 53–59.

(2) Prepare Special Anti-Money Laundering Legal Regulations for CryptoSDRs in Advance

FANTA, FASSIL, and others believe that specialized anti-money laundering regulations for cryptocurrencies will be more effective in increasing the cost of money laundering and reducing its crime rate.[100] The IMF should also require its member countries to incorporate corresponding anti-money laundering mechanisms for cryptoSDRs into their domestic laws and develop corresponding cooperation agreements on anti-money laundering for cryptocurrencies at the government level. In addition, China can reasonably draw on the model of New York State in the US and, based on existing anti-money laundering and counterterrorism financing laws and regulations such as the Anti-Money Laundering Law, the Measures for Anti-Money Laundering and Anti-Terrorist Financing Management of Payment Institutions, and the Measures for the Administration of Nonbank Payment Institutions' Online Payment Businesses, prepare in advance a specialized supervisory and management measure for cryptoSDRs that has the nature of departmental regulations. This measure should comprehensively regulate the supervisory mechanism of cryptoSDRs, including definitions, registration, capital requirements, management and protection of customer assets, substantial changes in business, changes in control rights, supervision and inspection, reporting and financial information disclosure, anti-money laundering mechanisms, network security mechanisms, business continuity and postdisaster recovery, and consumer protection, to facilitate timely and effective regulation and guidance of cryptoSDRs in the future while limiting and preventing risks associated with cryptoSDRs, including money laundering. Alternatively, China can develop a specialized departmental regulation on anti-money laundering and counterterrorism financing for cryptoSDRs, which makes specific and detailed provisions for the anti money laundering regulatory mechanism of cryptoSDRs. Additionally, China should actively clarify relevant provisions regarding jurisdiction and applicable law in international treaties in specialized regulations. For example, the principles of international anti-money laundering crime jurisdiction in Article 15 of the United Nations Convention against Transnational Organized Crime and Article 42 of the United Nations Convention against Corruption, including territorial jurisdiction, personal jurisdiction, passive personality jurisdiction, protective jurisdiction, and universal jurisdiction, can all be transformed into domestic law.

(3) CryptoSDRs Service and Trading Providers Should Establish Anti-Money Laundering Standards

To strengthen anti-money laundering supervision of cryptoSDRs, the IMF also needs to establish corresponding anti-money laundering standards for cryptoSDR service providers and transaction providers in member countries. Member country governments are also required to establish mandatory anti-money laundering regulations for cryptoSDR services and transaction providers within their borders, including

[100] FASSIL FANTA, HASAN M MOHSIN. Anti-Money Laundering Regulation and Crime: A Two-Period Model of Money-in-the-Utility-Function [J]. Journal of Economic Cooperation and Development, 2011(32), pp. 1–20.

(1) establishing an internal anti-money laundering control policy and procedural system based on risk prevention; (2) keeping records of cryptoSDR transactions; (3) strengthening customer identification and authentication; (4) establishing a reporting mechanism for large-scale cryptoSDR transactions; (5) establishing a monitoring and reporting mechanism for suspicious cryptoSDR transactions; (6) requiring the boards of directors and senior management of cryptoSDR services and transaction providers to designate qualified responsible persons to fully oversee anti-money laundering review procedures, including but not limited to coordinating and supervising the implementation of daily anti-money laundering review procedures, submitting anti-money laundering reports to the competent anti-money laundering authority at least once a year, and if necessary, hiring external anti-money laundering experts as consultants.[101]

At the same time, China can refer to Singapore's relevant measures, establish targeted anti-money laundering obligations for cryptoSDRs, and prepare in advance for the classification of supersovereign cryptocurrency—cryptoSDRs to be ready for their emergence.

(4) Establish a System of Evidence Gathering and Data Exchange

To improve the efficiency of combating money laundering crimes that use cryptoSDRs, the IMF may require member countries to establish an electronic evidence preservation system. As cryptoSDRs are essentially a distributed ledger, the transaction process, private keys, and identity information of all parties involved are considered electronic evidence. The storage and preservation of electronic evidence have high requirements, and the risk of damage or loss of electronic evidence is increased in the process of cross-border evidence exchange and formation of evidence chains in international judicial assistance due to differences in technology levels, evidence requirements, and standards across countries.

To combat money laundering crimes involving cryptoSDRs and other cryptocurrencies, electronic evidence preservation can be achieved through various means such as taking photos, copying, printing, and utilizing the tamper-proof characteristics of blockchain technology. In addition, investigators and cross-border evidence exchange personnel should receive professional training on cryptoSDRs, including technical principles, program functions, application of related equipment, and formats and methods for cross-border exchange of cryptoSDRs evidence.[102]

Furthermore, in the context of cross-border data exchange during the anti-money laundering process, relevant rules regarding data flow across borders according to the Budapest Convention and the Tallinn Manual 2.0[103] should be strictly

[101] Shi Xiuxia. Legal Regulation of the Risk of Money Laundering Using Virtual Currency [J]. Southern Finance, 2016(6), pp. 81–88.

[102] DORAN, MICHAEL DENNIS. A Forensic Look at Bitcoin Cryptocurrency [M]. Ann Arbor: ProQuest LLC, 2014, p. 19.

[103] ERIC TALBOT JENSEN. The Tallinn Manual2.0: Highlights and Insights [EB/OL] at https://www.law.georgetown.edu/international-law-journal/wp-content/uploads/sites/21/2018/05/48-3-The-Tallinn-Manual-2.0.pdf. Accessed 6 May 2022.

observed. To protect national information sovereignty and restrict cybercrime, further improvements should be made.

Under Article 8, Section 5 and Article 12, Section 7 of the IMF Agreement, member countries are obligated to report their financial information to the IMF, while the IMF also has a responsibility to disclose information regularly. Therefore, at the beginning of the birth of cryptoSDRs, only through cooperation between the IMF and member and nonmember countries in establishing a unified electronic evidence preservation system and sharing information, can effective measures be taken to combat money laundering crimes involving cryptoSDRs and improve the efficiency and success rate of cross-border recovery of corrupt assets involving cryptoSDRs. Otherwise, even if a law enforcement agency in one country initiates an investigation into cryptoSDRs-related crimes, it is difficult to obtain complete identity information of money laundering and terrorist financing criminals.[104]

(5) Enhance the Search and Confirmation Capabilities of CryptoSDRs

At the early stage of the birth of cryptoSDRs, the IMF and its member and nonmember countries should not only strengthen their anti-money laundering regulatory supervision but also enhance their search and recognition capabilities for cryptoSDRs. The search and recognition of cryptoSDRs must be carried out through relevant technologies such as computers, information networks, and blockchains, and relevant personnel should be trained to master and strengthen the technology for searching and recognizing Internet assets and establish specialized institutions or departments to combat crimes related to cryptoSDRs. Using technologies such as IP address information, big data, and social network information, holders of cryptoSDRs and other cryptocurrencies can be identified and recognized, and technological means can be used to freeze the assets of cryptoSDRs and other cryptocurrencies. In addition, periodic reporting obligations of cryptoSDR wallet platforms and exchange service providers should be strengthened, and a global information sharing and mutual assistance mechanism for cryptoSDR assets and their holders should be gradually established through conventions or bilateral treaties to improve international cooperation and assistance mechanisms for the cross-border recovery of cryptoSDRs.

(6) Cross-Border Recovery of CryptoSDRs as Corrupt Assets among Member States

As a corrupt asset, cryptoSDRs are recovered across borders among member countries, which is different from recovering other types of cryptocurrencies across borders or from nonsovereign states. Due to the traceability and real-name registration of cryptoSDRs in cross-border transactions among member countries, the law enforcement agencies of corrupt countries can obtain a chain of evidence of cryptoSDRs as a corrupt asset by applying to the IMF. Based on this, the probability of international cooperation and recovery of corrupt assets will be greatly increased. In addition, it is also easier to obtain evidence, as the transparent blockchain mechanism

[104] Shi Xiuxia. Legal Regulation of the Risk of Money Laundering Using Virtual Currency [J]. Southern Finance, 2016(6), pp. 81–88.

of cryptoSDRs allows for clear visibility of the flow of corrupt assets, regardless of whether they are transferred through relatives, friends, or companies (such as hidden shareholders).

Even if corrupt assets are laundered and divided through anonymous means, such as combining with nonsovereign cryptocurrencies, evidence can still be obtained through corresponding international and regional conventions, judicial assistance treaties, and other means, as mentioned above, to recover cryptoSDRs as a corrupt asset. Moreover, when some nonsovereign cryptocurrencies are auctioned, cryptoSDRs can be used as the unit of currency for valuation and auction and ultimately recovered as a currency unit.

(7) Promote the Development of International Judicial Assistance

First, because money laundering through cryptoSDRs is usually a transnational crime, strengthening international cooperation will help reduce the crime rate of anti-money laundering.[105] In this regard, the IMF can require member states that have accepted cryptoSDRs to strengthen the mutual recognition of court judgments and extradition systems. In addition, China promulgated the "Civil Procedure Law" (trial implementation) in 1982, which for the first time in the form of procedural law stipulated the conditions and procedures for mutual recognition and enforcement of judgments between China and other countries and signed bilateral judicial assistance agreements with more than ten countries, including Poland and France, in 1987. China has also joined the "New York Convention" to promote and safeguard the mutual recognition and enforcement of foreign arbitration awards and signed extradition treaties with more than 50 countries. Currently, China still needs to conclude treaties on mutual recognition of court judgments and extradition with more countries to more effectively carry out anti-money laundering work and cross-border enforcement and recovery.

Second, procedural provisions should be improved to ensure that China's courts' confiscation judgments are recognized and enforced by other countries. In the judicial systems of major recipient countries of criminal assets such as the UK, the US, and Canada, very strict legal standards are used to protect citizens' legitimate property rights. Especially in the design of confiscation systems, great emphasis is placed on protecting citizens' legitimate property rights: not only is the initiation of the confiscation process required to be conducted by law enforcement agencies clearly defined by law, but the courts also need to review each warrant, and specific remedies are provided for property holders and interested parties. China should learn from other countries' meticulous procedural provisions and improve existing confiscation systems. Only by establishing scientific and specific legal procedures and using procedural justice to protect citizens' legitimate property rights can China's court confiscation judgments be recognized and enforced by other countries, and overseas assets successfully recovered.[106]

---

[105] JORAS FERWERDA. The Economics of Crime and Money Laundering: Does Anti-Money Laundering Policy Reduce Crime? [J]. Review of Law & Economics, 2009(5), pp. 903–929.

[106] Zhang Yanqiang, Wu Di. On Legal Issues Related to Cross-Border Asset Recovery. International Law Review, 2017(5), pp. 60–83.

Last but not least, establish a reasonable and pragmatic mechanism for sharing criminal assets. In 2016, China signed a "China-Canada Agreement on the Repatriation of Fugitive Offenders and the Enforcement of Sentences" with the Canadian government, which provides a good reference for China to sign similar cross-border agreements on the recovery of criminal assets with other countries. China should establish a specialized mechanism for sharing criminal assets in the process of improving the legal framework for international criminal judicial assistance and make specific and complete provisions for the principles, proportion, institutions, methods, and related supporting measures of asset sharing. The establishment of a reasonable system for sharing criminal assets will be beneficial for China to promote the cross-border recovery of cryptocurrency criminal assets, including cryptoSDRs, in a long-term, effective, and stable manner.[107] When sharing criminal assets related to cryptoSDRs, smart contracts can also be used to guarantee the interests of both parties in the flow of criminal assets out of and into the country, effectively ensuring the distribution of interests and the initiative for cross-border cooperation.

In summary, combining the characteristics of cryptoSDRs, it is necessary to establish an international judicial assistance mechanism for cross-border recovery of cryptoSDRs and require all contracting countries to make provisions in their domestic legislation for providing judicial assistance in the prosecution of crimes involving cryptoSDRs, actively cooperating with requests for judicial assistance from other contracting countries, to achieve effective crackdown on crimes involving cryptoSDRs and successful recovery of relevant assets.

(8) Conduct Research on Intelligent Regulation

The decentralized nature and institutional advantages of blockchain technology enable the Internet to become a technologically constrained and trusted value network. CryptoSDRs are essentially on a public ledger on the blockchain, and every transaction on the blockchain will be monitored, verified, and recorded. When a transaction is generated and recorded on the blockchain, it means that the transaction will be broadcast to the entire network and become "known to all". If the blockchain node servers does not verify the sending address, receiving address, transfer amount, and currency of the transaction, such broadcasts can be almost immediately canceled, which can invalidate the sending address, receiving address or transaction itself of money laundering perpetrators, thus directly blocking money laundering criminal activities without the need for human intervention and monitoring. From this perspective, the openness and traceability of cryptoSDRs are actually more in line with anti-money laundering regulatory requirements and the evidentiary chain requirements for cross-border recovery than cash currencies. Through blockchain technology, cryptoSDRs can be organically integrated with anti-money laundering analysis and early warning work. Regulators can not only see how cryptoSDRs flow through the entire circulation system but also have a comprehensive observation and grasp of the entire

[107] Huang Yan. Research on Legal Systems of Cross-border Asset Recovery between China and Canada [J]. Times Law, 2016 (1), pp. 90–98.

money laundering process. At the same time, smart contract technology can automatically execute mortgages, clearing, and repayment, which can reduce the trust crisis between transaction parties and system risks and is a significant improvement over the soft constraints in the original regulatory mechanism. Therefore, it can be seen that the core goal that blockchain technology wants to achieve is essentially consistent with the purpose of financial regulation, that is, to achieve market transparency, efficiency, certainty, and stability at a low cost.[108] The agencies under the IMF also need to have corresponding research functions for smart supervision to ensure that cryptoSDRs can better serve the international monetary system under the dual credit of international organization credit and technical credit.

Currently, government regulatory agencies have invested a significant amount of manpower and resources in the construction of anti-money laundering regulatory systems. If the market accepts blockchain technology, it could be considered to encode the anti-money laundering system and regulatory rules into blockchain and generate smart contracts. This could then be used with artificial intelligence algorithms to identify illegal activities such as money laundering in cryptoSDRs. Once suspicious transactions involving cryptoSDRs are detected, compliance monitoring for anti-money laundering can be triggered immediately, greatly reducing the costs of human intervention and supervision.

(9) Strive for Leadership in the Establishment and Operation of CryptoSDRs

CryptoSDRs have inherent international characteristics and the endorsement of international organizations, which enable member countries to share information on money laundering fund flows. Under the premise of fulfilling corresponding information exchange and judicial assistance obligations among member countries, the real-name system under globalization can better trace the entire chain of evidence of money laundering crimes, including the flow of money laundering assets and criminals. Therefore, if China takes the lead in creating and promoting cryptoSDRs and actively uses the anti-money laundering supervision system of cryptoSDRs, it will be beneficial for China and other countries around the world to combat money laundering crimes.

In addition, China's pursuit of leading and actively promoting cryptoSDRs will allow more assets to be priced and settled through cryptoSDRs, which will help make asset transparency more accessible. Through this method, corruption and criminal assets that have been laundered through various means and to different countries can be more easily traced and undoubtedly increase the success rate of the cross-border recovery of corrupt assets.

In summary, although most countries in the world currently have a relatively negative attitude toward Bitcoin, they have implemented various laws and regulations to restrict Bitcoin and other cryptocurrencies. However, there are still many countries that maintain a positive attitude toward it and have enacted corresponding laws and regulations to recognize and regulate it. This will have a good reference role for

[108] Huang Rui. Regulatory Research on Financial Blockchain Technology [J]. Academic Forum, 2016 (10), pp. 53–59.

the upcoming cryptoSDRs, especially in the early stages of its creation, where its legal status and regulatory level in IMF member and nonmember countries may differ, requiring the IMF and its member countries to modify corresponding laws and regulations to give it legal currency status and legal recourse.

In addition, cryptoSDRs bring both opportunities and challenges to Internet finance. First, cryptoSDRs can use the unique distributed features and encryption algorithms of blockchain technology to ensure the security of transactions. With its irreversible transaction feature and traceability characteristic, it can reduce the role of "people" in transactions and weaken the subjectivity and impact of humans, making its risk control more objective and real and avoiding losses caused by human error. At the same time, the use of blockchain technology's distributed storage function by cryptoSDRs makes the system transparent, open, and unchangeable, which is conducive to improving the effectiveness of financial supervision. By monitoring the flow of each fund in real time, it can avoid postaudits and reduce the error rate of settlement and payment.

However, with the rapid development of cryptocurrencies and the emergence of cryptoSDRs, the challenges they bring are also very evident. Money launderers and terrorists can take advantage of the anonymity and difficulty in tracing in non-IMF member countries during the initial stages of cryptoSDRs to use illegally obtained assets for money laundering and other criminal activities. It can be said that cryptocurrencies provide a shortcut for money laundering and terrorist financing crimes to be carried out in nonmember countries. Only through the cooperation of the IMF and judicial authorities of various countries and the establishment of a unified regulatory mechanism for cryptocurrencies can money laundering crimes be effectively prevented and stopped.

In the future, cryptoSDRs as corrupt assets can be pursued internationally and domestically, but their cross-border recovery methods have special characteristics. The inherent characteristics of cryptoSDRs and related electronic evidence, as well as current incomplete laws, lagging regulatory methods, and immature technologies, make the cross-border recovery of cryptoSDRs as corrupt assets face many difficulties. However, by continuously improving and upgrading relevant legal regulations and through the enactment of specialized laws on judicial assistance in cryptocurrencies by various countries, the establishment of a unified international cooperation mechanism and treaty, and active international judicial cooperation, the success rate of cross-border recovery of cryptoSDRs as corrupt assets will increase. At the same time, our country is actively participating in and pursuing the creation and use of cryptoSDRs, leading more countries to join cryptoSDRs and more assets to be traded and stored through cryptoSDRs. This will be beneficial for the detection and recovery of corrupt assets laundered to various countries, greatly improving the success rate of cross-border recovery.

Chapter 4
Research on Legal Issues in the Mature Period of CryptoSDRs

As an increasing number of countries accept and recognize cryptoSDRs until all countries eventually adopt them as the world's main supersovereign currency, a new international monetary system will be established. CryptoSDRs will penetrate various industries and profoundly change the world's landscape and people's lives. International trade, the financial industry, and information technology will also enter a period of rapid development, and the world will become increasingly interconnected, with the concept of a "community with a shared future for mankind" gaining recognition worldwide.

At this point, the anonymity issue that arose during the early stages of cryptoSDR creation in non-IMF member countries will be resolved as cryptoSDRs become widely adopted and mature. When the vast majority, or even all, countries become members of cryptoSDRs, their governments and central banks will have the ability to read domestic cryptoSDR transaction information and enforce real-name registration. Therefore, cryptoSDRs holding and transaction information will be transparent to the governments and central banks of all member countries, and illegal activities such as money laundering that may have arisen due to the anonymity in the early stages of the currency's creation will no longer exist.

As cryptoSDRs become integrated into various industries worldwide, many legal issues will inevitably arise. Countries will need to improve and upgrade their current laws to address the impact of cryptoSDRs on their economies, financial systems, regulation, taxation, and other aspects after their widespread adoption. At the same time, as cryptoSDRs become the world's main supersovereign currency and possibly the only supersovereign cryptocurrency, their impact on various countries will not be the same, and each country will need to prepare in advance and think about how to respond.

L. Zeng, *A Study on the Creation, Impact and Legal Issues of Crypto Special Drawing Rights*, Modern China and International Economic Law,
https://doi.org/10.1007/978-981-99-9975-0_4

4.1 Legal Issues Concerning the Combination of CryptoSDRs and the Financial Industry

After cryptoSDRs become widespread, using the blockchain characteristics inherent in the currency, many changes can be made to the financial industry worldwide. By comparing cryptoSDRs with existing blockchain-based projects in the financial industry, we can better analyze the impact they will have on various industries.

Since Satoshi Nakamoto designed Bitcoin, many derivative applications based on blockchain have emerged. From a practical perspective, the continuous optimization and development of blockchain technology will bring two positive impacts to the Internet finance industry.

First, due to its powerful decentralized structure, blockchain technology can ensure the security of user personal information data by encrypting the transaction activities of both parties during the operation of the entire information system, thus achieving the purpose of maintaining data safety. Furthermore, since all relevant data and users involved in the transaction activity can be effectively saved and recorded in the information database, it can facilitate the regulation of transaction activity. Additionally, because each node server is independent and tamper-proof, it can ensure that the information data system is not vulnerable to network hacking and attacks. In summary, during the entire transaction process in blockchain, there are few manual operation steps, and most of the activity is performed by machines, which can ensure the objectivity and effectiveness of capital operation.

Second, the development and optimization of blockchain technology can expand the coverage of the Internet information database, optimize the storage structure and operation system of user information and transaction data, and improve the problem of information asymmetry among different industries and enterprises, promoting fair and reasonable competition and optimizing the industry structure. Additionally, data expansion of the information database can ensure the economic benefits of enterprises and the circulation range of transaction funds, thus achieving the purpose of controlling the direction of capital flow. Because blockchain has the feature of decentralization, node servers can ensure the sharing, transparency, and openness of information data and prevent the system from being attacked by network hackers, which can facilitate real-time dynamic supervision of all transaction activities and projects on the system trading platform, ensuring the safety and effectiveness of capital flow and guaranteeing the success rate and accuracy of transactions.

Moreover, with the birth of cryptoSDRs, the characteristics of blockchain technology will promote the reform and development of infrastructure construction in the financial industry and the information system technology system. First, the decentralized ledger record rules generated by the blockchain technology utilized by cryptoSDRs will have a certain impact on the record of financial trading instruments, and the construction of a decentralized system generated by the development of blockchain technology will result in the reform of the settlement procedures of the entire financial and economic system. Second, from a practical perspective, the coverage of cryptoSDRs will be very extensive, and it can be used and combined in many industries and fields, especially in the financial industry, where it can construct a more complete information system on the basis of the traditional financial system. Additionally, as a typical example, major international stock exchanges such as NASDAQ have begun to conduct research on the combination of blockchain technology and financial information services, occupying a favorable market position in the reform of Internet information technology and financial systems. NASDAQ has already developed a convenient shareholder meeting voting system by combining blockchain technology and voting systems. Finally, cryptoSDRs can also impact and innovate the entire Internet financial system environment and promote the overall ecological reform of the financial industry. Currently, the vast majority of Internet finance is still based on traditional financial models, with the Internet added on top, and the overall credit system and operating framework structure have not been improved and optimized.

The emergence of cryptoSDRs can help the Internet finance system achieve data transparency, system coconstruction, and decentralized accounting processing. It can effectively ensure information and data equality among various industries and within the industry and can greatly solve the problem of asymmetric information and data.[1] Additionally, by combining cryptoSDRs with shareholder equity, credit systems, and enterprise risk control systems, the use of decentralized accounting processing technology can simplify the system, improve the professionalism of services and business models, and ensure efficient overall operation. In the process of international payment settlement and business processing, a relatively stable and simple information processing system can be used to grasp and control overall market transactions.[2]

Based on the cases and characteristics of cryptoSDRs combined with different financial industries, the author analyzes the specific legal issues that may arise in China.

4.1.1 Legal Issues of CryptoSDRs Combined with Payment and Clearing

The popularity of cryptoSDRs will show huge advantages in international transaction activities, establishing a simple and effective interactive platform for both parties, ensuring efficient transactions, and reducing transaction costs to a certain extent.

To date, the banking system is essential in all commercial and financial transaction activities. As a traditional transaction settlement method, it needs to complete the entire payment process through multiple steps and calculation procedures, which

[1] Wang Chao. Financial Innovation and Legal Reform from the Perspective of Blockchain [J]. Prosecutorial Sky, 2016(20), pp. 66–67.

[2] He Feng, Geng Xin. Innovation and Transformation of Financial Infrastructure Based on Blockchain. Financial Theory and Practice, 2016(10), pp. 58–61.

significantly increases the complexity of transaction activities and increases operating and management costs.

In the complete payment process, each information system processing institution has an exclusive accounting processing system, which needs to build a special interactive platform between different systems. Each transaction activity and project that occurs on the trading platform needs to be registered and processed by the banking system. At the same time, there are many steps and procedures when settling accounts between the two parties, resulting in a lack of convenience and flexibility in the entire transaction settlement payment system, which significantly increases management and operating costs. For example, in the process of international currency settlement and capital flow, the funds paid by the paying party will be credited to the other party's account within 2–3 days, resulting in low settlement efficiency and the excessive occupation of funds in circulation, thereby increasing the cost of capital circulation.

The use of blockchain technology for cryptoSDRs can provide a simplified process for traditional payment systems by directly connecting the two parties involved in the transaction, thus eliminating the involvement of third-party intermediaries. This ensures the efficiency and simplicity of fund flows and payment processes. The payment system built on the basis of cryptoSDRs can achieve dynamic real-time settlement in international currency transactions, ensuring that transaction costs are always in a stable state and streamlining related transaction procedures to increase transaction speed. Additionally, cryptoSDRs have a certain degree of anonymity, which ensures fair and reasonable transactions and promotes shared building and sharing. During the payment settlement process, cryptoSDRs can safeguard the security of user information and effectively reduce the risk and loopholes in the fund settlement process, increasing the efficiency of fund circulation and reducing the space for funds to be used in the flow process.[3]

Currently, cross-border payment settlements mainly use the Society for Worldwide Interbank Financial Telecommunications (hereafter referred to as the "SWIFT"), established in the 1970s as a nonprofit organization for efficient international currency payment services in the global trade market, to form centralized processing of trade settlements worldwide. SWIFT has a daily transmission volume of 5 million messages and a transmission fund of trillions, covering over 200 countries and regions and providing data services for more than 11,000 financial institutions. In the early 1980s, Hong Kong banks connected with SWIFT through data connections, and the Bank of China also joined SWIFT in 1983, indicating that China is gradually connected with the international financial trading market and continuously improving its degree of currency internationalization. In the process of economic development, major domestic trading institutions and banks have also been linked to SWIFT. As a highly internationalized data information transmission system, SWIFT mainly provides data information transmission and business settlement services to

[3] Zhang Rui. Traditional Finance Innovation and Reform Based on Blockchain. Southwest Finance, 2016(10), pp. 18–23.

major financial institutions, ensuring efficient technology and comprehensive diversity of the system. To expand the coverage of data transmission, SWIFT established the third global information service transmission center in Hong Kong in the mid-1990s, ensuring that China can also obtain Chinese-language information technology support.[4]

In fact, there is not only SWIFT in the world's cross-border payment settlement systems but also the Cross-border Interbank Payment System (hereafter referred to as the "CIPS") developed by China for Chinese yuan, the EURO1 system of the European Banking Association, the Pan-European Automatic Real-time Gross Settlement Express Transfer (hereafter referred to as the "TARGET"), and the US dollar clearing system (hereafter referred to as the "CHIPS"). However, because SWIFT was established earlier and has slow system updates, it has many problems that have been criticized by countries around the world. First, SWIFT's long-term monopoly in the international payment settlement industry has resulted in weak technical innovation, extremely low efficiency, and not only long cross-border account crediting times but also large remittances that often require paper-based certificates and charge a fee based on 0.001% of the settlement amount, resulting in excessive user costs. Second, as a nonprofit international organization, SWIFT should have the independence and neutrality of third-party service platforms, but in reality, it has lost its impartiality and has a credit overdraft problem.[5]

Therefore, in this diverse and competitive environment, SWIFT could be marginalized or even replaced in the following three situations. First, if there is a technological update and more professional, convenient, efficient, and cost-effective technologies then SWIFT emerges to provide services for cross-border payment settlement systems, such as blockchain technology and cryptoSDRs. Second, SWIFT institutions lose credibility due to internal corruption or external interest transfers. Third, if international organizations or governments use policies or legal means to prohibit SWIFT from being used by international organizations or in a certain country.

Currently, SWIFT is still the largest cross-border payment settlement system globally, but after the popularization of cryptoSDRs, it is likely to become the biggest challenger to SWIFT in terms of technology and policy, satisfying the first or third situation. The check payment system accounts for nearly half of the entire financial industry. Generally, the cost of each check is approximately US$8, plus corresponding nondaily losses, which will lead to US$550 billion in off-balance sheet expenses for financial enterprises worldwide based on the traditional payment settlement system. In addition, the high cost of international remittance and exchange and the possibility of leakage of user and enterprise transaction data and identity

[4] SWIFT. The Global Provider Of Secure Financial Messaging Services [EB/OL]. https://www.swift.com/about-us. Accessed 6 May 2022.

[5] Yang Dong, Chen Zheli. Research on the Positioning and Nature of Legal Digital Currency [J]. Social Sciences Digest, 2020(10), pp. 71–73.

information during the process of fund flow and information exchange pose a great threat to the security of the entire transaction activity.[6]

Unlike SWIFT, the cross-border payment and settlement system formed by cryptoSDRs through the underlying blockchain technology can reduce intermediate links, be independent of the traditional financial network, achieve direct transactions between peers, not only reduce the cost of cross-border payment and settlement but also greatly improve the efficiency of international payment and clearing, and flatten the currency circulation by eliminating the dollar information monopoly formed by commercial banks in various countries. By realizing interconnection through the underlying system, the exchange links can be minimized, and the speed of cross-border fund flow can be greatly improved, thereby solving the problems of slow arrival speed, long settlement cycle, low efficiency, and high cost that currently exist in SWIFT. Moreover, the features of tamper-proofness and transparency provided by blockchain technology can enable all participants to supervise it together, ensuring that its neutrality and independence will not be affected by external interference.[7] Therefore, after the popularization of cryptoSDRs, they will be a strong competitor to SWIFT and may even replace it. Of course, it is not ruled out that SWIFT may provide clearing services for cryptoSDRs, but even if this service is indeed more convenient for SWIFT's member banks in the early stage, it will be redundant later. This is because cryptoSDRs can achieve payment and clearing by themselves without relying on other traditional clearing platforms.

To date, in the field of cross-border payments, there are several companies that can be used as references for cryptoSDRs:

(1) Ripple: Ripple is a US-based fintech company that is committed to building a global integrated network financial transmission protocol through blockchain technology to facilitate international trade and replace SWIFT's cross-border payment platform. Currently, Ripple has provided technical services for many different banks around the world to access its network. Member banks that access the system can still maintain their original accounting methods and can access and use Ripple's "Interledger" protocol with relatively small changes in their original systems.[8]
(2) Circle: Circle is a highly innovative US financial industry company that mainly studies cryptocurrencies, with Bitcoin as its main focus. The company's main research direction is to use the blockchain data network constructed by Bitcoin to promote the simplification of the international fund flow system and effectively reduce currency transaction costs. In 2016, the company received the first e-money license issued by the UK, enabling its users to achieve real-time transfer of funds between the US dollar and pound sterling settlement units.

[6] Li Jun. Technology and Law: Dual Tracks of Blockchain Financial Development [J]. Journal of Shanghai Lixin Accounting and Finance College, 2017(3), pp. 54–59.

[7] See footnote 5.

[8] Zhou Meili, Gu Chenjie, Li Min. Legal Issues of Blockchain Finance. Finance Horizon, 2017(8), pp. 69–76.

(3) Visa B2B Connect: In 2017, the company launched the B2B international fund flow payment system, which was tested and verified by 30 banks worldwide. It can ensure the efficient operation of the currency transaction system based on blockchain technology, ensure real-time processing of account information during fund financing, and effectively reduce management costs.[9]

The legal issues faced by the combination of cryptoSDRs and payment settlements are similar to those faced by the combination of blockchain and payment settlements. These mainly include the following aspects:

First, there is no effective and reasonable policy system formed worldwide in the field of nonsovereign cryptocurrencies represented by Bitcoin, nor is there a relatively consistent understanding of the legal status of Bitcoin, which leads to a certain degree of policy conflicts in the international payment system, which is not conducive to the development of nonsovereign cryptocurrencies such as Bitcoin. The situation of nonsovereign cryptocurrencies is similar to the problems that may be encountered in the initial stage of the birth of cryptoSDRs. For example, IMF member countries accepting cryptoSDRs are allowed to freely and legally circulate, and their legal currency status can be maintained through policy formulation. However, nonmember countries may classify cryptoSDRs as virtual commodities, do not recognize their legal currency status, and even prohibit their circulation and possession by nationals. CryptoSDRs have fewer policy restrictions on nonmember countries, and their issuance and circulation are mainly realized through blockchain technology. Organizations and institutions in nonmember countries can only conduct reasonable supervision and cannot intervene. Therefore, they cannot effectively prevent some criminal activities that violate national laws and regulations in nonmember countries. Moreover, for nonmember countries, the relevant security structure of the information system and legal responsibilities of cryptoSDRs still have relatively ambiguous boundaries.[10]

Second, the issuance and circulation of cryptoSDRs through the IMF and central banks of various countries raise concerns about the imperfect legal framework and legal loopholes. To address issues such as the legal basis for cryptoSDRs, central banks can issue relevant written documents for effective interpretation, and corresponding laws and policies can be developed as safeguards. Existing legal policies can also be modified and optimized to clarify issues related to the transfer of rights and responsibilities of cryptoSDRs. Regarding the legal issues regarding the construction of cryptoSDR data, international organizations and governments can provide legal protection for user data security and privacy in relevant areas. To ensure the maintenance of various hierarchical systems, collaboration and cooperation among governments and relevant departments are needed.

Third, after the widespread adoption of cryptoSDRs, they are bound to be extensively used in international payment and settlement businesses. As it possesses the

[9] See footnote 6.

[10] See footnote 8.

credit endorsement of international organizations and is designed for easy globalization of regulation, it is likely to be recognized by governments, financial institutions, and individuals of major countries worldwide. Therefore, its emergence will inevitably squeeze the business volume of nonsovereign cryptocurrencies and sovereign cryptocurrencies in cross-border payments and settlements. Of course, as a tool for cross-border payment and settlement, it will also face legal issues such as foreign exchange supervision and the financial sovereignty of various countries. However, these legal issues can be resolved through relevant agreements among member countries of the IMF and compliance with the IMF Agreement, making it a convenient, fast, and legitimate major tool for international payment and settlement.

4.1.2 Legal Issues of CryptoSDRs Combined with Digital Banknotes

In the operation process of relevant credit loan projects in commercial banks, the most basic reference condition is the credit evaluation of the business subject itself. When commercial banks handle loan businesses for business objects, they need to conduct a detailed investigation and evaluation of the situation of the business subject beforehand. With the customer's permission, they can obtain corresponding credit evaluation data from the central bank's credit reporting system as a reference material for handling the loan.[11] The low degree of completeness of the institutional system in the entire financial market and its limitations in the time and space domains result in significant information asymmetry between fund transaction parties, which makes it impossible to guarantee fair and reasonable transactions and causes significant differences in the value evaluation of the entire transaction target. As the information data of investors is relatively complex, it is difficult to obtain information in the entire financial market, and the utilization of information decreases accordingly. Banks usually need to conduct a detailed analysis of the specific situation of the applicant in the process of handling credit loan applications. Compared with companies with short information production cycles and high frequencies, such as insurance companies, the information costs incurred by individual investors are higher. The accuracy of market operation data is also relatively low, which has certain limitations. Therefore, the analysis and acquisition of operating data and transaction data of business subjects by third-party information data agencies can effectively improve the efficiency of business handling. However, there are still problems such as low integrity of information data and high-cost consumption.

The main purpose of building the entire credit system is to ensure the cooperation, sharing, and transparency of market information data. As the underlying technology of the blockchain for cryptoSDRs can ensure the traceability of information data and transaction activities, it can effectively regulate the relevant organizations'

[11] Cheng Hua, Yang Yunzhi. Research on the Development Trend of Blockchain and the Response Strategies of Commercial Banks. Financial Regulatory Research, 2016(1), pp. 73–91.

supervision of transaction activities and projects on the trading platform. With the continuous development of the financial industry and strict requirements for data accuracy, commercial banks around the world have invested considerable manpower and financial resources in customer credit evaluation and review procedures to ensure the security of the entire financial transaction system and effectively reduce potential risks.[12] Moreover, the widespread adoption of cryptoSDRs can also ensure that all data in the entire information system can achieve transparency, thereby ensuring the security and effectiveness of data information use and greatly reducing the occurrence of illegal operations and fraud. The effective integration of blockchain technology and the market credit rating system can provide a reference for cryptoSDRs. The CertChain website is a practical case of the organic combination of blockchain technology and the credit rating system. The website can directly extract valid information from the database through blockchain technology without the participation and intervention of third-party intermediaries, forming an integrated analysis module of the market. Through corresponding algorithmic compilation and technical means, secure transactions can be realized, and the privacy of both parties to the transaction can be guaranteed while simplifying the transaction process and reducing business operation management costs.[13]

When the relevant business of commercial banks can be organically integrated with cryptoSDRs, it can greatly ensure the security of bank user information data and effectively record and store various transaction activities and transaction projects that occur on the trading platform. The immutability of blockchain technology ensures the effectiveness and accuracy of operations and greatly avoids the occurrence of fraudulent events. At the same time, user personal information data can be effectively connected with transaction activity data through smart contracts to simplify various banking operations. The bank's information system can also ensure the legitimacy of transaction activities by real-time monitoring of various transaction activities in the distributed ledger processing system.[14]

The traditional credit rating system of commercial banks can be organically integrated with cryptoSDRs, and the emerging Internet finance industry can also be integrated with cryptoSDRs. The key to Internet finance is to provide effective security guarantees for transaction activities and reasonably avoid potential risks and threats, providing reasonable data support for the credit rating system in the entire information system and enterprise valuation. The market information database generated by cryptoSDRs can also achieve this goal.

The introduction of cryptoSDRs can ensure the effective development and improvement of the enterprise's credit rating system while enabling the sharing and coconstruction of data within the industry.[15] Companies with low credit values can

---

[12] See footnote 3.

[13] Qin Yi. The Impact of Blockchain on the Global Financial Industry [J]. Contemporary Financier, 2016(2), pp. 43–46.

[14] See footnote 3.

[15] Melanie Swan. Blockchain: Blueprint for a New Economy and Introduction [J]. Financial Electronicization, 2016(3), p. 96.

be included in the information system to ensure the industry's healthy development. Traditional data information platforms have certain limitations, but the introduction of cryptoSDRs can ensure the decentralization of information storage systems and the independence of various node servers and better regulate and protect privacy under the management of central banks of various countries.

The establishment of cryptoSDRs and blockchain technology credit rating systems can guarantee the effectiveness of enterprise credit ratings from three aspects. First, the credit evaluation system established based on the two technologies has strong privacy protection for user data and transaction activities. Second, the storage and record form of information can guarantee the traceability of data, and in the process of sharing and coconstruction of databases, it can force financial enterprises to be responsible for the security, effectiveness, and authenticity of data. Finally, this system can effectively promote the enthusiasm of financial enterprise data sharing and promote the sustainable development and operation of credit rating systems. By encouraging the use and sharing of data by fintech companies through policy tilt, the problem of information asymmetry can be effectively solved.[16]

Legally, in the early days of the birth of cryptoSDRs, similar problems to those faced by Bitcoin will also exist in nonmember countries, mainly because the fund settlement system supported by cryptoSDRs has strong anonymity in nonmember countries. Therefore, it is necessary to reconstruct and optimize the corresponding laws and regulations to ensure the legitimacy of all transaction activities. At the same time, since cryptoSDRs support the sharing of various data information, user identity information and various transaction records will be made public on information systems based on blockchain, which will have a certain impact on the security of users' personal information. Therefore, relevant policies need to be formulated at the legal system level to protect users' personal information security.[17]

When cryptoSDRs are used by most countries, the credit system of enterprises and individuals in each country will be more perfect. By combining blockchain with credit, cryptoSDRs will provide more comprehensive credit information on the chain, and credit information on the blockchain will be more accurate. Moreover, legal issues related to privacy protection and anti-money laundering involved in credit reporting will also be solved because of the real-name system and global regulation of cryptoSDRs. At the same time, when cryptoSDRs become a supersovereign currency, banks in various countries will also use cryptoSDRs as the main currency to absorb savings, lend, and perform international settlements, which is conducive to banks obtaining more detailed fund flow and customer credit records and facilitating the realization of banks' compliance obligations in absorbing loans, lending and anti-money laundering.

---

[16] Zhang Xiuguang, Li Zhengdao. Prospects, Analysis, and Challenges of "Blockchain + Internet" in the Financial Field. Modern Management, 2016(6), pp. 4–6.

[17] See footnote 8.

4.1.3 Legal Issues of CryptoSDRs Combined with Insurance

With the continuous development and optimization of Internet technology, research on blockchain technology and cryptoSDRs is also gradually advancing. This progress will gradually enable dynamic updates of personal information storage and records, which will help to ensure the security and convenience of transaction activities. For example, in the insurance industry, when the insured encounters travel issues such as flight delays, smart contract technology will automatically handle the corresponding payment, effectively improving the efficiency of business processing and enhancing the user experience. The use of cryptoSDRs can guarantee the openness and sharing of information, effectively solve the problem of information asymmetry between transaction parties, and ensure the fairness and equality of transactions. The combination and use of blockchain technology make transaction behavior and activity traceable, and market-related departments can effectively regulate transaction activities on trading platforms. In addition, the use of cryptoSDRs can effectively guarantee the legitimacy of transaction behavior and enhance the confidentiality of user personal information data.

Thus far, a case that can serve as a reference for the use of cryptoSDRs is the cooperation between the emerging blockchain technology company Edgelogic and the financial insurance company Aviva. This collaboration aims to provide technical guidance for the development and optimization of the field by combining blockchain technology with gemstone insurance services. Establishing an account processing system based on blockchain technology can accurately record and store basic information and data of gemstones and quickly query the accurate information and corresponding ownership relationship of gemstones through blockchain technology.[18]

In payment compensation work, insurance institutions are the key to the entire insurance industry, maintaining the flow and operation of funds. However, due to the high normal operating costs of institutions, the combination of cryptoSDRs and smart contracts eliminates the need for the participation and intervention of third-party intermediaries, simplifying project processes. Corresponding blockchain technology can effectively guarantee the effective storage and recording of user data information on trading platforms, which is conducive to the management and query of transaction history information.[19]

In the insurance information system based on cryptoSDRs, various transaction data and user information can be shared and transparently open to government regulatory agencies and insurance companies. In addition, blockchain technology can ensure the traceability of information, which has a good preventive effect on insurance fraud and can provide convenient solutions. Based on a complete credit system, P2P mutual insurance business systems are developed, and funds in the form of cryptoSDRs are raised and pooled in a fund pool, which can formulate complete rules

[18] Xu Tao. Research on the Development Status and Application Value of "Blockchain+" Education [J]. Distance Education Journal, 2017(2), pp. 19–28.

[19] See footnote 6.

and systems for payment compensation issues of various users. In traditional Internet insurance business, third-party intermediaries need to be involved, which to a certain extent causes problems such as information asymmetry and increases the complexity of the business process, thereby reducing the efficiency of project processing. After technological optimization, Internet insurance integrates cryptoSDRs with P2P business, realizing the transparency and automation of insurance fundraising, investment, and payment compensation while strengthening the transparency of data information, establishing an open and transparent information database, and clarifying the scope of fund circulation.[20]

In summary, purchasing insurance through cryptoSDRs clarifies ownership and compensation obligations while enabling automatic payment of insurance premiums and claims. Cross-chain technology allows for automatic calculation of information such as the insured's credit rating and anti-money laundering compliance at the time of insurance purchase, as well as targeted customization and recommendation of insurance products, automatic payment of insurance premiums, promotion of relevant insurance policies, collection of information during the insurance period, and subsequent recommendations for related insurance products. This even includes automatic payment of medical expenses during the insurance claim period and automatic distribution of dividends for bonus-type insurance. Transparent flows of insurance premium payment and claim compensation can help insured individuals carry out reasonable and legal tax planning and compliance with relevant insurance laws and regulations.

Currently, the key legal and regulatory issues related to cryptoSDRs and insurance business are focused on peer-to-peer mutual aid insurance. The "Trial Measures for the Supervision of Mutual Insurance Organizations" issued by the China Insurance Regulatory Commission in 2015 mainly target centralized insurance businesses that require the participation of third-party intermediaries, with corresponding regulatory measures and policies for various institutions and enterprises. In the future, in P2P mutual aid insurance, as cryptoSDRs are used, it is necessary to optimize and adjust legal and regulatory systems and management measures within a reasonable scope. Relevant departments should formulate targeted management methods and solutions.[21]

4.1.4 Legal Issues of CryptoSDRs Combined with Financial Audits

With the widespread use of cryptoSDRs, they can safeguard the accuracy of user information and transaction data, as well as the security of the entire information system because the data in each node server are unmodifiable. This is beneficial for

[20] See footnote 8.

[21] See footnote 8.

relevant organizations and government regulatory departments to conduct real-time supervision and management of transaction activities on the platform.

On the blockchain of cryptoSDRs, data collection and storage of information are more complete and accurate, providing technical support for online audit projects of related enterprises. With the continuous development of Internet technology, information collection and analysis in online auditing must be based on a relevant database. In the past, traditional Internet auditing work may have led to a decline in work efficiency due to insufficient information collection and recording. Currently, with the promotion of cryptoSDRs, projects and businesses can be optimized and promoted from two aspects:

First, cryptoSDRs can optimize the information storage format of online audit business, effectively improving the efficiency of project completion and ensuring the efficient promotion of various businesses.

Second, the audit warning mechanism is the most critical function in project business. The traditional audit warning mechanism requires dynamic management and updating of various information data based on manual services, while cryptoSDRs combine relevant technologies to achieve intelligence and automation in data supervision and platform management, reducing the error rate of manual operations, effectively ensuring the security and integrity of information data, and achieving dynamic management of data information in the true sense. In addition, this technology can ensure the independent backup of processed information, thus realizing the security and effectiveness of transaction information data. Business processing personnel can achieve online network auditing functions by connecting to the corresponding audit terminal independently, without the participation of data collection modules.[22]

CryptoSDRs have a positive role in optimizing the information storage format, effectively promoting the process of information collection, and ensuring efficient and convenient business processing.[23] In the "13th Five-Year Plan," the central government promotes the informationization strategic process based on big data, and local governments also cooperate with local Internet enterprises to invest a large amount of capital in research and development and construction of Internet data storage and algorithm technology. Internet data storage and algorithm technology have made significant progress, effectively realizing the input and storage of various information data and ensuring dynamic updates and real-time supervision of various data through their own algorithms, providing effective technical support for information data collection and analysis, and preparing for the integration and development of the auditing industry and cryptoSDRs.[24]

One case that can be used as a reference for combining cryptoSDRs with financial auditing is the blockchain technology research undertaken by Deloitte Accounting

[22] Fu Shaoying. Issues and Countermeasures Faced by Networked Auditing. Theoretical Reports, 2014(4), p. 34.

[23] Chen Wei, Yin Ping. Feasibility Analysis of Networked Auditing Based on Cost–Benefit Perspective. Audit and Economic Research, 2007(1), pp. 36–39.

[24] Huang Guanhua. Research on Improving the Networked Audit Approach with Blockchain [J]. Fiscal Science, 2016 (10), pp. 84–91.

Firm since 2014. This research is dedicated to combining blockchain technology with auditing business to effectively promote the optimization of the industry structure system. Currently, through cooperation and technological exchanges with various sectors of society, Deloitte has established an audit practice plan based on blockchain technology. Price water house Coopers (hereafter referred to as the "PwC") also began investing in blockchain technology in 2016, recruiting Internet technology talent and cooperating with companies worldwide.[25]

The legal issues faced by the combination of cryptoSDRs and financial auditing are the applicability issues stipulated by the Accounting Law and relevant financial regulations, particularly the legal issues of data auditing, customer information security, privacy protection, automatic supervision, and compliance involved in intelligent investment consulting and related asset auditing processes. The combination of cryptoSDRs and financial auditing will be more beneficial to achieve truly automated supervision and compliance, automatically warning suspicious behavior, and automatically comparing data, making financial auditing more accurate and secure.

Compared with the situation where the combination of cryptoSDRs and the financial industry involves more legal issues, the combination of cryptoSDRs and nonfinancial industries involves less legal regulation and even obtains more financial and policy support in China. The blockchain industry park established in Haikou City, Hainan Province of China, is designed to support the combination and development of blockchain technology and related nonfinancial industries. However, these combinations still face related legal issues, such as the combination of cryptoSDRs with music copyright creation and distribution, which will involve the provisions and protection of copyright stipulated by the Intellectual Property Law of the People's Republic of China; the combination of cryptoSDRs and voting, which will involve the Administrative Law of the People's Republic of China, the Company Law, the Constitution of the People's Republic of China, and so on. The use of cryptoSDRs in the field of communication will be subject to regulations on information and communication security, privacy protection, and the Advertising Law of the People's Republic of China. The combination of cryptoSDRs with the notarization industry needs to comply with the relevant provisions of the Notarization Law of the People's Republic of China. The use of cryptoSDRs in domain name management needs to comply with the relevant requirements of the Measures for the Administration of Internet Information Services. The application of cryptoSDRs in the medical field also needs to comply with the regulations of the Drug Administration Law of the People's Republic of China, the Measures for the Handling of Medical Accidents, and other regulations.

In summary, cryptoSDRs can convert various financial assets into digital assets on the blockchain for management and trading, such as cross-border payments and securities trading. The tamper-proof nature of blockchain data ensures the maximum security and trustworthiness of financial assets. We are currently in the early stages of blockchain technology development, and it is important to stay up-to-date with the latest developments and research directions in Internet technology, constantly

[25] See footnote 11.

expanding the use cases of blockchain technology, optimizing the integration of blockchain technology with the financial industry, and effectively enhancing China's position in the world of Internet technology research, making China a strong player in the field of blockchain finance.[26]

At the same time, after the widespread adoption of cryptoSDRs, using cryptoSDRs' real-name system, global supervision, and transparent fund flow, combined with cross-chain technology, can make the current applications of blockchain technology in these financial business scenarios more comprehensive and perfect, allowing cryptoSDRs to truly achieve their intended effects. By actively participating and seeking to lead the birth of cryptoSDRs, China can further lead the application of cryptoSDRs in financial scenarios and gain corresponding benefits, becoming a new international rule maintainer in the era of cryptoSDRs.

4.2 The Legal Issues of Personal Information Protection and Cross-Border Data Transfer Under the Background of CryptoSDRs

After the widespread adoption of cryptoSDRs, a global information and value network for the free flow of financial information and personal wealth will be formed, which will have an impact on the legal regulations for personal information protection and data cross-border flow. However, due to the different legislative provisions of various countries regarding personal information protection and data cross-border flow, some countries' legislation in personal information protection and data cross-border flow even contradicts the globalization trend of cryptoSDRs. Therefore, it is necessary to explore and study the corresponding laws and regulations and adjust them in accordance with the characteristics of cryptoSDRs.

4.2.1 The Origin of the Regulation of Personal Information Protection and Data Cross-Border Flow

With the continuous development of science and technology, human society has experienced different stages of human relationship networks, such as blood relationships in clans, geographical relationships in regions, occupational relationships based on the division of labor,[27] and network relationships after the emergence of information networks.[28] Especially after the second industrial revolution, the emergence

[26] See footnote 16.

[27] Sun Liping. Introduction to Sociology [M]. Beijing: Capital University of Economics and Business Press, 2014, pp. 82–109.

[28] Wang Zhicheng. Analysis of the Alliance Blockchain Model for Personal Credit System in the Internet Era [J]. Credit Investigation, 2019(8), pp. 26–32.

of the Internet has greatly changed the way human information is transmitted, and the emergence of network relationships has made personal information particularly important. Therefore, the protection of personal information has begun to receive attention. Contemporary personal information protection actually originates from the regulation of the cross-border flow of personal information by European and American political economies. In the mid-twentieth century, the US gained advantages in all aspects of the Internet field and, with the advantage of network hardware and software, obtained all kinds of data, including personal information, worldwide, forming an absolute advantage in the field of computers.

In this situation, the ECC was concerned about the long-standing advantage the US held in various data fields and the continuous acquisition of data from member countries of the European Community. In a report from 1973, it was stated that there was an urgent need to improve the data processing capabilities of European Community companies to break the dominance of American companies in the computer field and strive to establish a powerful computer industry within the European Community as soon as possible. Therefore, European Community countries have passed legislation to strengthen the protection of computers and data and have protected personal data as an important legal right, to some extent setting restrictions on the free cross-border flow of personal data. However, the US has a different view, believing that the free cross-border flow of data is the cornerstone of democracy and freedom and that the law should serve the free flow of data. As a result, European countries and the US have contradictory legislative concepts and economic interests, and their political and economic games are becoming increasingly prominent.

At the same time, to reduce the negative impact on the economy caused by differences in cross-border data flow regulations among European countries, the ECC adopted the "Guidelines on Privacy Protection and Cross-Border Data Transfer" in 1990. Although the "Guidelines" are not binding, they have set a precedent for the design of the legal systems of international organizations and European countries in the future, especially providing important legislative references for the General Agreement on Trade in Services (hereafter referred to as the "GATS") in 1994 on cross-border data flows. The scope of the GATS covers cross-border consumption, payments, establishment of companies abroad, and dispatching personnel to third-party countries to provide services, showing that the cross-border flow and protection of personal information generated by cross-border e-commerce activities are also included. The protection of personal information under the GATS is achieved through restrictions on cross-border trade in services to protect individual privacy and personal accounts.[29] This legislative model has had a profound impact on the legislative rules of various countries in the world regarding the protection and cross-border flow of personal information.

[29] WTO. GATS Art. 14 General Exceptions [EB/OL]. https://www.wto.org/english/docs_e/legal_e/26-gats_01_e.htm. Accessed 6 May 2022.

4.2.2 The Concept of Personal Information Protection

According to the provisions of the "Civil Code of the People's Republic of China," personal information refers to "various types of information recorded electronically or by other means that can be used to identify a specific natural person alone or in combination with other information, including the individual's name, date of birth, ID card number, biometric information, address, telephone number, email address, whereabouts, etc."[30] The definition of personal information in the "Personal Information Protection Law of the People's Republic of China (Draft)" published in 2020 is as follows: "Personal information refers to various types of information recorded electronically or by other means that are related to identified or identifiable natural persons, excluding anonymized information. The processing of personal information includes activities such as collection, storage, use, processing, transmission, provision, and disclosure of personal information."[31] It can be seen that the main feature of personal information is its identifiability.[32]

The protection of personal information mainly starts from two aspects: the personality rights and property rights of personal information. First, personality rights are the rights connected to the body and personality of a civil subject that are stipulated in China's laws. These rights exist with the existence of the civil subject and disappear with their demise. The personality rights of personal information are reflected in the information that outlines the personal characteristics of an individual, such as their name, gender, nationality, and ID card number, and are unique to each individual. Similar to the basic principles of personality rights, the processing of personal information also requires the principle of "informed consent." Personal information can only be processed with the explicit consent of the parties involved after being fully informed.

Second, the property rights of personal information mainly refer to the right of the information subject to naturally possess, use, dispose of, and benefit from the information created by them, especially the right to use personal information for any form of profit, including using personal information to register accounts with financial institutions to obtain financial services or using personal credit reports to obtain loans. For example, Article 65 of the "Personal Information Protection Law of the People's Republic of China (Draft)" stipulates: "If personal information processing activities infringe upon the rights and interests of the information subject, the person responsible for the personal information processing shall bear compensation liability according to the losses suffered by the information subject or the benefits gained by

---

[30] People's Republic of China. "Civil Code of the People's Republic of China." [EB/OL]. Available at: http://www.npc.gov.cn/npc/c30834/202006/75ba6483b8344591abd07917e1d25cc8.shtml. Accessed 6 May 2022.

[31] People's Republic of China. "Full Text of the Personal Information Protection Law (Draft) of the People's Republic of China." [EB/OL]. Available at: https://www.sohu.com/a/426584424_780954. Accessed 6 May 2022.

[32] Wang Liming. On the Legal Protection of Personal Information Rights—Centered on the Distinction between Personal Information Rights and Privacy Rights [J]. Modern Law Science, 2013(35), pp. 62–72.

the personal information processor. If it is difficult to determine the losses suffered by the information subject or the benefits gained by the personal information processor, the amount of compensation shall be determined by the people's court according to the actual situation." It can be seen that the "Personal Information Protection Law of the People's Republic of China (Draft)" provides protection for personal information in terms of both personality rights and property rights.

According to Article 1046 of the "Civil Code of the People's Republic of China," the main personal information rights include the right to access, copy, object, replicate, request correction, and request deletion. In addition, the personal information rights defined in Article 3 of the EU's General Data Protection Regulation (hereafter referred to as the "GDPR") also include the right to be forgotten, the right to control, and the right to remedy.

4.2.3 *Legal Regulations on Personal Information Protection and Cross-Border Data Flow*

Due to differences in legislation regarding the protection of personal information and the cross-border flow of data in different countries, the degree of protection of personal information varies. Particularly concerning the issue of restricting data cross-border flow, countries have different attitudes. Countries such as the US advocate for the free flow of data across borders, while the EU primarily aims to protect citizens' personal information and imposes restrictions on the free flow of data across borders.

(1) Legal Regulations on Personal Information Protection and Cross-Border Data Flow in China

In China, legislation on the protection of personal information and the cross-border flow of data is not yet comprehensive, and specialized laws and regulations have not been established. Instead, relevant provisions can be found scattered throughout different legal texts. For example, Article 38 of the Constitution of the People's Republic of China stipulates that the personal dignity of citizens of the People's Republic of China shall not be violated. Article 253 of the Criminal Law of the People's Republic of China stipulates that those who steal, sell, or provide others with citizens' personal information shall bear criminal responsibility if the circumstances are serious. The Consumer Rights and Interests Protection Law of the People's Republic of China prohibits operators from disclosing, selling or illegally providing consumers' personal information and provides corresponding remedies, including stopping infringement, eliminating the impact, restoring reputation, offering apologies and compensating for losses. The relevant financial laws and regulations, such as the Commercial Bank Law of the People's Republic of China, the Securities Law of the People's Republic of China, and the Insurance Law of the People's Republic of China, also contain provisions on the protection of personal financial information.

The Information Security Technology Personal Information Security Specification, which has been implemented since 2018, stipulates that information collection agencies need to follow the principles of authorization, legality, and minimization, that is, the principle of meeting the minimum requirements for personal information collection in terms of type, quantity, and frequency under the premise of the consent of the information subject and legal behavior. Additionally, the fourth chapter of the fourth compilation of the Civil Code of the People's Republic of China, which was implemented in 2021, provides clear legal definitions and interpretations of personal information and privacy rights and specifies their protection principles and infringement penalties.

The EU has maintained a world-leading position in the regulation of personal information protection and cross-border data flow and established personal information protection as a basic constitutional right in the European Convention on Human Rights enacted in 1960. Subsequently, Germany enacted the Hesse Data Protection Act in 1970, and the European Community and the EU successively enacted a series of laws and regulations on personal information protection and cross-border data flow, such as the Convention for the Protection of Individuals with regard to Automatic Processing of Personal Data and the Directive on the protection of individuals with regard to the processing of personal data and on the free movement of such data. This has gradually improved the EU's legal framework and principles for personal information protection.

When European countries transform corresponding documents and international treaties into domestic law, they can generally be divided into four categories:

The first type, represented by countries such as Ireland, Belgium, and Austria, explicitly defines the right to personal information as a tool for serving privacy and other rights.

The second type, as in Slovakia and Hungary, includes provisions for protecting personal information as an independent fundamental right in their constitutions.

The third type, such as Germany, although without specific provisions for protecting personal information in their constitutions, has established the right to personal information through judicial trials in their constitutional courts.

The fourth type, as in Finland and the Netherlands, authorizes their government departments to legislate for the protection of the right to personal information through their constitutions.

It is precisely because of the differences in the domestic laws of European countries that there have been increasing divergences in the rules on the protection of personal information and cross-border data flow. Therefore, in April 2016, the EU passed the GDPR, which is known as the "strictest personal information protection law," and came into effect in May 2018. The GDPR has a very broad scope of application, covering any company or organization that collects, stores, transmits, or processes personal information of citizens of EU member states, including companies that are not members of the EU and even those that are not located within the EU.[33] One of the most important principles of the GDPR is to strictly limit the conditions under which companies, organizations, and governments can use personal information to maximize the protection of personal information and privacy.

Another important aspect of the GDPR is the strict manual review of decision-making algorithms of artificial intelligence, including requiring the provision of decision-making mechanisms and detailed explanations. At the same time, the GDPR also stipulates the rights of data subjects, including the right to know, the right to consent, the right to object, the right to be forgotten, the right to data portability, the right to oppose, and the right to remedy, to protect personal information and cross-border data flow from all aspects.

In summary, one of the important goals of the GDPR is to maximize the protection of personal information from the harm of technological black boxes and uncontrolled data.[34]

(2) Legal Regulations on Personal Information Protection and Cross-Border Data Flow in the US

Unlike the EU's uniform legislative model, the US employs a decentralized legislative approach, with laws and regulations related to personal information protection and cross-border data flow dispersed across more than 40 legal documents. These include the Gramm–Leach–Bliley Act (hereafter referred to as the "GLBA"), also known as the Financial Services Modernization Act, which stipulates how financial institutions should handle nonpublic personal data; the Fair Credit Reporting Act (hereafter referred to as the "FCRA"), which protects consumers from errors by credit reporting agencies; the Health Insurance Portability and Accountability Act (hereafter referred to as the "HIPAA"), which governs the protection of protected health information; the Family Educational Rights and Privacy Act (hereafter referred to as the "FERPA"), which governs how educational institutions protect the education-related information they collect; the Video Privacy Protection Act (hereafter referred to as the "VPPA"), which prohibits the disclosure or release of personally identifiable information from audiovisual materials such as DVDs without the consumer's consent; the Children's Online Privacy Protection Act (hereafter referred to as the "COPPA"), which regulates how online service providers collect, disclose, or use personal information of children under 13 years old; the Computer Fraud and Abuse Act (hereafter referred to as the "CFAA"), which prohibits computer hacking and the unauthorized collection and use of computer data, and imposes corresponding legal responsibilities; the Electronic Communications Privacy Act (hereafter referred to as the "ECPA"), which protects electronic information and communication privacy; the Federal Trade Commission Act (hereafter referred to as the "FTC Act"), which protects personal information data in trade; and The Securities Act of 1933, which requires listed companies to take strict measures to prevent personal information

[33] Wang Ying. Discussion on the Current Status of Data Security Legislation in the Era of Digital Economy [J]. Legal System Expo, 2020(2), pp. 215–216.

[34] Lei Man. Burial of the soul in the black box [EB/OL]. https://www.huxiu.com/article/319074.html. Accessed 6 May 2022.

leaks and to timely disclose such leaks to the Securities and Exchange Commission. The Consumer Financial Protection Agency Act (hereafter referred to as the "CFPA") also prohibits financial institutions from engaging in unfair or fraudulent practices against consumers. Although decentralized legislation covers a wider and more comprehensive range of protection, it lacks a well-structured system and may lead to difficulties in legal application and even conflicts in practice. Therefore, establishing a unified and sound legal framework for personal information protection and cross-border data flow is crucial.

(3) Legal Regulations on Personal Information Protection and Cross-Border Data Flow in Russia

Unlike the strict personal information protection policies of the EU and the encouragement of free cross-border data flow in the US, Russia has adopted a policy of isolation from the global Internet. In 2015, the Russian Personal Data Law came into effect, requiring all operators in Russia to store citizens' personal information permanently in databases within their borders. Subsequently, Russia disconnected the Internet from its national network to defend its national network sovereignty against invasion, and in February 2019, it passed the Russia Sovereignty Internet Law. Meanwhile, Russian President Putin signed the Digital Economy National Project Law, which aims to defend the country's network sovereignty through the creation of an independent LAN with Russia's self-owned network "RuNet."

4.2.4 The Conflict Between CryptoSDRs and Personal Information Protection and Cross-Border Data Flow

As blockchain technology is used as the underlying technology for cryptoSDRs, there will inevitably be records of holder information and related financial information flow on the blockchain. Therefore, when cryptoSDRs become more popular, personal information protection and cross-border data flow will inevitably be affected, and the relevant technical and legal issues are worth researching and exploring.

(1) Conflicts between the Unalterable and Traceable Characteristics and the Right to Rectification and the Right to Be Forgotten in Personal Information Protection

Due to the blockchain technology used as the underlying framework for cryptoSDRs and the inherent characteristics of blockchain technology, such as tamper-proof and traceability, there is a conflict with the right to correction and the right to be forgotten in personal information rights.

In traditional financial institutions, when the information subject believes that the stored information is inaccurate or incomplete, they can apply to the information storage organization to correct the incorrect or incomplete information.[35]

---

[35] Shi Chao. Governance Logic of Trust Creation and Application of Blockchain Technology [J]. Eastern Methodology, 2020(1), p. 15.

GDPR Article 16 stipulates: "The data subject shall have the right to obtain from the controller without undue delay the rectification of inaccurate personal data concerning him or her. Taking into account the purposes of the processing, the data subject shall have the right to have incomplete personal data completed, including by means of providing a supplementary statement."[36] However, as an application of blockchain technology, cryptoSDRs may not be able to avoid the problem of flaws caused by personal information errors. First, when the information subject uploads information or the system autonomously captures user information, errors may occur, and the authenticity and accuracy of personal information on the blockchain cannot be guaranteed. Second, according to Article 17 of the GDPR, "The data subject shall have the right to obtain from the controller the erasure of personal data concerning him or her without undue delay and the controller shall have the obligation to erase personal data without undue delay," but because blockchain information can often only be added and not deleted or revoked, it is difficult to update and revoke personal information such as user account information, identity information, certificates, and proof information, which will inevitably conflict with relevant personal information protection laws and regulations. Although cryptoSDRs can adopt a mode of adding, updating, and modifying in the central server of the IMF, for blockchain technology, after information is put on the chain, it can only be covered by adding new information to old information, which is also contradictory to the right to be forgotten. Third, Article 1034 of the Civil Code of the People's Republic of China stipulates: "The provisions on privacy shall apply to the private information in personal information, and in the absence of such provisions, the provisions on the protection of personal information shall apply."[37] After sensitive information or private parts of personal information that are not suitable for public disclosure are put on the chain, it will also have adverse effects on the information subject, and the traceability feature of blockchain makes it impossible to completely erase this information, resulting in conflicts with corresponding laws and regulations on personal information protection.

(2) Conflicts between Anonymity and the Right to Control and Consent in Personal Information Protection

Article 1035 of the Civil Code of the People's Republic of China stipulates: "In handling personal information, the principle of legality, legitimacy and necessity shall be followed, excessive processing shall not be conducted, and the following conditions shall be met: (1) The consent of the natural person or his/her guardian shall be obtained, except as otherwise provided by laws and administrative regulations; (2) The purpose, method and scope of processing information shall be explicitly stated."[38] GDPR Article 7 states: "The data subject shall have the right to withdraw his or her consent at any time. It shall be as easy to withdraw as to give consent." The control of personal information is reflected in the rights of information subjects

[36] Intersoft Consulting. General Data Protection Regulation [EB/OL]. https://gdpr-info.eu/. Accessed 6 May 2022.

[37] See footnote 30.

[38] See footnote 31.

to possess, use, benefit from, and dispose of their personal information. The right to consent means that others cannot collect or process personal information without the information subject's consent. Traditional financial institutions allow users to reset their account passwords by providing limited identification information when storing and maintaining their personal information. However, when conducting small payments, cryptoSDRs can be used for anonymous transactions that are similar to cash payments, and the characteristic of cash is that it cannot be retrieved once lost. In this case, cryptoSDRs rely more on blockchain technology, which has extremely strong anonymity. If the private key is lost, the account and its controlled funds will not be able to be retrieved, which conflicts with the control and consent rights required by personal information protection regulations. However, for large payments, cryptoSDRs can use real-name account registration, and even if it is lost, the account and password can be retrieved through valid personal identification information, effectively resolving the conflict between the anonymity of cryptocurrency and the control and consent rights of personal information protection.

(3) Conflicts between Remedies, the Liability Subject, and the Right to Remedy in Personal Information Protection

According to general judicial rules, when a person's rights are infringed upon, arbitration, litigation, or mediation can be used to protect one's legitimate rights and interests and hold the infringer accountable for corresponding civil, criminal, or administrative responsibilities. According to GDPR Articles 26, 80, and 82, when information subjects believe that information controllers or users have harmed their rights, they have the right to lodge a complaint with regulatory authorities or file a lawsuit with judicial authorities. However, after the widespread adoption of cryptoSDRs, the existing legal framework will face new challenges, especially in the attribution of legal responsibility and the use of remedy rights. First, in small transactions, due to the strong anonymity of cryptoSDRs and the fact that data are stored on node servers, it is difficult to confirm the true infringer behind the system data tampering, especially when small transactions are anonymously attacked.[39] Second, even if the specific infringer can be identified and confirmed, according to the current regulations on personal information protection in various countries, the requirements for blockchain-related technologies are not sufficient, and there are no regulations specifically for cryptoSDRs. Only the responsibilities of cryptocurrency service providers are regulated, and there is no clear regulation on how to provide remedies for losses caused by hacking or other damage.

(4) Conflicts in the Application of Subject Rights and Responsibilities

The anonymity of blockchain technology makes it difficult to attribute legal responsibility to relevant parties. Compared to open-source cryptocurrencies such as Bitcoin, cryptoSDRs use a consortium blockchain, which clarifies the rights and responsibilities mainly involving the two parties in the transaction, the IMF as the super node

[39] Wang Qingsong. The Nature Definition and Rule Path of the Internal Relations of Blockchain System [J]. Legal Science, 2019(5), pp. 130–142.

server and central banks of various countries as the validating node servers. The super node server is mainly responsible for monitoring the authorization and access of the blockchain network and supervising and handling abnormal situations. Under normal circumstances, it does not directly process personal data and only processes personal information or related data in special circumstances when the central super node server is the eligible responsible entity under Article 4(7) or Article 26(1) of the GDPR. At this time, the central banks of various countries' node servers, as auxiliary validating and modifying node servers, are joint controllers as defined under Article 26 of the GDPR. Therefore, the IMF as the monitoring entity is generally not responsible for on-chain data processing activities. The central super node server of the IMF and node servers of central banks of various countries generally enjoy immunity privileges, but if they intentionally infringe upon personal information or cause substantial harm to personal data, they will no longer enjoy immunity privileges.

(5) Legal Conflicts of Cross-Border Free Flow of Personal Data Recommendations

With the popularity of cryptoSDRs, the flow of personal information and financial data between countries will become more frequent and smooth, but various national laws and regulations, including the GDPR, which value the protection of personal information, are not conducive to the free flow of data across borders. According to Article 45 of the GDPR, any transfer of personal data to third countries or international organizations must meet the requirements of human rights, fundamental freedoms, and relevant legislation, including compliance with national security and criminal law provisions, among others.[40] The IMF, as an international organization, is also required to support the use of cryptoSDRs. However, some countries may not be able to meet the GDPR's requirements for transferring personal data of EU citizens, thereby causing inconvenience for EU citizens using cryptoSDRs and even creating legal conflicts between multiple countries and international organizations.

4.2.5 The Coordination Between CryptoSDRs and Personal Information Protection and Cross-Border Data Flow

National laws and regulations on personal information protection and cross-border data flow all provide for the right to correction and the right to be forgotten, mainly to enable data subjects to exercise their information rights and eliminate outdated or incorrect information. Therefore, it is necessary to resolve conflicts from both institutional and technical aspects to facilitate the wider adoption of cryptoSDRs.

(1) Provide Remedies for the Right to Rectification in Small-Scale Payments

When conducting large-scale transactions, cryptoSDRs require real-name authentication and payment. However, for anonymous transactions of small amounts,

[40] Intersoft Consulting. General Data Protection Regulation [EB/OL]. https://gdpr-info.eu/art-45-gdpr/. Accessed 6 May 2022.

blockchain technology can be upgraded to enable free selection between real-name and anonymous transactions and to update or overwrite incorrect information on the blockchain. At the same time, based on timestamp technology, information can be stored on the cryptoSDR blockchain in chronological order, the latest information can be confirmed based on the principle of timeliness, and the latest data shall prevail. For privacy and sensitive information, on-chain automatic review mechanisms can be used, and even some smart contract functions can be added to automatically supervise and prohibit the on-chain uploading of private and sensitive information while also prompting users or storing information off-chain for easy modification or deletion in the future.

(2) Provide Remedies for the Right to Be Forgotten

Among personal information, there is often some outdated or unwanted information, especially in the credit aspect, that one does not want others to know. To avoid the reliance of credit institutions or the auditors of information subjects on outdated information, which may affect the interests of information subjects, it is necessary to delete this information technically. However, because blockchain technology is tamper-proof, it is necessary to add the function of deletion to the IMF super node server. At the same time, to avoid the problem of the inefficient and heavy workload of the IMF super node server caused by dealing with too many trivial matters, permission to modify a small amount of information can be delegated to the central bank node servers of various countries. To prevent central banks from abusing these powers, the IMF can be empowered to regularly inspect and supervise central bank node servers. In the blockchain of cryptoSDRs, some smart contracts can also be added to automatically set the effective time limit of credit information (such as 5 years) through the side chain so that it complies with relevant laws and regulations. Outdated credit information can be automatically overwritten and stored offline, helping information subjects exercise their right to be forgotten more effectively.[41]

(3) Improve Legal Regulations of CryptoSDRs

Although China has already introduced laws and regulations related to personal information protection and blockchain technology, such as the Civil Code of the People's Republic of China and the Reference Framework for Blockchain and Distributed Ledger Technology, these laws and regulations will not be able to adapt to new situations when cryptoSDRs become popular. Especially for provisions related to personal information protection and cross-border data flow, relevant departments need to issue corresponding application guidelines and management regulations, such as implementing a monitoring and early warning system, regularly conducting risk assessment work, improving the information reporting system, establishing crisis emergency response mechanisms, and organizing crisis handling drills irregularly. At the same time, corresponding laws should be enacted to clarify the responsible subjects and accountability principles. First, when the cryptoSDR system is subjected to hacker

[41] Li Xinmiao. Protection of Personal Information Rights in the Business of "Blockchain + Personal Credit Reporting". Securities Law Review, 2019(1), p. 14.

attacks, the hackers should be held accountable in accordance with the relevant provisions of criminal law. Second, for the technical service providers and administrators of cryptoSDRs, their corresponding management responsibilities should be strengthened, and a punitive compensation system and the principle of fault presumption should be established. Third, when the managers of central bank node servers of various countries fail to regulate properly, administrative litigation and administrative review can be used to require them to fulfill their administrative obligations and bear responsibilities. At the same time, appropriate compensation should be given to users for the losses incurred. Finally, a bottom-line clause should be set up to hold the infringers responsible for any infringement of personal information rights according to the degree of responsibility and the damage caused.

(4) Improve Cross-Border Data Sharing Systems of Various Countries

The GDPR, as a milestone in legislation regulating the protection of personal information and cross-border data flow, has played a crucial role in the protection of personal information. However, it places significant limitations on the free flow of data across borders, which is not conducive to the globalization of data flow. Especially with the increasing use of cryptoSDRs for cross-border payments, the international flow of personal information and financial data will inevitably increase. Therefore, with regard to the free flow of cryptoSDRs across borders, the basic starting point for legislation in each country should be the free flow of cross-border data, and each country should adjust its laws and regulations on personal information protection and cross-border data flow based on its own actual situation, with the principles of protection and openness as the foundation. This should form a global cross-border data sharing system, which should be incorporated into international treaties and systems and integrated into the domestic laws of member countries of the IMF to facilitate the recognition and support of cryptoSDRs in the laws of member countries and to achieve their free circulation worldwide.

Taking Russia as an example, if it wishes to join and use cryptoSDRs, it needs to legislate to recognize the legal status of cryptoSDRs before its domestic network becomes an independent Internet, actively cooperate with the IMF's requirements for the domestication of the data sharing system, and legislate to maintain network connectivity with the World Wide Web to protect its network sovereignty and strengthen its response to liberalization's impact and have positive effects on its economic development. At the same time, if Russia is concerned about the adverse effects on social stability caused by the sudden opening up of cross-border data flow across the country, it can refer to the UK's "regulatory sandbox" model for innovative financial technology and conduct pilot tests in some technologically advanced cities before gradually promoting them nationwide.

In short, after the widespread use of cryptoSDRs, it is necessary to form a consensus and system for the protection of personal information and the free flow of cross-border data among member countries of the IMF and internalize it into the domestic laws of each member country to support the use and popularization of cryptoSDRs. For the conflicts and impacts that may arise due to differences in laws and regulations among member countries, the GDPR model can be used to formulate a unified international treaty for coordination.

Chapter 5
The Impact of CryptoSDRs and China's Countermeasures

The birth of cryptoSDRs will inevitably have a significant impact on China's industrial development, economic operation, legal formulation, policy transmission, currency finance, and other aspects. Especially since China's financial system is not yet perfect, foreign exchange policies are still mainly based on foreign exchange controls, and the internationalization of Chinese yuan is not yet sufficient, it will be more affected. Therefore, the Chinese government needs to think ahead and adopt a new international monetary strategy.

5.1 The Impact of CryptoSDR Monetization

In the future, before the birth of cryptoSDRs, although the US dollar weakened, no sovereign currency of any country could replace the unique status of the US dollar. The birth and popularization of cryptoSDRs will inevitably have a huge impact on countries around the world and the existing international monetary system. Especially for traditional industrialized countries, the impact will be greater, while for developing countries, the impact will be relatively smaller, mainly reflected in the fact that developing countries can gradually reverse their disadvantaged position and obtain more equitable treatment in the new international order. At the same time, the new international monetary system will also better reflect the changes in the current world pattern due to the readjustment of the proportion of shares and responsibilities of various countries in the IMF and cryptoSDRs.

L. Zeng, *A Study on the Creation, Impact and Legal Issues of Crypto Special Drawing Rights*, Modern China and International Economic Law,
https://doi.org/10.1007/978-981-99-9975-0_5

5.1.1 The Impact of CryptoSDRs on Developed Countries

CryptoSDRs will form a new international monetary system, will consequently generate different rules of rights and obligations for different countries, and will also have varying degrees of impact on traditional developed countries.

Due to the US dollar's position as the major international currency, there are certain defects in the current international monetary system that need to be adjusted through the new international monetary system formed by cryptoSDRs.

(1) Elimination of the Defects of Unrestricted Overissuance of the US Dollar

For a long time, the international supply of the US dollar has become disorderly and flooded. This flood of international liquidity has pushed the prices of assets to rapidly expand into bubbles, causing a decline in global economic stability and ultimately resulting in a global economic crisis. During the economic crisis, the US implemented two loose monetary policies in total for its own interests, and the US Federal Reserve even transferred the crisis by greatly increasing the issuance of US dollars. However, existing international laws and regulations do not formulate relevant legal sanctions for the act of issuing too much currency to transfer economic crises, so the US does not need to bear any legal responsibility for this behavior.[1]

Under the background of the formation of a new international monetary system by cryptoSDRs, cryptoSDRs will become a more stable and creditable international currency through monetization, gradually replacing the US dollar's international status as the major currency. The status of the US dollar will be lowered to that of sovereign currencies such as the euro, the pound, and Chinese yuan. Countries will gradually reduce their use of the US dollar for national reserves, international trade, financial bond markets, and bulk commodity transactions, and in private cross-border transaction markets, they will increasingly choose to use cryptoSDRs for transactions and payments. Finally, the legal defects of the current international monetary system that are unconstrained will be resolved.

(2) Change in the Situation Where the United States Enjoys Rights Without Fulfilling Obligations

The new international monetary system under the leadership of cryptoSDRs will make the rights and obligations of countries more equitable in the new world order. Currently, as the main issuer of major international currency, the US enjoys the following special privileges:

First, it earns huge seigniorage. The primary source of seigniorage is the US dollars that freely flow internationally, which are liabilities issued by the US that carry no interest and do not need to be repaid. Seigniorage also comes from US

[1] CHRISTOPHER J BRUMMER. How International Financial Law Works and How It Doesn't [J]. Georgetown Law Journal, 2011(99), p. 261.

Treasury bonds, which can be financed at low-interest rates internationally. Additionally, seigniorage comes from the low cost of financing the US in the global financial market.[2]

Second, it earns an inflation tax. The US Federal Reserve issues more US dollars to devalue the currency, thereby benefiting US exports and reducing foreign debt.

Third, it avoids exchange rate risk. In the international economic market, payment and settlement are mainly completed through the US dollar, so the US does not have to bear the risk and crisis of currency exchange rate fluctuations, which is conducive to the stable development of its foreign exchange and trade.

Fourth, it fills the domestic savings gap. The circulation of the US dollar is conducive to low-cost foreign capital entering the US, thereby filling the gap in domestic capital that cannot be financed through domestic savings.

Due to the substitutive effect of cryptoSDRs on the US dollar in the international currency circulation field, the recognition and acceptance of the US dollar by governments and people around the world will be disrupted. Therefore, the seigniorage and inflation tax brought to the US by the US dollar will be inherited by cryptoSDRs and be more fairly distributed among member countries under the new rules of the IMF.

(3) Adjustment of Unfair Treatment Where the United States Seeks Unilateral Benefits and Ignores the Principle of Fair and Mutual Benefit

After the Asian financial crisis in the late twentieth century, emerging economies were forced to accept a foreign exchange asset structure dominated by the US dollar to quickly restore normal operation of the economic and financial system. This move was highly unfair to developing countries and emerging economies, as it undermined fair and reasonable trading in the market. Developing countries were forced to exchange valuable physical resources for bonds with extremely low yields. The valuable resources and wealth of developing countries did not make an effective contribution to their economic growth but rather promoted the economic growth of developed countries. At the same time, the US loose monetary policy led to the tightening of the value of US dollar currency reserves in various countries, causing countries around the world to fall into the "dollar trap."[3]

After the birth of cryptoSDRs, the US dollar will no longer be the main foreign exchange reserve for developing countries and emerging economies. The US will also no longer be able to unilaterally export low-yielding bonds in exchange for the resources and wealth of developing countries. Developing countries will no longer be trapped in the "dollar trap" due to holding large amounts of US dollars. The direct effect of this is to force the US to change its policy of long-term trade deficits and restore the normal status of the US dollar. Therefore, the US must assume international responsibilities that match the rights it has gained and abide by corresponding international rules like other countries.

---

[2] Li Daokui, Yin Xingzhong. New Structure of the International Monetary System: Research on the Post-Financial Crisis Era [J]. Financial Research, 2010 (2), pp. 31–43.

[3] PAULKRUGMAN. China's Dollar Trap [EB/OL]. https://wenku.baidu.com/view/021614e4ec3a87c24028c478.html. Accessed 6 May 2022.

At the same time, the new international monetary system formed by cryptoSDRs will have a certain impact on the currency and international status of traditional developed countries such as the eurozone, the UK, Japan, and Canada. Under the current international monetary system, the EU and the euro did not achieve the expected international status equivalent to the US dollar due to events such as the Eurozone debt crisis. Therefore, in the new international monetary system, the status of the euro may be elevated relative to the US dollar, and it will have a greater opportunity to compete with the US dollar on an equal footing. Traditional developed countries such as the UK, Japan, and Canada also have the opportunity to improve their financial status and obtain corresponding international seigniorage tax distribution. However, if cryptoSDRs achieve great success, they may lead to currency substitution in non-IMF member countries, and cryptoSDRs may be used in parallel with the local currency in these countries in the short term. However, in the long run, cryptoSDRs will replace the local currency of these countries and become a unified supersovereign currency worldwide.

5.1.2 The Impact of CryptoSDRs on Developing Countries

After the birth of cryptoSDRs, a new international monetary system emerged that will have a significant impact on developing countries and emerging economies. These impacts are mainly reflected in changing the disadvantageous position of developing countries in the existing international monetary system, giving them a fairer international status, particularly for small countries with weak economic power and vulnerable currencies.

In the current international monetary system, the currencies of developing countries mostly belong to "small country currencies." According to McKinnon's theory of the "original sin of small countries," the currencies of small countries can only avoid speculative attacks by aligning with those of major economies.[4] In normal times, small countries with current account deficits have to rely on borrowing foreign debt to maintain their economic operations. Prolonged borrowing often leads to currency depreciation, thereby increasing the burden of debt and leading to debt crises. The Mexican peso crisis of 1995 is a typical example of this phenomenon. However, for small countries with current account surpluses, their currencies continue to appreciate, and foreign exchange reserves accumulate, resulting in domestic currency expansion and further causing asset prices to rise and leading to serious economic bubbles.

At the same time, the currencies of developing countries must align with the major international currency; otherwise, due to changes in the monetary policies or exchange rates of major economies, arbitrage opportunities may easily arise, causing severe damage to small country currencies. In the various financial crises, it is difficult

[4] R MCKINNON. Optimum Currency Areas [J]. American Economic Review, 1963(53), pp. 717–725.

to see small country currencies come out unscathed. Since the Southeast Asian financial crisis in 1997 and the global financial crisis in 2008, countries such as Pakistan, South Korea, Indonesia, India, the Philippines, Ukraine, Argentina, Brazil, South Africa, and other regions in Asia, Latin America, and Africa have all experienced capital outflows and significant exchange rate fluctuations, leading to a precarious financial industry and severe impact on the economy.

During the initial birth of cryptoSDRs, some countries joined this new international monetary system, which was equivalent to regional currency cooperation. Regional currency cooperation is a "collective insurance mechanism" that helps maintain the stability of the regional monetary system and thereby promotes the stability of the international monetary system. The practice of European monetary integration has shown that regional cooperation can effectively reduce the region's dependence on the US financial system and the US dollar and is an effective mechanism for promoting regional currency order and stability. Developing countries and emerging economies, due to their weak economic strength, are vulnerable to the impact of international speculative capital, leading to currency market instability, and therefore especially need this "collective insurance mechanism."[5]

When cryptoSDRs gain major international currency status and can freely circulate worldwide, it will be easy for developing countries and emerging economies to experience currency substitution, especially for countries that have already undergone "dollarization," such as Cambodia, Laos, Zimbabwe, and others. At the same time, countries with financial and exchange controls will face the risk of financial liberalization and exchange control failure. However, the promotion of cryptoSDRs will have a more positive impact on developing countries and emerging economies.

First, promoting cryptoSDRs can help these countries eliminate the "dollar trap" and the influence of the US on their economies. When the US dollar is no longer the major international currency, these countries can choose cryptoSDRs to escape from the dilemma of holding a large amount of US dollars.

Second, by using a more stable currency, the supersovereign cryptocurrency cryptoSDRs, these countries can eliminate the potential risk of their currency being targeted by international speculative capital. The domestic financial market will also become more stable, making it easier to cope with financial and exchange liberalization. International trade will no longer need to bear exchange rate risks and costs due to currency unification, which can effectively improve their trade capacity and commodity competitiveness. The financial environment will also become stable, without worrying about the speculative space being exploited by international speculative capital.

Third, these countries do not need to treat the US dollar as their primary foreign exchange reserve, thereby avoiding the passive responsibility of bearing the depreciation of the US dollar and absorbing US domestic inflation. Choosing a more stable cryptoSDR as a national reserve, they can adjust the reserve amount at any time, and they may not even need foreign exchange reserves because when they no longer issue their own currency, they do not need foreign exchange reserves to maintain their

[5] EDOARDO CAMPANELLA. The Triffin Dilemma Again [J]. Economics, 2010(3), pp. 1–18.

currency exchange rate stability. Therefore, most of their foreign exchange reserves can be released as disposable capital for the country.

Finally, these countries can receive the distribution of seigniorage tax and enhance their international status. Although developing countries and emerging economies will no longer issue their own currency, they may lose seigniorage tax revenue and lose the regulatory tools of their own currency policy. However, they can obtain some currency policy regulatory capabilities and seigniorage tax revenue by participating in the monetary policy committee of the IMF and further enhance their international status. The distribution of their international rights and obligations will also become more equitable.

5.1.3 The Impact of CryptoSDRs on the International Monetary System

As cryptocurrencies gradually replace the US dollar as the new international currency, a new international monetary system will inevitably emerge to replace the current "systemless system"—the Jamaica international monetary system. This will change the chaotic situation of frequent financial crises and unequal rights and responsibilities among countries under the current international monetary system and lead the current international monetary order to a stable, orderly, and more equitable new international monetary system.

There is no doubt that the fundamental cause of the series of global financial crises since the Bretton Woods system and the Jamaica Agreement is the fundamental flaw of the current international monetary system. Whether it is the US dollar or any country's sovereign currency as the major international reserve currency, they are all unstable and fragile and inevitably lead to systemic internal flaws in the current international monetary system. Therefore, the new international monetary system formed by supersovereign cryptocurrency cryptoSDRs will fundamentally solve this inherent flaw and make the international monetary system more stable. It is an effective method to break through the current impasse of the international monetary system.

First, promoting cryptoSDRs is the fundamental solution to the "Triffin Dilemma." Under the current international monetary system, the "Triffin Dilemma" has undergone a change in its manifestation: first, if the US Federal Reserve restricts the issuance of the US dollar to control domestic inflation, it will limit the supply of international reserve currencies, leading to global deflation. Second, if the US Federal Reserve adjusts the issuance of the US dollar according to the needs of various countries, it will continue to cause the US to be in a long-term deficit, worsen its international balance of payments, and cause large-scale asset bubbles and inflation domestically, making the US dollar unable to maintain the value stability that a major international currency should have and ultimately leading to the collapse of the dollar-dominated monetary system.

From the current international monetary system, this contradiction cannot be solved by any country's sovereign currency. However, by issuing supersovereign currency cryptoSDRs, the "Triffin Dilemma" can be fundamentally solved: first, cryptoSDRs are not sovereign currency, are not affected by any country's international balance of payments situation, and do not need to take care of any country's domestic interests separately; second, the IMF does not need to consider the domestic monetary policy needs of sovereign countries and can directly consider the currency needs of the international community when formulating monetary policies. Therefore, the introduction of cryptoSDRs can fundamentally solve the "Triffin Dilemma."

Second, implementing cryptoSDRs is an effective means of maintaining global financial stability. Maintaining global financial stability is one of the primary goals of the international monetary system. As the issuing country of the major international reserve currency, the US has continued to adopt loose monetary policies and maintain a long-term trade deficit, releasing asset bubbles and inflation into the international community and leading to frequent global financial crises. At the same time, the continuous overissuance of the US dollar by the US Federal Reserve has caused the dollar to continuously depreciate and led to the flooding of liquidity in the international community, posing a huge risk to global financial stability.[6]

As a supersovereign currency, cryptoSDRs have a value composed of a basket of currencies, making them more stable than sovereign currencies. Moreover, the formulation of its monetary policy is not based solely on the interests of the issuing country but rather on global financial stability and the balance of interests among countries. Therefore, the emergence and widespread use of cryptoSDRs can better maintain global financial stability and development.

Third, implementing cryptoSDRs can maintain the balance of rights and obligations among countries. Along with the birth of cryptoSDRs, the IMF has undergone reforms to better reflect the rights and positions of developing countries and emerging economies in the current international financial environment, more accurately reflecting the existing world economic and political landscape. This will make the new international monetary system more stable and balanced, more in line with the interests of developing countries and emerging economies, enabling them to participate in international affairs and share benefits on an equal footing. In particular, for China's "A Belt and a Road" initiative, the introduction of cryptoSDRs will play a huge role in promoting the steady realization of the goal of a "community with a shared future for mankind."

Fourth, implementing cryptoSDRs can achieve inclusive finance on a global scale. As explained in the Libra white paper mentioned earlier, there are still 1.7 billion adults worldwide without bank accounts, and Libra's vision is to provide financial services to every individual anywhere in the world.[7] Although Libra has been put

---

[6] Li Renzhen, Xiang Yaping. Analysis of Legal Paths to Strengthen the Role of SDR. Journal of Wuhan University (Philosophy & Social Sciences Edition), 2012(3), pp. 59–64.

[7] DIEM. Libra Whitepaper [EB/OL]. https://www.diem.com/en-us/white-paper/. Accessed 6 May 2022.

on hold, the birth of cryptoSDRs can achieve the historical mission that Libra could not complete. In the future, with the global popularity of smartphones and the global circulation of cryptoSDRs, people in any corner of the world can use cryptoSDRs conveniently, quickly, and efficiently. Even people in remote areas can enjoy financial technology services from developed countries, quickly obtain low-interest loans, and lift themselves out of poverty, thus achieving inclusive finance on a global scale and making the international monetary system fairer and more stable.

Fifth, there are other advantages. Compared with other sovereign currencies or international reserve assets, cryptoSDRs indeed have undeniable advantages: (1) value stability. CryptoSDRs use a basket of currencies as the basis for their pricing, ensuring their stability as a major international reserve currency with stable international purchasing power. (2) Permanently increasing liquidity. The allocation of cryptoSDRs to the world reserve assets and international liquidity permanently increases without any means of recall or risk, reducing the systemic risk and credit risk of the entire monetary system. (3) Low cost. CryptoSDRs are generated through electronic devices, and the costs of issuance and circulation can be neglected, while the current major international currencies are mainly issued and circulated in the form of paper cash, which incurs higher costs. (4) Independent monetary policy. The IMF adjusts the issuance of cryptoSDRs dynamically based on global economic trade and international liquidity demand without being influenced by any individual sovereign country's domestic demand and monetary policy.[8]

5.1.4 *The Impact of CryptoSDRs on China*

After the widespread adoption of cryptoSDRs, the impact on China can be divided into two aspects: on the one hand, it will impact China's current monetary sovereignty and monetary policy; on the other hand, if China can strive for dominance in the cryptoSDR system, it can better balance the current situation where its national and monetary strengths are not proportional.

(1) The Impact on China's Monetary Sovereignty and Monetary Policy

The widespread adoption of cryptoSDRs will create a new world currency and financial system, which not only benefits the optimization of resource allocation but also improves the efficiency of global financial services. However, because blockchain technology can operate outside the constraints of traditional financial networks in various countries, whether China actively or passively accepts cryptoSDRs, the existence of cryptoSDRs is highly "substitutable" and "disruptive," which may pose serious challenges to China's monetary sovereignty, monetary policy, and related regulations.

When Chinese yuan, DC/EP, and cryptoSDRs are in circulation in China at the same time, cryptoSDRs will inevitably have a certain degree of substitutability for

[8] See Footnote 6.

Chinese yuan and DC/EP, which will weaken China's monetary sovereignty to a certain extent and will have a certain impact on the basic currency, money supply, circulation speed, monetary policy transmission mechanism, interest rate policy, and other aspects.

First, the impact of cryptoSDRs on the underlying currency is mainly to reduce the circulation of cash, while the legal deposit reserve and excess deposit reserve of banks will increase. CryptoSDRs in circulation in China will store more national assets in electronic form, including cryptoSDRs and DC/EP, resulting in a significant reduction in the circulation of Chinese yuan cash. With the popularization of electronic payment methods, people have more convenient and flexible access to deposits and withdrawals, which requires banks to have more currency reserves to meet the demand for withdrawals. Therefore, banks need to allocate more excess deposit reserves and raise the legal deposit reserve. Furthermore, after the widespread acceptance of cryptoSDRs, pricing for financing, deferred sales, credit, and financial products related to economic activities may use cryptoSDRs. Once cryptoSDRs have credit capacity, there will be monetary multipliers and derivative deposits. At this point, if only the reserve equivalent to M0 is used, it may lead to insufficient guarantee of Chinese yuan exchange and further fluctuations in Chinese yuan value.

Second, the popularization of cryptoSDRs has an impact on the money supply. Central banks in various countries consider the money supply as an important economic indicator, and after the widespread circulation of cryptoSDRs, the planned, predictable, anti-interference, and controllable nature of the money supply will face enormous challenges. CryptoSDRs have a substitution effect on circulating Chinese yuan cash, which will change the domestic currency structure, and combined with the effect of the monetary multiplier, the total money supply will change, making it more difficult for the Central Bank of China to control the total money supply and adjust monetary supply policies.[9]

Third, the popularization of cryptoSDRs has an impact on the velocity of money circulation in China. The velocity of money circulation refers to the frequency of currency use during a specific period of time. The popularity of cryptoSDRs not only makes domestic electronic payments as convenient as traditional ones but also makes cross-border payments and transactions easier, thereby increasing the speed of money circulation and accelerating China's economic development. However, it also poses greater challenges to the regulation of currency and financial activities.

Fourth, the popularization of cryptoSDRs will have an impact on China's interest rate policy. China currently implements a prudent monetary policy, which corresponds to a "dual-track system" of interest rate policy: on the one hand, the market determines the monetary interest rate completely and autonomously, and on the other hand, the central bank still decides the benchmark interest rate in terms of deposits and lending. In 2018, the Governor of the People's Bank of China, Yi Gang, said at the Boao Forum for Asia that China's current "dual-track system" of interest rates would continue to be reformed in the future, gradually unifying the rates on the two

[9] Jiang Shaohua. Research on the Impact of Electronic Payment Development on Central Bank Monetary Policy [M]. Beijing: Economic Science Press, 2013, pp. 17–89.

tracks.[10] Although China has started to implement the loan prime rate (hereafter referred to as the "LPR") in reforming its interest rate policy, there are still problems such as weak transmission of the interest rates adjusted by the central bank's monetary policy to the credit market. The interest rates of commercial banks still have to be priced through the benchmark lending rate, and the effect of LPRs has not been fully realized. After cryptoSDRs begin to circulate in China, instability of the money supply may occur, and the quantity adjustment effect of monetary policy will be lower than that of price control. The role of the central bank in interest rate regulation will become more important. The instability of the money supply will also significantly increase the difficulty of controlling interest rates through the autonomous pricing of bank interest rates and the interest rate corridor mechanism. Furthermore, since the interest rate of cryptoSDRs is determined by the IMF and is not subject to any country's influence, it will to some extent affect China's interest rate policy formulation and effectiveness.

Fifth, the popularization of cryptoSDRs has an impact on China's monetary policy transmission mechanism. After the popularization of cryptoSDRs, China can still obtain an independent monetary policy by participating in the decision-making of the IMF and implementing certain policy interventions in domestic currency circulation. Currently, China's monetary policy transmission mainly starts from the central bank to commercial banks, financial institutions, enterprises, and individuals, and finally to various economic variables such as prices and employment. After the popularization of cryptoSDRs, cross-border payments will increase the breadth of the financial market, and the activity of financial products, transaction investment, and arbitrage mechanisms will increase the depth of the financial market. However, the active financial market may lead to the rapid transmission of China's monetary policy, causing the central bank to overreact to the financial market or not be able to take appropriate measures to effectively guide it in a timely manner, resulting in poor execution of the monetary policy.[11]

(2) The Impact on China's International Financial Status

After the widespread adoption of cryptoSDRs, China can improve its international status and financial influence by actively participating in and pursuing the creation and promotion of cryptoSDRs and striving to lead the way in the establishment of the new international monetary system, tilting the balance in favor of developing countries, including China.

First, the birth and widespread adoption of cryptoSDRs will weaken the US dollar's international dominance, allowing China to enhance its international status and lead the establishment of the new international financial order.

---

[10] People's Bank of China. "Q&A Record of Governor Yi Gang at the 2018 Boao Forum for Asia Annual Conference Subforum on 'Normalization of Monetary Policy'." [EB/OL]. Available at: https://www.financialnews.com.cn/jg/ld/201804/t20180411_136295.html. Accessed 6 May 2022.

[11] Li Zhen, Liu Yingge, Dai Yicheng. Impact of Libra Stablecoin on China's Monetary Policy and Response Strategies. Journal of Xi'an Jiaotong University (Social Sciences Edition), 2020(3), pp. 55–63.

Second, the weight of the Chinese yuan in international payment and settlement is still very low compared to the country's second-largest global economy and its significant foreign trade and investment scale. By actively participating in and leading the creation and promotion of cryptoSDRs, China can align its national interests with the monetary policies of cryptoSDRs, further promoting the internationalization of its financial sector and expanding the scale of its foreign trade and investment. This will enable China's monetary policy influence to be expanded worldwide through the circulation of cryptoSDRs, thus achieving a world financial status commensurate with China's economic and political strength.

Third, promoting the development of cryptoSDRs can not only improve China's international status but also help the country become less dependent on cross-border settlement systems such as SWIFT. Although China has been using the CHIPS Chinese yuan cross-border settlement system since 2012, it still heavily relies on the SWIFT system in international information and communication links and does not have completely independent operating capabilities. However, cryptoSDRs can optimize China's financial system, improve the country's financial security coefficient, and protect its financial sovereignty.

Moreover, China can take advantage of the opportunity to promote cryptoSDRs and build a world-class big data monitoring and warning system to prevent financial crises and strengthen global anti-money laundering regulatory cooperation. The emergence and widespread adoption of cryptoSDRs make it possible to monitor the creation, trading, and settlement data of international currencies. By desensitizing large amounts of currency flow data and dynamically monitoring and analyzing the circulation of cryptoSDRs using big data, cloud computing, and other technologies, the inherent logic and relevance of these data can be identified, providing more specific and effective information for currency regulation and policy-making and improving the accuracy of monetary policy. Based on a big data mining risk prediction model, multiple dimensions of information are repeatedly verified and adjusted, and sensitive information in currency circulation is identified in a timely and effective manner, thereby improving risk monitoring and early warning capabilities and helping prevent frequent cyclical financial crises. At the same time, it strengthens the regulatory and anti-money laundering cooperation of countries around the world, enabling real-time monitoring of cryptoSDR trading data and transaction identity information, thereby enhancing the regulatory and anti-money laundering capabilities of countries worldwide and preventing negative impacts on the new international monetary system caused by cryptoSDRs.

Finally, cryptoSDRs can help China enhance its global governance capabilities and currency regulation level. By establishing and promoting the use of cryptoSDRs, China can obtain improvements in blockchain technology and information on the international monetary system and financial system. At the same time, through practical application and improvement of technologies such as artificial intelligence, big data, and cloud computing, the security and stability of the global use of cryptoSDRs can be enhanced, providing technical and policy support for the new international monetary system. Moreover, China's regulatory agencies and financial institutions can also use the cryptoSDR platform to continuously improve their own financial technology research and development, better regulate information risks, operational risks, and credit risks, deepen cooperation with technology companies, and further enhance the technology level, service concept, and safety and stability of China's financial industry.

(3) The Impact on the International Status of Chinese Yuan

In the basket of currencies for SDRs, there are five currencies: US dollar, euro, pound sterling, Japanese yen, and Chinese yuan. Based on the structure of national foreign exchange reserves, the expansion of the coverage of cryptoSDRs and the increase in the amount of reserve currencies held will have a direct impact on the international settlement and payment status of the sovereign currencies in the currency basket and their importance in the international monetary system.

In China's financial market, various financial assets have not yet achieved complete free circulation and exchange, and the entry of overseas capital is restricted, with limited funds being invested by foreign investors. Therefore, the continuous optimization and development of cryptoSDRs will help to continue pushing forward the internationalization process of the Chinese yuan and promote its holding in the international trading market. The important premise for Chinese yuan to become an international reserve currency is to maintain the stability of its value and exchange rate, and investors must have an expectation of appreciation for Chinese yuan.

However, since 2015, the appreciation of Chinese yuan has faced difficult challenges, and foreign short-selling groups have been watching closely. To ensure the value space of Chinese yuan, the Chinese government even reduced the supply of Chinese yuan in the international market to ensure the safety of Chinese yuan's value. However, this policy and measure also directly led to the decline in the value of offshore Chinese yuan in the offshore financial market and the decline in the status of Chinese yuan in the international market, hindering the process of Chinese yuan internationalization. Therefore, to continue promoting the internationalization of Chinese yuan, it is necessary to make conditional adjustments to Chinese yuan, expand the range of Chinese yuan holders, and ensure the supply of Chinese yuan in the international market. However, due to the lower degree of freedom of cash Chinese yuan exchange in the market, the process of Chinese yuan internationalization is also limited. After the emergence of cryptoSDRs, they can be used as carriers of Chinese yuan to introduce Chinese yuan into the international market. Due to the high acceptance and recognition of cryptoSDRs in the market, they can ensure the free circulation and widespread holding of Chinese yuan in the world trade market.[12]

Although the Chinese yuan is already an important component of the basket of currencies and the sovereign currency of the world's second-largest economy, it is almost impossible for it to achieve a level of international status comparable to the US dollar, let alone replace it, in the short term. Supporting the issuance and circulation of cryptoSDRs is beneficial for reducing the international status of the US dollar and narrowing the gap between Chinese yuan and the dollar. The emergence

[12] Shi Jianxun, Wang Panpan. Does Expanding the Use of SDR Help the Internationalization of Renminbi? [J]. World Economic Research, 2018(10), pp. 3–17 + 64 + 135.

and development of cryptoSDRs will have greater functions and impacts than any single currency of a sovereign country, becoming a supersovereign international currency and replacing the US dollar's international currency status, leading to a decline in the US dollar's status. Conversely, Chinese yuan may continue to increase its international status and continuously narrow the gap with the US dollar, thus enhancing its international status from a comparative perspective.

(4) Impact on Dependency on the US Dollar

Using cryptoSDRs as a pricing currency for international trade, international finance, and cross-border settlement can avoid the unfair trade wars that the US has with other countries under the dominance of the US dollar.

At the same time, expanding the use of cryptoSDRs helps accelerate the promotion of the diversification reform of the international monetary system, effectively weaken the US dollar's share and influence in the international currency trading market, reduce the dependence on the US dollar in transaction payment and settlement processes, and continuously reduce the dominant position of the US dollar in the world trading market while expanding the coverage of Chinese yuan in the international trade market.

Currently, the main loophole in the international trade monetary system is that the US dollar, as a national sovereign currency, is traded as a globalized currency in the trade market. Although other countries in the world support the reform of the international monetary system, there are still no specific measures and practical actions. The emergence of supersovereign cryptoSDRs provides an effective solution to reduce the world's currency market's dependence on the US dollar, continuously weaken the US dollar's participation in world trade payment and settlement processes, and continuously reduce the dominant status of the US dollar as a major international currency.

Based on a basket of currencies, SDRs have been supported and promoted by China since Chinese yuan entered the basket of currencies. This aims to limit the dominance of the US dollar in the world trade system, provide development space for other currencies, optimize the structure of the international currency trading system, continuously promote the influence and coverage of cryptoSDRs in the world trade market, and promote the diversified development of the world currency trading system. From the perspective of the US, as cryptoSDRs were led and developed by the US at the beginning, and currently, the US dollar has the largest proportion in the basket of currencies, the development of cryptoSDRs will not have a huge impact on the value of the US dollar. Therefore, the US has no reasonable reason to oppose the development of cryptoSDRs.

The development and expanded use of cryptoSDRs can effectively reduce the dominant position of the US dollar as a major international currency in the world trade market. This can help ensure that the trade structure in the international monetary system is more stable and diverse, which in turn can benefit the rapid development of the Chinese yuan in a more diversified trading system.

According to model analysis, the current proportion of the US dollar in international trade and foreign exchange reserves is higher than that of SDRs, while the proportion of the Chinese yuan in foreign exchange reserve currencies is lower than that of SDRs. Therefore, the development and optimization of cryptoSDRs can have a positive promoting effect on the internationalization process of the Chinese yuan, continually expanding its holdings and share in the international market.[13]

In summary, the emergence of cryptoSDRs can solve the inherent flaws of the current international monetary and financial system, effectively preventing global financial crises. For developing countries, the emergence of an international reserve currency with a more credible foundation than the US dollar can protect them from the threat of US financial sanctions.

If China can actively participate in or even lead the implementation of cryptoSDRs, it will have the opportunity to restructure the international monetary system, tilt the previously unequal international system toward developing countries, and promote the balance and stability of the international system. This will also benefit the promotion of the international status of the Chinese yuan, promote China's financial liberalization and trade development, and alleviate the international conflicts between traditional developed countries and emerging economies, achieving a harmonious development of the international monetary strategy of the internationalization of Chinese yuan and the monetization of cryptoSDRs.

Using cryptoSDRs in international trade can eliminate the cost of currency exchange between enterprises, individuals, and institutions, facilitating the globalization of international investment, trade, and financial products and promoting the development of global integration. At the same time, the technical characteristics of cryptoSDRs can make cross-border payments more secure and convenient. Cheap financial services in developed countries can also conveniently serve people in remote areas of poor countries, making the circulation of global wealth smoother and promoting the wider dissemination of inclusive finance.

The above discussion is based on the premise that China successfully leads the birth of cryptoSDRs and gains a significant degree of initiative and benefit. In this context, the impact is more favorable than unfavorable for China. However, if China passively accepts cryptoSDRs, there may be many adverse factors, including hindering the internationalization of Chinese yuan. The People's Bank of China may lose some or all of its currency issuance rights, and the government's ability to control the domestic financial market may decrease. At that point, China may lack sufficient preparation for the upcoming cryptoSDRs and may adopt a passive policy, developing the same resistance strategies as Bitcoin and other cryptocurrencies, gradually detaching itself from the international community and resulting in a decline in China's international status and influence. Therefore, this book suggests that China should actively participate in and lead the birth of cryptoSDRs to benefit its future development and currency strategy upgrade.

[13] See Footnote 12.

5.2 Chinese Yuan Internationalization in the Context of CryptoSDRs

The popularity of cryptoSDRs will to some extent squeeze the market share of Chinese yuan as a pricing tool in the international market, and the internationalization process of Chinese yuan will inevitably be affected at the beginning of the circulation of cryptoSDRs. However, China's currency and even national interests can be maximized by controlling the harmonious development of cryptoSDRs and the internationalization of Chinese yuan.

5.2.1 The Dilemma of Chinese Yuan Internationalization

In the context of the increasing popularity of cryptocurrency and the new globalization brought about by blockchain, Chinese yuan faces challenges in internationalization, financial liberalization, and foreign exchange control failure. When China's financial environment is not ready to respond to globalization, the internationalization of Chinese yuan remains difficult.

(1) Difficulties in Financial Liberalization

Various economic organizations around the world have made relevant regulations and restrictions on the internationalization of Chinese yuan from various perspectives. In various regulations and annual reports issued by the IMF, corresponding evaluations and valuations have been made on the exchange rates and trade restrictions among various currencies. If the level of restriction is high, the corresponding degree of openness should also be increased. The Organization for Economic Co-operation and Development (hereafter referred to as the "OECD") mainly regulates the degree of openness and sharing in the financial market through the "OECD Guidelines on Liberalization of Capital Flows," providing detailed and complete evaluations of various market flows and fund transaction systems, including various fund investments and trade exchanges. From the overall evaluation effect, the degree of openness in the financial market and trade market has achieved two-way opening, and effective supervision and management of various transaction modes, price-setting mechanisms, and currency exchange rates have been implemented to achieve dynamic monitoring and efficient management of the financial market.[14]

Since China's degree of financial liberalization is still relatively low, although there are many free trade zones serving as pioneers and experimental fields, the standards for financial access are still relatively high. If the financial door is immediately opened to support the internationalization of Chinese yuan, it will inevitably have a huge impact on China's economy. When China is not ready to respond to the changes

[14] Wu Guanghao. Connotation, International Experience and Inspiration of Financial Opening [J]. Northern Finance, 2018(10), pp. 95–98.

and impacts brought about by financial liberalization, these issues still deserve the attention of China's regulatory authorities.

(2) Difficulties in Exchange Rate Fluctuations

After the emergence of cryptoSDRs, Chinese yuan is likely to experience faster exchange rate fluctuations due to the availability of a more convenient supersovereign cryptocurrency for exchange. Therefore, it is necessary to plan the process of Chinese yuan internationalization and effective measures to respond to exchange rate fluctuations in advance. Since Chinese yuan joined the SDR currency basket, many scholars have suggested that the reform of the Chinese yuan exchange rate can learn from the experience of the eurozone's exchange rate target zone system and gradually lift exchange rate intervention. After the emergence of cryptoSDRs, this experience can also be applied to promote Chinese yuan internationalization and reform the exchange rate system.

By analyzing the value system and currency exchange rate represented by the euro, it can be found that the fundamental goal of the exchange rate target zone system is to achieve balanced development and stable fluctuations of various currency exchange rates in the EEC. Although different from the exchange rate floating policy based on the market supply and demand relationship with a basket of currencies as a reference indicator that China will construct and implement, it still has a strong positive reference value for the reform and adjustment of the domestic currency exchange rate system.

First, on the basis of a complete government credit system, the currency exchange rate will gradually converge toward the central exchange rate. The main influencing factors of the currency exchange rate include investor expectations and fundamental factors. Fundamental factors can serve as a reference indicator for the government's adjustment of currency exchange rates, while investor expectations need to be dynamically adjusted and updated according to the government's relevant policies. Under normal circumstances, currency exchange rates will continue to converge toward the central area. However, when the stability of fundamental factors decreases and the sensitivity of the central currency exchange rate decreases, investors will have doubts about the government's credit system. The issuance of cryptoSDRs will greatly facilitate Chinese yuan exchange, but at the same time, it will also increase the degree of fluctuation in the Chinese yuan exchange rate, resulting in the inability to update and adjust the central exchange rate in real time and causing doubts about the government's credibility among investors.

Second, the efficiency and effectiveness of the exchange rate target zone will be affected by capital controls. The main purpose of implementing the exchange rate target zone in the European Monetary System is to ensure that the economic output of the eurozone member states gradually concentrates toward the central region. However, since there are no capital controls among the member states, all currency indicators are converging toward Germany. If China were to implement a similar exchange rate target zone mechanism with the US dollar, under the premise of free capital flow and trading, the short-term exchange rate of the currency would be mainly determined by interest rate differentials, and the long-term exchange rate would converge toward the US. However, if there were capital controls, the Central Bank of China could ensure the effectiveness and feasibility of various monetary policies over a longer period of time. At the same time, it could largely establish the government's credit system and guarantee its credibility.[15] However, when the introduction of cryptoSDRs causes the failure of capital controls over Chinese yuan, the government may not be able to maintain the effectiveness of its monetary policy and may further weaken its commitments.

The birth of cryptoSDRs will inevitably have an impact on the internationalization of Chinese yuan and exchange rate fluctuations. If appropriate countermeasures are not taken, they will have a negative impact on the international status of Chinese yuan and the exchange rate of Chinese yuan.

(3) Difficulties in the Failure of Foreign Exchange Controls

Krugman's "Impossible Trinity Theory" shows that fixed exchange rates, independent monetary policy, and free capital flow are three independent goals, and only two of them can be achieved simultaneously.[16] Currently, China adopts a managed exchange rate system and restrictive foreign exchange flow, and the Chinese yuan external account system and foreign exchange account system are set up and managed separately. After cryptoSDRs are successfully launched, they will inevitably become a globally freely circulating currency. Due to the characteristics of blockchain technology, cryptoSDRs can achieve free circulation and hold without relying on traditional financial systems. Therefore, China's foreign exchange control system will face the consequence of failure. Even if traditional physical methods such as laws and customs are used to intercept and restrict, it will not be possible to achieve the goal of prohibiting the circulation of cryptoSDRs because as long as there is a network, cryptoSDRs can be used. The existence of nonsovereign cryptocurrencies such as Bitcoin and Ethereum has enabled many criminals to transfer assets abroad through network money laundering, which has caused the failure of foreign exchange control. The credit and technology of cryptoSDRs are above these nonsovereign cryptocurrencies, which will inevitably lead to more nationals and overseas investors using the convenient exchangeability of Chinese yuan and cryptoSDRs for cross-border capital flow, thereby exacerbating the failure of China's foreign exchange control.

(4) Limited Help from CryptoSDRs to Chinese Yuan Internationalization

Zheng Liansheng and Zhang Ming believe that the inclusion of Chinese yuan in the SDR basket could be beneficial for the continued internationalization of Chinese yuan, effectively safeguarding its main position in world trade and the international monetary system and promoting the diversified development of domestic and international foreign exchange reserve systems. However, there is still considerable uncertainty as to whether the SDRs can become a supersovereign currency on the world

[15] Li Chong. Path Selection of RMB Exchange Rate Reform under the Current Situation [J]. Guangdong Economy, 2016(4), pp. 40–43.

[16] PAUL R KRUGMAN. A Model of Balance of Payment Crisis [J]. Journal of Money Cridet and Banking, 1979(11), pp. 311–325.

trading platform.[17] Pan Yingli believes that if SDRs cannot provide effective support at the physical level and cannot circulate widely in society, they will not have a significant positive effect on the internationalization and diversified development of Chinese yuan.[18]

From the perspective of Chinese yuan's international reserve status, its proportion of international reserves in the world monetary system is still low. Although China has become a powerful country in the global economy and trade, the status of Chinese yuan in the international trade system is still not high, and it is not commensurate with China's economic strength. The main reasons include the following:

From the perspective of the international environment, as the US dollar dominates the international foreign exchange reserve system and has a significant impact on the entire network system, the promotion of the international currency status of Chinese yuan will take a considerable amount of time.

From the perspective of the domestic environment, the flaws in Chinese yuan currency itself will also have a significant impact on its international foreign exchange reserve status. As Chinese yuan is still not convertible in the capital account, it poses a major obstacle to the promotion of Chinese yuan's international currency status. Moreover, due to the high proportion of US dollars used in China's international trade payment and settlement processes, even though China's economic strength ranks at the forefront of the world, the use of the US dollar as the main currency in its foreign transactions will still have a significant impact on the promotion of Chinese yuan's international status.[19]

Currently, the SDRs are not yet monetized and do not provide much help for the internationalization of Chinese yuan, but if the SDRs become cryptoSDRs as a super-sovereign currency, it will have a significant driving force for the internationalization of Chinese yuan.

5.2.2 Harmonious Development of Chinese Yuan Internationalization and CryptoSDRs Monetization

After the birth of cryptoSDRs, China must inevitably face the issue of how to internationalize Chinese yuan. The internationalization of Chinese yuan is not only a trend but also an indispensable part of China's financial rise. However, China may not respond adequately to the internationalization of Chinese yuan after the emergence of cryptoSDRs. At least, the current strategic path for Chinese yuan internationalization is not clear, and its effect is not yet evident. In this situation, China can consider

---

[17] Zheng Liansheng, Zhang Ming. Should the Chinese Government Strongly Promote the Inclusion of RMB in the SDR? International Finance, 2015(7), pp. 3–6.

[18] Pan Yingli. The Relationship between the Goal and Means of Renminbi Internationalization and an Evaluation of the Significance of Joining the SDR [J]. Exploration and Contention, 2016(1), pp. 79–82.

[19] See Footnote 12.

drawing lessons from the internationalization strategies of the Japanese yen and the German mark and summarizing a strategic roadmap for Chinese yuan internationalization that is suitable for China in the new international monetary system based on cryptoSDRs.

Japan and Germany both experienced rapid economic development after World War II, and their current accounts remained in surplus, facing significant pressure for currency appreciation. However, they chose completely different strategies in dealing with the issue of currency appreciation and the full liberalization of capital projects. This is similar to the current situation in China, especially with the impact of cryptoSDRs on foreign exchange liberalization in the future. Japan was worried that the full liberalization of capital projects would lead to sharp fluctuations in the yen exchange rate, which could trigger a deterioration of its balance of payments, financial market turmoil, and macroeconomic weakness, so it did not open up capital projects completely until 1980. In contrast, West Germany achieved trade liberalization and capital liberalization on the basis of trade surplus and economic growth in 1956. Due to the full liberalization of its capital account in the late 1950s, Germany experienced rapid economic growth and development in the 1970s and 1980s. At the same time, Germany made reasonable use of foreign investors' expectations for its currency by timely adjusting and using its monetary policy and continuously exporting marks to the international market through its domestic capital account, thus continuously enhancing the mark's position in the international monetary settlement system.[20]

After the successful export of the German mark in Germany, domestic inflation pressure was effectively reduced. Throughout the 1970s, Germany's annual growth rate was 5%, far below Japan's 9%. Meanwhile, on the international trade market, as the proportion of the German mark gradually increased, the expectations of appreciation and investment pressure on the mark gradually decreased. By using the appreciating mark for payment and settlement in international trade, Germany effectively reduced the frequency of using the US dollar, thus greatly reducing the losses caused by using the US dollar for trade settlement. It is worth noting that the mark quickly became the second-largest international reserve currency after the US dollar under this policy, and its share in global foreign exchange reserves steadily climbed from 2.1% in 1970 to 10.2% in 1980 and then rose to a high of 17.9% over the next decade.[21] The high share of the mark in international reserves became the basis for the later birth of the euro, as the sum of the proportion of the French franc, Italian lira, Spanish peseta, Dutch guilder, and other currencies in international reserves was less than 2%, making it impossible to form the euro.

In the 1970s and 1980s, Japan faced the same problem after experiencing rapid development. However, Japan's approach was to block the inflow of foreign currencies into the country and restrict the supply of yen to the outside world through the

[20] Compared to the volatility of the Japanese yen exchange rate, the volatility of the mark exchange rate is smaller at this time. After calculation, the standard deviation of the Japanese yen exchange rate fluctuation is 39.52, while the standard deviation of the mark exchange rate fluctuation is only 0.45.

[21] Calculated based on official IMF data, http://imf.org/external/np/sta/cofer/eng/cofer.pdf.

control of capital projects. This resulted in a period when investors and residents outside Japan did not have a reasonable expectation for the yen's appreciation. Japan did not actively export the yen to the international trade market or increase its share in international trade settlements and payments. Therefore, in the 1970s and 1980s, Japan's trade deficit in the international trade system reached $3 billion. The amount of currency funds involved in the trade was small, so the yen's share in the international currency reserve system did not increase significantly. Japan did not export enough yen to the international market, leading to continuous trade surpluses and rising domestic commodity prices, which became the root cause of the subsequent Japanese economic crisis.[22]

When Japan realized the necessity and importance of internationalizing the yen, it was already the late 1970s. In 1980, Japan began to implement a strategy to internationalize the yen and liberalize its capital account. For instance, between 1981 and 1985, Japan maintained a capital account deficit of 136 billion US dollars, while the yen's share as an international reserve currency of other countries increased from almost zero to 8%.[23] However, Japan was heavily dependent on the US in politics, military, and other areas and had to sign the Plaza Accord in 1985, which was led by the US and forced the yen to appreciate rapidly. Within a year of the Plaza Accord's implementation, the exchange rate between the yen and the US dollar increased from 320 yen per dollar to 80 yen per dollar.[24]

The continuous appreciation of the yen's value led to a continuous decrease in investors' expected returns on the yen. Meanwhile, Japan's domestic economic growth rate began to slow down, and the yen's position in the international market had become unable to compete with the US dollar and the British pound. In the international trade market, foreign investors had started to gradually reduce their holdings of yen, and the yen's share in international reserve currencies had also gradually declined. The Japanese government tried to ease the domestic economic crisis and reduce domestic inflation by continuously exporting yen to the international market. However, due to the lack of historical opportunities and development trends, various currency policies and economic measures in Japan had little effect, even if Japan intended to increase the yen's share in the international trade market. However, investors had formed a negative attitude toward the future returns on the yen, resulting in a lack of market and customer flow and making it impossible for the yen to sustain international scale expansion.[25]

Germany and Japan adopted two completely different strategies in solving the issue of their domestic currency internationalization, and as a result, the yen was forced to appreciate rapidly in a very short period of time, causing a severe decline in

[22] According to official data from the IMF, http://imf.org/external/np/sta/cofer/eng/cofer.pdf. Accessed 6 May 2022.

[23] IMF. International Financial Statistics [EB/OL]. http://www.worldbank.org. Accessed 6 May 2022.

[24] Liu Junmin, Zhang Yun. Liquidity Expansion Dilemma and Its Response from the Perspective of Virtual Economy. Reform, 2008(1), pp. 18–25.

[25] See Footnote 24.

exports and the Japanese economy lasting for decades. At the same time, the yen was exported less to foreign countries, resulting in insufficient external output of Japan's domestic inflation pressure and ultimately causing the expansion and collapse of the Japanese economic bubble. On the other hand, the German mark became the world's second-largest international reserve currency, leading to the birth and development of the euro.

The experiences of Germany and the lessons learned by Japan tell us that China should firmly grasp the opportunities of the times, seize the opportunity of the strong expectation for Chinese yuan appreciation, and utilize China's strong economic strength, especially its strong industrial economy. Under the strong leadership of the Chinese government and monetary authorities, there should be a vigorous push to promote the internationalization of Chinese yuan and actively increase Chinese yuan's overseas supply. At the same time, efforts should be made to actively increase Chinese yuan's weight in the basket of currencies that make up the SDRs, promote and lead the birth of cryptoSDRs, and prepare in advance for the free circulation of Chinese yuan and its exchange with cryptoSDRs. With the cooperation of the new international situation, Chinese yuan should be developed into the major international reserve currency accepted by more countries, realizing a new internationalization strategy of enhancing Chinese yuan's international status and harmonious development with cryptoSDRs.

Actively promoting the internationalization of Chinese yuan, increasing the output of Chinese yuan abroad, and increasing the supply of Chinese yuan in international trade and financial markets can effectively export the growing inflation pressure domestic and slow down the speed of Chinese yuan appreciation. It can also change the serious imbalance between China's economic strength and the status of Chinese yuan.[26] At the same time, while resolving the insufficient internationalization of Chinese yuan, actively promoting the birth and popularity of cryptoSDRs can effectively improve the international status of Chinese yuan, enhance China's voice in the international community, and reflect the leadership and responsibility of China as the world's second-largest economy. This can also promote the establishment of rules for the international monetary system of cryptoSDRs and the rebalancing of the world's structure.

From a practical perspective, as the process of Chinese yuan internationalization continues to advance and the development of supersovereign currency continues, the corresponding policy-making departments in China should also ensure the coordination and integration of Chinese yuan internationalization and the domestic rule of law system through legal regulations to ensure the progress of Chinese yuan internationalization. Since 2009, China has already introduced a number of policy regulations to safeguard the process of Chinese yuan internationalization, such as the "Administration Measures for Pilot Settlement of Cross-border Trade in Chinese yuan" jointly issued by the People's Bank of China, the Ministry of Finance, the

[26] Li Lingyun. Formation and Influence of the "Dual Standard" International Monetary System [D]. Tianjin: Nankai University, 2010, pp. 186–189.

Ministry of Commerce, the General Administration of Customs, the State Administration of Taxation, and the China Banking Regulatory Commission in 2009; the "Implementation Rules for the Administration Measures for Pilot Settlement of Cross-border Trade in Chinese yuan" issued by the People's Bank of China; the "Circular on Relevant Matters Concerning the Refund (hereafter referred to as the "Exemption") of Export Goods Settled in Chinese yuan for Cross-border Trade" formulated by the State Administration of Taxation in 2009; the "Circular on Issues Related to the Pilot Settlement of Cross-border Trade in Chinese yuan" issued by the General Administration of Customs in 2009; the "Circular on Relevant Issues Concerning the Expansion of Pilot Settlement of Cross-border Trade in Chinese yuan" jointly issued by the People's Bank of China, the Ministry of Finance, the Ministry of Commerce, the General Administration of Customs, the State Administration of Taxation, and the China Banking Regulatory Commission in 2010; the "Administration Measures for Pilot Settlement of Chinese yuan for Direct Investment across the Border" formulated by the People's Bank of China in 2010; the "Interim Measures for the Administration of Cross-border Chinese yuan Receipt and Payment Information Management System" issued by the People's Bank of China in 2010; the "Circular on Simplifying the Process of Cross-border Chinese yuan Transactions and Improving Relevant Policies" formulated by the People's Bank of China in 2013, etc. The introduction of these policy regulations has played an indispensable role in promoting the internationalization process of Chinese yuan, but because most of the rules and regulations formulated during this period are only at the departmental level and are mainly in the form of notices and measures, the efficiency of the relevant legal policies is generally low. At the same time, some of the rules and regulations are named "interim measures" and lack the longevity and stability of laws. In terms of legal nature, some of the relevant regulations and policies formulated since 2009 are only "interim measures" and are not true laws, so relevant government departments need to strengthen the legislative level to optimize and improve the legal system related to Chinese yuan internationalization.[27] Currently, the new internationalization strategy for the harmonious development of cryptoSDRs and Chinese yuan has not yet begun, and the Chinese government needs to attach great importance to it and prepare in advance. When formulating legislation, it is necessary to actively carry out research and layout on relevant laws and regulations through regulatory "sandbox" experiments.

Using the development process of international currencies as a classification criterion, international currencies can be divided into dominant currencies, key currencies, neutral currencies, and negotiating currencies. Dominant currencies refer to domestic currencies that are forced to be used in colonies or dependent countries. Key currencies are the currencies of sovereign countries that dominate the international trade market. Neutral currencies refer to currencies that have trading advantages in the international trade system but do not occupy a major currency position and have a lower internationalization tendency of the issuing country. Negotiating currencies

[27] Tu Yongqian, Qiu Ben. Legal Path and Rule of Law Construction for the Internationalization of Renminbi [J]. Political Science and Law Journal, 2015(5), pp. 13–22.

refer to currencies that are actively supported by some countries and promote the currency of the issuing country to occupy a dominant position in the international trade system.[28]

Chinese researchers in relevant fields believe that the policies and strategic directions demonstrated by the Chinese government in promoting the internationalization process of Chinese yuan are continuously deepening and comply with the concept and strategic model of negotiating currencies.[29] China's strategy and model for promoting Chinese yuan internationalization mainly involves external negotiation and cooperation, promoting coordinated development in regional areas, and ensuring the stability of Chinese yuan in the internationalization process.[30]

According to the "2020 Chinese yuan Internationalization Report" released by the People's Bank of China, Chinese yuan's market share in the global foreign exchange trading market was 4.3%, and its market share in major international payment currencies was 1.76%, ranking fifth.[31] According to the "Composition of Official Foreign Exchange Reserve Currencies" report released by the IMF, in the first quarter of 2021, Chinese yuan accounted for 2.45% of the global foreign exchange reserve holdings, equivalent to USD 287.463 billion.[32] These data indicate that Chinese yuan is currently only in a neutral currency position and has not yet reached a fully negotiating currency status. Although China has signed multiple currency swap agreements with ASEAN countries, its share in the international currency market is still very small. Furthermore, in the environment of the US trade war and the fortified world financial pattern, it is unrealistic for Chinese yuan to quickly increase its market share and rapidly internationalize in a short period of time.

Although cyptoSDRs will not be issued by any sovereign country, they can be attributed to the international currency attributes of key currencies, and thus, the theoretical model of key currencies can be used for strategic promotion and popularization. As a key currency, the promotion and popularization of cyptoSDRs globally are relatively easy, and Chinese yuan can effectively increase its internationalization share by taking advantage of the favorable opportunity of the continuous increase in the market share of cyptoSDRs. Even in some areas where cyptoSDRs are not easily accepted, Chinese yuan can enter and circulate with the help of cyptoSDRs,

---

[28] Li Yanfeng. Political and Economic Analysis of Renminbi Internationalization. Contemporary Economic Management, 2015(6), pp. 1–5.

[29] Cao Yong. Analysis of the Political and Economic Dual Perspectives of RMB Internationalization. Economic System Reform, 2010(2), pp. 20–24.

[30] Cao Yong. Analysis of the Political and Economic Dual Perspectives of RMB Huang Xueyin. Legal Thinking on the Internationalization of Renminbi-from the Perspective of Renminbi Joining the Special Drawing Rights [J]. China Market, 2017(12), pp. 122–125.

[31] People's Bank of China. "2020 Report on Renminbi Internationalization." [EB/OL]. Available at: https://www.sogou.com/link?url=hedJjaC291M1crEDB-pObOfhhvEf1fs_amZWDDqm0FvdLAEz2Et20878Pc-EdQ1DriuqOZE83Sr688U3F96Juq4to0wa_Tif. Accessed 6 May 2022.

[32] IMF. Currency Composition of Official Foreign Exchange Reserves (COFER) [EB/OL]. https://data.imf.org/?sk=E6A5F467-C14B-4AA8-9F6D-5A09EC4E62A4&sId=1408206195757. Accessed 6 May 2022.

complementing each other and achieving the harmonious development of Chinese yuan internationalization and cyptoSDRs. The specific approach is as follows.

(1) Construction of the Legal System for the Harmonious Development of Chinese yuan Internationalization and CryptoSDR Monetization

First, based on the characteristics of cryptoSDRs, amendments should be made to the People's Bank of China Law, and targeted monetary policies should be developed to effectively promote the development and transformation of various economic systems in China, taking into account the actual economic situation. At the same time, research on cryptoSDRs and their legal status should be included in legislative research on currency. Currently, progress in realizing the reserve currency function of Chinese yuan remains relatively slow, mainly due to the lack of targeted monetary policies and reform measures by the Central Bank based on China's current economic and monetary situation. Currently, domestic monetary policies are mainly adjusted through government actions, but the policies and regulations introduced by the government cannot completely integrate with the market operation mechanism, resulting in neglect of the market's dominant position and regulatory function. Furthermore, to avoid the influence of the international external environment on China's current domestic monetary policy, adjustments and optimization should be made to the domestic monetary policy.[33]

In addition, the monetization strategy of cryptoSDRs should be included in China's monetary strategy to achieve a new internationalization strategy in which Chinese yuan and cryptoSDRs can develop harmoniously and promote each other. Currently, Chinese yuan is already a member of the SDR basket of currencies, accounting for 10.92% and ranking third.[34] As China's international status and that of Chinese yuan continue to rise, China will have more international discourse power, which will help China lead the establishment of cryptoSDRs and the formulation of corresponding international monetary policies.

Second, in the process of adjusting and optimizing the legal framework for securities issuance, the lower limit of qualifications for securities issuers in the market should be adjusted to allow more foreign issuers to enter the domestic securities market to issue bonds and to form an internationalized domestic securities market. Meanwhile, research should be strengthened to introduce cryptoSDRs as settlement currencies for securities. Currently, the degree of internationalization of China's securities market is relatively low, resulting in strong market closure. As the existing legal system for securities regulation still regards the government as the main monitoring body and behavior orientation and lacks market supervision and regulation, it has become a significant obstacle to the influx of international capital. In addition, inconsistencies in various regulations and legal provisions have led to the inability of related businesses to obtain effective processing and resolution through

[33] Wang Guogang. The Multiple Functions of Renminbi Joining SDR [J]. China Finance, 2015(24), pp. 41–43.

[34] IMF. Special Drawing Rights (SDRs) [EB/OL]. https://www.imf.org/en/Topics/special-drawing-right. Accessed 6 May 2022.

legal means.[35] After Chinese yuan became a basket currency, international investors mainly obtained Chinese yuan from deposit outflows and investment project fund flows. If the funds invested by foreign investors are subject to restrictions on the qualifications of domestic legal entities, the holding of Chinese yuan in the international trade market will decrease.

Meanwhile, actively studying cryptoSDRs will help facilitate international capital inflows into China's securities market, creating an internationally oriented securities market that is in line with China's national conditions. Adjusting and optimizing the Securities Law should take into account the current bond issuance and trading models in the securities market, continuously promote the formation of diversified product and service models in the domestic financial market, and promote the optimization of the securities market structure. At the same time, a complete international securities issuance system and bond circulation system should be established to promote the inflow of foreign capital while enhancing Chinese yuan's dominant position in the international trade market.

Third, laws and regulations should be formulated in the field of foreign trade to continuously strengthen the construction of Chinese yuan's exchange rate mechanism, actively responding to the impact that cryptoSDRs may have on the foreign exchange reserve system. The experience of revising Japan's foreign exchange law shows that timely development of integrated foreign exchange management methods that meet market realities can promote the safety and freedom of securities and financial market transactions in China. At the same time, transparency in all types of transaction behavior and activities, as well as efficiency in business operations, should be increased to continuously promote Chinese yuan's position in the international trade system, ensure orderly progress in Chinese yuan's internationalization process, and proactively respond to the passive situation that may arise from the failure of foreign exchange controls caused by the free circulation of cryptoSDRs. Based on the current foreign exchange management legal system and combined with various policies and regulatory systems, an integrated and complete foreign exchange management legal system should be formed.

(2) Deepening Exchange Rate System Reform, Implementing a Managed Floating Exchange Rate System, and Focusing on CryptoSDRs

A good exchange rate adjustment mechanism should have both flexibility and stability. Currently, cryptoSDRs have not yet been fully implemented, and due to the relatively low level of policy and regulatory perfection in the domestic financial market, the market's ability to regulate itself is insufficient. Therefore, it is necessary to rely on the government to improve and adjust the entire financial market system. Based on a floating exchange rate policy, it is necessary to ensure the stability and balance of the exchange rate through the market's supply and demand relationship, allow the market to independently adjust and control the exchange rate, and empower

[35] Liu Daoyuan. Legal Dilemmas and Solutions for Internationalization Reform of China's Securities Market: A Reflection on the U.S. Securities Law System. Law and Business Research, 2016(4), pp. 173–182.

the central bank to stabilize and coordinate the financial market in the legal formulation of the floating exchange rate system to prevent falling into a liquidity trap during economic development.[36]

The primary condition for the internationalization of a currency is to ensure the stability of its exchange rate and the transparency of its currency valuation mechanism. Only by meeting these conditions can such a currency's proportion in the international monetary system continue to increase. On the basis of stable market supply and demand, a basket of currencies should be used as a reference sample for Chinese yuan exchange rate adjustment to effectively improve the defects of Chinese yuan's inability to develop independently and reduce its dependence on foreign currencies. When the degree of currency exchange rate fluctuation is large, it may cause financial market volatility. At this time, the central bank should stabilize the currency exchange rate and use measures such as repurchase agreements to adjust and control the supply and demand of both sides of the foreign exchange market, thus improving domestic and foreign trade markets as well as investment entities' expectations of the value of Chinese yuan.[37]

At the same time, when cryptoSDRs are introduced, changing the managed floating exchange rate system with a basket of currencies as the reference to a pegged exchange rate system with cryptoSDRs as the reference can effectively reduce the reliance on sovereign foreign currencies. According to Tinbergen's rule, a policy tool can only solve one currency or economic problem. Only through the integrated construction of policies can multiple problems be solved.[38] The formulation of currency exchange rates should be based on the current domestic market and foreign economic environment and undergo flexible adjustments and updates. By systematically reforming the Chinese yuan exchange rate formation mechanism and evaluation system, we can effectively realize dynamic management and real-time supervision of the exchange rate, ensure the stability of the capital market, and promote the integrated development of the securities and financial markets. Pinning the exchange rate to cryptoSDRs can better achieve the reform of the exchange rate system.

(3) Leveraging the Construction of the "A Belt and a Road" to Construct the Legal Foundation for Chinese yuan Internationalization and CryptoSDRs Monetization

The establishment of the Bretton Woods system laid the institutional foundation for the US dollar to become the major international currency, playing a crucial role in promoting the US dollar's sovereignty as a payment and settlement currency in global trade. China's "A Belt and a Road" initiative can also effectively promote economic exchanges and trade activities among countries along the route while

---

[36] Han Long. Ideas for Solving Major Legal Issues of RMB Internationalization. Law Science, 2016(10), pp. 40–49.

[37] Zuo Haicong, Cui Yu. Shortcomings and Reform Proposals of the Current RMB Exchange Rate System: Based on the Perspective of RMB Internationalization. Southern Finance, 2016(10), pp. 23–28.

[38] Yang Lihua. Research on the Effectiveness of Renminbi Exchange Rate Reform Mechanism—Based on the Perspective of Achieving the Reform Goals [J]. Southwest Finance, 2016(5), pp. 51–58.

effectively promoting the flow and interaction of funds and strengthening the degree of trade dependence between China and countries along the route, thus continuously advancing the internationalization process of Chinese yuan and improving its currency status in international trade activities. This also helps China participate in and pursue the creation of cryptoSDRs and the formulation of relevant monetary policies.[39] First, China should seize the opportunity of "A Belt and a Road" judicial construction, actively participate in the formulation of intergovernmental multilateral currency cooperation agreements,[40] cryptoSDR monetization legislation and other international economic rules, and continuously promote innovation in international economic business and legal construction in free trade zones in the process of judicial adjudication. Second, China should continuously optimize and promote the internationalization process of Chinese yuan, improve the currency status of Chinese yuan in the international trade system, and use China's "A Belt and a Road" initiative to continuously stimulate investors in the international market to invest in China's domestic economic construction, thereby reducing the pressure on China's foreign exchange reserves, increasing the proportion of international financial assets in China's domestic financial market and realizing the internationalization development of China's securities trading and financial trade market.[41] Third, by increasing the role and function of the Silk Road Economic Belt, the 21st-Century Maritime Silk Road, and the AIIB, China can continuously increase the overall use of Chinese yuan in foreign trade. The establishment of the AIIB in December 2015 provided a multilateral funding platform for the development of "A Belt and a Road." If we can continuously strengthen the frequency of Chinese yuan's use in the operation of the AIIB and increase the amount of Chinese yuan held by international investors, it will be beneficial to the realization of Chinese yuan's settlement, payment, and investment functions. Finally, China should accelerate the construction of the cryptoSDR exchange system and appropriately open up some cities for the circulation of cryptoSDR "sandbox" regulatory experiments. At the same time, China should continuously strengthen the system construction of Chinese yuan and improve the currency exchange mechanism of cryptoSDRs. By forming a commodity system with Chinese yuan as the currency unit in trade with countries along the "A Belt and a Road" route and increasing the use of Chinese yuan through trade agreements and cooperation exchanges among governments, China can achieve the goal of continuously increasing the proportion of Chinese yuan in the international trade market.[42]

The construction of the credit system for the Chinese currency, Chinese yuan, originates from the establishment of China's legal system and legal protections. In

---

[39] Lin Lefen, Wang Shaonan. One Belt One Road Initiative and Renminbi Internationalization. World Economics and Politics, 2015(11), pp. 72–90 + 158.

[40] He Rong. On China's Judicial Participation in the Formulation of International Economic Rules [J]. International Law Research, 2016(1), pp. 3–15.

[41] See Footnote 33.

[42] See Footnote 18.

fact, the creditworthiness of the currency is an objective expression of the completeness of the country's legal system. The People's Bank of China has clearly defined the legal status of Chinese yuan and its legal currency status within China. No entity or individual has the authority to refuse Chinese yuan payments or debt repayment.[43] The formulation of various laws and regulations also guarantees the legal status of Chinese yuan as the sole legal unit of measurement for transactions and settlements within China, and as a function of unlimited payment. Everyone must accept Chinese yuan payments for all debts, and the value of Chinese yuan should be determined by the state's regulatory policies.

The formulation of various policies and regulations also guarantees the establishment of Chinese yuan as a legal currency and the persistence of its credit system. The durability of the monetary credit system depends on the feasibility and effectiveness of the legal system that safeguards monetary credit. When the legal system is scientific and effective, it can promote the sustainable operation of the monetary system, thereby continuously optimizing and developing the domestic economy.[44]

It can be seen that the formulation of various laws and regulations in China will have a significant impact on the internationalization process of Chinese yuan. Therefore, it is necessary to continuously strengthen the updating and optimization of China's legal system, thereby enhancing the credibility of Chinese yuan in domestic and foreign markets and improving its international competitiveness.[45] After the integration and regulation of cryptoSDRs, China's relevant monetary laws and regulations will have a comparative advantage and can better promote the harmonious development of Chinese yuan internationalization and cryptoSDRs monetization.

The internationalization process of Chinese yuan should be promoted in conjunction with the construction of various domestic laws and regulations. The enhancement of Chinese yuan's status in the world trade market system should be combined with the construction of various supporting legal systems in the country. However, since the existing laws, policies, and regulations were formulated and implemented during the initial stage of Chinese yuan internationalization, they are no longer compatible with the current economic structure as Chinese yuan's international status increases. Therefore, they must be reformed and optimized to continuously promote the sustainable development of the domestic economy and improve the flaws in domestic policies and legal systems.[46] The harmonious development of Chinese yuan internationalization and the monetization of cryptoSDRs is still in the research stage and requires the participation of more government agencies and scholars to study and discuss and to establish corresponding policies and regulations.

---

[43] Liu Ying. Legal Analysis of the Development of Currency Forms: Impact of Electronic Currency on Legal System. Chinese Law, 2002 (1), pp. 81–92.

[44] Fried, Schwartz. A Monetary History of the United States (1867–1960) [M]. Translated by Ba Shusong, et al. Beijing: Peking University Press, 2009, p. 497.

[45] See Footnote 27.

[46] Xiang Yaping. Analysis of the Legal Path of RMB Internationalization [J]. Hebei Law Science, 2013(5), pp. 120–126.

Various interest groups in the US can fundamentally guarantee the US dollar's dominant position in the international currency settlement and payment system through the Western developed capitalist system, as well as America's strong economic power and total funds. In addition, the US has a certain degree of control over the prices of various traded goods in trade activities. Thus, the US can achieve its fundamental interests by manipulating the prices of international commodities.[47] For example, at the beginning of the twenty-first century, the international trading market saw a continuous rise in oil prices, even reaching $100 per barrel. The main reason for this was China's possession of the world's largest foreign exchange reserves, which greatly influenced US capital groups. Therefore, the US continuously raised the international trade price of oil by taking advantage of China's huge oil gap in domestic economic development, with the primary aim of consuming China's foreign exchange reserves.[48]

Thus, if China cannot obtain the pricing power of production materials and bulk commodities in the market competition process, it will lose its advantage in international trade competition, which will pose a significant obstacle to the internationalization process of Chinese yuan and China's strategic objectives for economic development. Therefore, the primary goal of Chinese yuan internationalization is to obtain the pricing power of the world's major production materials, which can further guarantee the sustainable development of China's domestic economy.[49]

In addition, China can gradually obtain pricing power over commodities in the world trade market through the priority pricing power of rare earth resources. Although China is a major exporter of rare earth resources, accounting for 90% of the world's total supply, it has not yet obtained the pricing power of rare earth resources in the world trade market. Therefore, even though rare earth resources are essential to industrial and innovative fields, their prices remain relatively low.

However, the pricing power of rare earth resources is not entirely controlled by the US, and China still has the opportunity to control the international pricing power of this commodity. Based on relevant regulations in the international trade market, China must establish a legal system for pricing and supplying reserves of rare earth resources domestically while protecting the country's natural resource reserves. Through timely adjustments and control of the pricing rules of rare earth resources in the international market, China can ensure that Chinese yuan obtains pricing and valuation rights over rare earth resources in the international trade market.[50]

If Chinese yuan is not sufficient to fully monopolize the international pricing power of rare earths, China can also indirectly promote the use of cryptoSDRs to control the international pricing power of rare earths to some extent, thereby

---

[47] Lang Xianping. How International Financial Speculators Plunder Wealth [J]. IT Times Weekly, 2009(6), p. 11.

[48] Data Briefing. International Crude Oil Price Trends and Major Events Since 1970 [EB/OL]. http://intl.ce.cn/specials/zxxx/201307/31/t20130731_24622321.shtml. Accessed 6 May 2022.

[49] Lan Yonghai, Jia Linzhou, Wen Tiejun. The U.S. Dollar's "Currency Hegemony" Strategy and China's Response [J]. World Economics and Politics, 2012(3), pp. 121–137 + 159–160.

[50] Song Wei. Bulk Commodities are the Breakthrough Point for Renminbi Pricing [J]. China Finance, 2013(23), pp. 55–56.

enhancing the international status of Chinese yuan and grasping the monetary policy-making power of cryptoSDRs as much as possible.

5.2.3 *Implementation of a Domestic Currency Mechanism to Respond to CryptoSDRs*

China, as the world's second-largest economy and especially as the advocate and strong supporter of the "A Belt and a Road" initiative, has continuously increased its international status and influence. It needs to take on the responsibility of reforming the current international monetary system to make it more in line with the current world pattern and international situation. By promoting the construction of a new international monetary system based on cryptoSDRs, it will be beneficial to balance the interests of traditional developed countries and emerging economies, promote the sustainable development of the international monetary system, and solve the inherent defects of the current international monetary system.

(1) Establishing a Sound Domestic Regulatory System

From the perspective of economic globalization, an integrated transaction supervision system should be formulated for the trade process between countries around the world to reduce management costs and improve the flexibility and convenience of business process handling. The construction of a unified regulatory system can promote the sharing of data information. A publicly transparent mechanism can ensure that all transaction activities are based on equal data information, which is conducive to policy supervision and management of all transactions in the trade market, safeguarding the legitimate interests of both supply and demand sides of commodities, expanding the coverage and influence of the trading market, and promoting economic integration and globalization.

In addition, the legalization of the financial market can promote all businesses and projects to be more reasonable and legitimate, thereby guaranteeing the efficiency of trade exchanges. China can draw on the historical experience of other countries in the construction of the legal system in the financial market. It can also combine the domestic economic environment and the development of the financial market to establish a financial market legal system with Chinese characteristics based on practice, guaranteeing the stable development of China's trade exchange market and promoting the sustainable circulation and use of Chinese yuan in the international market.[51] In particular, China should draw on the experience of developed countries in the financial field and clarify the rights and responsibilities of regulators in legal form. In addition, gradual unification of the cross-border flow of Chinese yuan can be achieved through the gradual unification of regulatory laws, regulations,

[51] Jiang Boke. New Compilation of International Finance (Third Edition) [M]. Shanghai: Fudan University Press, 2008, p. 270.

and corresponding measures between countries. Additionally, after the birth of cryptoSDRs, research on the legislative and regulatory status of cryptoSDRs can help China improve its regulatory laws and regulations to support the internationalization strategy of Chinese yuan.

(2) Strengthening Legal Regulations and Crackdowns on Cross-border Financial Illegal Activities

Currently, with the rise of cryptocurrencies, many funds in China are flowing out to foreign countries in the form of cryptocurrencies, causing a continuous loss of Chinese yuan assets. In fact, a portion of Chinese yuan circulating in foreign markets enters the international market through illegal channels. The outflow of Chinese yuan from the domestic market will lead to a continuous decline in the currency supply on the domestic trade market, resulting in a drop in commodity prices in China. Chinese yuan that enters the international market through illegal channels will not bring social resources and material wealth to China but instead will cause a continuous outflow of domestic economic resources, resulting in a decline in domestic capital flow, making it difficult to effectively promote infrastructure construction. The continuous outflow of funds results in a shrinking domestic investment scale, causing a continuous increase in the unemployment rate and having a significant impact on GDP.

At the same time, a portion of Chinese yuan that flows into the international market returns to the domestic market through investment, but this portion of the returned Chinese yuan does not belong to international capital in the true sense, leading to a continuous decline in China's fiscal revenue and having a negative impact on economic growth and social development. Therefore, the government must prevent such situations from happening through appropriate laws, regulations, and monitoring measures while increasing the inspection of incoming foreign funds to ensure the authenticity and safety of foreign capital flowing into the domestic market.[52]

As a more stable and legal alternative to nonsovereign cryptocurrencies, the emergence of cryptoSDRs will inevitably accelerate the outflow of Chinese yuan and the inflow of "foreign capital." Therefore, it is necessary to conduct corresponding research and preparation in advance, strengthen the supervision of currency circulation channels, and increase penalties for illegal capital flows to prevent the illegal outflow of domestic currency and avoid economic development instability caused by illegal currency outflow. To this end, the People's Bank of China's "Management Measures for Large and Suspicious Foreign Exchange Transactions of Financial Institutions" issued in 2003 clearly stipulates the evaluation standards and review procedures for large and suspicious foreign exchange transactions in which financial institutions participate. It is combined with the "Anti-Money Laundering Regulations for Financial Institutions" and the "Management Measures for Large and Suspicious Payment Transactions in Chinese yuan" to establish a legal system for financial

[52] Ma Ronghua. Empirical Analysis of the Impact of the Offshore Circulation of Renminbi on China's Economy [J]. Economic Research Journal, 2006(4), pp. 35–48.

management in the domestic financial market, ensuring the safety and stability of Chinese yuan flow on the basis of currency free flow.

(3) Establishing Effective International Cooperation Mechanisms

Domestic regulatory agencies need to establish management policies for offshore financial markets to ensure coordinated development between Hong Kong and mainland China. In 2003, Hong Kong established the world's first offshore Chinese yuan clearing system to safeguard the stable and sustainable development of its financial market. If Chinese yuan is to establish its primary currency status in a specific region and gradually achieve internationalization, it must start with the Hong Kong financial market.[53] At the same time, with the continuous development of the Hong Kong Chinese yuan securities and financial markets, it effectively reduces the securities issuance risks and settlement risks in mainland China's market and plays a positive role in safeguarding the stable development of the domestic financial market. As the internationalization of Chinese yuan continues to advance, it is necessary to establish Chinese yuan's function as an investment currency and promote the realization of its status as a reserve currency in the global integration process. Hong Kong is a critical pathway for Chinese yuan to go global, so it is necessary to formulate reasonable policies and regulations between the financial markets in Hong Kong and mainland China to support the free and secure flow of Chinese yuan. Moreover, in the construction of the system for the exchange between cryptoSDRs and Chinese yuan, the offshore Chinese yuan market in Hong Kong can also be used as a pilot to further open up the free exchange between Chinese yuan and cryptoSDRs and achieve the harmonious development of Chinese yuan and cryptoSDRs.

Second, it is necessary to continuously enhance China's trade and economic cooperation with other countries and safeguard the basic interests of all countries in the international monetary system through trade agreements. In the currency swap agreements signed between China and other countries, the participating countries have reached a consensus on currency transaction settlement and exchange, stipulating that the sovereign currencies of the participating countries can achieve free exchange and trading, guaranteeing the free flow of currencies in the economic and trade markets of all countries, and promoting the orderly development of economic markets and the efficiency of capital raising. Strictly speaking, currency swaps are not necessary factors in the internationalization process of a currency, but they can promote the orderly development of finance and economy and stimulate the development of trading activities, as well as reduce the management and capital-raising costs of trade.[54]

For China, signing currency swap agreements with other countries can significantly guarantee the internationalization of Chinese yuan, ensure its holding and impact in the global market, and facilitate the transaction convenience of various

[53] Wang Yuanlong. Research on Some Issues of RMB Internationalization [J]. Finance and Trade Economics, 2009(7), pp. 16–22 + 135.

[54] See Footnote 53.

economic entities in international trade. It can also promote the reasonable development of domestic and foreign trade markets, effectively reduce currency payment and settlement risks, and ensure the security and effectiveness of various transaction activities. When cryptoSDRs are introduced, Chinese yuan should also exchange a large amount of currency with the IMF. This exchange not only benefits the internationalization of Chinese yuan but also allows the Chinese government and people to hold a large amount of cryptoSDRs and reduce dependence on the US dollar.

At the same time, it is also necessary to strengthen trade cooperation between China and countries along the "A Belt and a Road," promote economic and cultural exchanges between countries, and construct a new type of international trade interaction system in trade relations. This includes the real-time updating and optimization of various economic systems, policies, and regulations to ensure the efficiency and stability of all activities. The development of product and service diversification in the trade system should be strengthened, and the development process of banking business should also be continuously advanced. The payment and settlement channels between commercial banks of various countries should be optimized to improve Chinese yuan's currency status in bilateral trade payment and settlement. Meanwhile, through government cooperation and exchanges, the free flow of Chinese yuan in overseas investment should be safeguarded to promote its function as an investment currency.

Although there are still many obstacles to the free exchange of Chinese yuan, as China's policies and systems gradually open up, the structure of its financial market has also been optimized and reformed, and the use of Chinese yuan in overseas investment has gradually increased. Of course, the domestic review procedures for fund connectivity and entry conditions also need to be adjusted and updated to ensure the free flow of Chinese yuan in the international trade market and continuously promote the internationalization process of Chinese yuan and the world integration development of the domestic financial market.[55] Additionally, it is necessary to accelerate the coordination and cooperation between the IMF and Central Bank of China to prepare in advance for the birth and operation of cryptoSDRs and to better serve the harmonious development strategy of the internationalization of Chinese yuan and the monetiization of cryptoSDRs.

The continuous optimization of China's financial market, along with the ongoing development of the monetary system and the continuous improvement of the domestic legal system, has a positive effect on the internationalization of Chinese yuan and the integrated development of the domestic financial market. Chinese yuan's position in the international monetary system is gradually increasing, and its usage and frequency in the world trade market are also constantly growing. China should seize the historical opportunity of the IMF's reform, actively expand the coverage of Chinese yuan, accelerate the organic connection between the Mainland and Hong Kong's financial markets, optimize the domestic policy system structure, and ensure

[55] Ma Ronghua. Analysis of the Benefits and Costs of the Offshore Circulation of Renminbi [J]. Journal of Shijiazhuang University of Economics, 2006(1), pp. 57–61 + 68.

Chinese yuan's dominant position in partial regional payments and transaction settlements. At the same time, the economic development modules of the "A Belt and a Road" and the AIIB ensure the effective development of Chinese yuan in the overseas fund circulation system. Through currency swap agreements and various economic development consensuses, ensure the free exchange and efficient circulation of Chinese yuan with other countries' currencies. By accelerating various business processes, simplifying transaction steps, improving the efficiency of business processing in the economic and trade system, continuously enhancing Chinese yuan's appreciation expectations among international investors, and thus ensuring Chinese yuan's continuous dominance in the international market, increasing its holdings in the world trade market, and continuously promoting the internationalization of Chinese yuan, China can enhance its global standing and influence.[56] At the same time, the government should actively promote the birth of cryptoSDRs and the construction of their related systems and lead the development of a new international monetary system.

(4) Improving the Foreign Exchange Regulatory System

The emergence of cryptoSDRs can serve as another currency tool for China. In the process of gradually relaxing the control of Chinese yuan, it can boost China's foreign capital financial communication and give Chinese yuan time to adjust so that Chinese yuan can transition from strict control to free circulation smoothly. At the same time, in the short term, it can effectively prevent fluctuations in Chinese yuan's exchange rate and alleviate the pressure of Chinese yuan depreciation.

According to the 2014 annual report released by the IMF, in various financial transactions and capital exchange projects, except for the two capital trading projects of the financial subitem and various commercial credit loan businesses, a series of policies and measures have been formulated for the other six capital trading control projects to ensure the efficient development and orderly promotion of various trading activities.[57] In the process of formulating various evaluation criteria and control systems, the IMF has issued clear certifications and approvals for various trading projects. However, some of the management methods and measures for certain projects do not conform to China's actual economic development situation.[58]

With the gradual opening up of China's financial market system and the gradual reduction of restrictions on the use of Chinese yuan in the international trade market, the circulation freedom of Chinese yuan in the international monetary system has gradually increased. The State Administration of Foreign Exchange in China issued

[56] Wang Yan, Li Zhiyong. Research on the Legal Guarantee of RMB Cross-border Flow Safety [J]. Journal of Yunnan University (Law Edition), 2010(2), pp. 35–42.

[57] INTERNATIONAL MONETARY FUND. Annual Report on Exchange Arrangements and Exchange Restrictions 2014[EB/OL]. https://www.imf.org/en/Publications/Annual-Report-on-Exchange-Arrangements-and-Exchange-Restrictions/Issues/2016/12/31/Annual-Report-on-Exchange-Arrangements-and-Exchange-Restrictions-2014-41643. Accessed 6 May 2022.

[58] ANDRÉS FERNÁNDEZ, MICHAEL W KLEIN, ALESSANDRO REBUCCI, etal. Capital Control Measures: A New Dataset [R]. IMF Working Paper, 2015.

the "Notice on Further Simplifying and Improving the Foreign Exchange Management Policies for Direct Investment" in February 2015, which stipulated that from June 1, 2015, foreign exchange registration and approval under direct investment would be canceled, and domestic and foreign investment entities could directly handle foreign exchange registration for direct investment at banks. In terms of foreign exchange capital inflows and domestic fund outflows, China has formulated relatively strict management measures and policies to ensure the safety of fund transactions and overseas investment management, reduce investment risks, and ensure the stability of the monetary system.

In practice, the adjustment of the Chinese yuan exchange rate has gradually developed into market-oriented reforms. The country began to implement market-led and regulated exchange rate changes to weaken the government's participation in the currency market and ensure the dominant role of the market.

In 2005, the People's Bank of China issued the "Announcement on Improving the Reform of Chinese yuan Exchange Rate Formation Mechanism," announcing that the exchange rate of Chinese yuan should no longer only follow the exchange rate changes of the US dollar but also take the market supply and demand relationship as a reference basis for dynamically updating and adjusting the exchange rate and strengthening the market's influence and dominant role in currency exchange rates.

In April 2012, the daily floating range of Chinese yuan against the US dollar was increased from the original 0.5 to 1%, and the maximum difference between the daily exchange rates for US dollar cash buying and selling provided by designated foreign exchange banks was expanded from 1 to 2% of the daily midpoint exchange rate.

In March 2014, the People's Bank of China issued a notice to increase the floating range of the Chinese yuan exchange rate against the US dollar in the interbank spot foreign exchange market from 1 to 2% starting on March 17, 2014. At the same time, the maximum difference between the daily exchange rates for US dollar cash buying and selling provided by designated foreign exchange banks was expanded from 2 to 3%.

Even if the above exchange rate system adjustments are made, to further promote the internationalization process of Chinese yuan, greater efforts and policy adjustments are needed to provide a more perfect institutional framework and economic and trade environment for optimizing and reforming the Chinese yuan exchange rate. A two-step approach can be taken to achieve this.

The first step is to increase the total amount of national debt issuance in China. The main reason for the relatively low amount of national debt issuance is due to the restrictions of relevant laws and regulations, as well as the low level of completeness of the entire market trading system. Therefore, China must lower the conditions for foreign capital entering the domestic financial market from the perspective of global economic integration while also increasing the total amount of Chinese yuan issuance in the international market, promoting the free circulation of Chinese yuan in the trade system. At the same time, China should provide institutional guarantees and policy support for the development of domestic financial and securities markets, promoting the diversified development of economic and trade markets. Additionally, it is necessary to ensure the stable development of various products and services in the market, avoid financial risks as much as possible, safeguard the sustained growth of the domestic economy, strengthen the innovative development and optimization of the economic system, and thus construct a currency and economic system based on the internationalization process.[59]

The second step is to promote the development of cryptoSDRs and form a new model of currency cooperation that harmoniously coexists and complements the internationalization of Chinese yuan and the monetization of cryptoSDRs. China can take the landing of cryptoSDRs as the second channel for China to move toward the world. Without completely lifting Chinese yuan control, financial liberalization and the improvement of China's international competitiveness can be achieved through cryptoSDRs, making China a true technological and financial powerhouse. At the same time, the introduction of cryptoSDRs can provide a flexible exchange rate cooperation mechanism for China, improve the international status of Chinese yuan, and form an exchange mechanism based on the Chinese yuan exchange rate.[60]

(5) Prepared for Financial Liberalization

With the free circulation of cryptoSDRs in various countries around the world, the currency policies of China, such as foreign exchange controls, may become ineffective. Therefore, before the implementation of cryptoSDRs, China needs to be prepared to face financial liberalization and reform.

First, to address the emergence of supersovereign cryptocurrency, China needs to formulate corresponding solutions and plans in advance. With the development and growth of cryptoSDRs, it can be ensured that they are freely circulated in the world trade system, and Chinese yuan and domestic financial markets will also be affected by supersovereign cryptocurrency. Therefore, the top priority today is to improve and optimize the domestic financial market legal system and regulatory framework to ensure that China can maximize its benefits in world monetary system reform and enhance the payment and settlement status of Chinese yuan in the world currency market.

At the same time, China can learn from the experience of the US, proactively open up the exploration of high-tech companies in the blockchain financial field, and learn from Singapore's experience to establish a "regulatory sandbox." At the same time, we should actively promote the combination of Alipay and WeChat with blockchain technology, take the opportunity of the "A Belt and a Road" initiative, establish currency interchange policies with neighboring countries, and encourage the use of Chinese yuan and DC/EP worldwide to alleviate the impact of supersovereign cryptocurrency on China.

However, it is still difficult to enhance the international status of Chinese yuan and DC/EP. The reality is that the advantage of the US dollar still exists, and the internationalization process of Chinese yuan and DC/EP is inevitably difficult. Therefore,

[59] Han Long. Perspective on Legal Barriers to Achieving RMB Internationalization. Journal of Suzhou University (Philosophy and Social Sciences Edition), 2015(4), pp. 62–72 + 191.

[60] Li Xiang. The Establishment of Asian Monetary Unit from the Development of Artificial Currency SDR and European Currency Unit. Shanghai: Fudan University, 2008, p. 23.

the ultimate solution is to further weaken the dominant position of the US dollar in the world trade market through the development and popularization of cryptoSDRs and to construct a new international monetary and financial system dominated by cryptoSDRs. In the process of building international monetary and financial rules and systems, China should consider the proportion of Chinese yuan in the international monetary system and ensure the continuous improvement of China's international status. In the future world of cryptoSDRs, a new monetary strategy that promotes the harmonious development of Chinese yuan internationalization and cryptoSDR monetization through economic, trade, and currency cooperation, such as the "A Belt and a Road" initiative, should be adopted to achieve currency dominance.

5.3 Suggestions for Perfecting China's Financial Legal System Under the CryptoSDR System

The application of blockchain technology is profoundly transforming the operation system of China's financial industry. However, the legal and regulatory construction in this field has fallen far behind and requires radical reforms and adjustments.

First, we need to strengthen technology research and development, optimize and promote innovation, and take this as the standard for legal construction. This includes defining in detail the legal nature of cryptoSDRs and blockchain technology. At present, all technology and project businesses are still in the early stages of research. Therefore, for some emerging start-ups, policy guarantees should be given from the legal system. Corresponding legal policies should be formulated to restrict trading behavior and transactions, avoid illegal activities, and protect the legitimate rights and interests of consumers and investors through the combination and optimization of blockchain technology and the financial industry. Because cryptoSDRs and blockchain technology are still in the early stages of research and integration with the financial industry has just begun, appropriate fault tolerance mechanisms should be established for some evaluation standards and corresponding application systems. Continuous modification and adjustment should be carried out in the process of the continuous development of blockchain in the financial industry. By drawing on successful foreign cases and regulations, start-ups should be supported in innovating and experimenting with products and services at the institutional level to ensure the safety of relevant products and financial services and to help investors and consumers avoid investment risks and security vulnerabilities. At the same time, corresponding policies and measures should be formulated for the management and supervision of communication, cooperation, and exchange in the relevant technology and financial fields.

Second, we should encourage the participation of all interest parties in the blockchain financial industry, reach consensus with all parties on the corresponding technical standards and policy schemes, and protect the legitimate rights and interests of all industry participants. To this end, the department responsible for legal and policy formulation should actively adopt proposals from all parties based on the standards of equality and democracy and plan a promising road for the optimization and development of blockchain technology and cryptoSDRs from practical needs, supporting the continuous innovation and development of the Internet technology financial field and system optimization. At the same time, the department responsible for regulatory and market supervision should actively encourage interest groups and trading parties to establish industry self-discipline organizations and teams independently, protect the legitimate rights and interests of all parties in the industry through laws, regulations, and market policies, clarify their obligations and responsibilities, and promote the sharing and building of the blockchain financial field, providing effective solutions for the management and supervision of this field.

Third, through the study and analysis of the legal regulations and policy systems in this field, it can be found that the existing industry regulations are no longer compatible with the development and innovation of technology. Currently, there remains a lack of comprehensive regulations in the field of financial services based on blockchain technology and cryptoSDRs. Therefore, it is necessary to start from practical application, accurately and comprehensively analyze the role and functions of cryptoSDRs and blockchain technology, actively adopt opinions from all parties, and strengthen international cooperation and communication in this technical field. In the initial stage of blockchain finance, corresponding policy measures should be formulated to protect and guide the development of emerging fields and give market dominance. The implementation of laws and policies should be gradually extended from the local level to full-scale authorization. During the trial phase of policies, dynamic management and analysis of the loopholes in corresponding indicators should be conducted, and the defects of relevant regulations and policies should be adjusted and corrected in a timely manner. Through the practical operation of policies, integrating opinions and suggestions from all parties, a complete legal system in this field can be gradually formed.

Fourth, with the help of corresponding supervision and management technology, the dynamic update and real-time monitoring of market information data and transaction activities should be guaranteed. Regulatory technology (hereafter referred to as "RegTech") is the practice and application of market supervision and management technology. It was first proposed and developed in the UK with the aim of providing effective data support for market supervision through scientific and technological means. The UK Financial Conduct Authority (hereafter referred to as the "FCA") believes that this market supervision and management technology can guarantee the legality and rationality of corresponding transaction activities and behaviors on platforms and ensure efficient and orderly market supervision by applying emerging technologies. With the continuous development of RegTech and the expansion of its market scope, regulatory authorities are also expanding their use of RegTech to ensure equal sharing of information data and avoid potential security risks and loopholes in information processing systems.

RegTech can effectively help regulatory authorities and regulatory departments form a systematic knowledge system on cryptoSDRs and blockchain technology. To promote the research and development process of financial technology in China, the

Central Bank of China has established the Financial Technology Committee. This committee is led by the government and actively strengthens international exchanges and cooperation, with the aim of promoting the development of China's high-tech financial innovation field and occupying a leading position in the global financial informationization field. Correspondingly, China should also strengthen the research and development and application of regulatory technology, establish and apply evaluation standards for supervisory measures in the financial technology field at the legal level, improve the operation mechanism of the market, ensure the healthy development and system optimization of China's financial technology, and promote the coordinated progress of the entire industry.[61]

Meanwhile, with the continuous advancement and optimization of RegTech, all node servers of blockchain should be integrated into the overall regulatory and policy system and effectively matched with blockchain technology and cryptoSDRs through corresponding policies and regulations. With the incorporation of smart contracts, not only can the trading of financial products and related services be effectively promoted, but regulatory policies can also be embedded into the financial regulatory system based on blockchain technology by compiling algorithms, thus achieving data-driven legal policies and ensuring the autonomy of regulatory supervision. By connecting regulatory agencies as node servers to the blockchain system, market supervisory authorities can more conveniently exercise transaction regulatory rights, achieving the organic combination of technology and regulatory management. In addition, the establishment of regulatory node servers can effectively help the trading system to timely identify unreasonable or illegal transactions, enabling timely prevention and punishment of illegal activities, thus ensuring the security and stability of the entire blockchain trading system. At the same time, as regulatory technology adopts autonomous management, the entire regulatory process can be more convenient and efficient, greatly reducing labor costs and error rates. With the continuous development of science and technology and the continuous improvement of corresponding market laws and regulations, market supervision in the financial field will gradually shift from institutional management to technological management.

In practice, market supervisory agencies can apply blockchain technology to financial market supervision through node server access, enhancing the security of various information data and achieving the recovery of tampered data. This technology combines regulatory policies with science and technology, making machines the main body of system supervision and avoiding technical interference and transaction information leakage caused by human factors. When triggered by compliance supervision, it can automatically access human management services, achieving the perfect combination of regulatory flexibility and integrity. For example, when hackers attack the system and tamper with more than 51% of the computing power node server information on the entire data chain, resulting in an information security crisis in the entire data information system, the regulatory node servers in the system will automatically access human management and judge the tampering behavior as

[61] Feng Guo, Wu Shuang. Technical Fusion: Application of Blockchain to Achieve Precision Poverty Alleviation. Journal of Shanghai Political Science and Law Institute, 2018, 2(33), pp. 24–32.

a malicious attack. The system will then automatically judge the behavior as invalid, repair and adjust the tampered data autonomously, and even roll back the transaction timeline, thus forming a secure and effective credit data system.

Fifth, optimize interest rate policies and comprehensiveness. Interest rates are the intermediate variables of China's monetary policy transmission mechanism. If uncertainty in the money supply arises due to the inclusion of cryptoSDRs, it will affect monetary policy through the transmission effect of interest rates, causing uncertainty in monetary policy. Therefore, China needs to appropriately optimize corresponding monetary policies, weaken quantity-type monetary policies, strengthen price-type monetary policies, further enhance the role of interest rate regulation, promote the deepening of interest rate market reform, and improve the adaptability and comprehensiveness of China's interest rate policies.

Sixth, strengthen foreign exchange supervision capabilities. Currently, China's foreign exchange trading and exchange control system is strictly and prudently regulated. Article 4 of the Foreign Exchange Management Regulations stipulates the following: "This regulation applies to the foreign exchange receipts and payments or foreign exchange operations of domestic institutions or individuals, as well as the foreign exchange receipts and payments or foreign exchange operations of foreign institutions or individuals within the territory of the People's Republic of China." In addition, Article 2 of the "Interpretation of the Supreme People's Court and the Supreme People's Procuratorate on the Application of Laws in Handling Criminal Cases of Illegal Business in the Payment and Settlement Industry and Illegal Buying and Selling of Foreign Exchange," which began to be implemented in February 2019, stipulates that "those who violate national regulations and engage in illegal buying and selling of foreign exchange or disguised buying and selling of foreign exchange, disturb the order of the financial market, and have serious circumstances shall be punished for the crime of illegal business operations according to Article 225, Paragraph 4 of the Criminal Law." Based on China's current foreign exchange management regulations, the exchange and trading between cryptoSDRs and Chinese yuan and DC/EP must be approved and authorized by the relevant regulatory departments of the Chinese government. The circulation of cryptoSDRs must also strictly comply with the laws and regulations in the field of foreign exchange supervision in China. Only by strictly following the regulations on foreign exchange quotas, exchange conditions, and registration and filing can cryptoSDRs be exchanged and circulated. Therefore, it is recommended that China's foreign exchange management department strengthen supervision from the following aspects. First, the foreign exchange supervision department should attach great importance to the evolution and development of cryptoSDRs, establish real-time monitoring of cross-border capital flows, and closely monitor changes in the foreign exchange market. Second, cooperate with foreign regulatory agencies to severely crack down on illegal foreign exchange trading, illegal capital outflows, and evasion of foreign exchange controls. Third, corresponding foreign exchange management norms and new standards should be formulated according to the new issues and situations arising from the appearance of cryptoSDRs. Finally, strengthen cooperation with the IMF and establish a data sharing mechanism.[62]

Seventh, actively participate and strive to lead the creation and operation of cryptoSDRs. Promoting the recognition and use of cryptoSDRs by countries around the world will benefit China in maintaining a considerable degree of control over Chinese yuan. By leading the creation of cryptoSDRs, China can gain international status and to some extent promote the internationalization of Chinese yuan while still maintaining a certain degree of financial control domestically. This allows China to have control over Chinese yuan domestically while enjoying financial liberalization under international mainstream payment tools by using both the regulated and relatively less free Chinese yuan and the leading cryptoSDRs in the world financial market. This maximizes China's participation in international politics, economy, and finance, making up for the lack of Chinese yuan freedom and allowing China to gain greater initiative in the international monetary and financial field, thereby having the capital and opportunity to become a world-class strong country.

To achieve this goal, China must clarify the financial development ideas and currency strategies for the harmonious development of the internationalization of Chinese yuan and the monetization of cryptoSDRs. Furthermore, China must further promote the globalization of Chinese yuan and the landing and popularization of cryptoSDRs. Encouraging the adoption of cryptoSDRs as the main supersovereign cryptocurrency in the world can balance the traditional advantage of the US dollar in international trade and promote the transformation of the international monetary system.[63]

At the same time, China must seek trustworthy partners globally to increase the penetration, usage, and acceptance of cryptoSDRs and Chinese yuan. Strengthening cooperation with international organizations and institutions such as the IMF and the International Settlement Bank provides high-quality financial services and payment tools to the world.[64]

[62] See Footnote 11.

[63] Sun Yexia. The Disadvantages of Sovereign Currency as a World Currency from the Perspective of Marx's International Currency Function [J]. Economist, 2019(1), pp. 94–101.

[64] Shi Jianxun, Liu Yu. The Significance and Countermeasures of the Legal Digital RMB on the Internationalization Strategy of RMB [EB/OL]. https://doi.org/10.14100/j.cnki.65-1039/g4.20201102.001. Accessed 6 May 2022.

Conclusion

The initial motivation for the issuance of cryptoSDRs was to fill the gap caused by insufficient gold or freely convertible currencies as international reserves and to maintain stability in the foreign exchange market. However, decades have passed since the international monetary system went through various stages, such as the "gold standard," the "gold exchange standard," the "Bretton Woods system," and the "Jamaica system" after the "Jamaica Agreement" in 1976. The inherent problems and shortcomings of the current international monetary system, which uses sovereign currencies as international currencies, including the "Triffin Dilemma," have not been resolved, and SDRs have not truly played their expected role in stabilizing the foreign exchange market and supplementing the shortage of international reserve currencies. Since the birth of Bitcoin in 2009, the traditional information Internet has been upgraded to a value Internet of credit transmission, and blockchain technology has facilitated innovation and upgrading in the traditional financial industry. "Blockchain + finance" has been upgraded from "financial Internet" to "Internet finance," ultimately achieving the global application of technology finance. In this book, the author proposes combining the supersovereign legal attributes possessed by SDRs with the credit of international organizations and blockchain technology to create a new supersovereign currency, cryptoSDRs, and based on this, build a new international monetary and financial system. This idea has an important fundamental role in solving the inherent flaws of the current international monetary system, promoting the development of emerging economies, enhancing the international status of Chinese yuan, and solving macrolevel issues such as international anti-money laundering cooperation and cross-border asset recovery. At the same time, after the birth of cryptoSDRs, they will also be of great help to various industries at the microlevel, especially in the fields of payment, banking business, credit system, equity certification, insurance business, financial audit, technology supervision, notarization, and energy. If China can actively participate and strive to lead the birth of cryptoSDRs, it may obtain an opportunity to lead the creation of a new international monetary system, adjust international rules according to the existing world pattern,

L. Zeng, *A Study on the Creation, Impact and Legal Issues of Crypto Special Drawing Rights*, Modern China and International Economic Law,
https://doi.org/10.1007/978-981-99-9975-0

and make the new international monetary system fairer and more stable. At the same time, this idea will also be conducive to the promotion of the international status of Chinese yuan, the promotion of financial liberalization and trade development in China, the enhancement of China's global governance capacity, and the practice of the international monetary strategy of harmonious development of Chinese yuan internationalization and cryptoSDRs monetization. In international trade, the popularization of cryptoSDRs can save exchange costs, make international investment and trade more convenient, promote global development, and facilitate international transactions for businesses, individuals, and institutions. At the same time, due to the technical characteristics of cryptoSDRs, cross-border payments will be more secure and convenient, and inclusive financial services can also serve countries around the world faster and more conveniently, making the flow of world resources and wealth smoother and promoting faster global economic development.

Although there are still issues with system stability, application security, and the singularity of business models in blockchain technology, the application and popularization of financial business scenarios may be affected by factors such as timeliness and workload. The implementation of cryptoSDRs also faces obstacles such as uneven distribution of shares, lack of strong support from international political entities, and insufficient currency attributes. However, with the rise of China, the development of technology, and people's pursuit and adaptation to globalized lifestyles around the world, the emergence of supersovereign cryptocurrency has become an inevitable trend. As a member of the cryptocurrencies competing with Bitcoin and Facebook's Libra, cryptoSDRs currently have inherent advantages and are most likely to become the major international currency of supersovereign status. Its emergence will also promote the birth of a new international monetary system, making the global economy and finance more stable and effectively avoiding frequent financial crises, thereby bringing about another takeoff of the global economy. At the same time, China needs to seize opportunities in the early development stage of blockchain technology, closely integrating it with its financial practices and international governance, to quickly improve its international financial status and build itself into world-class blockchain financial power. In the era of cryptoSDRs, utilizing its real-name system, global supervision, and complete and transparent capital flow and combining it with cross-chain technology, its application in various financial business scenarios will be more comprehensive and effective, truly exerting its due effect. With the rapid development of financial technology, China will have the ability to lead the application of cryptoSDRs in financial scenes empowered by it and gain the benefits it deserves, becoming the leader and defender of new international rules in the era of cryptoSDRs and a technological financial power with world-class leadership and influence.

Bibliography

Books

SSA AIYA, An International Monetary Fund Currency to Rival the Dollar? [M]. Washington DC: Cato Institute 2009(10), pp. 1–15
Chen An, Li Guoan. International Monetary and Financial Law [M]. Beijing: Peking University Press, 1999, p. 17, 71, 73
COHEN, BENJAMIN J. The Geography of Money [M]. Cornell: Cornell University Press, 1998, pp. 27–47
DORAN, MICHAEL DENNIS. A Forensic Look a t Bitcoin Cryptocurrency [M]. Ann Arbor: ProQuest LLC, 2014, p. 19
DUTTA M. Seminar on the EU and the Euro Revolution: The Theory of Optimum Currency Area Revisited [M]. Colorado: Colorado University Press, 2001, pp. 352–375
EICHENGREEN, BARRY. Globalizing Capital: A History of the International Monetary System [M]. Princeton: Princeton University Press, 1996, pp. 62–105
Federal Republic of Germany. German Criminal Code [M]. Translated by Xu Jiusheng and Zhuang Jinghua. Beijing: China Fangzheng Publishing House, 2004, pp. 40–43
French Republic. French Code of Criminal Procedure [M]. Translated by Yu Shutong, Xie Chaohua. Beijing: China University of Political Science and Law Press, 1998, pp. 232–235
Fried, Schwartz. A Monetary History of the United States (1867–1960) [M]. Translated by Ba Shusong, et al. Beijing: Peking University Press, 2009, p. 497
FRIEDRICHA. VON HAYEK. Denationalization of Money [M]. London: Institute of Economic Affairs, 1976, pp. 40–55
Jiang Boke. New Compilation of International Finance (Third Edition) [M]. Shanghai: Fudan University Press, 2008, p. 270
Jiang Shaohua. Research on the Impact of Electronic Payment Development on Central Bank Monetary Policy [M]. Beijing: Economic Science Press, 2013, pp. 17–89
Liao Fan. New Developments in International Financial Law [M]. Beijing: China Social Sciences Press, 2013, pp. 62–65
Morishita Tadashi. Introduction to International Criminal Law [M]. Translated by Ruan Qilin. Beijing: People's Public Security University of China Press, 2004, pp. 183–185
PRIMAVERA, DE FILIPPI, WRIGHT, et al. Blockchain and the Law: The Rule of Code [M]. Cambridge: Harvard University Press, 2018

L. Zeng, *A Study on the Creation, Impact and Legal Issues of Crypto Special Drawing Rights*, Modern China and International Economic Law,
https://doi.org/10.1007/978-981-99-9975-0

TRIFFEN, ROBERT. Gold and Dollar Crisis [M]. New Haven: Yale University Press,1960, pp. 50–67
SAIFEDEAN AMMOUS. THE BITCOIN STANDARD: The Decentralized Alternative to Central Banking [M]. New Jersey: John Wiley & Sons, Inc., 2018
Shi Danlin, Li Xiuping. Monetary and Banking Studies [M]. Beijing: Tsinghua University Press, 2012
Stiglitz, et al. Stiglitz Report: Reforming the International Monetary and Financial Systems in the Aftermath of the Global Crisis [M]. Translated by Jiang Shu. Beijing: Xinhua Press, 2011, p. 4
Sun Liping. Introduction to Sociology [M]. Beijing: Capital University of Economics and Business Press, 2014, pp. 82–109
Treaty and Law Department of the Ministry of Foreign Affairs of the People's Republic of China. The United Nations Convention against Corruption and Relevant Legal Documents [M]. Beijing: Law Press, 2004, p. 36
United Kingdom of Great Britain and Northern Ireland. Proceeds of Crime Act 2002 [M]. Translated by Huang Feng and Zhao Linna. Beijing: China University of Political Science and Law Press, 2010, pp. 185–187
United Nations Office on Drugs and Crime. Legislative Guide for the Implementation of the United Nations Convention against Corruption [M]. Vienna: United Nations Office at Vienna English, Publishing and Library Section, 2012, pp. 194–196
Yang Yuguan, Wu Gaoqing. Interpretation of the United Nations Convention against Corruption [M]. Beijing: People's Public Security University of China Press, 2004, p. 460
Zhao Bingzhi, et al. The United Nations Convention against Corruption and Relevant Important Documents [M]. Beijing: People's Public Security University of China Press, 2004, p. 56
Zhang Mao. US International Civil Litigation Law [M]. Beijing: China University of Political Science and Law Press, 1999, p. 14

Thesis

AKARTUNA ERAY ARDA, JOHNSON SHANE D, THORNTON AMY. Preventing the money laundering and terrorist financing risks of emerging technologies: An international policy Delphi study [J].Technological Forecasting & Social Change, 2022(179)
ALEXANDER M, HEIDEMAN. Can IMFcoin Be Scaruffi's Moneta Immaginaria [J]. Marquette Intellectual Property Law Review, 2019(23), pp. 137–150
BAHAMAZAVA KATSIARYNA,NANDA ROHAN. The shift of DarkNet illegal drug trade preferences in cryptocurrency: The question of traceability and deterrence [J]. Forensic Science International: Digital Investigation, 2022(40)
Bai Jinfu, Bai Xi. New Patterns of Currency Competition and Central Bank Digital Currency. Financial Theory and Practice Exploration, 2020(3), pp. 3–9
BARRY EICHENGREEN. The Dollar Dilemma: The World's Top Currency Faces Competition [J]. Foreign Affairs, 2009(5), pp. 47–49
BARRY EICHENGREEN. The Euro as a Reserve Currency, Journal of the Japanese and International [J]. Economies, 1998(12), pp. 8–24
BENIGNO PIERPAOLO,SCHILLING LINDA M,UHLIG HARALD. Cryptocurrencies, Currency Competition, and the Impossible Trinity [J]. Journal of International Economics 2022(103)
Blockchair [EB/OL]. https://blockchair.com/zh/bitcoin. Accessed 4 May 2023
C CALCATERRA,W A KAAL,V RAO. Stable Cryptocurrencies [J]. Washington University Journal of Law & Policy, 2020(61), pp. 193–228
Cao Yong. Analysis of the Political and Economic Dual Perspectives of RMB Internationalization. Economic System Reform, 2010(2), pp. 20–24
Chen Fengying, Tao Jian. Changes in the International Financial System and Reflections. Modern International Relations, 1998(12), pp. 33–35

Chen Lei. Legal Basis and Main Ways of International Cooperation in Tracing Stolen Assets in China. Rule of Law Research, 2013(12), pp. 32–39
Chen Wei, Yin Ping. Feasibility Analysis of Networked Auditing Based on Cost–Benefit Perspective. Audit and Economic Research, 2007(1), pp. 36–39
Cheng Enfu, Wang Cui. Possibility and Implementation Path of Creating a "Shiyuan" Currency. Haipai Economics, 2013(1), pp. 1–16
Cheng Hua, Yang Yunzhi. Research on the Development Trend of Blockchain and the Response Strategies of Commercial Banks. Financial Regulatory Research, 2016(1), pp. 73–91
CHRISTOPHER J BRUMMER. How International Financial Law Works (How And It Doesn't) [J]. Georgetown Law Journal, 2011(99), p. 261
DELL'ERBA M. Stablecoins in Cryptoeconomics from Initial Coin Offerings to Central Bank Digital Currencies [J]. 22 New York University Journal of Legislation and Public Policy, 2019(1)
DIDENKO AN, Buckley. The Evolution of Currency: Cash to Cryptos to Sovereign Digital Currencies [J]. Fordham International Law Journal, 2019(4)
Dong Yi, Tang Huayun, Zhang Dong. Recent Progress and Important Views on Blockchain Technology of International Financial Infrastructure Institutions. Bond, 2016(7), pp. 46–51
Duan Jinyu. Legal Barriers and Solutions for China's Digital Currency—A Case Study of Bitcoin. Northern Economy and Trade, 2020(3), pp. 62–64
DUTTA M. Theory of Optimum Currency Area Revisited: Lessons From the Euro/Dollar Competitive Currency Regimes [J]. Journal of Asian Economics, 2005(16), pp. 352–375
EDOARDO CAMPANELLA. The Triffin Dilemma Again [J]. Economics, 2010(3), pp. 1–18
EMILE VAN DER DOES DE WILLEBOIS, JEAN-PIERRE BRUN. Using Civil Remedies in Corruption and Asset Recovery Cases [J]. Case Western Reserve Journal of International Law, 2013(45), p. 620
FASSIL FANTA, HASAN M MOHSIN. Anti-Money Laundering Regulation and Crime: A Two-Period Model of Money-in-the-Utility-Function [J]. Journal of Economic Cooperation and Development, 2011(32), pp. 1–20
Feng Guo, Wu Shuang. Technical Fusion: Application of Blockchain to Achieve Precision Poverty Alleviation. Journal of Shanghai Political Science and Law Institute, 2018, 2(33), pp. 24–32
Fu Shaoying. Issues and Countermeasures Faced by Networked Auditing. Theoretical Reports, 2014(4), p. 34
Gao Hongmin, Li Gang. Fintech, Digital Currency and Global Financial System Restructuring. Academic Forum, 2020(43)
Gao Junyi. A Preliminary Study on the Issue of "Sharing Criminal Assets" in International Criminal Judicial Assistance. Public Security Research, 2005(12), pp. 72–78
GATABAZI PAUL, et al. Cryptocurrencies and Tokens Lifetime Analysis from 2009 to 2021 [J].Economies, 2022(10)
Ge Zhaoqiang. Research on International Monetary System Reform and RMB Internationalization. Journal of Capital University of Economics and Business, 2009(5), pp. 29–38
HALABURDA H. Blockchain Revolution Without the Blockchain [J]. Science Electronic Publishing, 2018(7)
Han Long. Ideas for Solving Major Legal Issues of RMB Internationalization. Law Science, 2016(10), pp. 40–49
Han Long. Perspective on Legal Barriers to Achieving RMB Internationalization. Journal of Suzhou University (Philosophy and Social Sciences Edition), 2015(4), pp. 62–72+191
He Bingmeng, Li Qian. Correct Understanding of the Essence of the Contemporary International Monetary and Financial System. Red Flag Manuscripts, 2007(11), pp. 35–38
He Dexu, Yao Bo. Practice, Influence and Countermeasures of Legalizing RMB Digital Currency. Financial Review, 2019(5), pp. 116–117
He Feng, Geng Xin. Innovation and Transformation of Financial Infrastructure Based on Blockchain. Financial Theory and Practice, 2016(10), pp. 58–61

He Qufu, Xu Xijing, Peng Rong. Prospects for the Development of Bitcoin in the Background of the Reform of the International Monetary System with a Supersovereign Currency Orientation [J]. Economist, 2017 (4), pp. 15–17+19

He Rong. On China's Judicial Participation in the Formulation of International Economic Rules [J]. International Law Research, 2016 (1), pp. 3–15

He Shulan. The Rise of Emerging Economies and the Reform of the International Monetary System [J]. International Economic Cooperation, 2012 (10), pp. 80–86

HOWDEN E. The Cryptocurrency Conundrum: Regulating an Uncertain Future [J]. Emory International Law Review, 2015(4), pp. 741–798

Huang Guanhua. Research on Improving the Networked Audit Approach with Blockchain [J]. Fiscal Science, 2016(10), pp. 84–91

Huang Meibo, Xiong Aizong. Special Drawing Rights and the Reform of the International Monetary System [J]. International Financial Research, 2009(8), pp. 47–54

Huang Meibo, Xiong Aizong. The Dilemma and Way Out of the Reform of the International Reserve Currency System [J]. China Market, 2011 (46), pp. 80–86

Huang Rui. Regulatory Research on Financial Blockchain Technology [J]. Academic Forum, 2016(10), pp. 53–59

Huang Xueyin. Legal Thinking on the Internationalization of Renminbi-from the Perspective of Renminbi Joining the Special Drawing Rights [J]. China Market, 2017(12), pp. 122–125

Huang Yan. Research on Legal Systems of Cross-border Asset Recovery between China and Canada [J]. Times Law, 2016(1), pp. 90–98

HUGHES S, MIDDLEBROOK S T. Advancing Framework for Regulating Cryptocurrency Payments Intermediaries [J]. Yale Journal on Regulation, 2015(2)

JA ROSENSWEIG. Single Reserve Currency: An Analysis Of The Benefits And Challenges With Implementing A Single Reserve Currency [J].Global Macroseconomic Perspectives, 2009, pp. 25–86

JACOB GOLDSMITH. The IMF Must Develop Best Practices Before Government-Backed Cryptocurrencies Destabilize the International Monetary System [J]. Emory International Law Review, 2020(2), pp. 595–638

JAMUS JEROME LIM, GEOFFREY MINNE. Learning from Financial Crises [J]. Word Bank Policy Research Working Papers, 2014

JEFFREY, A FRANKEL. What's In and Out in Global Money [J]. Finance & Development, 2009(9), pp. 13–17

Jia Liping. Theory, Practice, and Impact of Bitcoin [J]. International Financial Research, 2013(12), pp. 14–25

Jiang Liwen, Hu Yue. The Legal Nature and Challenges of Bitcoin [J]. Journal of Fujian Financial Management Cadre Institute, 2013(4), pp. 12–17

Jin Baisong. How to Reform the International Monetary and Financial System [J]. World Knowledge, 2008(23)

JOHN WILLIAMSON. The Future of the Reserve System [J]. Journal of Globalization and Development, 2010(2), Article 15

JORAS FERWERDA. The Economics of Crime and Money Laundering: Does Anti-Money Laundering Policy Reduce Crime? [J]. Review of Law & Economics, 2009(5), pp. 903–929

JOSE ANTONIO OCAMPO. Building an SDR-Based Global Reserve System [J]. Journal of Globalization and Development, 2010(2), pp. 11–12

JOSE ANTONIO OCAMPO. Recasting the International Financial Agenda [J]. International Capital Markets: Systems in Transition, 2002

KARIAPPA BHEEMAIAH. The Blockchain Alternative: Rethinking Macroeconomic Policy and Economic Theory [J]. Apress, 2017

KUMAR ABHISHEK, et al. A Study of the Impact of Crypto Currency on the Indian Payment system [J]. Asian Journal of Management, 2022(12)

Lan Yonghai, Jia Linzhou, Wen Tiejun. The US Dollar's "Currency Hegemony" Strategy and China's Response [J]. World Economics and Politics, 2012(3), pp. 121–137+159–160

Lang Xianping. How International Financial Speculators Plunder Wealth [J]. IT Times Weekly, 2009(6), p. 11
Li Chong. Path Selection of RMB Exchange Rate Reform under the Current Situation [J]. Guangdong Economy, 2016(4), p. 11
Li Chong. Study on the Construction of Supersovereign International Monetary System [J]. Academic Research, 2014(2), pp. 62–70+159
Li Daokui, Yin Xingzhong. New Structure of the International Monetary System: Research on the PostFinancial Crisis Era [J]. Financial Research, 2010(2), pp. 31–43
Li Guoan. The Fragility of the International Monetary System and the Dilemma and Way Out of the Prevention and Control of International Financial Crises [J]. Strait Law, 2010(1), pp. 6–12
Li Jun. Technology and Law: Dual Tracks of Blockchain Financial Development [J]. Journal of Shanghai Lixin Accounting and Finance College, 2017(3), pp. 54–59
Li Lingyun. Formation and Influence of the "Dual Standard" International Monetary System [D]. Tianjin: Nankai University, 2010, pp. 186–189
Li Pengcheng. Micro-Exploration of the International Financial System Crisis. Journal of Guangdong Agricultural and Commercial Administrative Cadre Institute, 2000(3), pp. 50–54
Li Renzhen, Xiang Yaping. Analysis of Legal Paths to Strengthen the Role of SDR. Journal of Wuhan University (Philosophy & Social Sciences Edition), 2012(3), pp. 59–64
Li Shuren. European Monetary Integration and the International Monetary System. World Economy, 1998(1), p. 421
Li Xiang. The Establishment of Asian Monetary Unit from the Development of Artificial Currency SDR and European Currency Unit. Shanghai: Fudan University, 2008, p. 23
Li Xinmiao. Protection of Personal Information Rights in the Business of "Blockchain + Personal Credit Reporting". Securities Law Review, 2019(1), p. 14
Li Yanfeng. Political and Economic Analysis of Renminbi Internationalization. Contemporary Economic Management, 2015(6), pp. 1–5
Li Yang, Huang Jinlao. Research on Dollarization Issues. Financial Research, 1999(9), pp. 56–62+81
Li Zhen, Liu Yingge, Dai Yicheng. Impact of Libra Stablecoin on China's Monetary Policy and Response Strategies. Journal of Xi'an Jiaotong University (Social Sciences Edition), 2020(3), pp. 55–63
Lin Lefen, Wang Shaonan. One Belt One Road Initiative and Renminbi Internationalization. World Economics and Politics, 2015(11), pp. 72–90+158
Lin Liangchun. Research on the Legal Issues of Bitcoin. Citizen and Law (Law Edition), 2015(10), pp. 8–11
Lin Xiaochi, Hu Yeqianwen. A Review of Research on Blockchain Technology. Financial Market Research, 2016(2), pp. 97–109
Liu Daoyuan. Legal Dilemmas and Solutions for Internationalization Reform of China's Securities Market: A Reflection on the US Securities Law System. Law and Business Research, 2016(4), pp. 173–182
Liu Junmin, Li Lingyun. Global Economic Imbalances and Financial Crisis in the Virtualization of World Economy. Social Sciences, 2009(1)
Liu Junmin, Li Lingyun. The 'Dual Standard' International Monetary System and the Global Financial Crisis. Asia-Pacific Economy, 2009(5), pp. 22–26
Liu Junmin, Zhang Yun. Liquidity Expansion Dilemma and Its Response from the Perspective of Virtual Economy. Reform, 2008(1), pp. 18–25
Liu Wei. Exploration and Risk Prevention of Digital Currency Issuance Mechanism Based on International Experience. Southwest Finance, 2017(11), pp. 51–58
Liu Ying. Legal Analysis of the Development of Currency Forms: Impact of Electronic Currency on Legal System. Chinese Law, 2002(1), pp. 81–92
Lou Yaoxiong, Wu Jun. Legal Analysis of Bitcoin Issues. Journal of Beijing University of Posts and Telecommunications (Social Sciences Edition), 2013(4), pp. 25–31

Lu Yibin. Exploration of Advancing World Monetary System by Referring to the Efficiency of Super-sovereign Currency: A Case Study of the Pros and Cons of Bitcoin. Finance World (Academic Edition), 2014(7), pp. 24–26
Ma Ronghua. Analysis of the Benefits and Costs of the Offshore Circulation of Renminbi [J]. Journal of Shijiazhuang University of Economics, 2006(1), pp. 57–61+68
Ma Ronghua. Empirical Analysis of the Impact of the Offshore Circulation of Renminbi on China's Economy [J]. Economic Research Journal, 2006(4), pp. 35-48
MARK V VLASIC, JENAE N NOELL. Fighting Corruption to Improve Global Security: An Analysis of International Asset Recovery Systems [J]. Yale Journal of International Affairs, 2010(106), p. 111
R MCKINNON. Optimum Currency Areas [J]. American Economic Review, 1963(53), pp. 717–725
Mei Haitao, Liu Jie. Current Status, Existing Problems, and Policy Suggestions of the Blockchain Industry [J]. Telecommunications Science, 2016(11), pp. 134–138
Melanie Swan. Blockchain: Blueprint for a New Economy and Introduction [J]. Financial Electronicization, 2016(3), p. 96
MENZIE CHIN, JEFFREY FRANKEL. Why the Euro Will Rival the Dollar [J]. International Finance, 2008(1), pp. 49–73
MOHAMMED AHMAD NAHEEM. China's dirty laundry-international organizations posing a risk to China's AML systems [J]. Journal of Money Laundering Control, 2018(2), pp. 189–202
Mundell, R. The Idea of a World Currency [J]. Economic Reform, 2010(2), pp. 56–58
NORMAH OMAR ZAITONHAMIN, WAN ROSALILI WAN ROSLI. Airing Dirty Laundry: Reforming the Anti-Money Laundering and Anti-Terrorism Financing Regime in Malaysia [J]. Global Jurist, 2016(16), p. 128
Pan Yingli. The Relationship between the Goal and Means of Renminbi Internationalization and an Evaluation of the Significance of Joining the SDR [J]. Exploration and Contention, 2016(1), pp. 79–82
PAUL R KRUGMAN. A Model of Balance of Payment Crisis [J]. Journal of Money Cridet and Banking, 1979(11), pp. 311–325
PETER B KENEN. The Substitution Account as a First Step Toward Reform of the International Monetary System [J]. Peterson Institute for International Economics, 2010, pp. 5–10
PETER B KENEN. Use of SDR to Supplement or Substitute for Other Means of Finance [J]. International Money and Credit: The Policy Roles, 1984, ch. 7
PLASSARAS NICHOLAS A. Regulating Digital Currencies: Bringing Bitcoin within the Reach of the IMF [J]. Chicago Journal of International Law, 2013(14), pp. 377–390
PLASTUN ALEX, KHOMUTENKO LUDMILA, BASHLAI SERHII. Is There Any Witching in the Cryptocurrency Market? [J]. Journal of Risk and Financial Management, 2022(15)
Qiao Yide, Xu Mingqi. Strengthening the Status and Role of the SDR in the International Monetary System [J]. International Economic Review, 2011(1), pp. 52–65+4
Qin Yi. The Impact of Blockchain on the Global Financial Industry [J]. Contemporary Financier, 2016(2), pp. 43–46
FRANKEL, ROSE. The Endogeneity of The Optimumcurrency Area Criteria [J]. The Economic Journal, 1998(108), pp. 1009–1025
Research Team of the Research Bureau of the People's Bank of China. Literature Review on International Monetary System Reform. Financial Development Review, 2010(3), pp. 143–158
RICHARD N COOPE. A Monetary System for the Future [J]. Foreign Affairs, 1984(63)
RICHARD N COOPER. Necessary reform? The IMF and international financial architecture [J]. Harvard International Review, 2009(04), pp. 52–55
ROBERT A MUNDELL. A Theory of Optimum Currency Areas [J]. American Economic Review, 1961(4), pp. 657–665
ROBERT ZOELLICK. A Monetary Regime for A Multipolar World [J]. Financial Times, 2010(2), p. 9
Shao Jie, Qian Yong. IMF Economic Assistance Plan and the Reform of International Financial Institutions [J]. New Finance, 1998(4), p. 871

Shi Chao. Governance Logic of Trust Creation and Application of Blockchain Technology [J]. Eastern Methodology, 2020(1), p. 15

Shi Jianxun, Wang Panpan. Does Expanding the Use of SDR Help the Internationalization of Renminbi? [J]. World Economic Research, 2018(10), pp. 3–17+64+135

Shi Jing. SDR and the Reform of the International Monetary System [J]. Economic Research Guide, 2012(33), pp. 56–58+134

Shi Xiuxia. Legal Regulation of the Risk of Money Laundering Using Virtual Currency [J]. Southern Finance, 2016(6), pp. 81–88

Shi Xiuxia. Prevention and Control Strategies for Money Laundering Crimes Using Virtual Currency [J]. Journal of the People's Public Security University of China (Social Science Edition), 2016(1), pp. 1–11

Shi Xiuxia. Research on Money Laundering Crimes Using Virtual Currency [J]. Journal of the People's Public Security University of China (Social Science Edition), 2017(33), pp. 32–41

Shu Shuang. A Brief Discussion on the Nature of Currency [J]. Economic Research Guide, 2012(3), pp. 97–98

Song Wei. Bulk Commodities are the Breakthrough Point for Renminbi Pricing [J]. China Finance, 2013(23), pp. 55–56

STEVEN DAVID BROWN. Cryptocurrency and criminality: The Bitcoin opportunity [J]. The Police Journal: Theory, Practice and Principles, 2016(89), pp. 327–339

Stiglitz, Joseph E. Global Financial Regulation and Financial Structure Reform: Research Report of the International Commission on Reform of the International Financial and Economic System. Shanghai Economic Review, 2010(Z1), pp. 26–27

Sun Yexia. The Disadvantages of Sovereign Currency as a World Currency from the Perspective of Marx's International Currency Function [J]. Economist, 2019(1), pp. 94–101

TREVOR I KIVIAT. Beyond Bitcoin: Issues in Regulating Blockchain Transactions [J]. Duke Law Journal, 2015(65), pp. 569–608

Tu Yongqian, Qiu Ben. Legal Path and Rule of Law Construction for the Internationalization of Renminbi [J]. Political Science and Law Journal, 2015(5), pp. 13–22

Wang Chao. Financial Innovation and Legal Reform from the Perspective of Blockchain [J]. Prosecutorial Sky, 2016(20), pp. 66–67

Wang Guogang. The Multiple Functions of Renminbi Joining SDR [J]. China Finance, 2015(24), pp. 41–43

Wang Liming. On the Legal Protection of Personal Information Rights—Centered on the Distinction between Personal Information Rights and Privacy Rights [J]. Modern Law Science, 2013(35), pp. 62–72

Wang Qingsong. The Nature Definition and Rule Path of the Internal Relations of Blockchain System [J]. Legal Science, 2019(5), pp. 130–142

Wang Sheng. Research on Blockchain-based Legal Currency System [J]. Economist, 2016(9), pp. 77–85

Wang Shuji. The Historical Evolution and Design Ideas of Super-Sovereign Reserve Currency [J]. Wuhan Finance, 2015(4), pp. 8–11

Wang Yan, Li Zhiyong. Research on the Legal Guarantee of RMB Cross-border Flow Safety [J]. Journal of Yunnan University (Law Edition), 2010(2), pp. 35–42

Wang Ying. Discussion on the Current Status of Data Security Legislation in the Era of Digital Economy [J]. Legal System Expo, 2020(2), pp. 215–216

Wang Yuanlong. Research on Some Issues of RMB Internationalization [J]. Finance and Trade Economics, 2009(7), pp. 16–22+135

Wang Zhicheng. Analysis of the Alliance Blockchain Model for Personal Credit System in the Internet Era [J]. Credit Investigation, 2019(8), pp. 26–32

Wu Guanghao. Connotation, International Experience and Inspiration of Financial Opening [J]. Northern Finance, 2018(10), pp. 95–98

Xiang Yaping. Analysis of the Legal Path of RMB Internationalization [J]. Hebei Law Science, 2013(5), pp. 120–126

Xu Shan, Luo Yangyang, Zhao Zheng. Analysis of Domestic and Foreign Research Status of Currency Internationalization [J]. Economic Research Reference, 2019(11), pp. 49–58
Xu Tao. Research on the Development Status and Application Value of "Blockchain +" Education [J]. Distance Education Journal, 2017(2), pp. 19–28
Yang Dong, Chen Zheli. Research on the Positioning and Nature of Legal Digital Currency [J]. Social Sciences Digest, 2020(10), pp. 71–73
Yang Lihua. Research on the Effectiveness of Renminbi Exchange Rate Reform Mechanism—Based on the Perspective of Achieving the Reform Goals [J]. Southwest Finance, 2016(5), pp. 51–58
YI EOJIN, AHN KWANGWON, CHOI MY. Cryptocurrency: Not far from equilibrium [J].Technological Forecasting & Social Change, 2022(177)
Yu Pinxian. Analysis of Legal Issues of Central Bank Digital Currency [J]. Journal of Shanghai University of International Business and Economics, 2020(2), pp. 88–102
Yu Zhigang. The Era of "Transnational Information Crime" and China's Choice of the <Cybercrime Convention>—Additionally, on the Reshaping of the Idea and Rules of Criminal Jurisdiction over Cybercrime [J]. Law Forum, 2013(2), pp. 94–104
Yu Zhonghua, Yu Wenshan. Blockchain Concept, Financial Meta-Logic and Reconstruction of the International Monetary System [J]. Regional Financial Research, 2020(7), pp. 5–13
Zeng Jinhai. Legal Analysis and Enlightenment of Cryptocurrency. Information Security and Communications Privacy, 2019(11), pp. 71–79
Zhang Bin. Research on Blockchain Security Risks [J]. Telecommunications Engineering Technology and Standardization, 2017(11), pp. 1–5
Zhang Chen. Research on the Realistic Risks of Bitcoin and the Legal Regulation in China [J]. Journal of Chongqing University of Posts and Telecommunications (Social Science Edition), 2014(5), pp. 27–31
Zhang Fulin, Zhang Wei. Balancing Dilemma and Financial Security: Changes and Problems in the International Monetary System. International Security Studies, 2018(6)
Zhang Jiteng. International Monetary System Reform from the Perspective of Blockchain and Supranational Digital Currency: Taking the Innovation and Attempt of E-SDR as an Example. International Perspective, 2019(11)
Zhang Lei. Reflections on the Application of Foreign Repatriation Laws: Starting with the Bo Xilai Case. Journal of Jilin University (Social Sciences Edition), 2017(1), pp. 106–116+205–206
Zhang Ming. International Monetary System Reform: Background, Reasons, Measures and China's Participation. International Economic Review, 2010(1), pp. 114–137
Zhang Qian, Zhang Hongxu. The Role of DC/EP in the Internationalization of RMB. Financial Observer, 2020(10), pp. 52–53
Zhang Rui. Traditional Finance Innovation and Reform Based on Blockchain. Southwest Finance, 2016(10), pp. 18–23
Zhang Xiuguang, Li Zhengdao. Prospects, Analysis, and Challenges of "Blockchain + Internet" in the Financial Field. Modern Management, 2016(6), pp. 4–6
Zhang Yanqiang, Wu Di. On Legal Issues Related to Cross-Border Asset Recovery. International Law Review, 2017(5), pp. 60–83
Zhang Yiping, Huang Shengbin. Alternative Accounts and International Monetary System Reform. International Trade Issues, 2011(1), p. 130
Zheng Hongguang. The Impact of the United Nations Convention against Corruption on Improving China's Overseas Asset Recovery Mechanism. Liaoning Rule of Law Research, 2007(3), pp. 59–62
Zheng Jianhua. Discussion on International Monetary System Reform: On the Internationalization of RMB. Macroeconomic Research, 2014(7)
Zheng Liansheng, Zhang Ming. Should the Chinese Government Strongly Promote the Inclusion of RMB in the SDR? International Finance, 2015(7), pp. 112–121+135
Zhou Meili, Gu Chenjie, Li Min. Legal Issues of Blockchain Finance. Finance Horizon, 2017(8), pp. 69–76

Zhou Ruijue. Legal Regulation of Blockchain Technology. Journal of Beijing University of Posts and Telecommunications (Social Sciences Edition), 2017(3), pp. 39–45
Zhou Xiaochuan. Thoughts on Reforming the International Monetary System. Theoretical Reference, 2009(10), pp. 4–5
ZIMMERMANN, CLAUS D. Cryptocurrency: The Concept of Monetary Sovereignty Revisited [J]. European Journal of International Law, 2013(24)
Zuo Haicong, Cui Yu. Shortcomings and Reform Proposals of the Current RMB Exchange Rate System: Based on the Perspective of RMB Internationalization. Southern Finance, 2016(10), pp. 23–28

Electronic Literature

51CTO. The fall of the online black market "Silk Road" [EB/OL]. http://netsecurity.51cto.com/art/201311/415727.htm. Accessed 6 May 2022
Babite. Bank of Canada unveils digital currency experiment, using blockchain to create CAD-Coin [EB/OL]. https://www.8btc.com/article/93547. Accessed 6 May 2022
BANK OF ENGLAND. Central Bank Digital Currency Opportunities, Challenges and Design, Bank of England [EB/OL]. https://www.bankofengland.co.uk/paper/2020/central-bank-digital-currency-opportunities-challenges-and-design-discussion-pape. Accessed 6 May 2022
Blockchain Industry Service Platform. 12 Countries Supporting Bitcoin Globally in 2018 [EB/OL]. https://www.greendeco.com.cn/29604.html. Accessed 6 May 2022
Blockchain Pencil. Estonia Promotes the Issuance of "National Digital Currency" [EB/OL]. https://blog.csdn.net/IJXR1A64JI53L/article/details/78870303. Accessed 6 May 2022
btctq.com. Swiss Economy Minister: Switzerland wants to become a "crypto-nation" [EB/OL]. http://www.btctq.com/a/01/569.html. Accessed 6 May 2022
CEIC DATA. US Foreign Exchange Reserves [EB/OL]. https://www.ceicdata.com/zh-hans/indicator/united-states/foreign-exchange-reserves. Accessed 6 May 2022
Chen Minxuan. Official issues first ICO license, can Bermuda become the next digital currency center? [EB/OL]. https://www.walian.cn/news/9454.html. Accessed 6 May 2022
China Blockchain Technology and Industry Development Forum. "2016 China Blockchain Technology and Application Development White Paper." [EB/OL]. Available at: http://chainb.com/download/工信部-中国区块链技术和应用发展白皮书 1014.pdf. Accessed 6 May 2022
China Central Commission for Discipline Inspection and National Supervision Commission website. "Full Text of the United Nations Convention Against Corruption." [EB/OL]. http://www.ccdi.gov.cn/special/lygz/flfg/201310/t20131008_11282.html. Accessed 6 May 2022
China News Network. "Guangzhou Financial 'Regulatory Sandbox' Pilot Lands." [EB/OL]. Available at: https://baijiahao.baidu.com/s?id=1668653511174163928&wfr=spider&for=pc. Accessed 6 May 2022
China Securities Regulatory Commission. "Notice on Preventing Risks of Bitcoin." [EB/OL]. Available at: http://www.csrc.gov.cn/pub/newsite/flb/flfg/bmgf/zh/gfxwjfxq/201401/t20140122_242972.html. Accessed 6 May 2022
COUNCIL OF EUROPE GLOBAL PROJECT ON CYBERCRIME AND MONEYVAL. Criminal Money Flows on the Internet: Methods, Trends and Multi stakeholder Counteraction [EB/OL]. http://www.coe.int/t/dghl/monitoring/moneyval/Typologies/MONEYVAL(2013)6_Reptyp_flows_en.pdf. Accessed 6 May 2022
COUNCIL OF EUROPE. Convention on Cybercrime [EB/OL]. https://www.coe.int/en/web/conventions/full-list/-/conventions/treaty/185. Accessed 6 May 2022
DANMARKS NATIONAL BANK. Central Bank Digital Currency in Denmark? [EB/OL]. https://www.nationalbanken.dk/en/publications/Documents/2017/12/Analysis%20-%20Central%20bank%20digital%20currency%20in%20Denmark.pdf#search=CBDC. Accessed 6 May 2022

Data Briefing. International Crude Oil Price Trends and Major Events Since 1970 [EB/OL]. http://intl.ce.cn/specials/zxxx/201307/31/t20130731_24622321.shtml. Accessed 6 May 2022

Data Source. Coin World Website Data [EB/OL]. https://bishijie.com/hangqing. Accessed 6 May 2022

DIEM. Libra Whitepaper [EB/OL]. https://www.diem.com/en-us/white-paper/. Accessed 6 May 2022

Du Huitang, Huoxing Finance. Breaking News! The Wall Street Journal reveals that Facebook's cryptocurrency has the support of seven major companies including VISA, PayPal, and Uber [EB/OL]. https://mp.weixin.qq.com/s/ya1gj1sY-bTu6WUUIYl2Lw. Accessed 6 May 2022

ERIC TALBOT JENSEN. The Tallinn Manual 2.0: Highlights and Insights [EB/OL]. https://www.law.georgetown.edu/international-law-journal/wp-content/uploads/sites/21/2018/05/48-3-The-Tallinn-Manual-2.0.pdf. Accessed 6 May 2022

FCA, Regulatory sandbox [EB/OL]. https://www.fca.org.uk/firms/innovation/regulatory-sandbox. Accessed 6 May 2022

FRED BERGSTEN. How to Solve the Problem of the Dollar? [EB/OL]. https://www.ft.com/content/75cb5f2e-a729-11dc-a25a-0000779fd2ac. Accessed 6 May 2022

HUMPAGE O F. Will Special Drawing Rights Supplant the Dollar? [EB/OL]. https://wallstreetpit.com/4204-will-special-drawing-rights-supplant-the-dollar/. Accessed 6 May 2022

IMF, 2021 General SDR Allocation [EB/OL]. https://www.imf.org/en/Topics/special-drawing-right/2021-SDR-Allocation. Accessed 6 May 2022

IMF. Currency Composition of Official Foreign Exchange Reserves (COFER) [EB/OL]. https://data.imf.org/?sk=E6A5F467-C14B-4AA8-9F6D-5A09EC4E62A4&sId=1408206195757. Accessed 6 May 2022

IMF. IMF COUNTRY INFORMATION [EB/OL]. https://www.imf.org/en/countries. Accessed 6 May 2022

IMF. IMF Members' Quotas and Voting Power, and IMF Board of Governors [EB/OL]. https://www.imf.org/external/np/sec/memdir/members.aspx. Accessed 6 May 2022

IMF. International Financial Statistics [EB/OL]. http://www.worldbank.org. Accessed 6 May 2022

IMF. Special Drawing Rights (SDRs) [EB/OL]. https://www.imf.org/en/Topics/special-drawing-right. Accessed 6 May 2022

INTERNATIONAL MONETARY FUND. Annual Report on Exchange Arrangements and Exchange Restrictions 2014 [EB/OL]. https://www.imf.org/en/Publications/Annual-Report-on-Exchange-Arrangements-and-Exchange-Restrictions/Issues/2016/12/31/Annual-Report-on-Exchange-Arrangements-and-Exchange-Restrictions-2014-41643. Accessed 6 May 2022

INTERNATIONAL MONETARY FUND. International Monies, IMF Executive Board Concludes the Meeting on Enhancing International Monetary Stability—A Role for the SDR? Washington D.C.: Prepared by the Strategy, Policy, and Review Department, 2011 [EB/OL]. https://www.imf.org/en/News/Articles/2015/09/28/04/53/pn1122. Accessed 6 May 2022

INTERSOFT CONSULTING. General Data Protection Regulation [EB/OL]. https://gdpr-info.eu/. Accessed 6 May 2022

INTERSOFT CONSULTING. General Data Protection Regulation [EB/OL]. https://gdpr-info.eu/art-45-gdpr/. Accessed 6 May 2022

IT Xiaobai Ge. Belarus signs new law, giving blockchain technology protection [EB/OL]. http://m.sohu.com/a/212408220_100035093. Accessed 6 May 2022

Jimu News. UK research agency predicts China will surpass the US and become the world's largest economy in 2030 [EB/OL]. https://baijiahao.baidu.com/s?id=1720194822613589762&wfr=spider&for=pc. Accessed 6 May 2022

Jinli International. Bitcoin platform was once used by criminals to launder money: daily trading reached over 40,000 coins [EB/OL]. http://max232.net/btb/kuangye/6252.html. Accessed 6 May 2022

KEVIN V TU, MICHAEL MEREDITH. Rethinking Virtual Currency Regulation in the Bitcoin Age [EB/OL]. https://ssrn.com/abstract=2485550. Accessed 6 May 2022

M. KUMHOF, C. NOONE. Central Bank Digital Currencies—Design Principles and Balance Sheet Implications [EB/OL]. https://www.bankofengland.co.uk/-/media/boe/files/working-paper/2018/central-bank-digital-currencies-designprinciples-and-balance-sheet-implications. Accessed 6 May 2022

Legal Daily. The first bitcoin network property rights infringement dispute is pronounced [EB/OL]. http://www.pkulaw.cn/fulltext_form.aspx?Db=news&Gid=c6403738c43b014dbdfb&from=singlemessage&isappinstalled=0#10006-weixin-1-52626-6b3bffd01fdde4900130bc5a2751b6d1. Accessed 6 May 2022

Lei Man. Burial of the soul in the black box [EB/OL]. https://www.huxiu.com/article/319074.html. Accessed 6 May 2022

Liu Cheng. How China is dismantling US financial hegemony [EB/OL]. http://www.banbijiang.com/book/story.php?id=46946. Accessed 6 May 2022

MARKUS BRUNNERMEIER, HAROLD JAMES, JEAN-PIERRE LANDAU. The Digitalization Of Money [EB/OL]. https://www.nber.org/papers/w26300. Accessed 6 May 2022

Ministry of Foreign Affairs. List of Signatory Countries for Judicial Assistance Treaties [EB/OL]. https://www.fmprc.gov.cn/web/ziliao_674904/tytj_674911/tyfg_674913/t1215630.shtml. Accessed 6 May 2022

NAKAMOTO S. Bitcoin: A Peer-To-Peer Electronic Cash System [EB/OL]. https://bitcoin.org/bitcoin.pdf

NEW YORK STATE DEPARTMENT OF FINANCIAL SERVICES (NYSDFS). BitLicense [EB/OL]. https://www.dfs.ny.gov/apps_and_licensing/virtual_currency_businesses/information_applicants. Accessed 6 May 2022

Nie Lin. IMF reform plan officially takes effect, China becomes the third largest shareholder [EB/OL]. http://www.jiemian.com/article/527073.html. Accessed 6 May 2022

NIKKEI. Japan eyes treating bitcoins the same as real money [EB/OL]. https://asia.nikkei.com/Politics-Economy/Policy-Politics/Japan-eyes-treating-bitcoins-the-same-as-real-money. Accessed 6 May 2022

Ostrich Blockchain. Gibraltar Launches Regulation to Protect Cryptocurrency Value and Reputation [EB/OL]. http://dy.163.com/v2/article/detail/D780A1PQ0511QUF7.html. Accessed 6 May 2022

PAUL KRUGMAN. China's Dollar Trap [EB/OL]. https://wenku.baidu.com/view/021614e4ec3a87c24028c478.html. Accessed 6 May 2022

Pencil Path. Understanding the Central Bank's Digital Currency with One Article [EB/OL]. http://m.sohu.com/a/345381277_649045/. Accessed 6 May 2022

People's Bank of China. "2020 Report on Renminbi Internationalization." [EB/OL]. Available at: https://www.sogou.com/link?url=hedJjaC291M1crEDB-pObOfhhvEf1fs_amZWDDqm0FvdLAEz2Et20878Pc-EdQ1DriuqOZE83Sr688U3F96Juq4to0wa_Tif. Accessed 6 May 2022

People's Bank of China. "Announcement by the People's Bank of China and 7 Other Departments on Preventing Risks of Token Issuance and Financing." [EB/OL]. Available at: http://www.sohu.com/a/169507895_523492. Accessed 6 May 2022

People's Bank of China. "Interim Measures for Statistics and Publication of Monetary Supply." [EB/OL]. Available at: https://www.pinlue.com/article/2018/09/1809/017273406401.html. Accessed 6 May 2022

People's Bank of China. "Notice of the People's Bank of China on Publicly Soliciting Opinions on the Draft Amendments to the Law of the People's Republic of China on the People's Bank of China." [EB/OL]. Available at: http://www.gov.cn/zhengce/zhengceku/2020-10/24/content_5553847.htm. Accessed 6 May 2022

People's Bank of China. "Q&A Record of Governor Yi Gang at the 2018 Boao Forum for Asia Annual Conference Subforum on 'Normalization of Monetary Policy'." [EB/OL]. Available at: https://www.financialnews.com.cn/jg/ld/201804/t20180411_136295.html. Accessed 6 May 2022

People's Republic of China. "Civil Code of the People's Republic of China." [EB/OL]. Available at: http://www.npc.gov.cn/npc/c30834/202006/75ba6483b8344591abd07917e1d25cc8.shtml. Accessed 6 May 2022

People's Republic of China. "Full Text of the Personal Information Protection Law (Draft) of the People's Republic of China." [EB/OL]. Available at: https://www.sohu.com/a/426584424_780954. Accessed 6 May 2022

People's Republic of China. "Provisions on the Management of Property Involved in Criminal Proceedings by the People's Procuratorates," Article 2. [EB/OL]. Available at: http://politics.people.com.cn/n/2015/0309/c70731-26662761.html. Accessed 6 May 2022

PIERRE-HENRI DE MENTHON, SABINE SYFUSS-ARNAUD. Interview with Christine Lagarde, President of the ECB [EB/OL]. https://www.ecb.europa.eu/press/inter/date/2020/html/ecb.in200108~f3ba434000.en.html. Accessed 6 May 2022

Qiu Bijun. 2018 Global Currency Circle Regulatory Trends: Different Attitudes from Various Countries, However, You Need to Know! [EB/OL]. https://www.qqbite.com/bitcoin/3196.html. Accessed 6 May 2022

RICHARD CLARIDA. With Privilege Comes…? [EB/OL]. http://www.pimco.com/LeftNav/Global+Markets/Global. Accessed 6 May 2022

RIKSBANK. The Riksbank to Test Technical Solution for the E-Krona, Riksbank [EB/OL]. https://www.riksbank.se/en-gb/press-and-published/notices-and-press-releases/notices/2020/the-riksbank-to-test-technical-solution-for-the-e-krona/. Accessed 6 May 2022

ROBERT ZOELLICK. The IMS Must be Reformed [EB/OL]. http://www.finance.sina.com.cn/roll/20101227/00053560431.shtml. Accessed 6 May 2022

Shi Jianxun, Liu Yu. The Significance and Countermeasures of the Legal Digital RMB on the Internationalization Strategy of RMB [EB/OL]. https://doi.org/10.14100/j.cnki.65-1039/g4.20201102.001. Accessed 6 May 2022

Sina Finance. Binance Suspected to Have Been Attacked, Causing Failure and a Sudden 10,000% Surge in VIA Price [EB/OL]. http://finance.sina.com.cn/stock/usstock/c/2018-03-08/doc-ifxpwyhv7094818.shtml. Accessed 6 May 2022

Sohu. Tunisia to Replace its National Digital Currency eDinar with Monetas Currency Driven by Blockchain [EB/OL]. https://www.sohu.com/a/235535833_100180465. Accessed 6 May 2022

Sunrye. Research report on the central bank's digital currency (DC/EP) [EB/OL]. https://learnblockchain.cn/2019/11/06/DC/EP-research/. Accessed 6 May 2022

Tencent. Breaking News: Cross-border Payment Platform CBP Officially Forms Strategic Partnership with Central Bank's Digital Currency DC/EP [EB/OL]. https://new.qq.com/rain/a/20210204A0BEI500. Accessed 6 May 2022

Tencent. Pilot Process of Central Bank's Digital Currency DC/EP - We Need to Learn to Adapt Quickly [EB/OL]. https://new.qq.com/rain/a/20210113A0785N00. Accessed 6 May 2022

THE FINANCIAL ACTION TASK FORCE (FATF). Money Laundering Using New Payment Methods [EB/OL]. http://www.fatf-gafi.org/media/fatf/documents/reports/ML%20using%20New%20 Payment%20Methods.pdf. Accessed 6 May 2022

THE FINANCIAL ACTION TASK FORCE (FATF). Virtual Currencies: Key Definitions and Potential AML/CFT Risks [EB/OL]. https://www.fatf-gafi.org/media/fatf/documents/reports/Virtual-currency-key-definitions-and-potential-aml-cft-risks.pdf. Accessed 6 May 2022

THE GLOBAL PROVIDER OF SECURE FINANCIAL MESSAGING SERVICES. SWIFT [EB/OL]. https://www.swift.com/about-us. Accessed 6 May 2022

TOBIAS ADRIAN, STABLECOINS. Central Bank Digital Currencies, and Cross-Border Payments: A New Look at the International Monetary System [EB/OL]. https://www.imf.org/en/News/Articles/2019/05/13/sp051419-stablecoins-central-bank-digital-currencies-and-cross-border-payments. Accessed 6 May 2022

Website of the China State Council Information Office. Signing of the Strategic Cooperation Framework Agreement for the "Maritime Silk Road" Fund [EB/OL]. http://www.scio.gov.cn/ztk/wh/slxy/htws/Document/1379029/1379029.htm. Accessed 6 May 2022

WORLD BANK, Key Development Data & Statistics [EB/OL]. http://www.worldbank.org. Accessed 6 May 2022
WTO. GATS Art.14 General Exceptions [EB/OL]. https://www.wto.org/english/docs_e/legal_e/26-gats_01_e.htm. Accessed 6 May 2022
Xie Juan. The Next Step for Financial Globalization: Opportunities for eSDR and SHC [EB/OL]. https://www.yicai.com/news/100426479.html. Accessed 6 May 2022
Zhang Liqing. Research on Global Financial Governance Should Start from Eight Major Issues [EB/OL]. https://wallstreetcn.com/articles/252900. Accessed 6 May 2022
Zou Jun. "Will Blockchain be the Protagonist in the Second Half of the Internet?" [EB/OL]. https://www.jianshu.com/p/635e95e09bd0?utm_campaign=maleskine&utm_content=note&utm_medium=seo_notes&utm_source=recommendation. Accessed 6 May 2022

Other Types of Literature

P ALESSANDRINI. M FRATIANNI. International Monies, Special Drawing Rights and Supranational Money [C]. Rome: Prepared for the 2009 Pre-G8 Summit Conference on" Global Financial Crises: National Economic Solutions, Geopolitical Impacts", 2009
ANDR-S FERN-NDEZ, MICHAEL W KLEIN, ALESSANDRO REBUCCI, et al. Capital Control Measures: A New Dataset [N]. IMF Working Paper 2015
BARRY EICHENGREEN, Global Imbalance and the Lessons of Bretton Woods [N]. NBER Working Paper, No. 10497, 2004
BARRY EICHENGREEN, MARC FLANDREAU. The Rise and Fall of the Dollar, or When did the Dollar Replace Sterling as the Leading Reserve Currency? [N]. NBER Working Paper, No. 14154 2008
BORDO, FLNADREAU. Core, Periphery, Exchange Rate Regimes, and Globalization [N]. NBER Working Paper, No. 8584, 2001
BORDO, FLNADREAU. Exchange Rate Regime Choice in Historical Perspective [N]. NBER Working Paper, No. 9654, 2003
M CARNEY. The Evolution of the International Monetary System [N]. New York City: Foreign Policy Association
P B CLARK, J J POLAK. International Liquidity and the Role of the SDR in the International Monetary System [S]. IMF Staff Position Note, 2002/02/217
ELIAS PAPAIOANNOUA, RICHARD PORTES, GREGORIOS SIOUROUNISE. Optimal Currency Shares in International Reserves: The Impact of the Euro and the Prospects for the Dollar [N]. CEPR Discussion Paper, No. 5734, 2006
Fan Chongyi. "Exclusion of Reasonable Doubt: New Standards for Criminal Evidence." [N]. Procuratorial Daily, May 16, 2012
GREENWALD, STIGLITZ. A Long Term Perspective On The Euro [N]. NBER Working Papers, No. 13815, 2008
LANDAU DOOLEY, GARBER DOOLEY. Management on Interest Rates and Exchange Rates in Center Countried[N]. NBER Working Paper, No. 10332, 2004
MATEO Y LAGO,R DUTTAGUPTA ISABLLE,GOYAL ABD R GOYAL. The Debate On The International Monetary System[S]. Imf Staff Position Note, 2009/09/26
M ODSTFELD, J C SHAMBAUGH, A M TAYLOR. Financial Stability, the Trilemma, and International Reserves [N]. NBER Working Paper, No. 14217, 2008
RAHBARI BECK. Optimal Reserve Composition in the Presence of Sudden Stops: The Euro and the Dollar as Safe Haven Currencies [N]. ECB Working Paper, No. 916, 2008
SERGIO ROSSI. Global imbalances and international monetary disorder: supranational [C]. Berlin: Paper for the 13th international conference of the Research Network on Macroeconomics and Macroeconomic Policies "The World Economy in Crisis: The Return of Keynesianism?" 2009, pp. 4–13

UNITED NATIONS. Toward a New International Financial Architecture [C]. New York: Report of the Task Force of the Executive Committee on Economic and Social Affairs of the United Nations, 2001

Zhang Tao. "SDR Boosts International Monetary System Reform." [N]. First Financial Daily, September 5, 2016

GPSR Compliance
The European Union's (EU) General Product Safety Regulation (GPSR) is a set of rules that requires consumer products to be safe and our obligations to ensure this.

If you have any concerns about our products, you can contact us on

ProductSafety@springernature.com

In case Publisher is established outside the EU, the EU authorized representative is:

Springer Nature Customer Service Center GmbH
Europaplatz 3
69115 Heidelberg, Germany

www.ingramcontent.com/pod-product-compliance
Ingram Content Group UK Ltd.
Pitfield, Milton Keynes, MK11 3LW, UK
UKHW020803290926
15470UKWH00003B/937
* 9 7 8 9 8 1 9 9 9 9 7 4 3 *